ESSENTIALS OF ENVIRONMENTAL LAW

Third Edition

Craig B. Simonsen
Managing Editor

Upper Saddle River, New Jersey 07458

Library of Congress Cataloging-in-Publication Data

Essentials of environmental law / Craig B. Simonsen, managing editor.—3rd ed.
   p. cm.
   Includes index.
   ISBN 0-13-228045-0
   1. Environmental law—United States.   2. Legal assistants—United States.   I. Simonsen,
Craig B.
   KF3775.E84 2007
   344. 7304¢ 6—dc22   2006002092

Editor-in-Chief: Vernon R. Anthony
Director of Production and
Manufacturing: Bruce Johnson
Senior Acquisitions Editor: Gary Bauer
Editorial Assistant: Linda Cupp
Development Editor: Athena Group, Inc.
Marketing Manager: Leigh Ann Sims
Marketing Coordinator: Alicia Dysert
Managing Editor—Production: Mary Carnis
Manufacturing Buyer: llene Sanford

Production Liaison: Denise Brown
Manager of Media Production: Amy Peltier
Media Production Project Manager: Lisa Rinaldi
Full-Service Production/Composition: Lindsey
Hancock/Carlisle Publishing Services
Senior Design Coordinator: Christopher Weigand
Cover Design: Kevin Kall
Printer/Binder: RR Donnelley & Sons
Cover Printer: RR Donnelley & Sons

Some of the material contained in Chapter Five is reprinted with permission from the publisher of
Environmental Law Resource Guide by Craig B. Simonsen. Copyright © 1995 by Clark Boardman
Callaghan, New York.
Scripture taken from the *Holy Bible*, NEW INTERNATIONAL VERSION®. Copyright © 1973, 1978,
1984 International Bible Society. All rights reserved throughout the world. Used by permission of
International Bible Society.

Pearson Education Ltd.
Pearson Education Singapore, Pte. Ltd.
Pearson Education Canada, Ltd.
Pearson Education—Japan

Pearson Education Australia PTY, Limited
Pearson Education North Asia Ltd.
Pearson Education de Mexico, S.A. de C.V.
Pearson Education Malaysia, Pte. Ltd.

10 9 8 7 6 5 4 3 2 1
ISBN: 0-13-228045-0

Dedication

For Nancy and Kevin

Who has gone up to heaven and come down? Who has gathered up the wind in the hollow of his hands? Who has wrapped up the waters in his cloak? Who has established all the ends of the earth? What is his name, and the name of his son? Tell me if you know!

Proverbs 30:4 (NIV)

Pearson Legal Series

Pearson Legal Series provides paralegal/legal studies students and educators with the publishing industry's finest content and best service. We offer an extensive selection of products for over 70 titles and we continue to grow with more new titles each year. We also provide:

- online resources for instructors and students
- state-specific materials
- custom publishing options from Pearson Prentice Hall representative, visit www.prenhall.com

To locate your local Pearson Prentice Hall representative, visit *www.prenhall.com.*

To view Pearson Legal Series titles and to discover a wide array of resources for both instructors and students, please visit out website at:

www.prenhall.com/legal_studies

Contents

Law Protecting Specific Environmental Media

Law Regulating Environmental Pollution

Law Protecting Specific Biota

Federal Environmental Processes

Appendices

Foreword

It is with great pleasure—and some humility—that I write this foreword. The pleasure comes from the fact that such a comprehensive, understandable teaching text has been written and compiled. The humility comes from the fact that I, instead of many others competent in the field of environmental law, was chosen to offer the foreword.

To put this book in its proper, important perspective, I think it is not only appropriate but necessary to look back at the establishment and development of the field of what we now know as environmental law. There were always laws governing the very basics of how we were to treat the environment—water, air, and solid waste. Prior to 1970, these laws were administered by dedicated, knowledgeable technical people, i.e., sanitary engineers. Frankly, they did a good job with statutes and regulations that gave them very little "muscle" to enforce standards that protected the environment. To be honest, in those days no public outcry would have forced policy makers to enact strict environmental laws that would enhance environmental conditions, not just maintain the status quo.

In the late 1960s, the public, the press, and others became aware of events that demonstrated that there was something seriously wrong and, in fact, foul with the environment. Just driving through Gary, Indiana, you could feel the pollution. A river with industrial discharges began to burn. Walking the streets of Los Angeles, your eyes watered and you did not see the sun until noon. Such conditions and others like them produced what were called "zealots," who took it upon themselves to become physically involved in trying to stop the degradation of the environment. One of these zealots was called "the fox." He (or she) combed the Fox River in Illinois and plugged discharge outfalls with rags, concrete, or anything else that would ebb the flow of discharges into the river.

Another type of zealot was the writer. Perhaps the one writer who is most often credited with popularizing concern for the environment is Rachel Carson. In her book *Silent Spring*, Carson described in detail how, if we continued our polluting ways, someday there would be no spring and, indeed, no earth for us to live on; the reign of man on earth would end. While the major concern of the book was to highlight the deleterious effects of DDT, the book clearly had an effect on many environmental activists in the United States. Other books and newspaper articles were also instrumental in drawing attention to environmental concerns.

As a result of the efforts of zealots and writers, citizens' groups, like the campaign against pollution in Chicago led by the Reverend Leonard Duby, became increasingly involved in public demonstrations against polluters. With greater numbers of citizens involved, it was not long before politicians joined their ranks.

In 1970, protection of the environment became a local, state, and national political issue. Ironically, the issue crossed political lines in that both Republicans and Democrats supported the establishment of new ways to protect the environment. The significance of this issue was demonstrated by the establishment of a National Earth Day in April of 1970. On that day, all people gathered and demonstrated to foster protection of the environment.

Protection of the Environment Was Equated with Protection of Life!

Because laws concerning the environment were deemed inadequate, the body politic, under pressure from the citizenry, called for new, innovative environmental laws. Thus, environmental law as we know it today was born.

To deal with the protection of the environment, there developed a series of laws, mostly by media—air, water, solid waste. Perhaps the most comprehensive state law at the time was the Illinois Environmental Protection Act, which brought the regulation of environmental control under one statute with a regulatory screen that included

- a technical group (the Environmental Protection Agency);
- a regulatory/enforcement court (the Pollution Control Board); and
- a research group (the Environmental Institute for Environmental Quality).

The federal government was also very active. Congress adopted the Clean Air Act in 1970, the Clean Water Act in 1972, and the Resource Conservation and Recovery Act in 1978. President Nixon, by executive order, created the U.S. Environmental Protection Agency (EPA) in the fall of 1970; this new agency was the consolidation of divisions in various agencies of the federal government.

Since those days, new laws have been enacted and existing laws have been amended. The new laws, among others, include

- The Toxic Substances Control Act
- CERCLA (Superfund)
- The Endangered Species Act
- The Emergency Planning and Community Right-to-Know Act

Because of such laws, governmental bureaucracies were established and grew rapidly. The EPA quickly became one of the larger federal agencies, and at some early point in time its regulations, codified in the *Code of Federal Regulations* (C.F.R.), became more voluminous than the regulations of the Department of the Treasury.

In addition, industrial bureaucracies were established. The managements of industrial facilities, also known as the "regulated community," soon learned that engineering and law groups, as their constituents, could not deal with the statutory and regulatory morals that were developing. They realized that what was needed were engineering and legal specialists who could review and interpret an ever-growing body of environmental laws and regulations and who could deal with government bureaucrats.

In addition to the growing government, industrial service groups began to form around this new field of environmental law and regulation. These groups included firms that would perform technical consulting on such matters as equipment control and operational changes. They also included lawyers.

The structure of laws enacted to protect the environment required that specific detailed regulations be developed to provide the regulated community with the requirements for compliance. The regulations lawyers, working with the engineers, had to put into words very technical requirements that had to be followed by the regulated community. The result was the proposal and adoption of complex, intricate regulations that were filled with new words, phrases, and cross-referencing sections.

So long and complicated were some of the phrases that acronyms were developed. For example, under the Clean Air Act, most stationary sources of contaminants must use "reasonably available control technology." Instead of using that long phrase, practitioners used the term "RACT." Similarly, under the Clean Water Act, most (if not all) dischargers of water (contaminated or otherwise) are required to have a National Pollutant Discharge Elimination System permit. This was referred to as an "NPDES" permit; some even tried to pronounce "NPDES" as a word. Thousands of new words and acronyms were developed as a result of environmental laws. A virtually new language was developed, and knowledge of this new language became a test of whether a person knew—or did not know—the requirements of environmental laws.

The complexity and volume of these new laws created the need to educate people coming into the field and to continually update the knowledge of the practitioners in the field of environmental law. In the early 1970s, few texts were written. Probably the earliest and most comprehensive was a book written by Professor David Carrie (a law professor at the University of Chicago Law School and the first chairperson of the Illinois Pollution Control Board) titled, brilliantly, *Environmental Law*. It was a solid attempt to compile existing laws in a text that would educate and challenge users about this burgeoning new field of law. There were other books for teachers and students, but it was hard to find any one book that could be considered comprehensive. In those days, I taught an environmental law course at the Chicago-Kent School of Law, and in that class I used handout material essentially of my own making. I'm not sure students grasped the subject entirely, but I did have one student who rose to be head of enforcement for Region V (in Chicago, Illinois) of the EPA. Unfortunately, he never gave his teacher any breaks!

A problem with writing materials in the 1970s was that by the time one finished a piece of work, it was usually outdated because laws and their attendant regulations were changing almost daily. Conversely, during the 1980s and early 1990s, while changes in the laws and regulations did occur, they did not do so at warp speed. It became time to develop learning tools that could have a permanent base and be used by teachers, students, and practitioners. *Essentials of Environmental Law* fits that bill.

In looking at the third edition of *Essentials of Environmental Law*, I marvel at its breadth and comprehensiveness. It so beautifully fits the purpose for which it was intended (a lawyer's phrase!). I believe that to be an effective educational tool, a book must have certain qualities, which I set forth below and explain how this book fits those qualities.

1. Thorough and Comprehensive

Any text on a particular subject must contain all of the relevant material related to that subject. Obviously, if one is to learn about a subject, one must have all the aspects and parts of it before him or her. The difficulty with writing a book on environmental law is the massive amounts of material that must be put together. This book compiles all of the laws, regulations, and pronouncements of environmental law. From air pollution to the intricacies of the Endangered Species Act, it lays out for the student or reader all relevant information. Teachers and students who use the book can rest assured that when they complete the text, they will have "run the gamut" of the field of environmental law.

Nothing of consequence is missed. For instance, the text includes numerous references to related materials so that readers can go beyond the four corners of the volume to see the "real thing" in terms of actual regulatory language, court cases, and the like. Having taught environmental law, I know that both teacher and student pray they have not "missed something." With this book, their prayers are answered.

2. Understandable

A text can be thorough and comprehensive, like the *Code of Federal Regulations,* but written in a way that is understandable. From the teacher's standpoint, this is important because to teach effectively, he or she must use material conducive to learning. By the same token, students must feel comfortable with text material so that they do not approach it as some archaic language that requires rote memory rather than full understanding.

One of the best aspects of this book is that it is written in such a way so as to allow the person who knows little or nothing about the field to grasp its elements. Laws and regulations concerning the environment are complex. This book makes the complex, simple. This is not to say that the study of environmental laws and regulations is an easy task, but it is to say that unless such laws and regulations are made understandable (or simple), fully comprehending them is an impossible task.

Teacher and students should take heart that, although lengthy, the text is both readable and understandable. With the proper effort of both teacher and student, learning can happen.

3. Organization

One objective of a comprehensive work is effective organization. A reader cannot be asked to jump from one place to another and still be expected to comprehend what is before him or her. All one has to do is read basic environmental statutes and regulations to understand that point. One section refers back to another, that section refers to another, and so on. In this book, material is organized in such a way that the reader does not need to "look back" to figure out where he or she is.

4. Detailed

A good teaching/learning text must provide a balance between simplicity and detail. The book must be simple enough to understand and absorb but must be detailed enough to provide the reader with a full examination of the subject matter. This book balances clarity with detail. The text is simple yet has the appropriate number of references to satisfy even the most detail-hungry reader.

5. Reference Text

A well-written book on any subject, particularly on environmental law, should be able to be used not only as a practitioner's tool but also as a teacher's tool. When a practitioner is faced with a real-life problem, he or she calls to mind all relevant laws and regulations that will help him or her reach a solution. Many times a problem is a multimedia one; that is, it involves air issues, water issues, solid waste issues, and so on. It is very beneficial to have a reference work that allows the problem solver to scan the various areas.

For example, the issue may begin with the control of an air emission source by the use of a wet scrubber. This control device adds a mist to flue gas and captures contaminants that otherwise would be emitted into the atmosphere. The scrubber will produce a slurry (water plus the contaminant collected) that must be dealt with: Should it be put into the wastewater treatment system or should it be landfilled? This book certainly allows the problem solver review of air laws, water laws, and solid waste laws. But it also allows him or her to look at other laws (e.g., Superfund) to see whether there is some applicability to the problem. This book is an excellent reference and resource for scanning relevant law.

In Conclusion

The American Association for Paralegal Educators (AAfPE) reviewed earlier editions of *Essentials of Environmental Law* and its corresponding syllabus and, seemingly in comparison, incorporated much of it into its "Model Syllabus: Environmental Law." The Model Syllabus mentions that the Syllabus Committee reviewed this text, and its contribution toward the final Model Syllabus is apparent.

For all of these detailed reasons, this book is a must for those who wish to learn about environmental law and for those practitioners in the field who simply need a reference text.

Before ending this foreword, I would like to take this opportunity to talk about Craig B. Simonsen. I first met him when he interviewed at our law firm for what was our first paralegal position. Craig was then (and continues to be) an enthusiastic learner, and I could see that he would be a strong asset to our firm—so he was hired. During the time I worked with Craig, I marveled at his intelligence, dedication, and, most of all, his organization. It was a great comfort to work with him because I could give him a task and know that it would be carried out competently and completely. He was also a delight to have around the office with his pleasant smile and dry sense of humor. It is clear from this text that Craig has honed his skills admirably since our early association.

Richard J. Kissel
of Counsel
Gardner Carton & Douglas

Preface

Everything You Need to Know About
Environmental Law, You Learned in Kindergarten

by Patrick A. Parenteau*

As you can tell from the title, I'm introducing a little levity, a bit of balance, into the serious business of environmental law. Environmentalists and lawyers who practice in the environmental field are so damned serious about regulations that they just squelch any kind of creativity or freedom of expression. They are a very sober crowd.

Somewhere along the line you might have noticed that there's a fair amount of jargon in the environmental field; you've got the EPA telling the PRPs to do the RI/FS under the NCP or they're going to be hit with a 106 order for treble damages with no pre-enforcement review. And after the RIGS, the PRPs are going to have to do the RD and the RA according the ROD based on the ARARs. Of course, this only applies to NPL sites and not CERCLIS sites. Clear enough?

And the jargon is not just confined to the pollution control side of the field; it infects natural resources management as well. For example, the BLM should have done an EIS on ORVs but elected instead to do a FONSI on EP and was successfully sued by SCLDF under NEPA and the APA. The court rejected BLM's defense that the EA was tiered to a programmatic EIS under the decadal management plan under FLPMA. That's what we lawyers in the field have to deal with day in and day out, and it probably mystifies normal people as to what all these acronyms–the alphabet soup of laws and regulations and technical terms–really mean.

Is it really that inaccessible to the common mind? Do you have to be part of some strange religion to understand the deep, dark secrets of environmental law?

---

* This essay is based on an address given September 10, 1992, at an environmental law seminar sponsored by the Federal Judicial Center and the Northwestern School of Law of Lewis & Clark College.

The preface is reprinted by permission of the publisher for "Everything You Need to Know About Environmental Law, You Learned in Kindergarten," by Patrick A. Parentceau, 23 *Environmental Law* 223–232 (1993).

No! It all comes down to a lot of commonsense understanding and simple principles. So what I thought I'd do is to go through Robert Fulghum's *All I Really Need to Know I Learned in Kindergarten*[1] and see whether the rules that were announced to us in kindergarten have any relevance to environmental law.

The first lesson is **Sharing.** Paraphrasing Chief Seattle, "The Earth doesn't belong to us, we belong to the Earth. We don't so much inherit the land from our forebears as we borrow it from our descendants."[2] I don't think we've improved on that clear, penetrating vision of our relationship with the earth with all our fancy ideas and technical jargon about environmental law and natural resource management.

Leopold, whose *A Sand County Almanac* is a conservation bible for many, talked about how we're all creatures of a place; the more we have a sense of the place, the more we understand the place, and the more we listen to the earth, the greater appreciation we'll have of the earth and the better care we will take of it under the classic stewardship ethic.[3]

Gifford Pinchot, founder of our national forest management system, also wrote about a conservation philosophy, one that would maximize the benefits for the greatest number of people through careful management and stewardship of nature resources. John Stuart Mill acknowledged in an economic context the utilitarian value of trying to get the maximum benefit from resources. The concepts of maximum sustainable yield and multiple use are the foundations of management of public lands.

It's no small task to manage RVs and backpackers on the same lands, jet boats and wind surfers on the same river, mining uses and wilderness experiences in the same forests. Furthermore, that's only in the context of current uses and doesn't consider generational aspects–what we leave behind for our children and grandchildren. Sharing everything is clearly something with which we're struggling in the area of natural resource management.

Biodiversity—the concept of maximizing the number of species in their natural evolutionary relationships to the systems that support them, whether it's the rainforests of South America or Indonesia, or the Douglas fir forests of the Northwest—is important to us all because ecosystems have all sorts of interesting interconnections that

---

[1] Robert Fulghum, *All I Really Need to Know I Learned in Kindergarten: Uncommon Thoughts on Common Things* (1988).

[2] Whether the Chief actually said this is open to question. See Paul S. Wilson, *What Chief Seattle Said*, 22 ENVTL. L. 1451 (1992).

[3] Aldo Leopold, *A Sand County Almanac, With Essays on Conservation from Round River* (Oxford University Press 1966).

we only dimly perceive. Biodiversity is shared both locally and globally. Forests and peatbogs fix carbon and prevent gases from reaching the upper atmosphere that may cause global warming. All of these things are phenomena that we're only beginning to understand.

The management and conservation of some of these biological resources have global and permanent implications for life on earth. Sharing those resources (and understanding how to share those resources) is a real challenge. Sharing is a simple rule but difficult to apply.

The second lesson is **Play Fair.** Playing fair in the environmental context means setting clear, understandable ground rules for everyone to follow. Government sets those rules, and industry is required to comply. Citizen groups play the role of watchdog to make sure everybody does what they are supposed to do and that the government enforces the rules. Environmental rules designed to protect air, water, and land are being enforced vigorously and diligently. But those rules must also be fair.

Frankly, environmental rules are not always fair. It's a constant struggle to adjust and modify those rules to make them more fair. Rules that aren't fair quickly lose support; a system that lacks fundamental fairness is doomed. In fact, you can make a cogent argument that unfair rules are worse than no rules.

From an industry standpoint, fairness means a level playing field. If government is going to intervene in the market context and "internalize the external costs" of environmental pollution, it must do so in a way that doesn't benefit one segment of the industry versus another. Of course, in the global market it's extremely complicated to try to maintain a competitive advantage between one country and another. But leveling the playing field is something that industry looks to government to do correctly and fairly.

The Superfund[4] is a good example of an unfair rule, and nobody makes any bones about it. Courts in their decisions are fond of saying fairness plays no role in the Superfund program. One can't say the Superfund is totally unfair, but one can certainly find examples of how the liability scheme sometimes overreaches as it is applied in a retroactive, unforgiving, all-consuming manner.

The rules also have to be applied fairly and enforced even-handedly. The main purpose of governmental enforcement of the rules is not so much punishing the malfeasant as it is to protect the people who do comply with the rules. It's a whole different way of looking at enforcement, but that's really what it's all about. If people are going

---

[4] Comprehensive Environmental Response, Compensation, and Liability Act (CERCLA), 42 U.S.C. §§ 9601 to 9675 (1988).

to go to the trouble to learn the rules, spend the money it takes to comply with the rules, hire the consultants, hire the lawyers, install and maintain the equipment, audit the performance, and make changes as necessary, at least they deserve to know that it's not going to place them at an economic disadvantage. That's what fairness in the enforcement context should mean.

Unfortunately, the expression "the government is fond of shooting the volunteer" is often true. Industries and businesses that step up to tackle an environmental problem, to undertake the auditing or compliance program, are too often the ones that government singles out for enforcement. Why? Because they have raised their profiles above the rest of the pack and make an easy target.

One of the major debates now is what use should be made of self-audits and internal environmental reports. The government insists on the right to access all information that business or industry might use in an audit. But is this fair? By auditing you look for problems in your compliance program. You look for violations. You document and track those problems to correct them, which costs time and money. Correction involves training programs and a lot of complicated investments in an area where the amount of regulation makes it inevitable that a business will be in violation at any given time. The sheer number of regulations, the fact that they're always changing, the fact that they're subject to interpretation, and the fact that the equipment on which you rely doesn't always announce that it's going to fail, make violation almost inevitable. The question is: how much can government use the information collected by businesses that are trying legitimately, in good faith, as good corporate citizens, to discover the problems and the violations they might have? There have been instances where the government has prosecuted businesses and individuals based on information gathered through self-audits. What kind of an incentive does that create for industry?

The Uniform Sentencing Guidelines[5] are another example of a good idea to objectify fair sentencing for criminal defendants. But unless they're intelligently applied with some judgment, they can work unfairly. Because of the strict liability nature of most environmental statutes, virtually every violation can be prosecuted as a criminal offense.

The third lesson is **Don't Hit People.** In the environmental context, hitting people comes down to introducing poisons and other chemicals into their environment. The "knowing-endangerment" provisions, the more recently added provisions of the Clean Air and Clean Water Acts,[6] recognize that businesses that work with

---

[5] U.S. Sentencing Commission, *Guidelines Manual* (1991).
[6] 42 U.S.C. § 7413(C) (1988); 33 U.S.C. § 1319(C) (1988).

hazardous materials now have a duty to take even greater care not to expose people unnecessarily and beyond the limits of their permits.

The fourth rule is **Put Things Back Where You Found Them.** John Muir said everything in the universe is hooked to everything else. Aldo Leopold said the first rule of intelligent tinkering is to save all the pieces.[7] The idea of putting things back where you found them is one of the primary principles of environmental management and environmental ethics. In strip mining, it means reclaiming the land. Sometimes what you reclaim is a little different than it was when you started, but you must make an effort to put the land back into its approximate former contours and replace the native species of plants and animals that were there before the mining operation began.

Restoration biology and restoration forestry are emerging concepts in the field of wetlands management and forest management. These are efforts to find, actively and affirmatively, areas that have been disturbed, altered, or damaged, where the biological functions and ecological systems have been diminished; then try to restore, recover, and nurture those areas to offset the ongoing losses and perturbations that we visit on the earth almost daily.

The fifth lesson is **Clean Up Your Own Mess.** That's Superfund writ large. In fact, clean it up even if it's not your own mess. The fundamental rule here, the principle, is "Polluter Pays." It's a good rule. Those who pollute should pay to clean it up. Internalize the costs of doing business so that ways will be found to minimize wastes. To take care of it properly, to treat it, to clean it up before it's released into the environment, is the Pogo Principle, the idea that we're all basically responsible. It relates to consumer behavior, what we buy, what we demand from the marketplace, whether we want white toilet paper in which dioxin has been used or brown toilet paper without dioxin.

The Pogo Principle has spawned a whole new movement. The Federal Trade Commission has adopted new "green label" regulations to regulate the accuracy of claims that products are "environmentally friendly." Groups like Green Seal and Green Cross are out there promoting the idea that as intelligent consumers we should create the demand for environment-friendly goods and services. "Reduce, re-use, recycle" is the battle cry of many environmentalists. It's a personal ethic kind of thing; maybe even a "family value."

The sixth lesson is **Don't Take Things That Aren't Yours.** This gives me a chance to talk about the great "takings" debate. My question is "Who's taking what?" The takings debate has resurfaced as a

---

[7] Leopold, *supra* note 3.

result of some court decisions favorable to landowners, including *Lucas*.[8] These decisions have given rise to movements whose battle cry is "wise use" (although I think their emphasis is on "use").[9] They've learned a little bit from environmentalists about oversimplifying and bumperstickerizing difficult issues. There's no question about it; property rights are really important. Whether they're sanctified or not, I don't know; I'm not a theologian. But they are certainly important. To a lot of people who own and try to use property, I'm sure it seems as though government regulations telling them what to do with their property are confiscations. And I'm sure in a lot of instances government regulation is, or comes very close to, confiscation of their property, or what they think is their property. Sometimes regulation is just downright stupid, and maybe we need a constitutional amendment prohibiting regulations.

But there is another way to look at this problem that doesn't imply a right or wrong answer. The *way* we look at things—the environmental issues—really does alter the context of what's being observed. The landowners see the government regulations as a taking. But from the public's standpoint, the private parties are the ones doing the taking. They're taking the public's right to clean water, clean air, biological diversity and the public's right to enjoy the amenities of public resources. Who's taking what? It's not easy to sort that out. It is a clash of values. It's not reducible to a simple legal formula. It's not answerable by scientific principles. It's not answerable by economic theories. It's a classic clash of legitimate values, and how we sort it out is always going to be difficult.

The seventh lesson is **Say You're Sorry When You Hurt Somebody.** Remember the *Exxon-Valdez*? How can we forget that? Remember the tanker running aground on Bligh Reef with the drunken captain talking to the Coast Guard: "We've fetched up, ah, hard aground . . . and, ah, evidently leaking some oil. . . ."[10] Have you got pictures in your mind? The enormous ugly black plume of crude oil seeping out of the hull, headed toward the pristine beaches and shoals of Prince William Sound and stretching 200 miles down the coast? When it came time to 'fess up, take the punishment, what did the president of Exxon Corporation say about the billion-dollar fine? "It won't affect our first quarter earnings." You know what happened when he said that? The plea agreement that had been worked out was thrown out by Judge Vanderhyde in Alaska, and I don't doubt it was because of the arrogance expressed by the president of Exxon.

---

[8] *Lucas v. South Carolina Coastal Council,* 112 S. Ct. 2886 (1992).
[9] Roberta Ulrich, *Multiple-Use Groups Alarm "Green" Forces,* The Sunday Oregonian, December 6, 1992, at A1, A28.
[10] *Hazlewood v. State,* 836 P.2d 943, 944 (Alaska Ct. App.) *reh'g denied* (1992).

In the end, there is something valuable about apologizing for visiting an insult on the earth, the same way you would if you punched someone in the nose without provocation, or even with provocation. And I think that it is clearly part of the learning, changing, evolving, and acculturizing experience that we say we're sorry when we've done something bad or stupid that results in environmental contamination or other environmental insult. I think courts are asking that more and more when they demand that senior corporate officers come to court at the plea agreement time and stand before God and everybody and say, "I'm sorry."

And that could be good for the soul, the same way it was for us in kindergarten. We didn't like it very much, but there is value in that process. Bad publicity is a big deterrent too. Jail, of course, is an even bigger deterrent. It does, as Samuel Johnson said about the imminent prospect of hanging, "concentrate the mind wonderfully."

The eighth lesson is **Wash Your Hands Before You Eat.** What can that have to do with the environment? The point is that personal characteristics and lifestyle have more of an impact on health and welfare than all of the environmental regulations combined. Smoking, drinking, eating. The risks imposed on us from some of these close-in impacts are infinitely greater than most of the ambient environmental risks that we spend so much time chasing.

To give you an example of the lengths to which we go to control industrial pollution in the natural environment, as opposed to naturally occurring hazards, consider dioxin, a by-product of bleaching wood pulp. There are nine operating pulp mills on the Columbia River. The ambient river standard for dioxin is 0.013 parts per quadrillion. That is not detectable in the natural environment of the river. You wouldn't be able to find it in that concentration, even if you went out looking for it with the most sophisticated equipment available. You'd have to go all the way back up to the plant's bleaching operation to find any detectable dioxin; our standard for the Columbia River is that stringent. It's based on a one in a million risk of cancer or other health problems.[11]

We have that kind of intense focus and regulation on dioxin, and yet radon, which is a naturally occurring hazard and carcinogen, is essentially unregulated and uncontrolled. People all over the area where radon is found, even Native Americans who fish from the rivers, can be exposed to a great deal more cancer risk from radon than they'll ever risk in a lifetime of exposure to dioxin.

---

[11] Office of Water Regulations and Standards, U.S. EPA, *Ambient Water Quality Criteria for 2,3,7,8-Tetrachlorodibenzo-P-Dioxin*, EPA 440/5-84-007 (1984).

When the EPA has done a self-analysis of its priorities,[12] it almost always concludes that what it is regulating is not among the greatest threats to human health or ecological health. The priorities truly are misplaced. They are the product of a political system that reacts to perceived problems. But from a standpoint of protecting human health and the environment, a lot of what we're regulating is less important than what is not being regulated.

The ninth lesson is **Flush.** The idea of flushing goes beyond the obvious. What it really suggests is "out of sight, out of mind." We put the trash in a container, and it goes away somewhere. We flush the toilet, and what is in it goes away somewhere. Magic.

No, it doesn't go away anywhere! There is no "away" in the environment. What goes up comes down. What goes into the ground goes into the groundwater and into the tap. What goes into the river goes into the fish, then into us. What goes out on the tide comes back on the beach. We thought we were regulating the tall smoke stacks to blow pollution away from the people below the stacks. We took a while to figure out that, once the pollution blew away, it came down somewhere else. It acidified the lakes of the Adirondacks and poisoned the Great Lakes. One of the most interesting phenomena that has been discovered about the Great Lakes is this: The greatest source of toxic contaminants is probably airborne from the smelters and utilities in Canada and the United States, rather than from the pipes that empty into the Great Lakes. Portland still hasn't learned the rule of dealing with what it flushes, as you will see when you take the CSO (combined sewer outflows) tour. A couple of hundred years of experience has not taught us that we should not crap in the places where we live and swim in the places where we crap. For all our sophistication, we do still have a few things yet to learn.

The tenth lesson is **Take a Nap.** In the environmental context, when I say take a nap, I mean chill out, take a break, time out, cease fire, lower the rhetoric, search for some common ground, give a reason a chance. Look for solutions instead of constantly dwelling on the problems and pointing the finger. Try alternative dispute resolution, try mediation, try mini-trials, try arbitration, try anything so that we can bring these values onto the table and talk about them—because that's where environmental conflict really rests.

The last rule is **Be Aware of Wonder.** Look around you. As Thoreau said, "The wonder of the natural world really is a tonic."[13]

---

[12] Science Advisory Board, U.S. EPA, *Reducing Risk* (1990).
[13] Henry David Thoreau, *Walden* (1966).

It's a classic spiritual value, one we have trouble expressing, one that's very personal. I'd like to close by including something from Wallace Stegner. In this 1960 letter to the U.S. Forest Service, Stegner is trying to get beyond the uniforms and protective layers the government clothes itself in when it approaches these issues. It grabs the Forest Service where it lives and where he thinks we all should live.

> Something will have gone out of us as a people if we ever let the remaining wilderness be destroyed; if we permit the last virgin forests to be turned into comic books and plastic cigarette cases; if we drive the few remaining members of the wild species into zoos or to extinction; if we pollute the last clear air and dirty the last clean streams and push out our paved roads through the last of the silence, so that never again will Americans be free in their own country from the noise, the exhausts, the stinks of human and automotive wastes. And so that never again can we have the chance to see ourselves single, separate, vertical and individual in the world, part of the environment of trees and rocks and soil, brother to the other animals, part of the natural world and competent to belong in it. Without any remaining wilderness, we are committed wholly, without chance for even momentary reflection and rest, to a headlong drive into our technological termite-life, the Brave New World of a completely man-controlled environment. We need wilderness preserved—as much of it as is left, and as many kinds—because it was the challenge against which our character as a people was formed. The remainder and the reassurance that it is still there is good for our spiritual health, even if we never once in ten years set foot in it. It is good for us when we are young, because of the incomparable sanity it can bring briefly, as vacation rest, into our insane lives. It is important to us when we are old simply because it is there—important, that is, simply as idea.[14]

---

[14] Wallace Stegner, *The Sound of Mountain Water* (Penguin 1997). 146–147.

Acknowledgments

In the writing of this textbook, I saw at every stage the hand of God moving. It is a great blessing in my life that my efforts have been combined with the efforts of these many outstanding men and women.

I gratefully acknowledge the valuable support, assistance, and encouragement of Nancy, my wife, and Kevin, my son. Also, I remember the loving assistance and support of Ida and Edward Kulach, my mother and my dear-departed stepfather; Ken and Ann Simonsen, my dear-departed father and stepmother; Carl and Patricia Simonsen, my brother and his wife; and so many other family members and friends.

Thanks to SeyFarth Shaw LLP, my employee, for allowing me, a paralegal, to write substantive client articles and newsletters, and to go as a speaker on substantive environmental law topics to meetings and conferences. This is an encouragement to me and, I think, somewhat unusual!

My heartfelt thanks go to Richard J. Kissel, author of the foreword. Dick Kissel was my first employer in environmental law. His foreword goes beyond a recommendation of the textbook; rather, he introduces environmental law and the practice it has become. It is an excellent addition to this edition.

Thanks to Patrick A. Parenteau for allowing me to include his interesting essay as preface to this work.

Thanks to Eric E. Boyd, who is well-accustomed to working with paralegals (me, particularly), who did an excellent job on the CAA chapter.

Thanks to Peter D. Holmes, who contributed the CWA chapter, and did excellent work.

Thanks to Charles W. Wesselhoft, a former paralegal who is now an environmental attorney, who contributed and updated the RCRA chapter.

Thanks to Professor James F. Berry for his vigorous support of this edition, and for his expert authoring of the TSCA, EPCRA, and NEPA chapters.

Thanks to Francine Shay, an environmental paralegal, and Jody L. Brooks, an environmental attorney, for the excellent work they have done on this edition's new chapter on endangered species. Special thanks also to Francine for her complete revision and update of Appendix E on Internet resources.

Thanks to David A. Piech, a former paralegal who is now an environmental attorney, for his authoring and updating the chapter on administrative law.

Thanks also to my students during those first years of my teaching environmental law courses and seminars. They encouraged me to write my own environmental law textbook for paralegals and then suffered through learning from earlier drafts. Their comments and suggestions have been valuable additions to this work.

Thanks to Lawrence E. Keller, an environmental engineer, and to Anne Chatham Ryan, formerly environmental counsel, for their review and comments on portions of earlier drafts of the original text.

Thanks to Frances Beall Whiteside, Steven B. Spector, Linda Furlet, and William Quimby for their efforts as editors and peer reviewers. Their input and comments on this text were valuable.

Thanks to Westlaw database publishers and to Susan Hyser, Account Manager, specifically, for their provision of temporary passwords to conduct much of the research and cite checking for this volume. Theirs is a very useful service to the legal and educational communities.

Thanks to the assistance and expertise of Carlisle Publishing Services for their careful proofreading and editing on the third edition. Also thanks to the staff at Pearson Prentice Hall for their assitance all the way through this project.

Finally, thanks to Enika Pearson Schulze, whose encouragement, assistance, and comments are always a great help. Her insightful courage in building a line of quality paralegal textbooks is a credit to her profession and to mine.

The Authors

Craig B. Simonsen holds a B.A. with honors and an M.A. in history from Northeastern Illinois University in Chicago, Illinois, and has a lawyer's assistant certificate from Roosevelt University's Lawyer's Assistant Program in Chicago. He is a senior paralegal at Seyfarth Shaw LLP in Chicago, Illinois. He has been an adjunct instructor for environmental law for the Paralegal Studies Program at Mallinckrodt College in Wilmette, Illinois, and the Roosevelt University Program. Mr. Simonsen has authored another Prentice Hall Legal Series title, *Computer-Aided Legal Research (CALR)* (2006), and on the internet a comprehensive computer-aided legal research manual and textbook. He also authored the *Environmental Law Resource Guide* (New York: Clark Boardman Callaghan, 1995), a paralegal practice series deskbook. Mr. Simonsen has also authored numerous Blackboard coursesites and textbook companion Web sites for various legal studies titles, including *Introduction to Law: Its Dynamic Nature* (2005), by Henry Cheeseman, for Prentice Hall. Additionally, Mr. Simonsen was the featured speaker on Internet research and resources for the Lake Michigan States Section of the Air & Waste Association in April 2005, and on environmental law at the 2005 Annual Convention of the National Federation of Paralegal Associations (NFPA). He has also authored numerous articles on environmental law and litigation support appearing in the *NFPA Reporter* and *The Paralegal*. Mr. Simonsen is founder and past chairperson of the Illinois Paralegal Association's Environmental Law Section.

James F. Berry is a biologist, college professor, and environmental attorney. He is a professor of biology at Elmhurst College in Elmhurst, Illinois, where he specializes in the fauna and ecology of wetlands and other sensitive areas, and in conservation biology. He also teaches environmental law courses for the Illinois Institute of Technologies' Environmental Management program, and occasionally for IIT Chicago-Kent Law School. As an attorney, Dr. Berry specializes in environmental, land use, and natural resources law. He is licensed to practice law in all state courts in Florida and Illinois, as well as in a number of federal district courts and courts of appeals. He is currently in private practice in Elmhurst, Illinois, having previously practiced with the law firm of Burke, Bosselman & Weaver in Chicago, Illinois, and Boca Raton, Florida. Dr. Berry's biological education includes B.S. and M.S. degrees from Florida State University, and a Ph.D. from the University of Utah. He received his law degree from IIT Chicago-Kent College of Law, having completed the law school's Program in Environmental and Energy Law. He is a member of many scientific and legal professional organizations, and has published over eighty scientific and legal articles and book chapters. He is a popular speaker on environmental issues for a variety of scientific, legal, and planning organizations and workshops, which have included the American Planning Association, the Chicago Bar Association, the Izaak Walton League of America, and the Midsouth Planning and Zoning Institute. Dr. Berry is also coauthor of *The Environmental Law and Compliance Handbook* (New York: McGraw-Hill, 2000).

Eric E. Boyd is a partner at Seyfarth Shaw LLP in Chicago, Illinois. He represents a wide variety of corporate clients in environmental regulatory compliance, litigation, and transaction matters. Mr. Boyd earned a J.D. degree from Indiana University, cum laude, where he was also executive editor of the *Indiana Law Journal*, and he holds a B.S. with honors from Northwestern University in Illinois. Mr. Boyd spends the majority of his time tracking and interpreting environmental laws and regulations. He has negotiated favorable air, water, solid, and hazardous waste permits for existing and new sources. He has obtained variances to allow clients to install controls in stages, and site-specific regulatory changes. He has negotiated with federal and state agencies regarding the cleanup of contaminated sites and has prepared comments and testimony on various state and federal air and waste regulations. He is a frequent speaker and author on air and hazardous waste developments. Mr. Boyd also has been involved in a variety of enforcement and environmental litigation matters. He has defended clients against local, state, federal, and citizen suits involving alleged violations of air, water, toxic chemicals, and waste regulations. He not only has successfully resolved such actions but has also kept clients out of litigation. He has also represented clients in private and governmental matters involving the cleanup of contaminated sites. He has represented insureds in environmental insurance coverage cases and has obtained favorable rulings and negotiated favorable settlements. Mr. Boyd has litigated matters before local, state, and federal agencies, Illinois courts, and federal courts.

Jody L. Brooks holds a B.S., with honors, in Management from Jacksonville University; a J.D., with honors, from the University of Florida, Levin College of Law; and an Environmental and Land Use Law Certificate from the University of Florida, Levin College of Law. Ms. Brooks is counsel for The St. Joe Company in Jacksonville, Florida, and advises the company's Regulatory Affairs division on environmental matters. Prior to going in-house, Ms. Brooks was an associate in the law firm of Lewis, Longman & Walker, P.A.

Peter D. Holmes is corporate counsel for BorgWarner Inc. in Auburn Hills, Michigan. Mr. Holmes began his practice in environmental law as an attorney with the U.S. Environmental Protection Agency's Office of General Counsel in Washington, D.C. He has taught environmental law as an associate professor at Western New England College School of Law and as an adjunct professor at Wayne State University Law School and Thomas M. Cooley Law School. He currently serves as chair-elect of the State Bar of Michigan's Environmental Law Section and is a certified hazardous materials manager. Mr. Holmes earned a B.S. in chemistry from Duke University, an M.S. in chemistry from the University of Michigan, and a J.D., magna cum laude, from the University of Michigan.

Richard J. Kissel, of-counsel in Gardner Carton & Douglas's Chicago office's Environmental Department, served as chairperson of that department from its inception until 1996. He has practiced environmental law since its beginning as a practice area. He codrafted the original Illinois Environmental Protection Act and was appointed by Governor Ogilvie to the first Illinois Pollution Control Board in 1970. He entered private practice in environmental law in 1973. Since that time, he has represented municipal and industrial clients in all aspects of environmental law, including air, water, solid waste, and Superfund. His varied background and experience as an in-house counsel, private practitioner, and government practitioner give him insight into the issues that face his municipal and industrial clients. Mr. Kissel is a frequent lecturer and writer on environmental law issues. He served as adjunct professor at Chicago-Kent College of Law and the University of Illinois School of Public Health. He was a contributor to the Illinois Continuing Legal Education Series on environmental law for many years. He received the Illinois Award from the Illinois Association of Wastewater Agencies. Mr. Kissel earned his J.D. at Northwestern University in Evanston, Illinois.

Patrick A. Parenteau holds a B.S. from Regis College, Denver, Colorado; a J.D. from Creighton University, Omaha, Nebraska; and an LL.M. in environmental law from George Washington University, Washington, D.C. Mr. Parenteau is the director of and a professor at the Environmental Law Center, Vermont Law School, South Royalton, Vermont. He has also served as of-counsel to and head of the environmental and natural resources practice group at the law firm of Perkins Coie in Portland, Oregon; as Commissioner of the Vermont Department of Environmental Conservation; and as Regional Counsel for Region I, United States Environmental Protection Agency. Mr. Parenteau is a faculty member of the Environmental Law Institute and has taught environmental law at the Willamette University School of Law, the Boston College Law School, and the

George Washington University National Law Center. He was a teaching fellow at the Lewis and Clark Law School. His publications include the essay prefacing this volume, "Everything You Wanted to Know About Environmental Law, You Learned in Kindergarten," 23 *Environmental Law* 223–232 (1993).

David A. Piech holds a B.S. in chemical engineering from the University of Notre Dame, Indiana; an M.B.A. from Loyola University in Chicago; and a J.D. from DePaul University School of Law in Chicago. Mr. Piech is an environmental attorney with Navistar International in Chicago, where he has worked on a wide range of environmental matters including clean air, clean water, solid and hazardous waste, Superfund, and product liability topics on both federal and state levels. Before becoming an attorney, Mr. Piech worked as a process engineer, quality engineer, and laboratory supervisor for several chemical manufacturers. While attending evening law school, he worked as an environmental paralegal at the Chicago firm of Ross & Hardies. Mr. Piech has held memberships in the Illinois State Bar Association, the American Bar Association, the Chicago Bar Association, the American Institute of Chemical Engineers, and the American Society of Quality Control.

Francine Shay, CP, holds a B.A., cum laude, from Brooklyn College of the City University of New York and is a National Association of Legal Assistants Certified Paralegal. Ms. Shay is a paralegal manager at Lewis, Longman & Walker, P.A., in West Palm Beach, Florida. Ms. Shay has been appointed to the Legal Studies Advisory Board for the West Palm Beach, Florida, campus of South University and serves on the Editorial Advisory Board of *Legal Assistant Today*, being featured as environmental paralegal in its May/June 1999 issue. She also serves as chair of the Public Relations Committee chair of the Paralegal Association of Florida, Inc., and as Career Network Chair for the Palm Beach County Chapter of the Association.

Charles W. Wesselhoft holds a B.S. in chemical engineering from Purdue University, West Lafayette, Indiana, and a J.D. from IIT Chicago-Kent School of Law in Chicago. Mr. Wesselhoft is a Deputy County Attorney for Pima County, Arizona, where he represents the County's wastewater treatment agency. Prior to his move to Arizona, Mr. Wesselhoft was in private practice in Chicago for over fifteen years, with a concentration in solid waste issues. He is registered in the state of Illinois as a professional engineer and has over twelve years of process and project engineering experience. Prior to practicing law, Mr. Wesselhoft worked for three years as an environmental law paralegal. He is a member of the Chicago Bar Association, the American Institute of Chemical Engineers, ASTM, and the State Bar of Arizona.

Introduction

Objectives of This Textbook

The objectives of this textbook are:

- To enable students to read and understand environmental documents, laws, rules, policy and guidance materials, and acronyms, enabling them to think critically, analyze, and interpret complex documents and events.
- To enable students to enter an environmental law practice as a paralegal, under the supervision of an attorney, to collect, organize and process environmental documents and information in support of administrative cases and litigation.
- To enable students to demonstrate effective researching and organizational skills within an environmental law practice area.
- To enable students to present research findings in written memorandum format and in oral presentation.

Essentials of Environmental Law

As illustrated in Patrick A. Parenteau's preface to this volume, everything you need to know about environmental law, you learned in kindergarten.

Well, almost everything.

AAfPE "Model Syllabus: Environmental Law"

Perhaps surprisingly, experience in environmental law or the sciences is not a requirement for an entry-level environmental law paralegal. As noted in the American Association for Paralegal Education's (AAfPE) *Model Syllabus: Environmental Law.*

Environmental Law courses in paralegal programs are taught with different philosophies—from a political science and economic approach to a technical/scientific approach and paralegal training approach. Actually, all these philosophies should exist in the "ideal" environmental law course. This Task Force [Model Syllabus Task Force on Environmental Law] has emphasized the paralegal training philosophy to reinforce AAfPE's goal to phrase course objectives as specific competencies and skills. However the complexity . . . of environmental law dictates that political science/economic and technical/scientific aspects be included, as shown by reading assignments and the bibliography.

An earlier edition of this textbook, with its syllabus and related course materials, was one of the models reviewed by the AAfPE's task force in the development of its *Model Syllabus*. This third edition, moreover, substantially updates all of its course materials to correspond to and to directly correlate with the AAfPE's *Model Syllabus: Environmental Law*.

A Paralegal in Environmental Law

Therefore, while the curriculum does cover topics in political science, economics, technology, and science, to be a paralegal in environmental law you need only an interest in the field, a willingness to learn about environmental law in all of its aspects, and an ability to organize information. The key point is that paralegal positions in this and in most law practice areas require information management and organizational skills, which are critical to advancement beyond the entry level.

To assist the student in gaining access to the environmental law field, this textbook indoctrinates the reader with literally hundreds of acronyms. The environmental law field is filled with so many long-winded terms that it has quite naturally become saturated with acronyms. As an aid to learning these acronyms, each chapter concludes with a glossary that lists and defines the many related acronyms.

The remainder of this introduction will review the history of the environmental law system and the historical legal responses to environmental contamination. It will conclude with a discussion of paralegal activities in an environmental law practice.

Legal Responses to Environmental Contamination

Before the 1970s and the enactment of federal environmental laws, there were limited responses to environmental contamination. Common law or "torts" (personal injury and property damage) were available as a cause of action to address civil wrongs. Several types of common law actions have been utilized in response to conduct alleged to involve environmental contamination.

Negligence has been utilized as a cause of action for personal injury and property damage arising out of exposure to hazardous wastes. Elements for a negligence case include the breach of a duty of due care, such as feasance, misfeasance, or nonfeasance, and require that such act is a violation of a standard of care, through negligence or recklessness. A reasonably close connection to the injury and actual damage or loss must also be shown.

Trespass, or an interference with another's possessory interest in land, has also been available in environmental torts. This type of case required an intentional, negligent, or ultrahazardous activity by the defendant.

Nuisance, or an unreasonable interference with another's use or enjoyment of his or her land, has been utilized in both private and public pollution actions. An invasion of a property interest is an example of a private nuisance. Relief might include an injunction as well as money damages. An unreasonable interference with a public right giving rise to an action by the public prosecutor is an example of a public nuisance.

Strict liability in tort for injury due to exposure to hazardous waste may be a viable cause of action. By itself, strict liability has been unevenly accepted among the states; but when coupled with negligence, it has been universally accepted.

Where an injury or damage is caused by a known product produced by identifiable manufacturers, there may be a cause of action for a product liability tort. These types of claims have been utilized more readily in recent history, with "toxic torts" growing into a specialty field of law. While the toxic tort case law builds on the more general practice of civil torts, there is now a body of case law that deals specifically with environmental torts.

One of the more tenuous toxic torts these days is medical monitoring.[1] A tort claim for medical monitoring seeks to recover the costs of periodic physical exams that are intended to detect the onset of physical injury but does not seek compensation for the anticipated harm itself. The plaintiff is someone who is not currently hurt, who wants the defendant to pay for medical testing that might detect a future injury that the plaintiff may never suffer.

The claims for medical monitoring have been seen related to exposures to asbestos, lead-based paint, tobacco, radiation, and drugs. The elements for a medical monitoring claim are

- Significant exposure
- Proven toxic substance
- Through tortious conduct
- Causing risk of developing serious latent disease

---

[1] This medical monitoring discussion summarizes research done by Andrew H. Perellis, Partner at Seyfarth Shaw LLP, Chicago.

- Periodic monitoring is warranted
- Examinations will facilitate early detection

The states are divided on whether a medical monitoring claim exists or not. Where this tort has been brought successfully, courts have used various methods of recovery, including lump sum payments, trust funds, and court-administered monitoring programs.

History of Environmental Protection

The history of environmental protection in the United States has been divided into three periods:

- 1840–1891   The Pre-Modern Period
- 1891–1969   The Conservationist Period
- 1969–Present   The Modern Period

These periods, as reviewed in detail in Anderson, Mandelker, and Tarlock, *Environmental Protection: Law and Policy* (Little, Brown and Company 1984), represent the development of ideas that continue to influence contemporary environmental law and policy.

1840–1891: The Pre-Modern Period

As early as the nineteenth century, New England Transcendentalists voiced reaction to the social disruption caused by the Industrial Revolution. Transcendentalists sought to emphasize the intuitive and spiritual above the empirical (scientific). The Transcendentalists attempted to develop a theory of the relationship between democracy and nature.

From these efforts came two major resource-use philosophies that continue to influence modern environmental law and policy. One, conservationism, became a major political movement. These philosophies were

- "preservationism," an elite philosophy concerned almost exclusively with preserving from development scenic portions of federal public lands; and
- "conservationism," the major philosophy that assumed the wisdom of developing and using the natural resources.

Key questions were (1) When should development occur? and (2) By whom should development be conducted? The only real issue was whether development should be through private or public ownership and utilization.

Pollution concerns during this early period were perceived, if perceived at all, as purely local public health concerns. Pollution prevention was not part of the early movements. The pre-modern period culminated in 1891 with the eventual withdrawal of entry of forest lands under the Homestead laws. The Homestead laws provided for the transfer of parcels of unoccupied land to homesteaders on payment of a nominal fee after five years of residence.

1891–1969: The Conservationist Period

This period saw the rise of a powerful progressive conservation movement applying the belief that, through resource planning, science could be used to better humanity and its conditions.

Importance was placed on the use and development of resources. An outgrowth of the conservationist philosophy, however, was the use of the state's police power over individual property rights to effect public resource policy. This use of power set the foundation for later legislative and judicial use of the regulation of private conduct that is especially prevalent in today's environmental regulation.

1969–Present: The Modern Period

The modern period began with the "environmental decade," beginning in about 1969. The idea of environmental law and environmental law practice has only evolved since that time. While a "natural resources law" had existed, it involved the proper use and exploitation of the environment and natural resources and lacked concern for environmental well-being. Environmental issues addressed before 1970, such as urban smog and sanitary controls, were purely local health concerns.

In 1970, the country was ripe for a positive political movement and agenda. With the evidence of visibly polluted lakes and rivers, the environmental cause was one of almost universal understanding and found little organized opposition. With the first Earth Day activities on April 22, 1970, the environmentalists illustrated to the country where improvements were necessary. Congress replied with an unprecedented response, passing the Clean Air Act.

The Clean Air Act in 1970 was the first major environmental statute, followed quickly by the Federal Water Pollution Control Act in 1972. By the mid-1970s, Congressional focus fell on toxic chemicals, and two laws were promulgated that regulated chemicals from premanufacture to ultimate disposal. Next came laws for municipal, solid, and hazardous waste handling and disposal. Then, in 1980, the hazardous waste site cleanup law was enacted. Finally, in 1986,

Congress enacted a new type of environmental law for community environmental emergency planning that compelled stringent public information requirements.

Paralegal Participation in Environmental Law

Environmental law has come of age and continues to be a fast-growing area. In any area of law, there is need for trained, knowledgeable attorneys, paralegals, and other support staff.

In environmental law practice, several skills are necessary. This is because administrative law practice and procedure are at the heart of most environmental cases (e.g., stemming from the agency decision-making process). The environmental practitioner must first be an administrative practitioner.

Environmental cases come to settlement by negotiation skills, a second facet necessary for a good environmental practitioner.

Finally, the environmental practitioner must be a litigator. From the very beginning of the administrative process, environmental cases must be prepared as if they will be litigated. An environmental paralegal's responsibilities will typically include all of those duties normally associated with litigation paralegals. Even where litigation does not follow, administrative cases are often hard-fought. Intensive preparation through document review and organization is necessary. These tasks then may involve

- Document organization and analysis
- Issue identification
- Witness and key file organization
- Drafting discovery documents and pleadings
- Case outlining
- Legal research and writing
- Factual, scientific, and technical research and writing
- Exhibit preparation
- Trial book preparation

An environmental paralegal may also perform tasks unlike peers in other practice areas. In particular, environmental paralegals may do the following types of projects:

- Review and analysis of environmental rule making
- Record (agency file) review and drafting testimony
- Research and writing on environmental sources of information
- Database analysis of environmental monitoring data
- Preparation of environmental allocations of responsibility
- Management and/or administration of pollution cleanup steering committee groups

- Managing multimillion dollar cleanup accounts, including review, processing, and payment of contractor invoices

The FOIA Request

The United States **Environmental Protection Agency (EPA or Agency)** is an administrative body that is subject to the federal **Freedom of Information Act (FOIA)**. Under FOIA, EPA files, with certain exceptions, are open to public inspection and for duplication. An environmental paralegal may spend considerable time preparing and processing FOIA requests.

For instance, where a client is in the process of buying XYZ Company in an acquisition, a "due diligence" review requires a complete investigation of XYZ Company's past and current environmental compliance. (*Due diligence* is a term of art applied in corporate transactions. The term basically means taking a careful and complete look at all aspects of the company being acquired.) The purchaser (in this example, our client) must review a complete set of environmental records to determine XYZ Company's compliance with environmental laws.

That usually means the preparation, submittal, and processing of FOIA requests to federal and state (most states have FOIA-like laws) environmental agencies. Processing FOIA requests can mean everything from taking telephone calls and monitoring the mail from the EPA, to visits to EPA offices for hands-on review and duplication of the file.

Environmental citizens' groups are also taking advantage of the FOIA laws to find and then to sue regulated entities, such as businesses and municipalities, for self-reported permit violations. After your client receives a resulting Notice of Intent to Sue letter, it is likely that your client, too, will want to review the EPA file to determine what the citizens' group has learned about the company and to make an estimate of the full extent of liability or exposure based on the self-reported permit violations.

The Rule-Making Process

Another section of the FOIA process requires that the Agency publish in the *Federal Register* (Fed. Reg.)

- notices of its rulemaking activities;
- proposed rules that explain the function and purpose of the proposed rule; and, when adopted,
- final rules.

An environmental paralegal may keep busy just following EPA rulemaking activities. Monitoring the daily *Federal Register* for notices, proposals, and final rules that may affect current or potential clients is an important task in staying abreast of developments.

When a rule-making activity does affect a client's interest, the client may wish to get involved in the **rule-making process.** The involvement may take the form of submitting written comments or testimony to the rule-making record. Such participation, if EPA officials have already made up their minds on the outcome of the rule, may simply be to preserve some perceived rights in a later dispute or appeal of the final rule. The involvement may require a review of the current agency/administrative record. The review should reveal what information is already in the file, including potential estimated impacts on the client's business activities.

For example, in early 1991, the EPA proposed air permit program regulations that would govern each state in adopting approvable air permit programs. A review of the administrative record in this proceeding suggested that the Agency proposed, rather than allowing flexibility, to adopt operational "flexibility" provisions that some industries found cumbersome.

In response, industrial representatives prepared and submitted into the administrative record comments and alternate proposed language to provide the operational flexibility envisioned under the statute. By submitting comments into the administrative record, the industry groups sought to change the outcome of the Agency's final rule making or, alternatively, to preserve a right to argue against the rule in a later dispute.

Preparation of Testimony

Paralegals may assist in the preparation of comments and hearing testimony. This will involve drafting testimony and collecting and analyzing other information for submission into the administrative record. Paralegals may also attend and participate in administrative meetings and hearings.

Besides federal rule making, every state has a counterpart agency to the federal EPA. The state agencies usually are subject to state freedom of information laws, with requirements similar to the federal scheme. Environmental paralegals may be involved in both the federal and state administrative rule-making processes.

Utilization of the Computer

Environmental paralegals may research and write about legal and nonlegal factual, scientific, and technical information. Paralegals may do online computer research in commercial legal and nonlegal databases, such as LexisNexis®, Westlaw, Dialog, and others.

The EPA maintains an extensive Internet Web site with documents and information concerning all of its programs. For links to access the EPA's Web site, refer to Appendix E for selected environmental resources on the Internet.

LexisNexis® and Westlaw provide comprehensive access to primary and secondary sources of environmental law. Dialog provides hundreds of full-text and reference records. Topics covered include environmental data, chemical substances, engineering, and geology.

Computer skills for the environmental paralegal are a requirement for career advancement. In environmental cases, information is either a big problem or a best asset.

Computer skills can be used in any number of ways to support environmental cases. For instance, in a Clean Water Act permit exceedance case, where over a three-year period the permittee (your client) had an unknown number of **permit limits exceedances**, computer spreadsheet analysis is quite useful. To understand your client's level of liability, you must determine exactly how often exceedances occurred, for what limited substances the exceedances occurred, and if there were any apparent trends in the exceedances that might illuminate the source of the problem. This information will also be required to prepare for negotiations with the agency or citizens' group on settlement terms. Once the information is abstracted from the occurrence documents (such as discharge monitoring reports) and placed into a computer format, the different analyses needed are easily performed and printed.

In a Superfund case, computer skills can be used to compile a **waste-in summary**. Typically in Superfund cases, contaminants have been released, or are threatened to be released, and will, or threaten to, endanger the public health and environment. Often the waste site has been abandoned by its owner and operator, but whether abandoned or not, under the federal Superfund law the generators of the waste are liable for completing a cleanup at the waste site.

A waste-in summary, or **nonbinding allocation of responsibility (NBAR)**, provides a detailed review from the available documentation of who sent what waste and in what amounts to the site. This waste-in list, much like an EPA NBAR, can become a basis for negotiations between the **potentially responsible parties (PRPs)** and is also a basis for establishing new PRP liability with the site. Once the information is abstracted from the occurrence documents (such as gate tickets and manifest forms) and placed into a computer database, the different analyses needed are easily performed and printed.

The environmental paralegal with computer skills who is able to perform these types of automated analyses will be highly respected in today's legal market. The appendices to this book will assist students in building these types of databases and in running these types of analyses. These abilities will enable both the paralegal and employer to market the paralegal's skills.

How This Textbook Will Help You

The purpose of this volume is to prepare paralegals to work in an environmental law practice, whether in a law firm, corporation, government, or other organization. It attempts to pique an interest in environmental law, to equip students with the knowledge and training they need to have in environmental law, and to promote practice area and organizational skills.

This textbook has been written by practicing paralegals, lawyers who are former paralegals, and by attorneys who work closely with paralegals in environmental law. It includes substantive reviews of major environmental laws, with practical discussion of how paralegals support attorneys, governments, businesses, and organizations in environmental law matters. Each chapter contains figures with reference documents, and other illustrative materials, cases for discussion, and a glossary of key terms and acronyms. A short bibliography at the end of each chapter provides readers with additional resource materials. Discussion questions explore the chapters in greater detail, and suggested projects allow further inquiry.

Appendix A presents a model for an NBAR database structure that is intended to prepare paralegals for hands-on involvement in an environmental law practice context. Appendix B provides a reference on case document management and indexing. Appendix C discusses a technique for organizing document image collections in a computer network environment. Appendix D provides an updated and expanded list of key contact telephone numbers for U.S. EPA offices. Appendix E provides an updated list of Internet addresses for selected environmental resources available on the Internet.

CHAPTER 1

The Clean Air Act

Eric E. Boyd

OBJECTIVES

The objectives of this chapter are for students to:

- Learn the terminology associated with the Clean Air Act (CAA).
- Learn the concepts and ideas that underlie the CAA law and regulatory program.
- Learn about specific sections and provisions of the CAA law and regulations.
- Learn about the processes and procedures used by the government and other parties to comply with and to enforce the law under the CAA.
- Learn about the particular jobs and functions that are performed by paralegals working for attorneys in CAA cases.

Introduction and History

The **Clean Air Act (CAA),** which is codified at 42 *United States Code* (U.S.C.) § 7401, *et seq.*, is the federal law designed to protect and enhance the quality of our nation's air resources. The CAA contains requirements for man-made sources of air pollution, including such things as cars and other transportation sources, mines, utilities, construction sites, and manufacturing plants. The requirements of the CAA are implemented through regulations and guidance promulgated by the **United States Environmental Protection Agency (EPA)** and state environmental agencies.

The CAA originated in legislation enacted in 1955. The most important CAA provisions, however, resulted from major amendments in 1970, 1977, and 1990.

The 1970 CAA Amendments required the EPA to establish **National Ambient Air Quality Standards (NAAQSs)** for criteria pollutants. The standards, which apply to outdoor air anywhere in the country, are designed to protect human health and welfare and the environment. The 1970 CAA amendments required each state to develop **State Implementation Plans (SIPs),** designed to help achieve the NAAQSs. The 1970 CAA amendments also required the EPA to provide assistance to help states to develop SIPs, to review and approve SIPs submitted by states, and to develop permitting requirements and New Source Performance Standards applicable to industrial categories of air pollution sources.

The 1977 CAA Amendments were necessary, in part, because the state State Implementation Plans had not resulted in the achievement of National Ambient Air Quality Standards throughout the country. The EPA had designated areas of the country as either having attained NAAQSs (so-called **attainment areas**), not having attained the NAAQSs (so-called **nonattainment areas**), or being unclassifiable. EPA's attainment designations are located at 40 *Code of Federal Regulations* (C.F.R.) part 81. The 1977 CAA Amendments contained a prohibition on the construction of new sources in nonattainment areas unless states revised their State Implementation Plans. In addition, the 1977 CAA Amendments included requirements for the **Prevention of Significant Deterioration (PSD)** of air quality in those areas that had attained the National Ambient Air Quality Standards.

The 1990 CAA Amendments radically expanded the scope and breadth of the CAA. Several of its provisions are discussed briefly here.

- Because many areas had failed to attain the ozone National Ambient Air Quality Standard even after twenty years of regulation under State Implementation Plans, the 1990 CAA Amendments set ozone nonattainment classifications and required the states to meet the ozone National Ambient Air Quality Standard by certain dates, depending on classification.
- Similarly, because only a handful of sources of **hazardous air pollutants (HAPs)** had been regulated up until that time, the 1990 CAA Amendments specifically listed 189 HAPs and required the EPA to develop standards for industrial categories of hazardous air pollutants by certain dates.
- Likewise, the 1990 CAA Amendments for the first time required major sources of air pollutants to obtain operating permits that include all applicable clean air regulatory requirements as well as monitoring, testing, recordkeeping, and reporting requirements.
- The 1990 CAA Amendments also mandated the phase-out of ozone-depleting substances.

- Finally, the 1990 CAA Amendments gave the EPA more enforcement tools and authority.

The effects of the 1990 CAA Amendments are still being felt.

The various CAA Amendments recognize that the type of air pollution control required in a given situation may depend on a number of factors. For instance, the types of controls for sources of criteria pollutants may depend on whether the area in which the source is located has attained the applicable National Ambient Air Quality Standards. The CAA, therefore, sets different requirements in **attainment areas** than for sources in **nonattainment areas.**

Similarly, the cost to install pollution controls on new equipment and facilities is often significantly less than it is to retrofit existing equipment and facilities with pollution controls. The CAA, therefore, sets more stringent control requirements for new equipment or facilities.

Finally, the nature of the pollutant will govern the kinds of control options that may be available. Although criteria pollutants were regulated as early as the 1970 CAA Amendments, controls for most sources of hazardous air pollutants were not required until the CAA Amendments of 1990. These factors are discussed more fully later in this chapter.

The remainder of this chapter is divided into five sections. The first section discusses the regulation of criteria pollutants and covers the National Ambient Air Quality Standards, State Implementation Plans, New Source Performance Standards, and the preconstruction review requirements in attainment and nonattainment areas. The second section discusses the regulation of hazardous air pollutants, including the regulations that resulted from the 1990 CAA Amendments and the developing residual risk review requirements.

The third section discusses the **Clean Air Act Permitting Program (CAAPP),** applicable to all major sources, and the steps facilities take in order not to be considered a **major source.** The fourth section discusses federal, state, and citizen enforcement of CAA requirements. Finally, the fifth section covers other important regulatory requirements under the CAA.

Regulation of Criteria Pollutants

The National Ambient Air Quality Standards are the basis for regulations of the criteria pollutants. There are two kinds of NAAQSs: **primary NAAQSs,** which are established in order to protect public health, and **secondary NAAQSs,** which are established in order to protect public welfare. 42 U.S.C. § 7409. NAAQSs have been established for ozone, carbon monoxide, sulfur dioxide, nitrogen oxides, lead, and particulate matter. *See* 40 C.F.R. part 50. Although the EPA established NAAQSs in the early 1970s, the CAA requires EPA to review the NAAQSs periodically. In fact, the EPA most recently promulgated NAAQSs for **fine particulate matter (PM2.5)** and an eight-hour standard for ozone in the late 1990s.

How areas are to reach the National Ambient Air Quality Standards is up to the states. Each state develops a State Implementation Plan designed to achieve the NAAQSs. State Implementation Plans must specify the manner in which the NAAQS will be achieved and maintained in each region of the state. 42 U.S.C. § 7410. The states develop regulations to control sources of air pollution based on **Reasonably Available Control Technology (RACT).** In order for a given control requirement to be considered reasonable, it must be technologically feasible and economically reasonable. Therefore, feasibility and cost as well as the financial circumstances of the affected facility are relevant in determining what constitutes RACT.

> Feasibility and cost as well as the financial circumstances of the affected facility are relevant in determining what constitutes RACT.

State Implementation Plans

The EPA retains authority with respect to the State Implementation Plan process. First, the EPA has developed a series of guidance documents and other background materials to aid states in developing SIPs. One series of these documents is called **Control Technology Guidelines (CTGs).** The EPA has numerous technical support documents and other memoranda relating to control strategies that can be useful to the **regulated community** (anyone that is covered by the rules at issue) and that can be found by paralegals who are trying to identify control strategies and costs for their specific client.

In addition, the EPA reviews each State Implementation Plan and approves, modifies, or disapproves it. If the EPA determines that an SIP will not be adequate to attain and maintain the National Ambient Air Quality Standards (based on the criteria set forth in 42 U.S.C. § 7410 and 40 C.F.R. part 52, subpart A (1997)), the CAA gives EPA the authority to require revision of the SIP or to promulgate a **Federal Implementation Plan (FIP).** The EPA also has authority to impose sanctions on nonattainment areas, including withdrawal of highway funding for the area (42 U.S.C. § 7509(b)) and a construction moratorium on all major sources of the pollutant for which the area has been classified nonattainment.

Initially, several industrial companies argued that the EPA should consider technological feasibility and economic reasonableness of control measures proposed by the states in their State Implementation Plans. See, for instance, *Lead Industries Association v. United States EPA,* 647 F.2d 1130 (D.C. Cir. 1980), and *American Petroleum Institute v. Costle,* 665 F.2d 1176 (D.C. Cir. 1982). The federal courts determined, however, that the EPA's review of SIPs is limited to whether or not they contain measures sufficient to assure the attainment and maintenance of the National Ambient Air Quality Standards. The courts ruled that the EPA is not required to consider technical feasibility or economic reasonableness when approving a SIP. These issues must be raised, therefore, before the states adopt the final SIP revisions.

In the 1990 CAA Amendments, Congress set different attainment deadlines for areas that had not attained the ozone National Ambient Air Quality Standards based on their existing levels of ozone. Nonattainment areas were designated as **marginal, moderate, serious, severe,** or **extreme.** These new designations required each state to "ratchet down" the controls on sources of air pollution. The scope of controls required depended on the classification status. In the most extreme areas, for instance, limits on individuals' activities, such as charcoal grilling and driving, were required. The EPA has also issued rules that will require significant reductions in nitrogen oxides by midwestern utilities to assist northeastern states in attaining the ozone and nitrogen oxide standards.

> Nonattainment areas were designated as marginal, moderate, serious, severe, or extreme.

Prevention of Significant Deterioration

To assist in meeting the National Ambient Air Quality Standards, the CAA requires State Implementation Plans to regulate the construction and modification of major stationary sources. One set of rules applies where a pollutant from a source is being emitted in an area that is nonattainment for that pollutant. Another set of rules applies if a source emits a pollutant in an area considered attainment or unclassifiable for a given pollutant.

If a major new source is proposed or a major source makes a major modification in an attainment area, the Prevention of Significant Deterioration (PSD) rules apply. The PSD rules are designed to protect areas with good air quality from suffering any significant deterioration in that air quality because of the installation of new sources. These PSD rules are triggered whenever a major new source is to be constructed or whenever there is a major modification to an existing major source.

Emitting more than 100 tons annually of certain listed pollutants generally qualifies a source as major. In a few cases, 250 tons annually are necessary. The Prevention of Significant Deterioration rules are also triggered for a major modification at a major source when there is a physical change or a change in the method of operations that results in a significant increase in emissions. As discussed further below, exactly when a "modification" for PSD purposes occurs is an unsettled area.

The information required in an application for a PSD permit includes a demonstration that:

- The source will use the **Best Available Control Technology (BACT).** The company must give detailed technical information to this effect. In no case can the emission rate exceed the applicable New Source Performance Standards.
- Operation of the source in addition to the effects of all nearby sources will not interfere with the attainment or maintenance of National Ambient Air Quality Standards.
- Operation of the source and all those nearby sources permitted subsequent to various effective dates since 1975 will not cause a significant deterioration of ambient air quality.

The EPA regulations governing the Prevention of Significant Deterioration program are located at 40 C.F.R. § 52.21 and generally apply unless a state has adopted its own PSD program in its State Implementation Plan.

CASES FOR DISCUSSION

Alaska Department of Environmental Conservation v. Environmental Protection Agency et al., 124 S.Ct. 983, 57 ERC 1801, 34 Envtl. L. Rep. 20,012 (2004).

This case concerns the authority of the EPA to enforce the provisions of the Prevention of Significant Deterioration program. Under that program, no major air pollutant-emitting facility may be constructed unless the facility is equipped with Best Available Control Technology. BACT, as defined in the CAA, means, for any major air pollutant-emitting facility, "an emission limitation based on the maximum degree of [pollutant] reduction . . . which the permitting authority, on a case-by-case basis, taking into account energy, environmental, and economic impacts and other costs, determines is achievable for [the] facility. . . ." 42 U.S.C. § 7479(3).

(continued)

CASES FOR DISCUSSION

Regarding EPA oversight, the Act includes a general instruction and one geared specifically to the PSD program. The general prescription, § 113(a)(5) of the Act, authorizes the EPA, when it finds that a state is not complying with a CAA requirement governing construction of a pollutant source, to issue an order prohibiting construction, to prescribe an administrative penalty, or to commence a civil action for injunctive relief. 42 U.S.C. § 7413(a). Directed specifically to the PSD program, the CAA at 42 U.S.C. § 7477 instructs the EPA to "take such measures, including issuance of an order, or seeking injunctive relief, as necessary to prevent the construction" of a major pollutant-emitting facility that does not conform to the Prevention of Significant Deterioration requirements of the Act.

In *ADEC v. EPA*, "the permitting authority" under § 7479(3) is the State of Alaska. The question presented was what role EPA has with respect to ADEC's Best Available Control Technology determinations, and, specifically, may the EPA act to block construction of a new major pollutant-emitting facility permitted by ADEC when EPA finds ADEC's BACT determination is unreasonable in light of the guides § 7479(3) prescribes? The Court held that the Act confers that checking authority on the EPA.

In supporting its case the EPA stressed Congress's reason for enacting the Prevention of Significant Deterioration program—to prevent significant deterioration of air quality in clean-air areas within a state and in neighboring states. That aim, the EPA urged, is unlikely to be realized absent an EPA surveillance role that extends to Best Available Control Technology determinations. The Agency cited in this regard to a House Report observation:

> "Without national guidelines for the prevention of significant deterioration a State deciding to protect its clean air resources will face a double threat. The prospect is very real that such a State would lose existing industrial plants to more permissive States. But additionally the State will likely become the target of "economic-environmental blackmail" from new industrial plants that will play one State off against another with threats to locate in whichever State adopts the most permissive pollution controls." H.R. Rep. No. 95-294, at 134 (1977).

New Source Review

A new source of air pollutants in an area designated nonattainment for those pollutants must comply with the nonattainment **New Source Review (NSR)** requirements. The CAA requires states to modify their State Implementation Plans to establish standards and procedures for preconstruction reviews to meet CAA requirements for these new sources. 42 U.S.C. § 7502. The exact NSR triggers will depend on the pollutants emitted and the classification of the area but generally track the Prevention of Significant Deterioration triggers.

The information required in an application for a New Source Review permit includes a demonstration that:

- The source will use the **Best Available Control Technology (BACT).** The company must give detailed technical information to this effect. In no case can the emission rate exceed the applicable New Source Performance Standard.
- Under the first nonattainment New Source Review requirement, the new or modified source must prove that it meets the **Lowest Achievable Emission Rate (LAER).** 42 U.S.C. § 7503(2) LAER is the lowest actual emission rate possible for a given source, which will be at least as stringent as Best Available Control Technology.
- Second, the new or modified source must show that it is already complying with existing regulatory standards in all facilities it operates in the state in which it is seeking a permit.
- The third nonattainment New Source Review requirement is to comply with federal emission offset requirements. The company must make, or get another company to make, an offsetting reduction in emissions of the same pollutant at another source in the area, so that the net emissions increase falls within an allowable growth margin or amounts to no increase at all.
- Fourth, the new source must show that the benefits of the project outweigh the environmental and social costs. This requirement is often applied in ozone nonattainment areas.

Additional requirements may apply as well, depending on where the source is located and what pollutants are involved.

On December 31, 2002, the EPA changed the federal regulations implementing the Prevention of Significant Deterioration and nonattainment New Source Review programs. *See* 67 *Federal Register* (Fed. Reg.) 80186, shown in Figure 1-1.

The changes affect whether a physical change or change in the method of operation of a source is considered a modification. The changes included:

- A change in the manner in which emissions baselines are determined for comparing pre- and post-change emissions. For instance, under the prior Prevention of Significant Deterioration

80186   Federal Register / Vol. 67, No. 251 / Tuesday, December 31, 2002 / Rules and Regulations

ENVIRONMENTAL PROTECTION AGENCY

40 CFR Parts 51 and 52

[AD–FRL–7414–5]

RIN 2060–AE11

Prevention of Significant Deterioration (PSD) and Nonattainment New Source Review (NSR): Baseline Emissions Determination, Actual-to-Future-Actual Methodology, Plantwide Applicability Limitations, Clean Units, Pollution Control Projects

AGENCY: Environmental Protection Agency (EPA).

ACTION: Final rule.

SUMMARY: The EPA is revising regulations governing the New Source Review (NSR) programs mandated by parts C and D of title I of the Clean Air Act (CAA or Act). These revisions include changes in NSR applicability requirements for modifications to allow sources more flexibility to respond to rapidly changing markets and to plan for future investments in pollution control and prevention technologies. Today's changes reflect EPA's consideration of discussions and recommendations of the Clean Air Act Advisory Committee's (CAAAC) Subcommittee on NSR, Permits and Toxics, comments filed by the public, and meetings and discussions with interested stakeholders. The changes are intended to provide greater regulatory certainty, administrative flexibility, and permit streamlining, while ensuring the current level of environmental protection and benefit derived from the program and, in certain respects, resulting in greater environmental protection.

EFFECTIVE DATE: This final rule is effective on March 3, 2003.

ADDRESSES: *Docket.* Docket No. A–90–37, containing supporting information used to develop the proposed rule and the final rule, is available for public inspection and copying between 8 a.m. and 4:30 p.m., Monday through Friday (except government holidays) at the Air and Radiation Docket and Information Center (6102T), Room B–108, EPA West Building, 1301 Constitution Avenue, NW., Washington, DC 20460; telephone (202) 566–1742, fax (202) 566–1741. A reasonable fee may be charged for copying docket materials. *Worldwide Web (WWW).* In addition to being available in the docket, an electronic copy of this final rule will also be available on the WWW through the Technology Transfer Network (TTN). Following signature, a copy of the rule will be posted on the TTN's policy and guidance page for newly proposed or promulgated rules: *http://www.epa.gov/ ttn/oarpg.*

FOR FURTHER INFORMATION CONTACT: Ms. Lynn Hutchinson, Information Transfer and Program Integration Division (C339–03), U.S. EPA Office of Air Quality Planning and Standards, Research Triangle Park, North Carolina 27711, telephone 919–541–5795, or electronic mail at *hutchinson.lynn@epa.gov,* for general questions on this rule. For questions on baseline emissions determination or the actual-to-projected-actual applicability test, contact Mr. Dan DeRoeck, at the same address, telephone 919–541–5593, or electronic mail at *deroeck.dan@epa.gov.* For questions on Plantwide Applicability Limitations (PALs), contact Mr. Raj Rao, at the same address, telephone 919–541–5344, or electronic mail at rao.raj@epa.gov. For questions on Clean Units, contact Mr. Juan Santiago, at the same address, telephone 919–541–1084, or electronic mail at santiago.juan@epa.gov. For questions on Pollution Control Projects (PCPs), contact Mr. Dave Svendsgaard, at the same address, telephone 919–541–2380, or electronic mail at *svendsgaard.dave@epa.gov.*

SUPPLEMENTARY INFORMATION:

Regulated Entities

Entities potentially affected by this final action include sources in all industry groups. The majority of sources potentially affected are expected to be in the following groups.

Industry group	SIC[a]	NAICS[b]
Electric Services	491	221111, 221112, 221113, 221119, 221121, 221122
Petroleum Refining	291	32411
Chemical Processes	281	325181, 32512, 325131, 325182, 211112, 325998, 331311, 325188
Natural Gas Transport	492	48621, 22121
Pulp and Paper Mills	261	32211, 322121, 322122, 32213
Paper Mills	262	322121, 322122
Automobile Manufacturing	371	336111, 336112, 336712, 336211, 336992, 336322, 336312, 33633, 33634, 33635, 336399, 336212, 336213
Pharmaceuticals	283	325411, 325412, 325413, 325414

[a] Standard Industrial Classification
[b] North American Industry Classification System.

Entities potentially affected by this final action also include State, local, and tribal governments that are delegated authority to implement these regulations.

Outline. The information presented in this preamble is organized as follows:

I. Overview of Today's Final Action
  A. Background
  B. Introduction
  C. Overview of Final Actions
   1. Determining Whether a Proposed Modification Results in a Significant Emissions Increase
   2. CMA Exhibit B

   3. Plantwide Applicability Limitations (PALs)
   4. Clean Units
   5. Pollution Control Projects (PCPs)
   6. Major NSR Applicability
   7. Enforcement
   8. Enforceability
II. Revisions to the Method for Determining Whether a Proposed Modification Results in a Significant Emissions Increase
  A. Introduction
  B. What We Proposed and How Today's Action Compares
  C. Baseline Actual Emissions For Existing Emissions Units Other than EUSGUs

  D. The Actual-to-projected-actual Applicability Test
  E. Clarifying Changes to WEPCO Provisions for EUSGUs
  F. The "Hybrid" Applicability Test
  G. Legal Basis for Today's Action
  H. Response to Comments and Rationale for Today's Actions
III. CMA Exhibit B
IV. Plantwide Applicability Limitations (PALs)
  A. Introduction
  B. Relevant Background
  C. Final Regulations for Actuals PALs
  D. Rationale for Today's Final Action on Actuals PALs
V. Clean Units

Figure 1-1 PSD/NSR Final Rule.

regulations, the term *actual emissions* was defined, in part, as "the average rate, in tons per year, at which the unit actually emitted the pollutant during a two-year period which precedes the particular date and which is representative of normal source operation." *See* former 40 C.F.R. § 52.21(b)(21)(ii).

The EPA could use a different time period for determining pre-change emissions if it determined that the different time period was "more representative of normal source operation." *Id.* Under the revised Prevention of Significant Deterioration regulations, the term *baseline actual emissions* is defined, in part, as "the average rate, in tons per year, at which the emissions unit actually emitted the pollutant during any consecutive twenty-four-month period selected by the owner or operator within the ten-year period immediately preceding either the date the owner or operator begins actual construction of the project, or the date a complete permit application is received by the Administrator." 40 C.F.R. § 52.21(b)(48)(ii);

- Use of past actual to future projected actual emissions, rather than past actual to future potential emissions, for triggering the requirements. The new Prevention of Significant Deterioration/New Source Review regulations define projected actual emissions as the maximum annual rate, in tons per year, at which an existing emissions unit is projected to emit a regulated New Source Review pollutant in any one of the five years (twelve-month period) following the date the unit resumes regular operation after the project, or in any one of the ten years following that date, if the project involves increasing the emissions unit's design capacity or its potential to emit that regulated New Source Review pollutant and full utilization of the unit would result in a significant emissions increase or significant net emissions increase at the major stationary source. 40 C.F.R. § 52.21(b)(41)(i). The method for determining projected actual emissions is spelled out at 40 C.F.R. § 52.21(b)(41)(ii)(a)–(c);
- Allowing plants flexibility by encouraging the use of plantwide applicability limits (PALs) so that the Prevention of Significant Deterioration/New Source Review requirements are not triggered as long as plantwide emissions remain below a certain level;
- Adding an exemption for clean units; and
- Codifying an existing exemption for pollution control and prevention projects.

The new Prevention of Significant Deterioration/New Source Review rules, although they are on appeal, were effective on March 3, 2003, in areas where the federal rules apply, and will be effective in other areas once a state amends its State Implementation Plan in response to the new rules. Another new rule clarifying the existing exemption for changes that constitute **routine maintenance, repair and replacement (RMRR),** promulgated at 68 Fed. Reg. 61248 (October 27, 2003), has been stayed pending a court challenge.

Under the new **actual-to-projected-actual applicability test,** a significant increase is projected to occur if the sum of the difference between the projected actual emissions and the baseline actual emissions equals or exceeds a significant amount. The regulations, however, require an owner or operator of a source to take certain measures "where there is a reasonable possibility that a project that is not a part of a major modification may result in a significant emissions increase and the owner or operator elects to use the method specified in paragraphs (b)(41)(ii)(a) through (c) of this section for calculating projected actual emissions." 40 C.F.R. § 52.21(r)(6).

Such sources, before beginning actual construction, must document and maintain a record of certain information but need not provide the information to the U.S. EPA unless the source is an existing electric utility steam generating unit. *See* 40 C.F.R. § 52.21(r)(6)(i) and (ii).

The owner or operator is thereafter required to monitor emissions of any regulated pollutants that could increase as a result of the project, and to calculate and maintain a record of annual emissions, in tons per year, on a calendar year basis. *Id.* § 52.21(r)(6)(iii). Figure 1-2 shows

DATE: ________ ILLINOIS ENVIRONMENTAL PROTECTION AGENCY PAGE 1 OF 2
DAPC - ANNUAL EMISSIONS REPORT - ________

ID NUMBER: ________ NAME: ________

- SOURCE DATA -

SOURCE IDS AND LOCATION

AIRS:	IEPA USE ONLY	LATITUDE:	
FINDS:	IEPA USE ONLY	LONGITUDE:	
FEIN:		YEAR OF DATUM:	
D&B:		SCALE:	
SIC 1:		METHOD:	
SIC 2:		ACCURACY:	
SIC 3:		DESCRIPTION:	

SOURCE ADDRESS

CONTACT: ________
PHONE: ________ EXT ________
FAX: ________

ANNUAL EMISSION REPORT MAILING ADDRESS

CONTACT: ________
PHONE: ________ EXT ________
FAX: ________

I certify under penalty of law that this document and all attachments were prepared under my direction or supervision in accordance with a system designed to assure that qualified personnel properly gather and evaluate the information submitted. Based on my inquiry of the person or persons directly responsible for gathering the information, the information submitted is, to the best of my knowledge and belief, true, accurate and complete.

AUTHORIZED SIGNATURE DATE

TYPED OR PRINTED NAME AND TITLE TELEPHONE NUMBER

IL 532 2217
APC 462 Rev. Dec-95

The Illinois EPA is authorized to require, and you must disclose, the information on this form pursuant to 35 Ill. Adm. Code 201.302(a, b) and 254. It is not necessary to use this form in providing the information. Failure to disclose the information may result in penalties as provided for in the Environmental Protection Act, 415 ILCS 5/42-45. This form has been approved by the Forms Management Center.

Figure 1-2 The Illinois Annual Emissions Report Form.

the Illinois Annual Emission Reporting form that is found on the Internet at http://www.epa.state.il.us/air/aer/forms/index.html.

The owner or operator must keep the annual emissions information for a period of five years for most changes, but for ten years if the project increases the design capacity of or potential to emit that regulated pollutant at the emission unit. *Id*. The owner or operator is required to submit a report to the EPA within sixty days after the end of any year in which:

> The annual emissions, in tons per year, from the project identified in paragraph (r)(6)(i) of this section, exceed the baseline actual emissions (as documented and maintained pursuant to paragraph (r)(6)(i)(c) of this section), by a significant amount (as defined in paragraph (b)(23) of this section), for that regulated NSR pollutant, and if such emissions differ from the preconstruction projection as documented and maintained pursuant to paragraph (r)(6)(i)(c) of this section.

Id. § 52.21(r)(6)(v). Exactly how the EPA will use the information is unclear, but it may result in triggering the Prevention of Significant Deterioration requirements and enforcement at some point after construction of the modification is completed.

A stationary source is a place or object from which pollutants are released and which stays in one place, such as power plants, gas stations, dry cleaners, incinerators, factories, and houses.

CASES FOR DISCUSSION

Chevron U.S.A., Inc. v. Natural Resources Defense Council, Inc., 467 U.S. 837 (1984).

The Court held that the EPA's plantwide definition is a permissible construction of the statutory term "stationary source."

EPA promulgated regulations in 1981 to implement the permit requirements of the CAA and to allow states to adopt a plantwide definition of the term "stationary source," under which an existing plant that contains several pollution-emitting devices may install or modify one piece of equipment without meeting the permit conditions if the alteration will not increase the total emissions from the plant, thus allowing a state to treat all of the pollution-emitting devices within the same industrial grouping as though they were encased within a single "bubble."

(continued)

CASES FOR DISCUSSION

The Court of Appeals set aside the regulations embodying the "bubble concept" as contrary to law. Although recognizing that the amended Clean Air Act does not explicitly define what Congress envisioned a "stationary source" to be, the Court of Appeals concluded that, in view of the purpose of the nonattainment program to improve, rather than merely maintain, air quality, a plantwide definition was "inappropriate," while stating it was mandatory in programs designed to maintain existing air quality.

The Supreme Court noted that "when a court reviews an agency's construction of the statute which it administers, it is confronted with two questions. First, always, is the question whether Congress has directly spoken to the precise question at issue. If the intent of Congress is clear, that is the end of the matter; for the court, as well as the agency, must give effect to the unambiguously expressed intent of Congress. If, however, the court determines Congress has not directly addressed the precise question at issue, the court does not simply impose its own construction on the statute, as would be necessary in the absence of an administrative interpretation. Rather, if the statute is silent or ambiguous with respect to the specific issue, the question for the court is whether the agency's answer is based on a permissible construction of the statute."

The Court concluded that "based on the examination of the legislation and its history . . . , we agree with the Court of Appeals that Congress did not have a specific intention on the applicability of the bubble concept in these cases, and conclude that the EPA's use of that concept here is a reasonable policy choice for the agency to make." *See* Figure 1-3 47 Fed. Reg. 15076 (4/7/1882), for the EPA's "Bubble Policy."

New Source Performance Standards

The CAA also requires the EPA to promulgate **New Source Performance Standards (NSPSs)** for new sources of air pollution. 42 U.S.C. § 7411. The EPA has adopted NSPSs for over sixty categories of sources covered by these regulations. *See* 40 C.F.R. part 60. The NSPSs are technology-based standards that apply in both attainment and nonattainment areas. Each NSPS contains control requirements as well as testing, monitoring, recordkeeping, and reporting requirements.

The New Source Performance Standards apply only to new sources, reconstructed sources, and modified sources. Determining

15076   Federal Register / Vol. 47, No. 67 / Wednesday, April 7, 1982 / Notices

ENVIRONMENTAL PROTECTION AGENCY

[PRM-FRL-1994-5]

Emissions Trading Policy Statement; General Principles for Creation, Banking, and Use of Emission Reduction Credits

May 12, 1982.

AGENCY: Environmental Protection Agency.

ACTION: Proposed policy statement and accompanying technical issues document.

SUMMARY: It is the policy of EPA to encourage use of emissions trades to achieve more flexible, rapid and efficient attainment of national ambient air quality standards.

This Policy Statement describes emissions trading, sets out general principles EPA will use to evaluate emissions trades under the Clean Air Act, and expands opportunities for states and industry to use these less-costly control approaches. Emissions trading includes several alternatives to traditional regulation: bubbles, netting, and offsets, as well as banking (storage) of emission reduction credits (ERCs) for future use. These alternatives do not alter existing air quality requirements; they simply give states and industry more flexibility to meet these requirements. EPA endorses emissions trading and supports its accelerated use by states and industry to meet the goals of the Clean Air Act more quickly and inexpensively.

This Policy Statement replaces the original bubble policy (44 FR 71779, Dec. 11, 1979) and sets forth minimum legal requirements for creation, storage or use of emission reduction credits in any emissions trade. It also provides criteria for "generic" SIP rules under which states can approve bubble or other trades without case-by-case federal SIP review.

EPA encourages states to continue adopting generic trading rules and approving individual trades. Until EPA takes final action on this proposal, it will evaluate state actions under the principles set forth here and illustrated in the accompanying Technical Issues Document.

EFFECTIVE DATE: This Policy Statement is effective as interim guidance upon publication. The deadline for submitting written comments is July 6, 1982.

ADDRESSES: Comments should be sent in triplicate if possible to: Central Docket Section (A-130), U.S. Environmental Protection Agency,

Washington, D.C. 20460, Attn: Doc. No. G-81-2.

DOCKET: EPA has established docket number G-81-2 for this action. This docket is an organized and complete file of all significant information submitted to or otherwise considered by EPA. The docket is available for public inspection and copying between 8:00 a.m. and 4:00 p.m., Monday through Friday, at EPA's Central Docket Section. A reasonable fee may be charged for copying.

FURTHER INQUIRIES:

Ivan Tether, Regulatory Reform Staff (PM-223), U.S. Environmental Protection Agency, 401 M Street, SW., Washington, D.C. 20460, (202) 382-2765,

or

Leo Stander, Office of Air Quality Planning and Standards (MD-15), Research Triangle Park, North Carolina 27711, (919) 541-5516.

SUPPLEMENTARY INFORMATION: Under Executive Order 12291, EPA must judge whether this action is "major" and therefore subject to the requirement of a Regulatory Impact Analysis. This action is not major because it establishes policies that are voluntary and can substantially reduce costs of complying with the Clean Air Act. Furthermore, it can reduce administrative complexity by reducing the number of trades which must be approved by EPA, can stimulate innovation in pollution control, and can allow state and local pollution control agencies to conserve scarce resources.

This Policy Statement was submitted to the Office of Management and Budget for review. Any comments from OMB to EPA are available for public inspection in Docket G-81-2. Pursuant to 5 U.S.C. 605(b), I hereby certify that this action will not have a significant economic impact on a substantial number of small entities. As a policy designed to allow firms flexibility and to reduce administrative complexity, it will impose no burdens on either small or large entities.

I. Introduction: Components of Emissions Trading

This statement details EPA policy on emissions trading. It presents the minimum conditions EPA considers necessary for emissions trades to satisfy the Clean Air Act. It simplifies past requirements and expands opportunities to use these more efficient alternatives.

A. What Is Emissions Trading?

Emissions trading consists of bubbles, netting, emission offsets, and emission reduction banking. These alternatives involve the creation of surplus reductions at certain emission sources

and use of these reductions to meet requirements applicable to other emission sources. Emission trades can provide more flexibility, and may therefore be used to reduce control costs, encourage faster compliance, and free scarce capital for industrial revitalization. Moreover, by developing "generic" trading rules (see section III below) states [1] and industry can be excused from SIP revisions, and attendant delay and uncertainty, for many individual bubbles or other trades.

B. The Bubble Policy and Today's Improvements

EPA's bubble policy lets *existing* plants (or groups of plants) decrease or be excused from pollution controls at one or more emissions sources in exchange for compensating increases in control at other emission sources. Bubbles give plant managers flexibility to develop less costly ways of meeting air quality requirements. Each bubble must be equivalent to the original emission limits in terms of ambient impact and enforceability. Bubbles cannot be used to meet technology-based requirements applicable to new sources.

This Policy Statement replaces the original bubble policy (Dec. 11, 1979; 44 FR 71779) and broadens opportunities for the bubble's use. Major changes include:

• Authorizing generic trading rules for all criteria pollutants;

• Extending use of the bubble to areas which lack approved demonstrations of attainment of the national ambient air quality standards;

• Expanding opportunities for use of bubbles as an alternative means of meeting reasonably available control technology (RACT) requirements;

• Reducing unnecessary requirements for detailed air quality modeling of the ambient impact of each trade;

• Reducing unnecessary constraints on trades involving open dust sources of particulate emissions;

• Allowing VOC and CO sources more time to implement bubbles under administrative compliance schedules, consistent with reasonable further progress and statutory deadlines for attaining ambient standards;

• Allowing sources to use the bubble to come into compliance, instead of having to be on a compliance schedule with original SIP limits to be eligible to bubble; and

[1] "States" includes any entity properly delegated authority to administer relevant parts of a State Implementation Plan (SIP) under the Clean Air Act.

Figure 1-3   The "Bubble Policy," at 47 Fed. Reg. 15076 (4/7/1982).

whether a source is a new source for NSPS applicability purposes is straightforward since each NSPS defines what a new source is. Similarly, whether a source is "reconstructed" is also relatively straightforward; the replacement of components of an existing facility to such an extent that:

(1) The fixed capital cost of the new components exceeds fifty percent of the fixed capital cost that would be required to construct a comparable entirely new facility, and

(2) It is technologically and economically feasible to meet the applicable standards set forth in this part.

40 C.F.R. § 60.15(b). Determining whether a source is "modified" for New Source Performance Standards purposes, however, raises some of the same issues as under the PSD/NSR programs. One difference, however, is that the NSPS provisions for modifications look to whether the emission rate, expressed as kg/hr of any pollutant discharged into the atmosphere for which a standard is applicable, increases, as opposed to the annual emission amounts under the NSR/PSD programs. 40 C.F.R. § 60.14.

Regulation of Hazardous Air Pollutants

The 1990 CAA Amendments greatly changed the federal government's regulation of hazardous air pollutants. Prior to the 1990 Amendments, the EPA had authority to establish emission standards for HAPs. The standards that were developed were known as **National Emission Standards for Hazardous Air Pollutants (NESHAPs).** Prior to 1990, however, NESHAPs for only seven HAPs were promulgated. *See* 40 C.F.R. part 61.

Figure 1-4 features an administrative complaint brought by the EPA under its § 113(d) authority, for National Emission Standards for hazardous air pollutants violations under § 112 of the Act, and specifically relating to the NESHAP for Secondary Aluminum Production, under 40 C.F.R. part 63, subpart RRR.

With the 1990 CAA Amendments, Congress mandated that the EPA regulate a greater number of hazardous air pollutants and HAP sources. Section 112(b) of the Act sets forth a list of 189 HAPs.[1] 42 U.S.C. § 7412(b).

---

[1] This list of 189 substances can be amended by the EPA or by petition. For example, caprolactam was delisted by petition in 1996, reducing the list to 188 substances. 40 C. F. R. part 63, subpart C.

UNITED STATES ENVIRONMENTAL PROTECTION AGENCY
REGION 5

IN THE MATTER OF:	) Docket No. **CAA-05- 2004** **0055**
	)
M & M Drying, LTD.	) **Proceeding to Assess a**
4125 Mahoning Road NE	) **Civil Penalty under**
Canton, Ohio 44705	) **Section 113(d) of the**
(**Respondent**)	) **Clean Air Act,**
	) **42 U.S.C. § 7413(d)**
	)

Administrative Complaint

1. This is an administrative proceeding to assess a civil penalty under Section 113(d) of the Clean Air Act (the Act), 42 U.S.C. § 7413(d).

2. The Complainant is, by lawful delegation, the Director of the Air and Radiation Division, United States Environmental Protection Agency (U.S. EPA), Region 5, Chicago, Illinois.

3. The Respondent is M & M Drying, LTD. (M & M Drying) a corporation doing business in Ohio.

Statutory and Regulatory Background

4. Under Section 112 of the Act, the Administrator of U.S. EPA promulgated the National Emission Standards for Hazardous Air Pollutants (NESHAP) for Secondary Aluminum Production at 40 C.F.R. Part 63, Subpart RRR.

5. The Secondary Aluminum Production NESHAP applies to the owner or operator of each secondary aluminum production facility. 40 C.F.R. §63.1500.

6. 40 C.F.R. §63.3 defines an "owner or operator" as any person who owns, leases, operates, controls, or supervises a

Figure 1-4 Section 113(d) Administrative Complaint in *M & M Drying, LTD.*

Hazardous air pollutants, or **HAPs,** also known as toxic air pollutants or air toxics, are those pollutants that cause or may cause cancer or other serious health effects, such as reproductive effects or birth defects, or adverse environmental and ecological effects. The list of HAPs is on the Internet at http://www.epa.gov/ttn/atw/orig189.html.

Hazardous air pollutants, or HAPs, also known as toxic air pollutants or air toxics, are those pollutants that cause or may cause cancer or other serious health effects, such as reproductive effects or birth defects, or adverse environmental and ecological effects.

Sections 112(c) and (e) require the EPA to list source categories for major and minor sources of HAPs and to establish emission standards for such categories by certain dates. *Id.* §§ 7412(c) and (3). Section 112(d) describes the factors that the EPA must consider in developing technology-based emission standards for source categories of HAPs. *Id.* § 7412(d). These standards are known as **Maximum Achievable Control Technology (MACT)** standards.[2] Section 112(h) allows the EPA to promulgate a design, equipment, work practice, or operational standard in lieu of an emission standard if it is not feasible to prescribe or enforce an emission standard. *Id.* § 7412(h). Section 112(g) requires MACT to be applied to modified or newly constructed sources, and provides that MACT will be determined on a case-by-case basis if the EPA has not established a standard at the time. *Id.* § 7412(g).

If the EPA does not establish a Maximum Achievable Control Technology standard for a category of hazardous air pollutant sources by the required dates, § 112(j) requires that MACT standards be developed for sources within the category on a case-by-case basis. *Id.* § 7412(j). This provision of the CAA is referred to as the **"MACT hammer."** Finally, if risk to public health remains after the promulgation of MACT standards for a source category, § 112(f) requires the EPA to promulgate standards that address the residual risk within eight (8) years after promulgation of the MACT standard. *Id.* § 7412(f).

Most of the Maximum Achievable Control Technology standards apply to major sources only. For the purpose of § 112, a major source

---

[2] The term "Maximum Achievable Control Technology" appears only in section 112(g) of the Act. Based on the legislative history, the EPA has concluded that the term also refers to the level of control required by section 112(d) emission standards. *See* 59 Fed. Reg. 26429, 26433 (May 20, 1994) (where the EPA promulgated its regulations for determinations under section 112(j) of the Act).

is a stationary source, or group of stationary sources, that has the potential to emit ten tons per year of any hazardous air pollutant or twenty-five tons per year of any combination of HAPs. In some cases, however, the MACT standards may govern smaller, or "area" sources as well. Area sources include such things as service stations, waste-water treatment lagoons, and dry cleaners.

The CAA provides some guidance as to how the EPA will establish emission standards for the source categories of hazardous air pollutants. Section 112(d) states:

> Emission standards . . . shall require the maximum degree of reduction in emissions of the hazardous air pollutants subject to this section (including a prohibition on such emissions, where achievable) that the Administrator, taking into consideration the cost of achieving such emission reduction, and any non-air quality health and environmental impacts and energy requirements, determines is achievable for new or existing sources in the category or subcategory to which such emission standard applies[.]

42 U.S.C. § 7412(d)(2). The Act further defines the application of certain measures, processes, methods, systems, or techniques to establish such emissions standards, including but not limited to measures which:

> (A) Reduce the volume of, or eliminate emissions of, such pollutants through process changes, substitution of materials or other modifications;
> (B) Enclose systems or processes to eliminate emissions,
> (C) Collect, capture or treat such pollutants when released from a process, stack, storage, or fugitive emissions point,
> (D) Are design, equipment, work practice, or operational standards (including requirements for operator training or certification), or
> (E) Are a combination of the above.

Id. The Act grants the EPA considerable flexibility in setting Maximum Achievable Control Technology standards.

The Act also describes how the **"maximum degree of reduction in emissions"** achievable for existing and new sources is to be determined. For new sources, the maximum degree of reduction in emissions "shall not be less stringent than the emission control that is achieved in practice by the best controlled similar source." 42 U.S.C. § 7412(d)(3). For existing sources, emissions standards:

> May be less stringent than standards for new sources in the same category or subcategory but shall be no less stringent than . . . the average emission limitation achieved by the best

performing 12 percent of the existing sources (for which the Administrator has emissions information) . . . in the category or subcategory for categories and subcategories with 30 or more sources, or the average emission limitation achieved by the best performing 5 sources (for which the Administrator has or could reasonably obtain emissions information) in the category or subcategory for categories with fewer than 30 sources.

Id. This is known as the **"MACT floor."** When a MACT floor is established, the Maximum Achievable Control Technology emission limitation standard must achieve an equal or greater level of control than the MACT floor. The section 112(d)(2) factors will determine whether a MACT emission limitation standard that achieves a level of control greater than the MACT floor should be required. *See* 59 Fed. Reg. 26429, 26443 (May 20, 1994).

The EPA has developed Maximum Achievable Control Technology standards for the majority of source categories. The MACT standards are located at 40 C.F.R. part 63. Each MACT standard contains applicable standards for new and existing sources, as well as monitoring, record-keeping, testing, and reporting requirements. Each MACT standard also discusses which provisions of the general requirements of 40 C.F.R. part 63, subpart A are applicable. The EPA lists the MACT standards on its Web site at http://www.epa.gov/ttn/atw/mactfnlalph.html.

Section 112(r) also addresses the prevention of accidental releases of certain hazardous air pollutants. 42 U.S.C. § 7412(r). The EPA promulgated a list of 100 substances that may cause death, injury, or serious adverse effects to human health if accidentally released. Sources where more than threshold quantities of these pollutants are held on site were required by 1999 to prepare and implement a **risk management plan (RMP)** to minimize accidental releases. 40 C.F.R. § 68.190. RMPs were required to be updated by June of 2004.

Operating Permits

The Clean Air Act requires all major sources of air pollutants to obtain operating permits known as Title V permits or **Clean Air Act Permit Program (CAAPP) permits.** The purpose of the Title V permit is to include all Clean Air Act requirements applicable to the source in one permit. Title V permits must list all emissions limitations and control requirements applicable to the source and include monitoring, record-keeping, testing, and reporting requirements sufficient to determine the source's continuous compliance with applicable requirements. CAAPP sources may rely on a **permit shield** that acts to shield the source from enforcement for violations of any requirements that are not covered by the CAAPP permit.

The Clean Air Act Permit Program is, for the most part, administered by the states. The EPA developed rules for state permit programs on July 21, 1992. States were thereafter required to develop and submit CAAPPs to the EPA for approval by November 15, 1993. State CAAPPs were required to include application schedules and procedures, monitoring and reporting requirements, permit fees, adequate personnel and funding provisions, hearing and judicial appeal opportunities, permit modification procedures, and allowance for changes that are not **modifications.** States also needed adequate authority to issue permits (for not more than five years); ensure compliance; enforce thorough civil and criminal penalty provisions; incorporate applicable requirements; and terminate, modify, or revoke permits.

Once the EPA approved a Clean Air Act Permit Program, **major sources** within the state were required to submit CAAPP permit applications (beginning in approximately November 1995). Draft permits were subject to public notice and comment as well as to EPA veto authority. The first round of CAAPP permits have been issued by the states. Since the CAAPP permits are effective for at most five years, the first wave of renewals has also begun.

Clean Air Act Permit Program sources must certify compliance at least annually with all applicable Clean Air Act requirements. The purpose of the compliance certification requirement is to make sure that responsible officials are involved early in the application, reporting, and compliance certification process. The term **"responsible official"** is defined in the federal Title V regulations as the following with respect to corporations:

> A president, secretary, treasurer, or vice-president of the corporation in charge of a principal business function, or any other person who performs similar policy or decision-making functions for the corporation, or a duly authorized representative of such person if the representative is responsible for the overall operation of one or more manufacturing, production, or operating facilities applying for or subject to a permit and either:
>
> (i) The facilities employ more than 250 persons or have gross annual sales or expenditures exceeding $25 million (in second quarter 1980 dollars); or
>
> (ii) The delegation of authority to such representatives is approved in advance by the permitting authority.

Figure 1-5 illustrates the Annual Compliance Certification form required under the Illinois Clean Air Act Permit Program rules. The

ILLINOIS ENVIRONMENTAL PROTECTION AGENCY
DIVISION OF AIR POLLUTION CONTROL
COMPLIANCE AND SYSTEMS MANAGEMENT SECTION
1021 NORTH GRAND AVENUE EAST, P.O. BOX 19276
SPRINGFIELD, ILLINOIS 62794-9276

CAAPP ANNUAL
COMPLIANCE CERTIFICATION

FOR AGENCY USE ONLY
ID NUMBER:
PERMIT #:
DATE:

THE CLEAN AIR ACT PERMIT PROGRAM (CAAPP) REQUIRES THAT EACH CAAPP PERMIT HOLDER SUBMIT AN ANNUAL COMPLIANCE CERTIFICATION FOR ALL EMISSION UNITS AT THE SOURCE AS REQUIRED BY 40 CFR 70.6 (c) (5), 39.5 (7) (p) (v) OF THE ENVIRONMENTAL PROTECTION ACT AND CAAPP PERMIT CONDITION 9.8. THE COMPLIANCE CERTIFICATION REPORTING PERIOD IS JANUARY 1 TO DECEMBER 31 AND IS DUE ON OR BEFORE MAY 1 FOR THE PRECEDING CALENDAR YEAR. THIS CERTIFICATION FORM CAN BE USED BY FACILITIES TO SATISFY THIS REQUIREMENT.

SOURCE INFORMATION

1) SOURCE NAME:

2) SOURCE ADDRESS:

3) CITY: 4) COUNTY:

5) TOWNSHIP: 6) STATE: 7) ZIP CODE:

8) DATE FORM PREPARED: 9) SOURCE ID NO. :

10) CAAPP PERMIT NO.:

11) CALENDAR YEAR OR REPORTING PERIOD COVERED BY THIS REPORT:

SOURCE COMPLIANCE INFORMATION

12) CHECK EITHER (a) OR (b) BELOW:

(a) _____ During the entire reporting period, this source was in **continuous** compliance with ALL terms and conditions contained in its CAAPP permit. The method used to determine compliance for each term and condition is the method specified in the permit.

(b) _____ With the exception of the items identified in Table 1 and Table 2, this source was in **continuous** compliance with all terms and conditions contained in the permit. The method used to determine compliance for each term and condition is the method specified in the permit, unless otherwise indicated.

NOTE: **Table 1 must be completed for all units and activities regardless of compliance status. Table 2 must be completed for all sources of intermittent or continuous noncompliance with any permit condition.**

Printed on Recycled Paper
401-CAAPP

Page 1 of 4

Figure 1-5   Illinois CAAPP Annual Compliance Certification Form.

form is available on the Internet at http://www.epa.state.il.us/air/caapp/401-caapp.pdf.

Any application, form, or report must also contain a certification by a responsible official that, based on information and belief formed after reasonable inquiry, the statements and information in the document are true, accurate, and complete. The certifications

---

UNITED STATES ENVIRONMENTAL PROTECTION AGENCY
REGION 5

IN THE MATTER OF:)
)
Picken's Plastics   )   **NOTICE AND FINDING OF VIOLATION**
Jefferson, OH   )
)   **EPA-5-04-OH-19**
Picken's Plastics   )
Ashtabula, OH   )
)
Proceedings Pursuant to   )
Section 113(a)(1) and (a)(3) of   )
the Clean Air Act, 42 U.S.C. §   )
7413(a)(1) and (a)(3)

NOTICE AND FINDING OF VIOLATION

The Administrator of the United States Environmental Protection
Agency (U.S. EPA), by authority duly delegated to the undersigned, is
issuing this Notice and Finding of Violation pursuant to Section
113(a)(1) and (a)(3) of the Clean Air Act. U.S. EPA hereby notifies
the State of Ohio and Picken's Plastics that U.S. EPA finds that
Picken's Plastics, located at 149 South Cucumber Street, Jefferson,
OH, and 4212 Ann Avenue, Ashtabula, OH are in violation of the Ohio
State Implementation Plan (SIP)and its Title V Operating Permit, as
follows:

Statutory and Regulatory Background

Jefferson - Plant #3 and Ashtabula - Plant #1

1.   On June 16, 1997, U.S. EPA approved 3745-21-07(G)(2) as part
      of the federally enforceable SIP for the State of Ohio. Fed.
      Reg. 62 FR 18520.

2.   OAC 3745-21-07(G)(2) states that a person shall not discharge
      more than forty pounds of organic material into the atmosphere
      in any one day, nor more than eight pounds in any one hour,
      from any article, machine, equipment, or other contrivance for
      employing, applying, evaporating or drying any photochemically
      reactive material, or substance containing such
      photochemically reactive material, unless said discharge has
      been reduced by at least eighty-five percent.

3.   On March 10, 2003, U.S. EPA approved 3745-31-05(A)(3) as part
      of the federally enforceable SIP for the State of Ohio. Fed.
      Reg. 68 FR 2909.

Figure 1-6   EPA Notice and Finding of Violation (NOV/FOV).

and reports required by Clean Air Act Permit Program permits provide enforcement agencies with a tremendous amount of information about the compliance status of CAAPP sources.

Figure 1-6 shows an EPA Notice and Finding of Violation
(NOV/FOV), issued to Picken's Plastics pursuant to §§ 113(a)(1)

and (a)(3) of the Clean Air Act, 42 U.S.C. §§ 7413(a)(1) and (a)(3). The notice was that the EPA found Picken's was violating the Ohio State Implementation Plan and its Title V Permit.

For the most part, the Clean Air Act Permit Program requirements apply only to major sources of pollutants. Whether a source is a major source depends on where it is located and on what and how much is potentially emitted. The term **potential emissions** generally refers to the amount a source can emit under worst-case conditions, not what the source actually emits in a given period of time. As such, sources have taken steps to limit their potential emissions in order to avoid the CAAPP permit requirements. The EPA has issued many guidance documents regarding ways sources can limit their potential emissions, including a January 25, 1995, EPA policy memorandum on "Options for Limiting the Potential to Emit of a Stationary Source Under Section 112 and Title V of the Clean Air Act." Some federal courts have also addressed the issue. *See National Mining Association v. EPA,* 59 F.3d 1351 (D.C. Cir. 1995).

Enforcement and Related Concerns

The Clean Air Act contains a number of enforcement tools. 42 U.S.C. § 7603. EPA inspectors have **field citation authority.** The EPA may issue administrative compliance or penalty orders for violations of the Act. The EPA may also bring a civil action for injunctive relief or to recover civil penalties in amounts of up to $32,500 per day.[3] States have their own enforcement authorities to deal with violations of the Act and Title V permit requirements.

The penalty policies of the EPA and most states consider at least two factors that potentially make the penalties for violations of CAA requirements significant. The first factor is the **gravity of the violation.** Violations of the **preconstruction** review requirements may be significant under this factor because of the amount of uncontrolled emissions that can occur before controls are added. The second factor is the **economic benefit** to the violator for delaying installation of the controls. This amount usually includes an amount saved for delaying the outlay of capital expenditures as well as an amount for the annual operating costs that were avoided as a result of the delay.

---

[3] Although the statute says $25,000, the amount has been raised for inflation by the EPA. *See* 69 Fed. Reg. 7121 (February 13, 2004).

If a company fails to add pollution controls when required, then the economic benefit resulting from that delay may be significant.

The CAA also contains **significant criminal penalties.** Any person who knowingly violates a requirement or prohibition of an SIP (after thirty days' notice or during a period of federally assumed enforcement), NSPS, NESHAP, inspection requirement, solid waste combustion requirement, preconstruction requirement, emergency order, ACO, APO, permit, acid rain requirement, or stratospheric ozone control can be subject to fines (up to $250,000 per person and $500,000 per organization) and a prison sentence (up to five years, but up to ten years if prior conviction has occurred.). In addition, any person who knowingly makes a false statement or conceals information, fails to report as required, or tampers with or fails to install a monitoring device may be subject to fines and up to two years of prison (up to four if there have been prior convictions). Any person who knowingly releases a HAP or extremely hazardous substance knowing that such release places another in imminent danger of death or serious injury is subject to fines (up to $1,000,000) and imprisonment (up to fifteen years).[4]

The CAA also makes certain negligent conduct criminal. Any person who negligently releases an HAP or an extremely hazardous substance and negligently places another in imminent danger of death or serious injury is subject to fines (up to $25,000 per person and $100,000 per organization) and imprisonment (up to one year, or two with prior conviction).

The CAA also contains a citizen suit provision. Citizen suits may be brought against anyone:

    a. alleged to have violated or to be in violation of an emission standard or limitation, or an Order issued by the EPA or State regarding such a standard or limitation, or

    b. proposing to construct or modify a major emitting facility without the necessary new source permits or in violation of such a permit.

A citizen suit may be brought only after sixty-day notice and if the EPA or the State has not "commenced and is diligently prosecuting a civil action" regarding the alleged violation.

---

[4] Perhaps the oddest criminal provision is that any person who knowingly fails to pay a fee owed to the United States is subject to fines ($25,000 per person or up to $100,000 for an organization) and up to one year of prison (two years with prior convictions).

CASES FOR DISCUSSION

Dow Chemical Co. v. United States, 476 U.S. 227 (1986).

The EPA and state agencies are endowed with considerable investigatory authorities. These authorities were expanded in *Dow v. United States*, where Dow operated a 2,000-acre chemical plant that included outdoor manufacturing equipment and piping conduits located between buildings and exposed to visual observation from the air. Dow maintained elaborate security around the perimeter of the complex, barring ground-level public views of the area. When Dow denied a request by the EPA for an on-site inspection of the plant, the Agency employed a commercial aerial photographer, using a standard precision aerial mapping camera, to take photographs of the facility from various altitudes, all of which were within lawful navigable airspace.

Upon becoming aware of the aerial photography, Dow brought suit in district court, alleging that the EPA's action violated the Fourth Amendment and was beyond its statutory investigative authority. The district court granted summary judgment for Dow, but the court of appeals reversed, holding that the EPA's aerial observation did not exceed its investigatory authority and that the aerial photography of Dow's plant complex without a warrant was not a search prohibited by the Fourth Amendment.

The Supreme Court held that the use of aerial observation and photography is within the EPA's statutory authority. It clarified by explaining that when Congress invests an agency such as EPA with enforcement and investigatory authority, it was not necessary to identify explicitly every technique that may be used in the course of executing the statutory mission. Further, although section 114(a) of the Clean Air Act, which provides for the EPA's right of entry to premises for inspection purposes, does not authorize aerial observation, that section appears to expand, not restrict, the EPA's general investigatory powers.

The Court concluded that the EPA's taking, without a warrant, of aerial photographs of Dow's plant complex from an aircraft lawfully in public navigable airspace was not a search prohibited by the Fourth Amendment.

Paralegal Responsibilities

Paralegals are frequently called upon in responding to EPA and state agency investigations. For instance, paralegals may be involved when the state solicits compliance information from potentially affected sources. The state agency will send a compliance inquiry letter when it suspects a violation has occurred.

Physical and operational data must be carefully reviewed and compiled before they are submitted to the agency. The agency is usually interested in the emission rates of given machinery and any existing pollution control equipment, as well as the feasibility and cost of reducing emissions. Similar procedures may be used by other state and local air quality regulatory agencies. Paralegals will take an active role in the collection of responsive documents, in analyzing the related documents and the source's compliance status, and in drafting the source's response.

> Paralegals are frequently called upon in responding to EPA and state agency investigations.

State agencies also solicit information when proposing new regulations. This is a time when a company may wish to review the proposed controls the agency is considering and develop a strategy for participating in the regulatory proceedings before the appropriate agencies.

Paralegals can be used to respond to proposed regulations by reviewing the agency record and industry journals and other literature to identify control strategies and costs. They can compile company and industry economic data. Environmental consultants can also be useful in compiling this type of information.

Other Issues

As discussed earlier, the NSR/PSD and CAAPP permit programs require sources to provide a large quantity of information to state agencies and to the EPA. Section 114(a) of the CAA also provides the EPA with authority to request information to assist it in developing plans to regulate air emissions, to determine whether a source is in compliance with applicable regulations, or "to carry out any provision of" the CAA. 42 U.S.C. § 7414.

Information provided to the EPA is available to the public through the federal and state freedom of information statutes. Although trade secret or otherwise confidential information would normally be exempt from disclosure to the public, "emissions data" contained in such submittals are specifically excluded from the definition of confidential information. In addition, sources are required to file detailed annual emissions reports with their state permitting agencies. The information submitted in such reports is often compared by the public against air emissions listed in the annual Toxic Release Inventory reports required to be submitted under the federal Emergency Planning and Community Right-to-Know Act.

A variety of Web pages listing air emissions information reported by facilities now exist. The EPA recently launched a Web site that allows citizens to identify the health effects of thirty-three toxic air pollutants in their community.

These trends, and the other developments discussed earlier, strongly indicate that paralegals will be called on more and more to assist in environmental compliance and enforcement under the Clean Air Act.

GLOSSARY OF CAA TERMS

acid deposition. A complex chemical and atmospheric phenomenon that occurs when emissions of sulfur and nitrogen compounds are transformed by chemical processes in the atmosphere and then deposited on earth in either wet or dry form.

air pollutant. Any substance in air that could, in high enough concentration, harm humans, other animals, vegetation, or material.

air pollution. The presence of contaminants or pollutants in the air that interfere with human health or welfare or produce other harmful environmental effects.

air quality criteria. The levels of pollution and lengths of exposure above which harmful health and welfare effects may occur.

air quality standards. The level of pollutants prescribed by regulations that is not to be exceeded during a given time in a defined area.

air toxics. Air pollutants that cause or may cause cancer or other serious health effects.

ambient air. Outside air beyond the fence line of an emitter's property.

area source. For purposes of § 112, any stationary source of hazardous air pollutants that is not a major source.

asbestos. Naturally occurring strong, flexible fibers that can be separated into thin threads and woven. These fibers break easily and form a dust composed of tiny particles that are light and sticky. When inhaled or swallowed, they can cause health problems.

attainment. Meets the NAAQS.

BACT. Best Available Control Technology.

CAA. Clean Air Act.

CAAPP. Clean Air Act Permitting Program.

CO. Carbon monoxide.

criteria air pollutants. Carbon monoxide (CO), sulphur dioxide (SO_2), nitrogen dioxide (NO_2), ozone (O_3), lead (Pb), and particulate matter (PM_{10}).

CTG. Control Technology Guideline.

emissions standard. The maximum amount of air-polluting discharge legally allowed from a single source, mobile or stationary.

field citation authority. Given to EPA inspectors under the 1990 Amendments.

FIP. Federal Implementation Plan.

GACT. Generally Available Control Technology.

HAP. Hazardous air pollutant.

indoor air. The breathable air inside a habitable structure or conveyance.

indoor air pollution. Chemical, physical, or biological contaminants in indoor air.

LAER. Lowest Achievable Emissions Rate.

MACT. Maximum Achievable Control Technology.

MACT hammer. A provision in § 112 of the CAA requiring the EPA to issue permits even if it has not promulgated an HAP standard.

major modification. A physical change in a source, including a change in the method of operations that results in an increase in emissions by more than a specified amount for the different criteria pollutants.

major source. For purposes of § 112 (Hazardous Air Pollutants), a stationary source or group of stationary sources that has the potential to emit ten tons per year of any hazardous pollutant or twenty-five tons per year of any combination of hazardous air pollutants. A major source for purposes of § 169a (PSD) is over 250 tons per year unless the source is listed as one of twenty-eight sources where the quantity for a major source is 100 tons per year.

mobile sources. Moving objects that release pollution from combustion of fossil fuels, such as cars, trucks, buses, planes, trains, lawn mowers, construction equipment, and snowmobiles.

NAAQS. National Ambient Air Quality Standard. Standards established by EPA under the Clean Air Act that apply to outdoor air throughout the country.

NESHAP. National Emission Standard for Hazardous Air Pollutants.

new source. New construction or modification of an existing source that will produce a significant increase in air pollutant emissions.

NO$_2$. Nitrogen dioxide.

NO$_x$. Nitrogen oxides.

nonattainment. Does not meet the NAAQS.

NOV. Notice of Violation.

NSPS. New Source Performance Standards.

NSR. New Source Review.

offset. Reductions in existing emissions that equal or exceed proposed new emissions.

Ozone (O$_3$). A reactive form of oxygen that is a bluish, irritating gas of pungent odor. It is formed naturally in the atmosphere by a photochemical reaction and is a beneficial component of the upper atmosphere. It is also an air pollutant in the lower atmosphere, where it can form by photochemical reactions.

ozone depletion. Destruction of the stratospheric ozone layer, which shields earth from ultraviolet radiation harmful to life. This destruction of ozone is caused by the breakdown of certain compounds that, when they reach the stratosphere, catalytically destroy ozone molecules.

ozone hole. A thinning of the ozone layer.

ozone layer. The protective stratum in the atmosphere, about fifteen miles above the ground, that absorbs some of the sun's ultraviolet rays, thereby reducing the amount of potentially harmful radiation that reaches Earth's surface.

ozone precursors. Chemicals that contribute to the formation of ozone.

particulate matter. Solid particles or liquid droplets suspended or carried in the air.

permit shield. CAAPP sources may rely on a "permit shield" that acts to shield the source from enforcement for violations of any requirements that are not covered by the CAAPP permit.

PM$_{10}$. Particulate matter with an aerodynamic diameter of less than ten microns.

PM$_{2.5}$. Particulate matter with an aerodynamic diameter of less than 2.5 microns.

potential emissions. Generally means the amount a source can emit under worst-case conditions, not what the source actually emits in a given period of time.

preconstruction. Gravity of violations of the preconstruction review requirements may be significant because of the amount of uncontrolled emissions that can occur before controls are added.

PSD. Prevention of Significant Deterioration. If a major new source is proposed or a major source makes a major modification in an attainment area, the PSD rules apply. The PSD rules are designed to protect areas with good air quality from suffering any significant deterioration in that air quality because of the installation of new sources. The PSD rules are triggered whenever a major new source is to be constructed or whenever there is a major modification to an existing major source.

RACT. Reasonably Available Control Technology.

regulated community. Anyone that is covered by the agency rules at issue. For instance, an air pollution stationary source regulated under the Prevention of Significant Deterioration program.

RMP. Sources where more than threshold quantities of pollutants are held on site were required by 1999 to prepare and implement a risk management plan (RMP) to minimize accidental releases.

RMRR. A rule clarifying the existing exemption for changes that constitute routine maintenance, repair, and replacement (RMRR), promulgated at 68 Fed. Reg. 61248 (October 27, 2003), has been stayed pending a court challenge.

SIP. State Implementation Plan.

SO$_2$. Sulphur dioxide.

stationary source. A place or object from which pollutants are released and that stays in one place, such as power plants, gas stations, dry cleaners, incinerators, factories, and houses.

TSP. Total suspended particulate matter.

unclassifiable. Not enough data available to classify the region attainment or nonattainment.

VOC. Volatile organic compound. Chemicals like gasoline and perchloroethylene that contain carbon and vaporize readily.

BIBLIOGRAPHY

Belden, Roy S. *The Clean Air Act.* (A.B.A. 2001).

Brownwell, F. William. *Clean Air Handbook* (3d ed. Hunton & Williams, 1998).

Clean Air Act Handbook (Robert J. Martineau & David P. Novello eds., 2d ed. A.B.A. 2004).

Clean Air Act Policy and Guidance: The Air Policy Compendium, available at http://www.epa.gov/compliance/resources/policies/civil/caa.

Garrett, Theodore L. & Sonya D. Winner, *A Clean Air Act Primer: Parts I – III.* 22 Envtl. L. Rep.: News & Analysis: 10159, 10235, and 10301 (1992).

Lave, Lester B., Eugene P. Seskin, & Michael J. Chappie, *Air Pollution and Human Health* (The Johns Hopkins University Press 1977).

Loewy, Steven A. *Indoor Pollution in Commercial Buildings: Legal Requirements and Emerging Trends,* Temp. Envtl. L. & Tech. J. 239 (1992).

Miskiewicz, James, & John S. Rudd, *Civil and Criminal Enforcement of the Clean Air Act After the 1990 Amendments,* Pace Envtl. L. Rev. 281 (1992).

The Plain English Guide to the Clean Air Act, EPA-400-K-93-001 (U.S. EPA 1993), *available at* http://www.epa.gov/oar/oaqps/peg_caa/pegcaain.html.

DISCUSSION QUESTIONS

1. Your firm represents Northanger Corporation, which manufactures plastic containers for products such as yogurt and cottage cheese. Northanger's manufacturing plant in Bar Harbor, Maine, is already classified as a major source of VOCs and particulates under the CAA. Northanger wants to expand into the cardboard carton market and needs to install several new pieces of equipment.

   Q. What categories of information would you ask the client to provide so that the attorney handling the file can decide how to proceed under the Clean Air Act? What questions would you ask the client? How would your conclusions change if the plant emitted hazardous air pollutants? What if the source was an area source under § 112?

2. B&D Manufacturing Co., a major manufacturer of ball bearings with plants in Peoria, Illinois, and San Diego, California, has contacted your firm to perform an environmental audit to make sure that it is in compliance with the provisions of the CAA and related state and federal regulations. Your firm has not represented B&D in the past. The attorney handling the file plans to send you to the Peoria plant for two days to inspect the physical plant and records kept on site. You will be traveling with an environmental engineer.

   Q. What would you do to prepare for your inspection?

3. Dodge and Weave Manufacturing has received an information request from the EPA under § 114 asking for its annual emission reports for the last five years and any and all operating records for its lead smelting operations. The

EPA has requested that copies of your response be sent to the EPA and the Department of Justice within twenty-one days.

Q. What sources of information should you review? Which plant personnel should be interviewed? What records outside the plant should be reviewed?

COMPUTER LABORATORY PROJECTS

1. Generate Facility Air Emissions reports and maps for a selected local property using the EPA's Internet tool at http://www.epa.gov/air/data/reports.html. Report your findings.

INTERNET SITES

- The full text of the Clean Air Act (CAA) is on the Internet at http://www.epa.gov/air/oaq_caa.html.

- Access clean air acronyms on the Internet at http://www.epa.gov/air/acronyms.html.

- The EPA Office of Air & Radiation Policy and Guidance Information is on the Internet at http://www.epa.gov/ttn/oarpg.

CHAPTER 2

The Clean Water Act

Peter D. Holmes

OBJECTIVES

The objectives of this chapter are for students to:

- Learn the terminology associated with the Clean Water Act (CWA).
- Learn the concepts and ideas that underlie the CWA law and regulatory program.
- Learn about specific sections and provisions of the CWA law and regulations.
- Learn about the processes and procedures used by the government and other parties to comply with and to enforce the law under the CWA.
- Learn about the particular jobs and functions that are performed by paralegals working for attorneys in CWA cases.

History of the Act

The **Clean Water Act (CWA),** 33 U.S.C. §§ 1251 to 1387 (2004), is the primary federal statute regulating water pollution. The CWA is the successor to several water pollution control statutes passed in the late 1940s to 1960s. The statute was created "to restore and maintain the chemical, physical, and biological integrity" of the waters of the United States. 33 U.S.C. § 1251(a) (2004). Regulations under the Act are found at 40 C.F.R. §§ 104 to 140 and 401 to 503 (2003).

The history of the CWA began with the **Rivers and Harbors Act of 1899 (Refuse Act),** created to protect the nation's navigable waters by prohibiting discharges of refuse matter other than sewage into those waters (and in some cases, their tributaries) without a permit from the **United States Army Corps of Engineers (COE).** This Act also prohibited construction "in or above" navigable waters without a COE permit. The Refuse Act traditionally was thought to apply only to discharges that obstructed navigation, but in the 1960s the Supreme Court broadened the application of the Refuse Act to include discharges of any industrial waste. *United States v. Standard Oil Co*., 384 U.S. 224 (1966); *United States v. Republic Steel Corp*., 362 U.S. 482 (1960), *reh'g denied*, 363 U.S. 858 (1960).

The **Federal Water Pollution Control Act Amendments of 1972,** commonly known as the Clean Water Act (CWA), established a new federal permit program that replaced the permit program under the Refuse Act. The CWA also changed the focus of the **Federal Water Pollution Control Act of 1948** from state-issued water quality standards to technology-based limitations issued by the United States **Environmental Protection Agency (EPA).** These limitations will be discussed in detail later.

Water quality standards were retained. The 1977 CWA Amendments focused on the control of toxic pollutants. Additional amendments addressing such issues as storm water discharges were adopted in the **Water Quality Act of 1987 (WQA).**

Subchapters of the Clean Water Act

The CWA is divided into six subchapters.

Subchapter I sets forth a declaration of goals and policies (§ 101). It also establishes various federal grant programs, such as grants for wet weather watershed pilot projects (§ 124).

Subchapter II addresses planning and construction grants for public sewage treatment plants. It encourages waste treatment management on an area-wide basis (§ 201). It established a federal grant program (§ 202), with such grants based on the EPA Administrator's approval (§ 203). It also encourages the development and implementation of area-wide waste treatment management plans (§ 208).

Subchapter III, which deals with effluent discharge standards, inspection, and enforcement, includes a no-discharge-without-a-permit policy carried over from the Rivers and Harbors Act of 1899 (§ 301). It requires the EPA to develop effluent limitations for point sources (§ 301), effluent standards or prohibitions for toxic pollutants, and pretreatment standards for discharges into publicly owned treatment works (§ 307). It provides the EPA with broad inspection and information-gathering powers (§ 308), stringent enforcement powers (§ 309), and it establishes strict liability for certain discharges of oil and hazardous substances (§ 311).

Subchapter IV established the **National Pollutant Discharge Elimination System (NPDES)** permit program to replace the Refuse Permit Program (§ 402) and a separate permit program administered primarily by the COE for discharges of dredged or fill material (§ 404). It also established a permit program for the disposal of sewage sludge (§ 405).

Subchapter V includes key definitions (§ 502), authorizes citizen suits (§ 505), provides for judicial review of certain EPA actions (§ 509), and preserves the right of states to impose more stringent discharge requirements (§ 510). Some of these sections are discussed in greater detail later.

Subchapter VI provides for EPA grants to the states to establish water pollution control revolving funds (§ 601).

The regulatory program of the CWA includes the NPDES permit program, which regulates point source discharges into waters of the United States based on federal categorical technology-based effluent limitations and state water quality standards. The program includes:

- A storm water discharge program;
- A pretreatment program for limitations on discharges to **publicly owned treatment works (POTWs)** to prevent pollutants in those discharges from interfering with or bypassing sewage treatment or causing toxicity in sewage sludge;
- A strict liability scheme for discharges of oil and hazardous substances to the waters of the United States; and
- Permits under § 404 for discharges of dredged or fill material to wetlands and other waters of the United States.

NPDES Permit System

The heart of the CWA is the **NPDES permit program.** Sections 301(a) and 402 of the CWA prohibit the discharge of any pollutant from a **point source** (a discrete, identifiable source of wastewater) to a water of the United States, except as authorized by an NPDES permit. NPDES permits are issued by the EPA or, if the EPA has approved its NPDES program, by the state. Currently, forty-five states have approved NPDES permit programs.

> The heart of the CWA is the National Pollutant Discharge Elimination System permit program.

The term *point source* is defined in § 502(14) of the Act, 33 U.S.C. § 1362(14) (2004), to mean:

> Any discernible, confined and discrete conveyance, including, but not limited to, any pipe, ditch, channel, tunnel, conduit, well, discrete fissure, container, rolling stock, concentrated

animal feeding operation, or vessel or other floating craft, from which pollutants are or may be discharged. This term does not include agricultural stormwater discharges and return flows from irrigated agriculture.

Point source has been interpreted broadly by the courts. In *United States v. Earth Sciences, Inc.*, 599 F.2d 368 (10th Cir. 1979), the court held that overflow from a mining sump used to collect surface runoff constituted a point source. In *Sierra Club v. Abston Const. Co.*, 620 F.2d 41 (5th Cir. 1980), the court held that simple erosion over the ground surface created a point source if strip mining activities had changed the surface or directed the waterflow.

In *Appalachian Power Co. v. Train*, 545 F.2d 1351 (4th Cir. 1976), however, the court held that unchanneled and uncollected rainfall runoff from material storage sites was not a point source. The Second Circuit held in *United States v. Plaza Health Laboratories, Inc.*, 3 F.3d 643 (2d Cir. 1993), that, at least in the context of criminal enforcement, a person who placed vials of blood at the edge of a river does not constitute a point source.

The U.S. Supreme Court granted certiorari in the case of *Miccosukee Tribe of Indians of Fla. v. South Fla. Water Mgmt. Dist.*, 280 F.3d 1364 (11th Cir. 2002). The Eleventh Circuit had held that a pumping system that moved water from a more polluted body of water to a separate, less polluted body of water required an NPDES permit. Although the pumping station did not itself add pollutants into the water it was moving, the court held that there was a discharge of pollutants because the pumping station caused the pollutants to enter the new body of water. The Supreme Court held that a pollutant may be discharged even though the point source is not the original source of the pollutant, but it vacated and remanded the decision for further factual determination by the lower court as to whether the two water bodies involved were truly separate or were simply two parts of the same water body. *South Fla. Water Management Dist. v. Miccosukee Tribe of Indians*, 124 S. Ct. 1537 (2004).

The term **waters of the United States** is interpreted by EPA to include virtually all surface waters in which the United States has an interest, including navigable waters, interstate waters and their tributaries, and waters that were in the past and may in the future be used in interstate commerce. Even a normally dry arroyo through which water might reasonably end up in a body of water in which there is some public interest is a water of the United States. *United States v. Phelps Dodge Corp.*, 391 F. Supp. 1181 (D. Ariz. 1975).

Navigable waters of the United States are those waters that are subject to the ebb and flow of the tide and/or are presently used, or have been used in the past, or may be susceptible for use to transport interstate or foreign commerce. A determination of navigability, once made, applies laterally over the entire surface of the waterbody, and is not extinguished by later actions or events which impede or destroy navigable capacity. 33 C.F.R. § 329.4.

Interstate waters and their tributaries, and waters that were in the past and may in the future be used in interstate commerce include:

- Waters used in interstate commerce.
- Interstate waters (i.e., Mississippi River).
- Intrastate lakes, rivers, streams, and wetlands:
  - ➡ Used by interstate travelers.
  - ➡ Sources of fish or shellfish sold in interstate commerce.
  - ➡ Used by industries engaged in interstate commerce.

In *Solid Waste Agency of Northern Cook County v. United States Army Corps of Engineers,* 531 U.S. 159, 168 (2001), the U.S. Supreme Court held that § 404 of the CWA did not apply to isolated wetlands or ponds visited by migratory birds. *SWANCC* thus narrows the reach of the CWA under the § 402 NPDES permit program, but the extent of its effect is uncertain. Most lower court cases have interpreted *SWANCC* to authorize CWA jurisdiction over otherwise "isolated" waters that are hydrologically connected in any way to navigable waters. *See, e.g., Headwaters, Inc. v. Talent Irrigation Dist.,* 243 F.3d 526 (9th Cir. 2001). But some lower courts require a more substantial nexus than a hydrological connection between the "isolated water" and a navigable water. *See, e.g., FD & P Enterprises, Inc. v. United States Army Corps of Engineers,* 239 F. Supp. 2d 509 (D.N.J. 2003).

CASES FOR DISCUSSION

Minnehaha Creek Watershed District v. Hoffman, 597 F.2d 617, 13 ERC 1009 (8th Cir. 1979).

Lake Minnetonka is a natural lake, navigable in fact, lying entirely within Hennepin County, Minnesota. According to the record, the total surface area of the lake is approximately 22.5 square miles, and the lake's depth averages forty feet. No permanent tributaries empty into Lake Minnetonka. The lake's single outlet is Minnehaha Creek, which flows eastward from Gray's Bay for approximately 20-22 miles, until it empties into the Mississippi River.

(continued)

CASES FOR DISCUSSION

In February 1975, the Army Corps of Engineers issued a "Determination of Navigability" that concluded that Lake Minnetonka and that portion of Minnehaha Creek above the Minnetonka Mills were "navigable waters of the United States," and were subject to Corps' jurisdiction under the Rivers and Harbors Act. The Corps also asserted its regulatory authority over the lake under both the Rivers and Harbors Act and under § 404 of the CWA.

The lower court held that both Lake Minnetonka and Minnehaha Creek above Minnetonka Mills were navigable waters since their capability of use for navigation was undisputed, but that they were not "navigable waters of the United States" as that phrase is used in the Rivers and Harbors Act because they were located entirely within one state and have no interstate waterway connection with other navigable waters. Also, the court held that the Corps lacked jurisdiction over the placement of riprap and the construction of dams in the lake and in the creek since, in its view, such activities do not constitute the "discharge of [a] pollutant" under §301 of the CWA, 33 U.S.C. § 1311.

The lower court reasoned that although "pollutant," as defined in § 502(6) of the CWA, 33 U.S.C. § 1362(6), includes "rock, sand, [and] cellar dirt," and riprap and dams incidentally require rock or sand for construction, such activities are not within the purview of the Act because they do not significantly alter water quality.

The Appellate Court concluded that entirely intrastate bodies of water, with no navigable interstate waterway linkage, are not subject to federal regulatory jurisdiction under the Rivers and Harbors Act. In addition, the Court concluded that:

> We believe that the construction of dams and riprap in navigable waters was clearly intended by Congress to come within the purview of §§ 301 and 404 of the Act. By including rock, sand and cellar dirt in the list of polluting substances, Congress recognized that the addition of these substances could affect the physical, as well as the chemical and biological, integrity of a waterbody. Since the construction of dams or riprap admittedly involves the placement of rock, sand or cellar dirt into the body of water, such activities would appear to come within the plain meaning of the Act.

Much of what paralegals do in supporting attorneys and clients in Clean Water Act cases revolves around the EPA's permitting of point sources. For a detailed discussion of what should be included

United States Environmental Protection Agency	Office of Water (4203)	EPA-833-B-96-003 December 1996

♻EPA   U.S. EPA NPDES Permit Writers' Manual

Figure 2-1 *NPDES Permit Writers' Manual,* EPA 833-B-96-003 (12/01/1996)

in an NPDES permit—from the Agency's perspective, see Figure 2-1, the *NPDES Permit Writers' Manual,* EPA 833-B-96-003 (12/01/1996), on the Internet at http://cfpub.epa.gov/npdes/writermanual.cfm?program_id545.

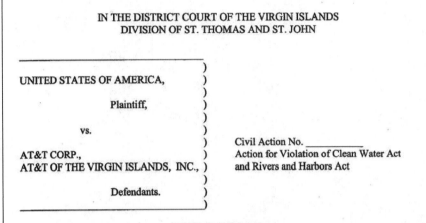

IN THE DISTRICT COURT OF THE VIRGIN ISLANDS
DIVISION OF ST. THOMAS AND ST. JOHN

UNITED STATES OF AMERICA,)
                    Plaintiff,)
             vs.)
) Civil Action No. _____
AT&T CORP.,) Action for Violation of Clean Water Act
AT&T OF THE VIRGIN ISLANDS, INC.,) and Rivers and Harbors Act
)
             Defendants.)

CONSENT DECREE

WHEREAS, Plaintiff the UNITED STATES OF AMERICA filed the Complaint herein against Defendants AT&T CORP. ("AT&T"), and AT&T OF THE VIRGIN ISLANDS, INC. ("AT&T VI"), alleging that Defendants violated Section 301(a) of the Clean Water Act ("CWA"), 33 U.S.C. § 1311(a), and Section 10 of the Rivers and Harbors Act ("RHA"), 33 U.S.C. § 403;

WHEREAS, the Complaint alleges that Defendants (1) violated CWA Section 301(a) by discharging pollutants into waters of the United States in Magens Bay, St. Thomas, the U.S. Virgin Islands ("The Site") without a CWA permit; (2) violated RHA Section 10 by modifying and altering an area within the navigable waters of the United States at the Site without authorization from the Secretary of the Army ("the Corps"); and (3) violated the terms and conditions of the Corps' authorization to perform certain work, as provided in the Corps' January 24, 1997 Letter of Permission (No. 1991150067 LP-DD);

Figure 2-2 CWA Consent Decree in *United States v. AT&T Corp.*

Figure 2-2 shows an EPA complaint for enforcement of section 301 of the CWA. As previously mentioned, section 301, among others, prohibits the discharge of any pollutant from a point source to a water of the United States, except as authorized by an NPDES permit.

Discharges to Groundwaters

Groundwaters are not considered waters of the United States, although the EPA claims that NPDES permit requirements apply to discharges to groundwater that is hydrologically connected to a water of the United States. Case law on this issue is split. *Cf. McClellan Ecological Seepage Situation v. Weinberger*, 707 F. Supp. 1182 (E.D. Cal. 1988), which held that an NPDES permit would be required if there was a discharge to groundwater that had direct hydrological connection to surface waters that constituted waters of the United States, with *Kelley v. United States*, 618 F. Supp. 1103 (W.D. Mich. 1985), which held that a discharge to groundwater without an NPDES permit did not violate the CWA even though the contaminants found their way into a surface water of the United States.

A **pollutant** is defined in § 502(6) of the CWA as:

Dredged spoil, solid waste, incinerator residue, sewage, garbage, sewage sludge, munitions, chemical wastes, biological materials, radioactive materials, heat, wrecked or discarded equipment, rock, sand, cellar dirt and industrial, municipal, and agricultural waste discharged into water.

In *Romero-Barcelo v. Brown*, 478 F. Supp. 646 (D.P.R. 1979), the court held that bombs from naval airplanes constituted pollutants discharged from a point source (the airplane).

The Permit Issuance Procedure

The seven-step permit issuance procedure is regulated under 40 C.F.R. part 124 (2003), which applies to EPA-issued permits as well as to state-issued permits if the state has incorporated EPA procedures into the state's NPDES program. Paralegals may be involved in the compilation, analysis, and completion of NPDES permits and permit applications.

Under step one, an NPDES permit application must be filed at least 180 days before the discharge is to begin. 40 C.F.R. § 122.21(c)(1) (2003). A renewal application must be filed at least 180 days before the previously issued permit expires (§ 122.21(d)).

The application must be made on either an EPA form or, in approved NPDES states, a state form. The state form must require at least as much information as the federal form. The application must be signed by a "responsible corporate officer," who must be at or above the level of a vice president, or by a plant manager of a facility who is authorized to make management decisions for the facility. 40 C.F.R. § 122.22(a)(1) (2003). Under § 122.21(b), if the owner and operator of the facility are two different entities, the operator must obtain the permit.

Under step two, state certification, the state or the appropriate interstate pollution control agency must certify that the EPA's proposed permit conditions will comply with all applicable federal and state effluent limitations and water quality standards. A state may choose to waive its right to certify and, if the state does not choose to certify the draft permit within sixty days, certification is deemed to be waived. CWA § 401(a)(1) (2004); 40 C.F.R. § 124.53 (2003).

Under step three, a fact sheet or statement of basis, together with a draft permit or intent to deny, is issued for public notice. 40 C.F.R. § 124.9 (2003).

The fourth step is an opportunity for public comment and an informal public hearing. Paralegals may be involved in the NPDES permitting process if comments on the draft permit are to be filed or a public hearing is held. The public comment and hearing process are explained in more detail in the Introduction and in Chapter Nine of this book.

Permit issuance is step five, with the permit generally made effective thirty days after issuance.

Under the sixth step, the EPA-issued permit may be appealed by filing a petition for review by the EPA's Environmental Appeals Board. 40 C.F.R. § 124.19 (2003). Paralegals may be involved in this administrative process through case preparation and initiation.

Judicial review is the seventh step in the permitting process, whereby the EPA's permit decision may be challenged in a U.S. Court of Appeals within 120 days of the issuance or denial of the permit by the EPA. CWA § 509(b)(1) (2004). Paralegals may be involved in CWA appeals through case preparation, research, writing, and document drafting.

NPDES permit conditions may be based on federal technology-based effluent limitations, more stringent state effluent limitations, **best management practices (BMPs),** health-based toxic effluent standards or prohibitions, water quality standards, and water quality management plans. Limited circumstances may allow for a modification of these standards. Figure 2-3 illustrates the EPA's guidance memorandum on "Best Management Practices (BMPs) in NPDES Permits," available on the Internet at http://www.epa.gov/npdes/pubs/bmps_npdes_permits.pdf.

In addition, **best professional judgment (BPJ)** may be used in writing permit limits. The BPJ process typically includes review of the EPA's five-volume *Treatability Manual*, which contains information on the toxic pollutant levels achievable by certain technologies.

The concept of **antibacksliding** generally precludes a renewed or reissued permit from applying a less stringent standard than the prior limits, including those based on BPJ. Figure 2-4 shows an EPA

UNITED STATES ENVIRONMENTAL PROTECTION AGENCY
WASHINGTON, D.C. 20460

AUG 1 9 1988

OFFICE OF
WATER

MEMORANDUM

SUBJECT: Best Management Practices (BMPs) in NPDES Permits –
Information Memorandum

FROM: James D. Gallup, Chief
Technical Support Branch

TO: Regional Permit Branch Chiefs
Region I – X

This memorandum provides information about the use of best
management practices (BMPs) in NPDES permits. Please make the
information available to your staff and your States as you deem
appropriate.

Figure 2-3   The EPA's "Best Management Practices (BMPs) in NPDES
Permits."

UNITED STATES ENVIRONMENTAL PROTECTION AGENCY
WASHINGTON, D.C. 20460

OFFICE OF
WATER

MEMORANDUM

SUBJECT: Interim Guidance on Implementation of Section 402(o)
Anti-backsliding Rules For Water Quality-Based Permits

FROM: James R. Elder, Director
Office of Water Enforcement and Permits (EN-335)

TO: Water Management Division Directors, Regions I-X
NPDES State Directors

Section 402(o) of the Clean Water Act (CWA), enacted in the
Water Quality Act of 1987, establishes anti-backsliding rules
governing two situations. The first situation occurs when a
permittee seeks to revise a technology-based effluent limitation
based on best professional judgment (BPJ) to reflect a
subsequently promulgated effluent guideline which is less
stringent. The second situation addressed by §402(o) arises when
a permittee seeks relaxation of an effluent limitation which is
based upon a State treatment standard or water quality standard.

Figure 2-4   The EPA's Guidance on Antibacksliding.

guidance document on antibacksliding, available on the Internet at http://www.epa.gov/npdes/pubs/owm0231.pdf. *See also* CWA § 402(o) (2004); 40 C.F.R. § 122.44(l) (2003). Exceptions to antibacksliding are allowed in limited circumstances. CWA § 402(o)(2) (2004); 40 C.F.R. § 122.44(l)(2)(i) (2003).

Permits may be terminated based on violation of permit conditions, failure to disclose relevant facts during the permit process, changes in conditions that require reduction or elimination of the discharge, or endangerment of health or the environment. 40 C.F.R. § 122.64 (a) (2003). Permit modification or revocation and reissuance may be based on any of the grounds for termination, notification of a proposed nonautomatic transfer of the permit, or any of the eighteen grounds listed in 40 C.F.R. § 122.62(a) (2003), which include:

- Alterations to the discharger's facility or activity;
- New information that, if known at the time of permit issuance, would have justified different permit conditions;
- The permittee's timely request for modification based on EPA's revision, withdrawal, or modification of the regulations or effluent guidelines on which the permit was based; and
- Changes required by the "reopener" conditions of the permit.

A permit may be transferred automatically when (i) EPA or the state is notified by the permittee at least thirty days before the proposed transfer takes place; (ii) a written agreement between the permittee and the transferee is submitted to the permit authority; and (iii) the EPA or the state does not notify the permittee of its intention to modify or revoke and reissue the permit. 40 C.F.R. § 122.61(b) (2003).

Permits may be terminated based on
➣ violation of permit conditions
➣ failure to disclose facts
➣ changes in conditions
➣ endangerment of health
➣ endangerment of the environment

The permit may be subject to minor modifications that do not require public notice and comment procedures to correct typographical errors, to increase the frequency of monitoring or reporting, to extend interim compliance dates up to 120 days, to allow for ownership or operational changes, to change the construction schedule for a new source, to delete an outfall whose discharge is terminated, or to incorporate pretreatment program conditions in a POTW's permit. 40 C.F.R. § 122.63 (2003).

The EPA authorizes a defense to permit violations that are caused by an **upset.** A permit upset is an exceptional incident involving non-compliance with technology-based effluent limitations due to factors beyond the permittee's reasonable control. To establish the defense, the permittee must identify the cause of the upset and provide oral notice to the permit authority within twenty-four hours, followed by a written report in five days. 40 C.F.R. § 122.42(n) (2003).

A permit **bypass** is an intentional diversion of waste effluent from the permittee's treatment facility. A bypass that does not cause effluent limits to be exceeded is authorized for essential maintenance. A bypass that causes effluent limits to be exceeded is authorized if the bypass was unavoidable to prevent loss of life, personal injury, or severe property damage, and there were no feasible alternatives. Notice is required in advance of an anticipated bypass and within twenty-four hours of an unanticipated bypass. 40 C.F.R. § 122.42(m) (2003).

Section 402(p) (2004) of the CWA, which was added by the 1987 WQA, requires NPDES permits for certain categories of storm water discharges. The EPA issued implementing rules in two phases. The Phase I storm water program required NPDES permits for storm water discharges from the following sources:

- "Medium" and "large" municipal separate storm sewer systems (located in incorporated places with populations of 100,000 or more);
- Eleven categories of "industrial activity," including construction that disturbs five or more acres of land;
- Discharges subject to a permit before February 4, 1987; and
- Discharges designated on a case-by-case basis as a significant contributor of pollutants.

40 C.F.R. § 122.26(a)(1) (2003).

The Phase II storm water program requires NPDES permits for storm water discharges from:

- Certain small municipal separate storm sewer systems; and
- Construction activity disturbing one to five acres of land.

Under the EPA's Phase II rules, any category of industrial activity (except construction) may be conditionally exempt from permit requirements for discharges composed entirely of storm water if the operator can certify that no industrial materials and activities will be exposed to rain, snow, snowmelt, or runoff. 40 C.F.R. § 122.26(g).

Most storm water discharges are regulated by general permits issued by the EPA or the state. General permits are intended to cover a large number of similar sources. Alternatively, storm water discharges may be regulated by individual NPDES permits.

40 C.F.R. § 122.41 (2003) establishes conditions applicable to all NPDES permits. Section 122.42 establishes additional conditions applicable to certain categories of NPDES permits. For example, all permittees must give twenty four-hour notice to the permit authority of any noncompliance that may endanger health or the environment, must properly operate and maintain their treatment facilities, and must retain monitoring records for at least three years.

Figure 2-5 shows the EPA's Discharge Monitoring Report (DMR) form. The DMR form is exemplary, as each state may require the use of a state form instead. The EPA form is available on the Internet at http://www.epa.gov/npdes/pubs/dmr.pdf.

Note that many states are now using "e-DMR" systems that allow dischargers to complete their forms and file in one process over the Internet. *See* "Illinois EPA Introduces the eDMR System" for a discussion of the system adopted in Illinois, available on the Internet at http://www.seyfarth.com/db30/cgi-bin/pubs/042604_OMM.pdf.

Credit for pollutants in intake water, known as **net limitations,** may be requested by a discharger when the applicable effluent limitations specify that they apply on a net basis or if the discharger can demonstrate that its treatment system would meet the applicable

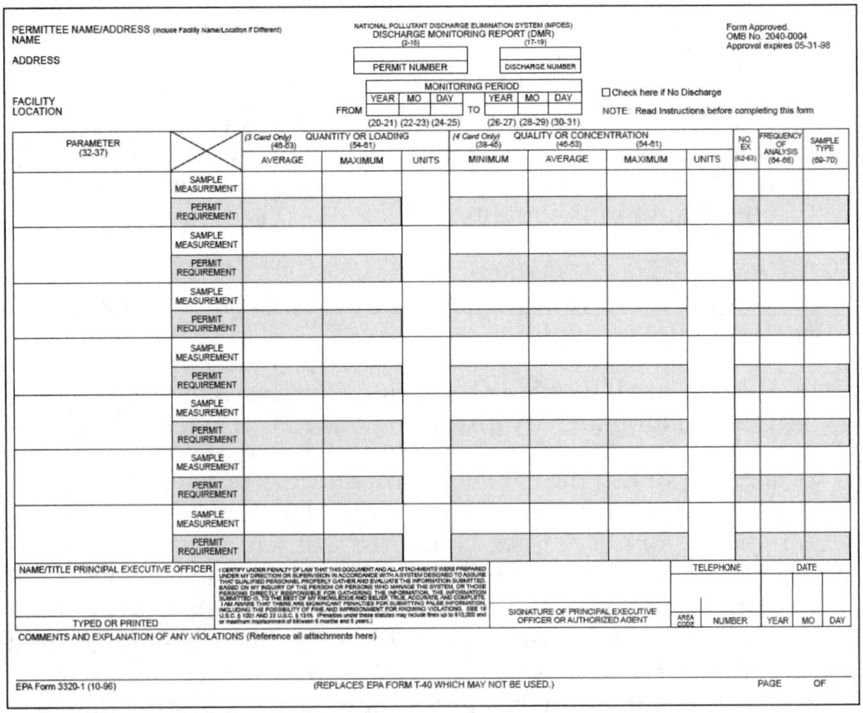

Figure 2-5 EPA's Discharge Monitoring Report (DMR) Form.

effluent limitations were it not for the presence of pollutants in the intake water. The credit may not exceed the amount necessary to meet the applicable limitation or the influent value, whichever is lower. To be eligible for a net limit, the intake water must come from the same body of water into which the discharge is made, unless the permit writer determines that there will be no environmental degradation. 40 C.F.R. § 122.45(g) (2003).

Under CWA § 402(k), compliance with an NPDES permit acts as a shield from other CWA requirements, except for health-based toxic effluent standards or prohibitions, or standards for sewage sludge under § 405(d) of the CWA, until the permit is modified, revoked and reissued, or terminated. 40 C.F.R. § 122.5(a)(1) (2003). In addition, new sources are granted a ten-year protection period from more stringent technology-based requirements, but not for water quality standards, health-based toxic effluent standards or prohibitions, or additional technology-based limits for toxic pollutants that are not controlled by new source performance standards. 40 C.F.R. § 122.29(d) (2003).

CASES FOR DISCUSSION

Sierra Club v. Abston Construction Company, Inc., 620 F.2d 41, 14 ERC 1984, 10 Envtl. L. Rep. 20,552 (5th Cir. 1980).

In this case, the issue was whether pollution carried in various ways into a creek from Abston's coal miners' strip mines amounts to "point source" pollution controlled by the Act. Sediment basin overflow and the erosion of piles of discarded material resulted in rainwater carrying pollutants into a navigable body of water. Because there was no direct action of the mine operators in pumping or draining water into the waterway, the lower court by summary judgment determined there was no violation of the Act because there was no "point source" of the pollution.

The Court, as taken from the statute, defined the term "point source" as any discernible, confined, and discrete conveyance, including but not limited to any pipe, ditch, channel, tunnel, conduit, well, discrete fissure, container, rolling stock, concentrated animal feeding operation, or vessel or other floating craft, from which pollutants are or may be discharged. 33 U.S.C. §1362(14). In this case, the Court found that although the point source definition "excludes unchanneled and uncollected surface waters," surface runoff from rainfall, when collected or channeled by coal miners in connection with mining activities, constitutes point source pollution.

Federal Effluent Limitations

NPDES permits serve to transfer general applicable effluent limitations into specific limitations applicable to each permittee. One of the primary sources of those effluent limitations are technology-based **effluent limitation guidelines** issued by the EPA under CWA § 304. The guidelines restrict the amount of a pollutant that may be discharged at the end of a pipe and are established for specific industrial categories. Thus, the EPA establishes separate limitations for such industries as steel manufacturing, food processing, and paper manufacturing.

> One of the primary sources of effluent limitations is technology-based effluent limitation guidelines issued by the EPA under CWA § 304.

These effluent limitations are enforceable only when incorporated into a permit. The effluent limitations reflect different levels of technology for industrial dischargers:

- **Best practicable technology (BPT),** which represents the minimum level of treatment required for all pollutants;
- **Best conventional technology (BCT),** which applies to discharges of conventional pollutants;
- **Best available technology (BAT),** which applies to discharges of toxic and nonconventional pollutants; and
- **Best available demonstrated technology (BADT),** for new sources, which is usually equal to BAT but in theory can be more stringent.

Under CWA § 301(b)(1)(a) (2004), BPT was required by July 1, 1977, for existing sources.

Under CWA § 301(b)(2)(E) (2004), BCT was required by March 31, 1989, for existing sources for conventional pollutants.

Under CWA §§ 301(b)(2)(C), (D), and (F) (2004), BAT was required by March 31, 1989, for existing sources of toxic pollutants and nonconventional pollutants.

Under 40 C.F.R. § 122.29(d)(4) (2003), BADT is required within ninety days from the date of operation for new sources.

Section 306 of the CWA requires that the EPA establish national standards of performance for new sources. A "new source" is a source on which construction begins after EPA proposes an applicable national standard of performance, if the final standard is issued in accordance with § 306. As indicated previously, the standards are based on best available demonstrated technology (BADT), which usually is equal to BAT. Because the standard must be achieved when the source begins to discharge, there is no compliance schedule. See, as shown in Figure 2-6, for greater depth on this topic, EPA's memorandum on "Clarification on the Procedure for Calculating Production-Based Effluent Limitations and to Provide Guidance on

UNITED STATES ENVIRONMENTAL PROTECTION AGENCY
WASHINGTON, D.C. 20460

DEC 18 1984

OFFICE OF
WATER

MEMORANDUM

SUBJECT: Calculation of Production-Based Effluent Limits

FROM: J. William Jordan, Chief
          NPDES Technical Support Branch (EN-336)

TO: Regional Permits Branch Chiefs

     The purpose of this memorandum is to clarify the procedure for calculating production-based effluent limitations and to provide guidance on the use of alternate limitations. Many effluent guidelines are expressed in terms of allowable pollutant discharge rate per unit of production. To determine permit limits, these standards are multiplied by an estimate of the facility's actual average production.

     Section 122.45(b) of the NPDES permit program regulations sets forth the requirements for calculating production-based effluent limitations. The central feature of this section is the requirement that limitations be based upon a "reasonable measure of the actual production of the facility", rather than upon design capacity. Interpretation of this requirement has proven confusing in the past. This memorandum provides recommendations for developing production-based limitations and alternate limitations. The Agency is also planning to revise this portion of the regulations, and has revised Part III of Application Form 2C, in order to clarify language which might lead to the use of inappropriate production-based limitations.

Background

     The proper application of production-based effluent limitation guidelines is dependent upon the methodology that is used to develop the guidelines. When most guidelines are developed, a single long term average daily production value and its relationship to flow are determined. This is combined with effluent concentration data collected from plants to form the basis of the guideline standards. Variability factors are developed on concentration data obtained from samples taken during periods of varying production. The variability factors and performance data are then used to derive the guideline standards.

Calculation of Limitations

     To apply these guidelines, permit writers should determine

Figure 2-6 "Clarification on the Procedure for Calculating Production-Based Effluent Limitations and to Provide Guidance on the Use of Alternate Limitations," December 18, 1984.

the Use of Alternate Limitations," December 18, 1984, available on the Internet at http://www.epa.gov/npdes/pubs/owm0427.pdf.

As a tradeoff for the imposition of stringent new source performance standards, new sources are protected for ten years against more stringent or revised technology-based requirements. CWA § 306(d) (2004). The ten-year protection does not apply to non-technology-based requirements, such as water quality standards or health-based toxic effluent standards or prohibitions under § 307(a).

Modifications and variances from the applicable effluent limitations are limited. For instance, an economic variance may be granted for BAT limitations for nonconventional pollutants. CWA § 301(c) (2004). A **water-quality-based variance** may be granted for BAT limits for five specific nonconventional pollutants and any other nonconventional pollutants listed by EPA. CWA § 301(g) (2004).

A **water-quality-based thermal variance** may be granted from effluent limitations for heat. See CWA § 316(a) (2004) and 40 C.F.R. § 125, subpart H (2003).

More stringent water-quality-related effluent limitations may be issued by the EPA when necessary to achieve or maintain water quality. CWA § 302(a) (2004). The CWA also authorizes for variances from these special limitations. CWA § 302(b)(2) (2004).

A variance for **fundamentally different factors (FDFs)** is available for BPT, BCT, and BAT effluent limitations if the discharger can demonstrate that its facility is fundamentally different from the other facilities considered by the EPA when it issued effluent limitation guidelines for that industry. CWA § 301(n) (2004); 40 C.F.R. § 125 subpart D (2003). FDF variances have seldom been granted by EPA. *See Georgia Pacific Corp. v. EPA*, 671 F.2d. 1235 (9th Cir. 1982) (upholding the EPA's denial of a request for an FDF variance). Paralegals may prepare initial regulatory and factual research and draft petitions for FDF variances.

It should be noted that a discharger cannot claim cost as an FDF factor. CWA § 301(n)(1)(A) (2004). Moreover, an FDF variance will not be granted on the basis of the applicant's economic inability to meet the cost of implementing the new uniform standard. *EPA v. National Crushed Stone Ass'n*, 449 U.S. 64 (1980).

Variances from BCT or BAT may also be based on innovative technology that will allow for a compliance date extension for up to two years. The technology must have industry-wide application and either achieve significantly greater effluent reduction than the limits that otherwise apply or meet those limits at a significantly lower cost. CWA § 301(k) (2004).

Finally, a permit modification may be granted for secondary treatment requirement for POTWs discharging into marine waters. To qualify for the modification, the POTW must meet nine specified conditions. *See* CWA § 301(h) (2004) and 40 C.F.R. part 125, subpart G (2003).

Other federal effluent limitations include:

- Health-based toxic effluent standards or prohibitions that have been established by the EPA for only six toxic pollutants (*see* CWA § 307(a)(2) (2004) and 40 C.F.R. § 129.4 (2003));
- Federal water-quality-related effluent limitations that have never been used but may be issued by the EPA to protect the water quality of specific bodies of water (CWA § 302(a) (2004)); and
- Best management practices to control toxic and hazardous pollutants from industrial activities (CWA § 304(e) (2004)).

Enforcement

Section 309 of the CWA contains stringent enforcement provisions. When the EPA finds a discharger in violation of the CWA, its regulations, or a permit, it may issue an administrative compliance order or bring a civil or criminal enforcement action in federal court.

Section 309 authorizes administrative Class I civil penalties of up to $11,000 per violation, but not to exceed a maximum of $32,500, and Class II civil penalties of up to $11,000 a day for each violation, but not to exceed a maximum of $157,500 (CWA § 309(g) (2004)). It authorizes judicial civil penalties of up to $32,500 a day for each violation (CWA § 309(d) (2004)). Finally, it authorizes criminal penalties of at least $2,500 and up to $25,000 a day for each violation or up to one year's imprisonment (or both) for negligent violations; at least $5,000 and up to $50,000 a day for each violation or up to three years' imprisonment (or both) for "knowing" violations; and up to $250,000 or up to fifteen years' imprisonment (or both) for "knowing endangerment" (CWA § 309(c) (2004)). Note that the maximum administrative and civil fines under the CWA and other federal environmental statutes are periodically adjusted for inflation by the EPA in accordance with the Federal Civil Penalties Adjustment Act of 1990, 28 U.S.C. 2461 (2004). *See* 69 Fed. Reg. 7121 (2004) for the EPA's most recent penalty adjustments.

There has been an increasing focus on the use of criminal enforcement under the CWA. In *United States v. Snook*, 336 F.3d 439 (7th Cir. 2004), the Seventh Circuit affirmed the conviction of the environmental manager of a petroleum refinery who selectively reported wastewater monitoring results and failed to report violations of the facility's NPDES permit. The environmental manager was sentenced to twenty-one months' imprisonment, two years of supervised release, and a $1,000 fine.

In general, federal jurisdiction is available for bringing CWA cases. For instance, § 505(a)(1) of the CWA gives citizens the right to bring civil actions in federal district court against any person "alleged to be in violation of" CWA requirements, or against the EPA for its alleged failure to perform a nondiscretionary duty. Citizen suits are not authorized against "wholly past" violations. Rather, a citizen-plaintiff must "allege a state of either continuous or intermittent violation, [with] a reasonable likelihood that a past polluter will continue to pollute in the future." *Gwaltney of Smithfield, Ltd. v. Chesapeake Bay Foundation, Inc.*, 484 U.S. 49 (1987). Successful citizen suits may result in the imposition of civil penalties or injunctive relief (or both) and the defendant's reimbursement of the citizen-plaintiff's attorneys' fees.

> CWA § 505(a)(1) gives citizens the right to bring civil actions against any person alleged to be in violation of CWA requirements.

To satisfy federal subject matter jurisdiction, a plaintiff's allegations of continuing violation must be made in good faith. The plaintiff must first provide sixty days' notice to the alleged violator, the EPA, and the state before filing a suit. The suit will be precluded if the EPA or the state has begun and is "diligently prosecuting" a civil or criminal suit before the citizen suit is filed. *See North & South Rivers Watershed Ass'n, Inc. v. Town of Scituate*, 949 F.2d 552 (1st Cir. 1991) (holding that State Department of Environmental Protection "diligently enforced" the state CWA, thus barring a citizen suit for the same violations under the federal CWA).

A defendant may defeat a plaintiff's CWA suit by moving for summary judgment and proving that the allegations of a continuing violation of the Act were false and raise no genuine factual issues. *Sierra Club v. Union Oil Co. of Cal.*, 853 F.2d 667 (9th Cir. 1988).

Pretreatment Programs

Publicly owned treatment works (POTWs) must meet limitations based on secondary treatment, as defined by regulation under CWA § 304(d) (2004). When a company discharges into city sewers leading to a POTW, it is known as an **indirect discharger** or an **industrial user.** Industrial users do not require NPDES permits but are subject to pretreatment standards and may require a pretreatment permit issued by the POTW authority. CWA § 307(b) (2004).

National pretreatment prohibitions issued by the EPA apply to all industrial users. 40 C.F.R. § 403.5 (2003). In addition, specific pretreatment standards issued by the EPA apply to specific categories of the industrial users in a manner similar to the BPT, BCT, and BAT effluent limitations applied to direct dischargers. Compliance is required within three years for existing sources and immediately for new sources. CWA § 307(a) (2004). The requirement to implement a pretreatment program is included in the POTW's NPDES permit.

Pretreatment standards were created to prevent industrial pollutants from interfering with or passing untreated through the POTW and to protect against contamination of sewage sludge. The standards apply to all discharges into POTWs and prohibit (i) fire or explosion hazards, (ii) corrosive discharges, (iii) solid or viscous obstructions, (iv) "slug" discharges, and (v) heat that would restrict biological activities.

> Pretreatment standards were created
> ➤ to prevent industrial pollutants from interfering with or passing untreated through the POTW
> ➤ to protect against sludge contamination.

The EPA requires a local pretreatment program when either:

- The POTW has a design flow over five million gallons a day and receives pollutants from industrial users that will cause pass through or interference or are subject to categorical pretreatment standards; or
- The state or EPA specifically requires a pretreatment program for a smaller POTW.

40 C.F.R. § 403.8(a) (2003).

In 1981, sections of the CWA pertaining to POTWs were amended to extend the deadline for secondary treatment from 1977 to 1988 upon a showing that federal financial assistance was not provided or construction could not be completed in time to achieve the applicable effluent limits by 1977. CWA § 301(i) (2004). In addition, the amended Act allowed secondary treatment to include "biological treatment facilities as oxidation ponds, lagoons, and ditches," if there would be no adverse affect to the receiving water quality. CWA § 304(d)(4) (2004).

Water Quality Standards

Water quality standards apply to every body of water and can form the basis for limitations on both point sources and nonpoint sources. Stream classifications are based on the actual or potential use designated for each segment of a water body; land standards are based on water quality **"criteria,"** which are the concentration limits necessary to support each designated use. EPA criteria information comes from the *Quality Criteria for Water, 1986* (the **Gold Book**), EPA 440/5-86-001 (1986), in which the EPA has set forth criteria for 137 pollutants based on the effect on the public's health and welfare, aquatic life, and recreation. CWA § 304(a) (2004). See also the EPA's compilation of national recommended criteria, *National Recommended Water Quality Criteria: 2002*, EPA 822-R-02-047 (Nov. 2002).

Under § 303, the CWA requires states to establish water quality standards and water quality management plans. These standards must be reviewed by the state at least once every three years and, when appropriate, revised or replaced to adopt new standards, which are subject to EPA review and approval. CWA § 303(c)(1) (2004).

NPDES permits issued to point source dischargers must impose limitations that go beyond the limitations of technology-based standards when necessary to meet applicable water quality standards or other state standards. CWA § 301(b)(1)(C) (2004). These additional limitations are known as **water-quality-based effluent limitations (WQBELs).**

In establishing water quality standards and water quality management plans, the water quality of the states located downstream must be considered. 40 C.F.R. § 131.10(b) (2003). The U.S. Supreme Court held in *Arkansas v. Oklahoma*, 503 U.S. 91 (1992), that a downstream state does not have the authority to block the EPA's issuance of a permit to a discharger located in the upstream state if it is dissatisfied with the upstream state's water quality standards. Instead CWA § 301(b)(1)(C) requires the EPA to impose any more stringent WQBELs necessary to comply with applicable water quality standards.

Finally, an antidegradation policy must be enforced to maintain and protect existing in-stream uses and existing high-quality waters. 40 C.F.R. § 131.12 (2003).

Under § 208 of the CWA, states are required to formulate area-wide water pollution control plans to control both point sources and **nonpoint sources**. The § 208 process has failed to make significant progress in controlling nonpoint source pollution. Therefore, the 1987 WQA created a new program under § 319 to address nonpoint sources. It require states first to prepare and submit for the EPA's approval assessment reports to identify:

- Waters that cannot meet water quality standards without control of nonpoint sources;
- The nonpoint sources that add significant pollution to those waters;
- The process for identifying BMPs and other measures to control pollution from those nonpoint sources; and

- The state and local programs for controlling nonpoint source pollution.

The states then must prepare and submit for the EPA's approval a management program for controlling nonpoint source pollution. Dischargers should participate in the § 319 process because programs, once they are approved, may be difficult to change.

CWA § 303(d) requires the states to identify waters for which existing controls are insufficient to meet water quality standards and to establish **total maximum daily loads (TMDLs)** for the pollutants at issue. TMDLs represent the maximum pollutant loading from both point and nonpoint sources that the water body can receive and still meet water quality standards for that pollutant, taking seasonal variations into account and including a margin of safety. The TMDLs must be allocated among current and future dischargers to the applicable segment of the water body. Section 303(d) includes deadlines for submission and approval of the lists of impaired waters and TMDLs. Citizen plaintiffs have been very successful in challenging the failure of the states and the EPA to meet those deadlines. *See, e.g., Friends of the Wild Swan v. EPA*, 74 Fed. Appx. 718 (9th Cir. 2003).

CWA § 304(e) requires states to also identify "toxic hot spots." The states must prepare two lists: one list for waters that are not expected to meet water quality standards after implementation of technology-based effluent limitations due to toxic pollutants from any source, and a second, shorter list for those waters for which the failure to meet water quality standards is due to toxic pollutants from nonpoint sources. For each segment of the waters included on the lists, the state must develop and implement (after EPA approval), an **individual control strategy (ICS)** to reduce toxic pollutants from point sources discharging into that water segment. For point sources, an ICS typically is incorporated into NPDES permit conditions. *See Dioxin/Organochlorine Center v. Clarke*, 57 F.3d 1517, 1520 (9th Cir. 1995).

Oil and Hazardous Substances

Section 311 of the CWA prohibits the discharge of oil or hazardous substances into waters of the United States in harmful quantities and imposes liability for the costs of remediating such discharges. **Harmful quantities** of oil are those that violate applicable water quality standards or cause a sheen, sludge, or emulsion in the receiving waters or on the shoreline of those waters. 40 C.F.R. § 110.3 (2003). The EPA has designated approximately 300 hazardous substances, which are listed by name, synonym, and **chemical abstract number (CAS #).** 40 C.F.R. part 116 (2003).

> CWA § 311 prohibits the discharge of oil or hazardous substances into waters of the United States in harmful quantities.

To try to prevent such discharges, EPA regulations under § 311 require that **spill prevention, control, and countermeasure (SPCC)** plans for oil spills be prepared by owners and operators of nontransportation-related facilities that have an aboveground oil storage capacity of more than 1,320 gallons or an underground oil storage capacity of more than 42,000 gallons. 40 C.F.R. § 112.3 (2003).

Figure 2-7 illustrates 40 C.F.R. § 112.7, the "General requirements for Spill Prevention, Control, and Countermeasure Plans." This complete document (rule) with all of the general requirements is available on the Internet at http://www.access.gpo.gov/nara/cfr/waisidx_04/40cfr112_04.html.

Section 311(b)(5) of the CWA requires notification to the National Response Center by the person in charge of a discharging facility or vessel "immediately" upon discovering a discharge by the facility of a **reportable quantity (RQ)** of oil or other hazardous substances. Under § 311(a) of the CWA, oil is defined to include "oil in any form" while the EPA's definition adds various forms of animal and vegetable oil, petroleum-based oil, synthetic oils, and mineral oils. 40 C.F.R. § 112.2 (2003).

Any person in charge of a facility or vessel who fails to notify the government of a reportable discharge is subject to criminal fines in accordance with Title 18 of the *United States Code,* or imprisonment for up to five years, or both. *Apex Oil Co. v. United States*, 530 F.2d 1291 (8th Cir.), *cert. denied*, 429 U.S. 827 (1976), rejected the corporate defendant's argument that only individuals could be "persons in charge" who are subject to criminal penalties for reporting violations.

> Failure to notify the government of a discharge or release is a criminal offense punishable by a fine in accordance with Title 18, imprisonment for as long as five years, or both.

Section 311(f) authorizes the federal government to seek reimbursement from the owner or operator of the vessel or facility causing the discharge of the government's costs to clean up the discharge. The owner/operator can establish a defense if it can prove that the discharge was caused solely by an act of God, an act of war, negligence on the part of the U.S. government, or any act or omission of a third party. Section 311 does not alter the owner's/operator's potential liability to the states or private parties.

SPCC Plan within six months of the review to include more effective prevention and control technology if the technology has been field-proven at the time of the review and will significantly reduce the likelihood of a discharge as described in §112.1(b) from the facility. You must implement any amendment as soon as possible, but not later than six months following preparation of any amendment. You must document your completion of the review and evaluation, and must sign a statement as to whether you will amend the Plan, either at the beginning or end of the Plan or in a log or an appendix to the Plan. The following words will suffice, "I have completed review and evaluation of the SPCC Plan for (name of facility) on (date), and will (will not) amend the Plan as a result."

(c) Have a Professional Engineer certify any technical amendment to your Plan in accordance with §112.3(d).

§112.6 [Reserved]

§112.7 General requirements for Spill Prevention, Control, and Countermeasure Plans.

If you are the owner or operator of a facility subject to this part you must prepare a Plan in accordance with good engineering practices. The Plan must have the full approval of management at a level of authority to commit the necessary resources to fully implement the Plan. You must prepare the Plan in writing. If you do not follow the sequence specified in this section for the Plan, you must prepare an equivalent Plan acceptable to the Regional Administrator that meets all of the applicable requirements listed in this part, and you must supplement it with a section cross-referencing the location of requirements listed in this part and the equivalent requirements in the other prevention plan. If the Plan calls for additional facilities or procedures, methods, or equipment not yet fully operational, you must discuss these items in separate paragraphs, and must explain separately the details of installation and operational start-up. As detailed elsewhere in this section, you must also:

(a)(1) Include a discussion of your facility's conformance with the requirements listed in this part.

(2) Comply with all applicable requirements listed in this part. Your Plan may deviate from the requirements in paragraphs (g), (h)(2) and (3), and (i) of this section and the requirements in subparts B and C of this part, except the secondary containment requirements in paragraphs (c) and (h)(1) of this section, and §§112.8(c)(2),112.8(c)(11),   112.9(c)(2), 112.10(c),   112.12(c)(2), 112.12(c)(11),112.13(c)(2),   and   112.14(c), where applicable to a specific facility, if you provide equivalent environmental protection by some other means of spill prevention, control, or countermeasure. Where your Plan does not conform to the applicable requirements in paragraphs (g), (h)(2) and (3), and (i) of this section, or the requirements of subparts B and C of this part, except the secondary containment requirements in paragraphs (c) and (h)(1) of this section, and §§112.8(c)(2), 112.8(c)(11),   112.9(c)(2),   112.10(c), 112.12(c)(2), 112.12(c)(11), 112.13(c)(2), and 112.14(c), you must state the reasons for nonconformance in your Plan and describe in detail alternate methods and how you will achieve equivalent environmental protection. If the Regional Administrator determines that the measures described in your Plan do not provide equivalent environmental protection, he may require that you amend your Plan, following the procedures in §112.4(d) and (e).

(3) Describe in your Plan the physical layout of the facility and include a facility diagram, which must mark the location and contents of each container. The facility diagram must include completely buried tanks that are otherwise exempted from the requirements of this part under §112.1(d)(4). The facility diagram must also include all transfer stations and connecting pipes. You must also address in your Plan:

(i) The type of oil in each container and its storage capacity;

(ii) Discharge prevention measures including procedures for routine handling of products (loading, unloading, and facility transfers, *etc.*);

Figure 2-7   40 C.F.R. § 112.7, General Requirements for Spill Prevention, Control, and Countermeasure Plans.

Section 404 Permits

Under § 404 of the CWA, permits are required for the discharge of dredged or fill material into waters of the United States. The permits are not required for discharges from normal agriculture and **silviculture** activities, from the maintenance of levees, dams, or bridges, from construction of farm ponds or sedimentation basins, or from the construction or maintenance of farm or forestry roads (§ 404(b)). **Dredged material** is defined as material that is excavated or dredged from a water body, and **fill material** is defined as any material that is placed in waters of the United States where it has the effect of replacing water with dry land or changing the water body's bottom elevation. 40 C.F.R. § 232.2.

The § 404 permits, which must meet EPA guidelines, are issued by the **U.S. Army Corps of Engineers (COE)**. Under the CWA, the COE maintains control of permits in navigable waters and their primary tributaries, but subject to EPA approval, states may take over most of the responsibility for the § 404 program. To date, only Michigan and New Jersey operate approved § 404 programs. Dredge and fill discharges may require individual permits or may be authorized by general or nationwide permits issued for activities determined by the COE to have minimal adverse impact on the environment.

CASES FOR DISCUSSION

Solid Waste Agency of North Cook County v. Army Corps of Engineers, 531 U.S. 159 (2001).

In *SWNACC*, the water in question consisted of permanent and seasonal ponds ("isolated wetlands") with no hydrological connection to other waterways. The United States claimed federal jurisdiction over the ponds through the Migratory Bird Rule, 33 C.F.R. § 328.3. The "Migratory Bird Rule" refers to an explanation, in the preambles to 1986 Army Corps of Engineers regulations and 1988 EPA regulations, that waters that are or may be used as habitat for migratory birds are an example of waters whose use, degradation, or destruction could affect interstate or foreign commerce and therefore are "waters of the United States." 51 Fed. Reg. 41217 (1986); 53 Fed. Reg. 20765 (1988). The Court ruled that the Migratory Bird Rule exceeded the authority granted under § 404(a) of the Clean Water Act.

(continued)

CASES FOR DISCUSSION

In another § 404 case, *United States v. Rapanos*, 339 F.3d 447 (6th Cir. 2003), John Rapanos owned a 175-acre plot of land in Michigan. Rapanos decided to sell a portion of that land to developers, but to make the land more attractive, Rapanos began to clear the trees and eradicate the wetlands that were on the property. Rapanos then approached the Michigan Department of Natural Resources with a development plan, and was told that the land contained wetlands and a permit would be necessary for development to begin.

Rapanos hired a wetlands consultant, who found at least forty-nine acres of wetlands on the property. After receiving the report, Rapanos threatened to fire him and sue if he did not destroy any paper evidence of the wetlands on the property. Despite warnings from the Michigan Department of Natural Resources and the EPA, Rapanos began destroying the wetlands on his property by filling them with earth and sand.

At trial, Rapanos successfully argued to the district court that *SWANCC*, through its frequent use of the phrase "wetlands adjacent to water," required that wetlands be directly adjacent to navigable water to be subject to the CWA.

The Sixth Circuit disagreed with such an expansive reading of *SWANCC* and held that because the wetlands were adjacent to the Labozinski Drain, especially in view of a hydrological connection between the two, the Rapanos wetlands were covered by the CWA. Any contamination of the Rapanos wetlands could affect the Drain, which, in turn could affect navigable-in-fact waters. Therefore, the court reinstated the district court's sentence of Rapanos to three years of probation and ordered him to pay a fine of $185,000.

Conclusion

The Clean Water Act is the primary federal statute regulating water pollution. The CWA is the successor to several water pollution control statutes passed in the late 1940s through 1960s. The statute was created "to restore and maintain the chemical, physical, and biological integrity" of the waters of the United States.

The CWA, among other things, institutes a permitting program for discharges of pollutants into the nation's waters. In the process, paralegals can find many tasks. For instance, paralegals may be involved in the compilation, analysis, and completion of NPDES permits or permit applications. Paralegals may be involved in the

NPDES permit review process if comments on the draft permit are to be filed or a public hearing is held. Paralegals may be involved in the CWA administrative decision-making and rule-making process and in CWA appeals through case preparation, research, writing, and document drafting. Paralegals may also prepare initial regulatory and factual research and draft petitions for variances.

GLOSSARY OF CWA TERMS

ALJ. Administrative law judge.

antibacksliding. A concept that precludes a renewed or reissued permit from a less stringent standard than the BPJ limits.

aquatic ecosystems. Saltwater or freshwater ecosystems, including rivers, streams, lakes, wetlands, estuaries, and coral reefs.

aquifer. An underground geological formation, or group of formations, containing water.

arroyo. A watercourse in an arid region.

BAT. Best available technology economically achievable.

BADT. Best available demonstrated technology.

BCT. Best conventional technology.

BMPs. Best management practices. The schedules of activities, prohibitions practices, maintenance procedures, and other management practices to prevent or reduce the discharge of pollutants to waters of the United States.

BPJ. Best professional judgment. The method used by permit writers to develop technology-based NPDES permit conditions on a case-by-case basis using all reasonably available and relevant data.

BPT. Best practicable technology currently available.

bypass. An intentional diversion of waste effluent from the permittee's treatment facility.

CAS #. Chemical Abstract Number.

COE. U.S. Army Corps of Engineers.

criteria information. The concentration limits necessary to support each designated use.

CWA. The Clean Water Act.

dredged material. Material that is excavated or dredged from a water body.

effluent. A liquid waste stream that emanates from a point source.

EPA. U.S. Environmental Protection Agency.

FDF. Fundamentally different factors. These may be asserted by an NPDES permittee in an attempt to obtain a variance from NPDES permitting standards.

fill material. Any material commonly used to replace water with dry land or to change a water body's bottom elevation.

FWPCA. Federal Water Pollution Control Act of 1948.

groundwater. Subsurface water that occurs beneath the water table in soils and geologic formations that are fully saturated.

ICS. Individual Control Strategy.

industrial user. A company that discharges effluent into city sewers; also known as an *indirect discharger*.

influent. A liquid waste stream that flows from a point source into a POTW or other permitted source.

net limits. There is a credit for pollutants in intake (influent) waters.

nonpoint source. An effluent source that is obscure or not quantifiable, such as city street runoff or farm runoff.

NPDES. National Pollutant Discharge Elimination System.

oil. Oil in any form. An oil spill above the RQ is reportable under § 311 of the CWA. The EPA's definition includes animal and vegetable oil and petroleum-based oil.

point source. Any discernible, confined, and discrete conveyance, including, but not limited to, any pipe, ditch, channel, tunnel, conduit, well, discrete fissure, container, rolling stock, concentrated animal feeding operation, or vessel or other floating craft, from which pollutants are or may be discharged. This term does not include return flows from irrigated agriculture.

pollutant. Dredged spoil, solid waste, incinerator residue, sewage, garbage, sewage sludge, munitions, chemical wastes, biological materials, radioactive materials, heat, wrecked or discarded equipment, rock, sand, cellar dirt and industrial, municipal, and agricultural waste.

POTW. Publicly owned treatment works.

Refuse Act. Rivers and Harbors Act of 1899.

RQ. Reportable quantity.

runoff. That part of precipitation, snowmelt, or irrigation water that runs off the land into streams or other surface water. It can carry pollutants from the air and land into receiving waters.

silviculture. A branch of forestry dealing with the development and care of forests.

SPCC. Spill prevention, control, and countermeasures.

TMDL. Total maximum daily loads.

upset. An exceptional incident involving noncompliance with technology-based effluent limitations.

water clarity. A measure of how clear a body of water is.

water quality criteria. Levels of water quality expected to render a body of water suitable for its designated use. Criteria are based on specific levels of pollutants that would make the water harmful if used for drinking, swimming, irrigation, fish production, or industrial processes.

water quality standards. State-adopted and EPA-approved ambient standards for water bodies. The standards define the water quality goals of a water body by designating the uses of the water and setting criteria to protect those uses.

waters. All water in which the United States has an interest, including navigable waters of the United States, interstate waters and their tributaries, and waters that may be used in commerce.

watershed. An area of land from which all water that drains from it flows to a single water body.

wetland ecosystems. Areas that are inundated or saturated by surface or groundwater at a frequency and duration sufficient to support, and that under normal circumstances do support, a prevalence of vegetation typically adapted for life in saturated soil conditions.

WQA. Water Quality Act of 1987.

WQBELs. Water-quality-based effluent limitations.

BIBLIOGRAPHY

The Clean Water Act Handbook (Mark A. Ryan ed., 2d ed. A.B.A. 2003).

Findley, Roger W., & Daniel A. Farber, *Environmental Law in a Nutshell* (6th ed. West 2004).

Houck, Oliver A. *The Clean Water Act TMDL Program: Law, Policy, and Implementation* (2nd ed. Envtl. L. Inst. 2002).

Houghton, Mary J., *The Clean Water Act Amendments of 1987* (BNA 1987).

Industrial User Permitting Guidance Manual (U.S. EPA 1989).

NPDES Permit Writers' Manual (U.S. EPA 1996).

Quality Criteria for Water, 1986 (the "Gold Book"), EPA 44015-86-001 (U.S. EPA 1986).

Rogers, William H., Jr., *Environmental Law* (2nd ed. West 1994).

Storm Water Permit Manual (Thompson Publishing Group).

U.S. EPA Enforcement Policy for Noncompliance with Section 404 of the FWPCA (U.S. EPA 1976).

DISCUSSION QUESTIONS

1. Under the NPDES permit system, it is unlawful for any person to discharge any pollutant from a point source into navigable waters without an NPDES permit.

   Q. How would a paralegal determine the type of pollutant that is the subject of the discharge?

   Q. What types of pollutants are excluded from the definition of *pollutants?*

2. The permit issuance section of the Clean Water Act applies to EPA-issued and state-issued permits.

   Q. What authority would a paralegal go through to obtain permit issuance for a direct discharge in Michigan? Would the paralegal go to the federal or state authority?

   Q. When an upset occurs for a permitted source, who must be notified and under what time frame? What information must be included in the notice?

3. POTWs must meet effluent limitations based on secondary treatment as defined in EPA's regulations.

   Q. If there is a modification of secondary treatment requirement for POTWs discharging into marine waters, what source can a paralegal use to look for the nine conditions that must be met with regard to water quality standards and toxic controls?

COMPUTER LABORATORY PROJECTS

1. Learn how to read and complete wastewater discharge monitoring reports (DMRs) at http://www.adeq.state.ar.us/ftproot/Pub/water/dmr/reports_files/frame.htm.
2. Research whether discharge monitoring report filers in your state must file paper or electronic reports (e-filing), or if either way of filing is optional. Prepare a summary memorandum for class presentation.

INTERNET SITES

- The full text of the Clean Water Act (CWA) is on the Internet at http://www.epa.gov/r5water/cwa.htm.

- The EPA's water Web site is on the Internet at http://www.epa.gov/water.

CHAPTER 3

The Resource Conservation and Recovery Act

Charles W. Wesselhoft

OBJECTIVES

The objectives of this chapter are for students to:

- Learn the terminology associated with the RCRA.
- Learn the concepts and ideas that underlie the RCRA law and regulatory program.
- Learn about specific sections and provisions of the RCRA law and regulations.
- Learn about the processes and procedures used by the government and other parties to comply with and to enforce the law under the RCRA.
- Learn about the particular jobs and functions that are performed by paralegals working for attorneys in RCRA cases.

History of the Act

The **RCRA** is the **Resource Conservation and Recovery Act,** 42 U.S.C. §§ 6901–6992k (1991). It was first enacted as an amendment to the Solid Waste Disposal Act in 1976 (Pub. L. No. 94-580) and was substantially revised in 1978 (Pub. L. No. 95-609) and, again, in 1984 (Pub. L. No. 98-616). Its purpose is to provide "cradle-to-grave" management of solid waste. Regulations under the Act are found at 40 C.F.R. §§ 260 to 281.

Congress's stated goal in enacting RCRA is that "wherever feasible, the generation of hazardous waste is to be reduced or eliminated as expeditiously as possible. Waste that is nevertheless generated should be treated, stored, or disposed of so as to minimize the present and future threat to human health and the environment." 42 U.S.C. § 6902(b) (1991). Subtitle C of RCRA covers hazardous waste. Subtitle D covers nonhazardous waste.

The RCRA program is administered by the EPA through its **Office of Solid Waste.** The EPA was also authorized to promulgate rules to further the purposes of the Act. Its first rule making under the program was in 1980 and has continued unabated since then. The rules currently cover anyone who generates, treats, stores, transports, or disposes of hazardous waste and anyone who operates a nonhazardous municipal solid waste landfill. The EPA continues to consider promulgation of rules governing nonhazardous industrial waste landfills.

An organizational chart of the EPA is shown in Figure 3-1. This chart can also be accessed at http://www.epa.gov/epahome/organization.htm.

What is a **solid waste?** For purposes of RCRA, it is:

Any garbage, refuse, sludge from a waste treatment plant, waste supply treatment plant, or air pollution control facility and other discarded material, including solid, liquid, semi-solid, or contained gaseous material resulting from industrial, commercial, mining, and agricultural operations, and from community activities, but does not include solid or dissolved material in domestic sewage, or solid or dissolved material in irrigation return flows or industrial discharges which are point sources subject to permits under section 1342 of Title 33, or source, special nuclear, or byproduct material as defined by the Atomic Energy Act of 1954, as amended (68 Stat. 923). 42 U.S.C. § 6903(27) (1991).

The EPA has amended the statutory definition in its hazardous waste rules to provide that a solid waste is any discarded material that is not subject to one or more of a variety of exclusions. For purposes of the rules, **discarded material** is any material that is abandoned, recycled, or inherently wastelike. Each of these terms is also defined and subject to its own set of exclusions.

> A solid waste is any discarded material that is not subject to one or more of a variety of exclusions.

There are some important points to recognize regarding the definition of *solid waste*. First, the material must be classified as a waste. Many industrial byproducts are reused as the bases for other manufacturing processes. If the material has another legitimate use, it is not a waste. Controversy often exists over what constitutes a legitimate use.

In addition, to be classified as a "solid" waste, the material does not need to be solid. The definition includes liquids and even some

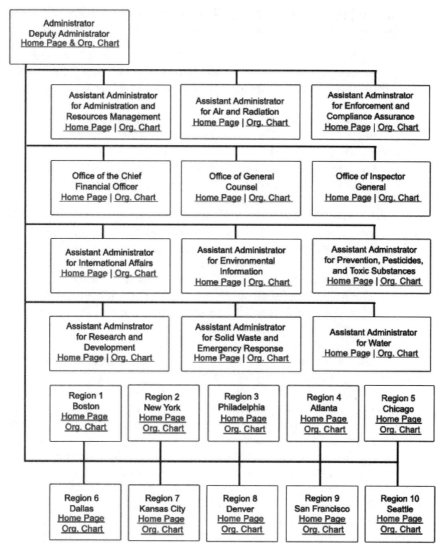

Figure 3-1   Organizational Chart of the EPA as Shown at http://www.epa.gov/
epahome/organization.htm.

gaseous materials. Therefore, such materials as solvents would be
solid waste when discarded, even though they may contain no solid
material.

To be a "solid" waste, the material does not need to be solid.

Subtitle D—State or Regional Solid Waste Plans

RCRA Subtitle D applies to nonhazardous waste generators, transporters, treaters, storers, and disposers. The only portion of this subtitle that is currently subject to federal regulation is that covering municipal solid waste disposal facilities. Rules pertaining to these facilities were promulgated in 1991 and first became effective in October 1993. As with Subtitle C, the states may develop their own programs covering these facilities provided the state rules are at least as stringent as those in the federal program.

The **Municipal Solid Waste Landfill (MSWL)** rules are found at 40 C.F.R. part 258. The rules apply only to landfills that accept household waste.[1] Therefore, a facility that accepts only nonhazardous industrial waste is not subject to federal regulation. There are, however, nonbinding federal guidelines concerning solid waste disposal found at 40 C.F.R. subchapter I. Note also that most states have extensive rules pertaining to industrial solid waste disposal facilities.

The MSWL rules provide minimum design and performance criteria for covered landfills. These include such things as siting criteria, liner standards, leachate collection standards, groundwater monitoring standards, and closure requirements. They also provide standards for corrective action if the landfill begins to affect the surrounding environment adversely.

Many states have special siting criteria for MSWLs that are the direct result of the **Not-in-My-Back-Yard ("NIMBY")** syndrome. Community activists have been unsatisfied with the response they have received from state regulatory agencies and, as a result, have persuaded state legislators in those states to provide them with a statutory right to review MSWL siting decisions.

An example is the Illinois "SB 172" siting criteria. Environmental Protection Act, 415 ILCS 5/39(c) (1992). The SB 172 process requires that the local county board or the governing body of the impacted municipality hold a series of hearings to allow public input into the proposed siting decision. The governing body is required to decide whether the selected site is appropriate based on nine specified criteria. See 415 ILCS 5/39.2(a) (1992). In Illinois, the SB 172 process has greatly slowed the opening of new landfills.

Paralegals will typically be involved in the complicated siting process. Siting is usually a complex and time-consuming operation.

---

[1] Household waste means any solid waste (including garbage, trash, and sanitary waste in septic tanks) derived from households (including single and multiple residences, hotels and motels, bunkhouses, ranger stations, crew quarters, campgrounds, picnic grounds, and day use recreational areas). 40 C.F.R. § 258.2 (2003).

Much research will have to be done on waste generation and transportation throughout the region of the proposed site. The siting application is a complex document that requires organizational skills. Reports and exhibits to support the siting application may also need to be prepared and may need review and comment.

Subtitle C—Hazardous Waste Management

Subtitle C of RCRA provides for the control of hazardous waste generation, transportation, treatment, storage, and disposal. The Act defines "hazardous waste" as:

> Solid waste, or combination of solid wastes, which because of its quantity, concentration, or physical, chemical, or infectious characteristics may—
>
> (A) Cause, or significantly contribute to an increase in mortality or an increase in serious irreversible, or incapacitating reversible, illness; or
> (B) Pose a substantial threat or potential hazard to human health or the environment when improperly treated, stored, transported, or disposed of, or otherwise managed.

42 U.S.C. § 6903(5) (1991).

Note that, to be designated hazardous waste, the material must first be classified as solid waste. If it meets that test, then the impact on human health or the environment is examined.

To be a hazardous waste, the material must first be a solid waste.

CASES FOR DISCUSSION

American Portland Cement Alliance v. EPA, 101 F.3d 772, 43 ERC 1705, 27 Envtl. L. Rep. 20,535 (DC Cir. 1996).

The issue in this case was whether the court had jurisdiction under RCRA to review petitions challenging the "Regulatory Determination on Cement Kiln Dust," issued by the EPA, at 60 Fed. Reg. 7,366 (Feb. 7, 1995). In the Regulatory Determination, the EPA decided that cement kiln dust did not warrant full hazardous waste regulation under Subtitle C of RCRA and that it should instead be subject to tailored standards to be developed by the EPA.

(continued)

CASE FOR DISCUSSION

Petitioner Safe Cement Alliance of Texas, *et al.* (Safe Cement), a coalition of environmental and citizens' groups, which included persons residing near cement kilns, challenged as arbitrary and capricious the EPA's decision not to apply full Subtitle C regulation. Both Safe Cement and EPA contend that the court had jurisdiction to review Safe Cement's petition. Petitioner American Portland Cement Alliance, *et al.* (American Portland), a trade association, maintained that the court lacked jurisdiction over the petition because the EPA's Regulatory Determination did not constitute one of the three actions designated as reviewable under RCRA, but was simply a determination to undertake rule making in the future.

Alternatively, American Portland sought review of its petition, which maintained that the EPA's decision to subject kiln dust to tailored standards is legally, technically, and scientifically flawed. The court found that the Regulatory Determination was not reviewable under RCRA and dismissed the petitions for lack of jurisdiction.

Characteristic Hazardous Waste

As a result of the congressional mandate in RCRA, the EPA developed a set of rules for determining whether a waste is hazardous. The cornerstone of this program is the **characteristic hazardous waste determination procedure** found at 40 C.F.R. § 261.3 (2001). The program contains four basic characteristics in determining whether solid waste is in fact hazardous:

1. Ignitability
2. Corrosivity
3. Reactivity
4. Toxicity

Solid waste, if it has one or more of these characteristics, is hazardous. Such wastes are typically referred to as **characteristic wastes.**

Ignitability Characteristic

The ignitability of a material is measured by its ability to begin to burn under certain conditions. This is determined by the chemical composition of the material or its flash point. The flash point is measured by any of several laboratory procedures. Ignitability data typically are available in various chemical handbooks. Ignitable wastes are identified as **D001** wastes.

Corrosivity Characteristic

A material is considered corrosive under RCRA if it has a pH of less than or equal to 2, or greater than or equal to 12.5, or if it corrodes steel above a specified rate. The pH of a material can be easily measured by electronic instruments or by dye-soaked paper tape. Rate data concerning a material's ability to corrode steel usually are available in engineering handbooks. Corrosive wastes are identified as **D002** wastes.

Reactivity Characteristic

Reactivity is a measure of the material's ability to change its state rapidly. An example is an explosive such as nitroglycerin. It is normally a liquid but, under certain conditions, it burns extremely rapidly and produces a large volume of gas and a shock wave. For most reactive materials that appear in normal commerce, extensive data exist in chemical handbooks and in the U.S. Department of Transportation shipping regulations. Reactive wastes are identified as **D003** wastes.

Toxicity Characteristic

The toxicity of a material is determined by using the **Toxicity Characteristic Leaching Procedure (TCLP)**. The TCLP is a laboratory method whereby a sample of the material is mixed with acetic acid solution for a specified period of time. The waste solids are then filtered out and the remaining solution is analyzed for a number of heavy metals and organic compounds. A waste is hazardous if those compounds are detected in the solution in quantities greater than the limits provided at 40 C.F.R. § 261.24(b) (2002). Toxicity characteristic wastes are identified as **D004** through **D043** wastes, depending on the compound detected.

> Four basic characteristics that make a solid waste hazardous are
> - ignitability
> - reactivity
> - corrosivity
> - toxicity

As noted in the preceding characteristic descriptions, each of the "characteristic" wastes is identified by a three-digit number preceded by a "D." These are generally called **D wastes.** A waste may have more than one characteristic, and all documentation referring to the waste should include all of the applicable identifiers. For example, chromic acid is a D002 waste because it has a pH of less than 2. It would also be a D007 (toxicity characteristic) waste because a TCLP would produce a chromium concentration of more than 5.0 mg/l.

"Listed" Wastes

The EPA was given the authority to list wastes as hazardous based on the waste's "toxicity, persistence, and degradability in nature, potential for accumulation in tissue, and other related factors such as flammability, corrosiveness, and other hazard characteristics." 42 U.S.C. § 6921(a) (1991). The EPA examined typical industrial waste streams and determined that a number of them nearly always have either one of the four characteristics identified above or contain compounds that have been determined to meet one of the other statutory criteria. These compounds or compound classes are listed by the EPA at 40 C.F.R. §§ 261.31 through 261.33.

> The EPA was given the authority to list wastes as hazardous wastes based on the waste's
>
> ➤ toxicity, persistence, and degradability in nature
> ➤ its potential for accumulation in tissue
> ➤ other related factors such as flammability and corrosiveness

The tables of wastes are divided into four groups. The **F wastes** are general classes of compounds such as all "halogenated solvents used in degreasing" (for instance, F001). 40 C.F.R. § 261.31.

K wastes are those that are industry- or process-specific. An example is K005, which is "[w]astewater treatment sludge from the production of chrome green pigments." 40 C.F.R. § 261.32. Finally, **P and U wastes** are compound-specific and include off-spec materials and spill residues. 40 C.F.R. § 261.33.

"Mixture" and "Derived From" Rules

As has been discussed, there are two basic classes of hazardous wastes, i.e., those that are **"characteristic" hazardous** and those that are **"listed" hazardous.** For permitting and handling purposes, there is really no distinction between the two classes. The distinction lies in the wastes' futures. A **characteristic waste** remains so only as long as that characteristic exists. Once the characteristic is removed, it is no longer a hazardous waste and can be generally dealt with in a much less restricted manner. A **listed hazardous waste** normally is a hazardous waste forever.

> Pursuant to the mixture rule, any nonhazardous waste with which a hazardous waste is mixed becomes a part of that hazardous waste.

Any nonhazardous waste with which a hazardous waste is mixed becomes a part of that waste. 40 C.F.R. § 261.3(a)(2)(iv) (2001). This is the so-called **mixture rule.** An example of the mixture rule in action for a listed waste is the situation in which a waste solvent is added to waste oil in a drum. Assuming that the waste oil is not a characteristic hazardous waste, it is in itself not a hazardous waste under RCRA.

However, when the waste solvent F003 (a listed hazardous waste) is added to the drum of waste oil, the whole drum of material instantly becomes F003 waste and remains so throughout its treatment, storage, and disposal. Alternatively, the addition of hydrochloric acid (a D002 characteristic waste because it has a pH of less than or equal to 2) to the drum of waste oil would make the whole drum of material D002 waste *only* if the resulting mixture also has a pH of less than or equal to 2. If the resulting mixture of hydrochloric acid and waste oil does have a pH of less than 2, it can be treated to raise the pH and thereby remove the hazardous characteristic. The treated mixture would then be nonhazardous for further treatment, storage, and disposal purposes.

The **"derived from" rule** deals with residues resulting from the treatment of listed hazardous wastes. Characteristic waste treatment residues are hazardous *only* if the residue exhibits a hazardous waste characteristic. 40 C.F.R. § 261.3(c)(2)(i) and (d)(2) (2001). However, under the "derived from" rule, residues from the treatment of most listed hazardous wastes remain listed hazardous wastes. The EPA determined that, in general, the residues from listed hazardous treatment retain the hazardous constituents of the parent waste.

Due to substantial public comment during the re-promulgation[2] of the mixture and derived from rules, the EPA has somewhat eased

---

[2] The "mixture" and "derived from" rules were the subject of a procedural challenge in *Shell Oil Co. et al v. EPA*, 950 F.2d 741 (D.C. Cir. 1991). In that case, the Court found that the EPA had failed to provide proper public notice when it promulgated the "mixture" and "derived from" rules. The rules were vacated and remanded to the EPA for repromulgation. The EPA published its final rule-making decision in this matter at 66 Fed. Reg. 27266 (May 16, 2001).

the severity of the "derived from" rule. Some listed hazardous wastes were listed solely because they exhibited a hazardous characteristic. Under the new rule, if the listed waste was listed solely due to ignitability, corrosivity, or reactivity (but not toxicity) and the treatment removes that characteristic, the treatment residue is no longer a listed hazardous waste. 40 C.F.R. 261.3(g) (2001).

Using the preceding example of the solvent/oil mixture, the drum of waste solvent/waste oil mixture could be distilled to recover the ignitable solvent portion. The distillation process would remove nearly all of the solvent (and, therefore, the ignitability characteristic) from the waste oil so the waste oil would no longer be an F003 waste even though it was "derived from" the listed F003 mixture. On the other hand, if the waste oil is F010 (quench oil from metal heat treating where cyanides are used) and it is treated to remove virtually all of the cyanide, the resulting oil would still be considered F010 waste.

Be aware that the Land Disposal Restriction (LDR) requirements (discussed later) still apply to residues listed wastes treated to remove the ignitibility, corrosivity, or reactivity hazardous characteristic unless the treatment occurred at the point of generation. 66 Fed. Reg. 27266 at 27269 (May 16, 2001).

Pursuant to the "derived from" rule, residues from the treatment of hazardous wastes listed for toxicity remain hazardous wastes regardless of whether the resulting residue is truly hazardous.

Universal Wastes

There are a number of waste streams that present unique management problems. They contain compounds that would bring the waste into the RCRA hazardous waste program, but management of these wastes pursuant to the full RCRA regulatory package presented a substantial burden to business and consumers. To ease this burden, the EPA developed the universal waste rules found at 40 C.F.R. part 273. These special rules apply to batteries, pesticides, thermostats, and lamps (for example, fluorescent and mercury vapor bulbs). Standards are set in the rules for small quantity waste managers (less than 11,000 pounds at any one time), large quantity managers, transporters, and destination facilities. Persons operating under these rules are generally exempt from the mainstream RCRA rules.

The Permit Program

Anyone who treats, stores, or disposes of a hazardous waste is potentially subject to the RCRA permit program.[3] 40 C.F.R. § 270.1(c) (1999). When RCRA first became effective, there were many facilities that were already engaged in hazardous waste **treatment, storage, and disposal (TSD).** Those that wished to continue after the effective date were required to file Part A of the RCRA TSD permit application. These facilities are known as **interim status** facilities until such time as they receive a full RCRA TSD permit. Interim status facilities are regulated under 40 C.F.R. part 265.

To receive the full permit, the interim status facility must file Part B of the application. Deadlines for the filing of the Part B applications for certain interim status facilities are found at 40 C.F.R. § 270.73 (1998). The EPA (or the state administrator) may, at its discretion, call for the Part B application. If the interim status facility fails to file its Part B by the required date, it loses its interim status and thereafter is operating without a permit. Once the interim facility has filed Part B, it may continue to operate as an interim facility until the full permit is granted or denied by the appropriate federal or state authority. New facilities must file both Part A and Part B and have the permit issued *prior* to initiating TSD activity.

> Anyone who treats, stores, or disposes of a hazardous waste is potentially subject to RCRA's permit program.

Many states have been given authority to administer the RCRA permit program, provided they develop state laws that are "no less stringent" than the federal version of RCRA. These states are allowed to operate fairly autonomously. The federal EPA has the right, however, to comment on any permit application, and it has the right to terminate state-issued permits on certain grounds. It should also be noted that the EPA has the right to enforce state RCRA law independently and will likely do so if it believes the state's enforcement efforts are inadequate.

---

[3] There are exceptions to this statement. For example, a generator may store for up to ninety days, or a generator may treat waste in a totally enclosed treatment system without a permit. (See page 76 for discussion of generators.)

CASES FOR DISCUSSION

Edison Electric Institute v. EPA, 996 F.2d 326, 36 ERC 1913, 23 Envtl. L. Rep. 21,006 (CA DC 1993).

In this case, a petition for review of the EPA's interpretation of the RCRA hazardous waste storage provision was brought by electric utility associations and power companies. The review was denied.

The court found that the EPA's interpretation of RCRA rendered it unlawful to store wastes for indefinite periods pending the development of adequate treatment techniques or disposal capacity. The petitioners contended that this interpretation was both inconsistent with the statute and unreasonable as applied to generators of wastes containing both hazardous and radioactive components, for which there were currently few lawful treatment or disposal options. The court decided that the EPA's interpretation was not only permissible, but was, in fact, mandated by the terms of the statute.

TSD Rules

RCRA rules provide very specific and highly technical standards for the design, construction, operation, and closure of TSD facilities. These rules are provided at 40 C.F.R. part 265 for interim status facilities and 40 C.F.R. part 264 for RCRA permitted facilities. There are separate sections in both parts for certain types of treatment operations, for storage operations, and for certain types of disposal operations. There are also general requirements for all TSD facilities such as "Preparedness and Prevention," "Contingency Planning and Emergency Procedures," and manifesting requirements.

Generator Status

Unless an exemption exists, all facilities that store hazardous waste are required to have a permit or interim status. Many industrial facilities generate hazardous waste as part of their manufacturing process. To require continuous removal of the waste to a permitted TSD facility would be prohibitively expensive and nearly impossible. To require these facilities to obtain TSD permits would place too heavy of a burden on the permit authority; therefore, an exemption was developed that allows these facilities to store hazardous waste on site for up to ninety days without a permit.[4]

Generators are regulated under 40 C.F.R. part 262. Figure 3-2 shows 40 C.F.R. part 262, with the subpart and section index illustrated. The complete rule is available on the Internet at http://www.access.gpo.gov/nara/cfr/waisidx_03/40cfr262_03.html.

Part 262 requires that the generator facility apply for and obtain an EPA generator identification number. It also requires that generators comply with the various portions of 40 C.F.R. part 265, including the personnel training requirements, tank storage standards, contingency planning, and facility preparedness. Finally, generators must prepare manifests for all hazardous waste shipments and keep records of these manifests for three years following shipment.

> Unless an exemption exists, all facilities that store hazardous waste are required to have a permit or interim status.

Manifests

The EPA has developed a system for keeping track of hazardous waste shipments. Each shipment is to be accompanied by a six-part hazardous waste manifest that is prepared by the generator. The EPA's uniform hazardous waste manifest form is shown in Figure 3-3. The form is available on the Internet at http://a257.g.akamaitech.net/7/257/2422/14mar20010800/edocket.access.gpo.gov/cfr_2002/julqtr/pdf/40cfr262.108.pdf (look on page two). Also, check out the Minnesota Pollution Control Agency's "Manifest Tip Sheet" for an up-close view of how to complete a uniform hazardous waste manifest form, on the Internet at http://www.pca.state.mn.us/publications/w-hw5-10.pdf.

The manifest includes information on the identity of the generator, the nature and quantity of the waste being shipped, and the transporter's identity. The manifest also includes a certification by the generator that the generator has made the best practicable effort to reduce the volume and toxicity of the waste and has selected a method to treat, store, or dispose of the waste in such a way as to

---

[4] Small-quantity generators (those that generate more than 100 kilograms but fewer than 1000 kilograms of hazardous waste within a calendar month) may store waste for up to 180 days provided certain additional requirements are met. Small-quantity generators who must transport their wastes more than 200 miles are allowed to store without a permit for up to 270 days. 40 C.F.R. § 262.44 (1987).

Pt. 262

PART 262—STANDARDS APPLICABLE TO GENERATORS OF HAZARDOUS WASTE

Subpart A—General

Sec.
262.10 Purpose, scope, and applicability.
262.11 Hazardous waste determination.
262.12 EPA identification numbers.

Subpart B—The Manifest

262.20 General requirements.
262.21 Acquisition of manifests.
262.22 Number of copies.
262.23 Use of the manifest.

Subpart C—Pre-Transport Requirements

262.30 Packaging.
262.31 Labeling.
262.32 Marking.
262.33 Placarding.
262.34 Accumulation time.

Subpart D—Recordkeeping and Reporting

262.40 Recordkeeping.
262.41 Biennial report.
262.42 Exception reporting.
262.43 Additional reporting.
262.44 Special requirements for generators of between 100 and 1000 kg/mo.

Subpart E—Exports of Hazardous Waste

262.50 Applicability.
262.51 Definitions.
262.52 General requirements.
262.53 Notification of intent to export.
262.54 Special manifest requirements.
262.55 Exception reports.
262.56 Annual reports.
262.57 Recordkeeping.
262.58 International agreements.

Subpart F—Imports of Hazardous Waste

262.60 Imports of hazardous waste.

Subpart G—Farmers

262.70 Farmers.

Subpart H—Transfrontier shipments of hazardous waste for recovery within the OECD

262.80 Applicability.
262.81 Definitions.
262.82 General conditions.
262.83 Notification and consent.
262.84 Tracking document.
262.85 Contracts.
262.86 Provisions relating to recognized traders.

262.87 Reporting and recordkeeping.
262.88 Pre-approval for U.S. Recovery Facilities. [Reserved]
262.89 OECD Waste Lists.

Subpart I—New York State Public Utilities

262.90 Project XL for Public Utilities in New York State.

Subpart J—University Laboratories XL Project—Laboratory Environmental Management Standard

262.100 To what organizations does this subpart apply?
262.101 What is in this subpart?
262.102 What special definitions are included in this subpart?
262.103 What is the scope of the laboratory environmental management standard?
262.104 What are the minimum performance criteria?
262.105 What must be included in the laboratory environmental management plan?
262.106 When must a hazardous waste determination be made?
262.107 Under what circumstances will a university's participation in this environmental management standard pilot be terminated?
262.108 When will this subpart expire?

APPENDIX TO PART 262—UNIFORM HAZARDOUS WASTE MANIFEST AND INSTRUCTIONS (EPA FORMS 8700–22 AND 8700–22A AND THEIR INSTRUCTIONS)

AUTHORITY: 42 U.S.C 6906, 6912, 6922–6925, 6937, and 6938.

SOURCE: 45 FR 33142, May 19, 1980, unless otherwise noted.

Subpart A—General

§ 262.10 Purpose, scope, and applicability.

(a) These regulations establish standards for generators of hazardous waste.

(b) 40 CFR 261.5(c) and (d) must be used to determine the applicability of provisions of this part that are dependent on calculations of the quantity of hazardous waste generated per month.

(c) A generator who treats, stores, or disposes of hazardous waste on-site must only comply with the following sections of this part with respect to that waste: Section 262.11 for determining whether or not he has a hazardous waste, § 262.12 for obtaining an EPA identification number, § 262.34 for accumulation of hazardous waste, § 262.40 (c) and (d) for recordkeeping,

160

Figure 3-2 The First Page of 40 C.F.R. Part 262, With Subpart and Section Index Illustrated.

Please print or type. (Form designed for use on elite (12-pitch) typewriter.) Form Approved. OMB No. 2050-0039

UNIFORM HAZARDOUS WASTE MANIFEST	1. Generator ID Number	2. Page 1 of	3. Emergency Response Phone	4. Manifest Tracking Number

5. Generator's Name and Mailing Address   Generator's Site Address (if different than mailing address)

Generator's Phone:

6. Transporter 1 Company Name   U.S. EPA ID Number

7. Transporter 2 Company Name   U.S. EPA ID Number

8. Designated Facility Name and Site Address   U.S. EPA ID Number

Facility's Phone:

9a. HM	9b. U.S. DOT Description (including Proper Shipping Name, Hazard Class, ID Number, and Packing Group (if any))	10. Containers No.	Type	11. Total Quantity	12. Unit Wt./Vol.	13. Waste Codes
	1.					
	2.					
	3.					
	4.					

14. Special Handling Instructions and Additional Information

15. **GENERATOR'S/OFFEROR'S CERTIFICATION:** I hereby declare that the contents of this consignment are fully and accurately described above by the proper shipping name, and are classified, packaged, marked and labeled/placarded, and are in all respects in proper condition for transport according to applicable international and national governmental regulations. If export shipment and I am the Primary Exporter, I certify that the contents of this consignment conform to the terms of the attached EPA Acknowledgment of Consent.

I certify that the waste minimization statement identified in 40 CFR 262.27(a) (if I am a large quantity generator) or (b) (if I am a small quantity generator) is true.

Generator's/Offeror's Printed/Typed Name   Signature   Month   Day   Year

16. International Shipments ☐ Import to U.S.   ☐ Export from U.S.   Port of entry/exit: _____

Transporter signature (for exports only):   Date leaving U.S.:

17. Transporter Acknowledgment of Receipt of Materials

Transporter 1 Printed/Typed Name   Signature   Month   Day   Year

Transporter 2 Printed/Typed Name   Signature   Month   Day   Year

18. Discrepancy

18a. Discrepancy Indication Space ☐ Quantity   ☐ Type   ☐ Residue   ☐ Partial Rejection   ☐ Full Rejection

Manifest Reference Number:

18b. Alternate Facility (or Generator)   U.S. EPA ID Number

Facility's Phone:

18c. Signature of Alternate Facility (or Generator)   Month   Day   Year

19. Hazardous Waste Report Management Method Codes (i.e., codes for hazardous waste treatment, disposal, and recycling systems)

1.   2.   3.   4.

20. Designated Facility Owner or Operator: Certification of receipt of hazardous materials covered by the manifest except as noted in Item 18a

Printed/Typed Name   Signature   Month   Day   Year

EPA Form 8700-22 (Rev. 3-05) Previous editions are obsolete.   DESIGNATED FACILITY TO DESTINATION STATE (IF REQUIRED)

GENERATOR / TRANSPORTER / INTL / DESIGNATED FACILITY

VOID

Figure 3-3 The EPA's Uniform Hazardous Waste Manifest Form.

minimize future environmental harm. The manifest form can vary from state to state, but it must contain all of the elements of the federal model form.

Once the generator has completed the manifest and transferred custody of the waste to the transporter, the transporter must sign and date the manifest and give a copy to the generator. Each transporter who takes custody of the waste in the chain between the generator and the ultimate destination (the TSD facility) must sign, date, and retain a copy of the manifest form. The TSD facility signs the last two copies, retains one, and sends the last copy back to the generator.

Each entity in the chain of custody has the responsibility to note any discrepancies between the waste types and volumes on the manifest and those being received. Each has the right to refuse delivery of the shipment if the manifest does not properly reflect the shipment. If delivery is refused, the shipment is sent back to the generator. If the generator has not received a copy of the completed manifest from the TSD facility within forty five days of shipment, the generator is required to file an exception report with the administering agency. This requirement does not apply for those situations in which a noncomplying shipment is returned.

> Each entity in the chain of custody has the responsibility to note any discrepancies between the waste types and volumes on the manifest and those being received.

Land Disposal Restrictions

Congress determined that, for a number of listed hazardous wastes, disposal in a hazardous waste landfill is not sufficiently protective of human health and the environment. It decided that some degree of treatment for these wastes is required prior to land disposal. The resulting land disposal restrictions are found at 42 U.S.C. §§ 6924(b)–6924(k) (1991).

Congress's concern was that these wastes would leak from the disposal site when subjected to typical disposal conditions. In general, the wastes subject to land disposal restrictions must be incinerated or stabilized in such a way as to prevent toxic contaminants from leaving the disposal site.

The EPA was directed to divide the universe of listed hazardous wastes into three groups and to examine the wastes in each group, in sequence, for their potential to impact the environment after disposal. This resulted in the so-called **first third, second third, and third third waste lists.** The EPA completed the reviews of each group and promulgated rules found at 40 C.F.R. part 268. These rules provide the proper treatment method for each listed hazardous waste. The rules also provide performance standards for the resulting treated waste.

In some cases, the treatment is sufficient to remove or encapsulate all hazardous components from the waste, and the resulting residue can be delisted by the EPA if the waste generated by the treatment process does not "meet any of the criteria under which the waste was listed." The **delisting procedure** is found at 40 C.F.R. § 260.22 (1994) and requires that a very extensive petition be filed with the EPA. Review of these petitions by the EPA often takes several years or more.

Underground Storage Tank Program

A stand-alone portion of RCRA is the **Underground Storage Tank (UST)** program. The rules for this program, found at 40 C.F.R. part 280, apply to all nonexempt USTs. Exemptions exist for tanks regulated by the RCRA hazardous waste program, for small tanks, for tanks containing *de minimis* concentrations of regulated substances and tanks used for wastewater treatment, among others. The rules provide minimum design and operational standards for all USTs. Existing USTs that cannot meet these standards must be closed by certain specified dates.

Under the rules, a UST is defined as a tank plus any underground piping connected to the tank that has at least ten percent of its combined volume underground. The federal UST regulations apply only to USTs storing either petroleum or certain hazardous substances.

According to EPA, when the UST program began (in about 1986), there were approximately 2.1 million regulated tanks in the United States. Since then, many of the USTs have been closed (removed from service) because of substandard construction systems. Until the mid-1980s, most USTs were made of untreated steel, which would be likely to corrode over time and allow the UST contents to leak into the environment. Faulty installation or inadequate operating and maintenance procedures also cause USTs to release their contents into the environment.

The potential hazard from a leaking UST is that the petroleum or other hazardous substance can seep into the soil and contaminate groundwater, a source of drinking water for nearly half of all Americans. A leaking UST can present other health and environmental risks, including the potential for fire and explosion.

Most of the approximately 2.1 million USTs contain petroleum, including marketers who sell gasoline to the public (such as service stations and convenience stores) and nonmarketers who use tanks solely for their own needs (such as fleet service operators and local governments). The EPA also estimated that about 25,000 tanks hold other hazardous substances covered by the UST regulations.

The owner or operator of the UST is required to report the suspected or actual release from a tank and to investigate. If it is determined that the tank has leaked, the owner or operator must initiate a specified sequence of events for full investigation and remediation of the release, a process that includes the filing of progress reports with the administering agency at specific intervals.

> The owner or operator of any tank that may have leaked or is possibly leaking is required to report the suspected leakage and investigate the possibility.

State Program Authority

Congress recognized that the EPA has neither the manpower nor the in-depth knowledge of the regulated community to administer RCRA regulations fully at the permit level. For that reason, individual states may develop and administer their own RCRA programs. Each state's RCRA program must be at least as stringent as the federal regulations. Most states that have taken RCRA authority have adopted the RCRA rules either verbatim or have incorporated them by reference. RCRA-authorized states have the authority to issue permits, administer the manifest programs, and enforce the rules with both civil and criminal actions. In those states, the EPA retains and exercises authority to review and approve/disapprove RCRA permits issued by the state. It also retains and often exercises the authority to enforce the RCRA rules, either in tandem with the state or independently. See the discussion regarding the *Harmon* decision. If it decides that the state is improperly administering the program, the EPA may rescind that state's authority.

Enforcement

Congress provided the EPA with very strong enforcement capabilities. These provisions are found at 42 U.S.C. § 6928 (1991), and they include both civil and criminal penalties. The EPA has the authority to issue compliance orders and to demand civil penalties as part of those orders. It may also initiate civil actions in the U.S. district courts for RCRA violations. Civil penalties may be up to $25,000 per day for each violation.

Figure 3-4A and Figure 3-4B show the EPA's use of RCRA's enforcement authority through a consent decree to clean up a hazardous waste site.

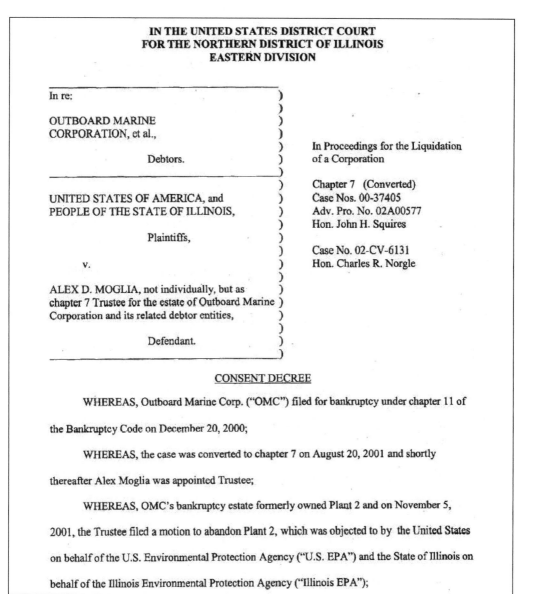

IN THE UNITED STATES DISTRICT COURT
FOR THE NORTHERN DISTRICT OF ILLINOIS
EASTERN DIVISION

In re:

OUTBOARD MARINE
CORPORATION, et al.,

        Debtors.

UNITED STATES OF AMERICA, and
PEOPLE OF THE STATE OF ILLINOIS,

        Plaintiffs,

    v.

ALEX D. MOGLIA, not individually, but as
chapter 7 Trustee for the estate of Outboard Marine
Corporation and its related debtor entities,

        Defendant.

In Proceedings for the Liquidation
of a Corporation

Chapter 7 (Converted)
Case Nos. 00-37405
Adv. Pro. No. 02A00577
Hon. John H. Squires

Case No. 02-CV-6131
Hon. Charles R. Norgle

<u>CONSENT DECREE</u>

WHEREAS, Outboard Marine Corp. ("OMC") filed for bankruptcy under chapter 11 of

the Bankruptcy Code on December 20, 2000;

WHEREAS, the case was converted to chapter 7 on August 20, 2001 and shortly

thereafter Alex Moglia was appointed Trustee;

WHEREAS, OMC's bankruptcy estate formerly owned Plant 2 and on November 5,

2001, the Trustee filed a motion to abandon Plant 2, which was objected to by the United States

on behalf of the U.S. Environmental Protection Agency ("U.S. EPA") and the State of Illinois on

behalf of the Illinois Environmental Protection Agency ("Illinois EPA");

Figure 3-4A RCRA Consent Decree *In Re Outboard Marine Corporation.*

Figure 3-4B shows page 2 of the Outboard Marine Corporation consent decree, the authorizing, statutory language.

If the EPA believes that the RCRA violation was the result of a person's **knowing** act, it may recommend criminal charges against the person. Criminal actions are brought by the Department of Justice. "Knowing" treatment, storage, or disposal of a waste without a

WHEREAS, on May 3, 2002, the United States on behalf of U.S. EPA and State of Illinois on behalf of Illinois EPA filed an Adversary Proceeding, <u>United States and State of Illinois v. Alex D. Moglia, not individually, but as Chapter 7 Trustee for the Estate of Outboard Marine Corporation</u>, Adv. Pro. No. 02A00577 (the "Adversary Proceeding"), which seeks injunctive relief against the Trustee to enforce, <u>inter</u> <u>alia</u>, compliance with Section 7003 of the Solid Waste Disposal Act, commonly known as the Resource Conservation and Recovery Act ("RCRA"), 42 U.S.C. § 6973. Specifically, the Complaint seeks to require OMC's bankruptcy estate to take cleanup action pursuant to RCRA with respect to a chlorinated solvent groundwater plume (the "Groundwater Plume") emanating from property commonly known as Plant 2 located at or near 80-100 Seahorse Drive in Waukegan, Illinois. The Complaint also seeks compliance with the District Court's Order and Consent Decree pursuant to the Comprehensive Environmental Response, Compensation and Liability Act of 1970, 42 U.S.C. §§ 9601 <u>et seq.</u> ("CERCLA") in <u>United States and State of Illinois v. Outboard Marine Corp.</u>, Civil Action No. 88-C-8571 (N.D. Ill) requiring, <u>inter</u> <u>alia</u>, performance of operation and maintenance of polychlorinated biphenyl ("PCB") containment cells situated near Waukegan Harbor and Lake Michigan and public beaches. The Complaint also alleges various violations of the Illinois Environmental Protection Act, 415 ILCS 5/1 <u>et</u> <u>seq.</u> (the "Illinois Act");

WHEREAS, on January 2, 2003, the District Court withdrew reference of the Adversary Proceeding from the Bankruptcy Court;

WHEREAS, in July 2002, the parties hereto entered into a Settlement Agreement ("First Settlement Agreement"), which permitted the Trustee to abandon Plant 2 upon the completion of specified work and making of a required payment but reserved the parties rights and defenses with respect to the Adversary Proceeding;

Figure 3-4B   Page 2 of the RCRA Consent Decree *In Re Outboard Marine Corporation.*

permit or "knowing" shipment of the waste without a manifest can result in fines of up to $50,000 per day and/or imprisonment for up to two years (a felony). Actions that result in a "knowing endangerment" of another person can result in a fine of up to $250,000 and/or imprisonment for up to fifteen years.

If the "knowing endangerment" activity was committed by an organization, it can be fined up to $1,000,000.

> "Knowing" treatment, storage, or disposal of a waste without a permit or "knowing" shipment of the waste without a manifest can result in fines of up to $50,000 per day and/or imprisonment for up to two years.

It is interesting to note that "knowing," when used in this context, does not mean that the person charged actually knew that he or she was violating the law, but rather that the person *should* have known that the activity was regulated. A typical example is found in *United States v. Johnson & Towers, Inc.*, 741 F.2d 662 (3d Cir. 1984), wherein the defendants were convicted of the disposal of hazardous wastes without a permit. The defendants claimed that they were unaware of the permit requirement and, therefore, had not "knowingly" violated the law. The court below agreed with this argument and dismissed that count of the complaint. The Third Circuit, however, reversed and remanded the case to the district court. It interpreted "knowing" to include situations in which the defendant is *inferred* to have knowledge that such defendant is regulated. The Court favorably cited *United States v. International Minerals and Chemical Corp.*, 402 U.S. 558 (1971), stating that, for dangerous waste materials, the "probability of regulation is so great that anyone who is aware that he is in possession of them [waste materials] or dealing with them must be presumed to be aware of the regulation." *Id.* 565.

CASES FOR DISCUSSION

United States v. Hansen, 262 F.3d 1217, 53 ERC 1203, (CA GA 2001), *cert. denied*, 535 U.S. 1111, 122 S. Ct. 2326 (2001).

In this case, two of the defendants challenged their convictions, and particularly the jury's determination that they had violated RCRA's knowing endangerment provision. Generally, a jury may convict a defendant of knowing endangerment only if the government proves that the defendant knowingly caused the illegal treatment, storage, or disposal of hazardous waste and knew that such conduct placed others in imminent danger of death or serious injury.

In this case, though, neither defendant was even physically present at the plant site when the endangerment allegedly occurred. Instead, both defendants worked at the corporate headquarters in another state.

(continued)

CASES FOR DISCUSSION

From there, they oversaw operations of six plants located across the eastern United States, including the Brunswick plant at issue. Defense counsel argued that the district court had erroneously permitted the jury to convict the defendants of knowing endangerment based solely upon their corporate positions within the company and without any regard to whether they had actual knowledge of any alleged endangerment.

The Eleventh Circuit disagreed and affirmed the defendants' convictions. The Court decided that the government may establish that a defendant acted knowingly merely by showing that the defendant had knowledge of the general hazardous character of the chemical and knew that the chemical had the potential to be harmful to others. The Eleventh Circuit concluded that the testimony of several former employees sufficiently demonstrated that the defendants knew that the Brunswick plant did not comply with various environmental standards and also knew that this failure to comply posed a danger to the plant's employees. Former employees testified that they had discussed the plant's deteriorating condition and the environmental compliance problems with the defendants. Employees further testified that the defendants had received reports detailing that hazardous wastes were improperly present at the plant and the danger associated with their presence.

The Supreme Court denied certiorari.

Citizen's Suits

In addition to the EPA and the Justice Department, citizens can act as "private attorneys general" to seek to enforce RCRA or to force the EPA to comply with its statutory duties. The citizens' suit provisions of RCRA are found at 42 U.S.C. § 6972 (1991).

This authority has two restrictions. First, a citizen may not file a suit if the EPA (or its designated agent) has already initiated an enforcement action. This generally requires that suit be filed in a court, as opposed to the mere issuance of a Notice of Violation.

Second, the citizen must identify the cause of action and provide the EPA at least sixty days' notice prior to filing the suit. The notice, in the form of a letter, is meant by Congress to spur the EPA into action to initiate its own suit. If the EPA does not file its own suit, it may intervene in the citizen's suit. Likewise, if the EPA does initiate its own action as a result of the notice letter, the citizen has a statutory right to intervene.

Citizens can act as private attorneys general to seek enforcement of RCRA or to force the EPA to comply with its statutory duties.

Use of the RCRA citizen's suit provisions in actions to force cleanup of properties has recently become popular. Actions against present and past owners, operators, and generators for hazardous waste activities are allowed if the defendant's activity contributed to a potential or actual "imminent and substantial endangerment to health or the environment." 42 U.S.C. § 6972(a)(1)(B). What makes this provision popular is the ability to recover attorneys' fees if the action is successful.[5] 42 U.S.C. § 6972(e). The provision also allows a current property owner to force a previous owner to clean up a mess without the current owner becoming directly involved in the removal action or remediation.

The disadvantage to such an action is the threshold required to prove that the endangerment may be "imminent and substantial." The mere presence of contamination in soil or groundwater is insufficient. If the "risk of harm is remote in time, completely speculative in nature, or *de minimis* in degree," relief will not be granted. *United States v. Reilly Tar & Chemical*, 546 F. Supp. 1100, 1109 (D. Minn. 1982). RCRA does not allow a citizen's suit to recover the prior costs of cleaning up toxic waste where the site does not continue to pose a danger to health or the environment at the time of suit. *Meghrig et al. v. KFC Western, Inc.*, 516 U.S. 479 (1996).

One final note regarding enforcement involves the conflict between federal EPA and state environmental agencies. RCRA gives approved states the authority to conduct enforcement activity. 42 U.S.C. § 6926(b). The EPA, on the other hand, believes that it has the authority to overfile when it does not like a state's resolution of an RCRA enforcement action. This issue became a major bone of contention as the result of *Harmon Industries, Inc. v. Browner*, 191 F.3d 894 (8th Cir. 1999). In that case, Harmon Industries (Harmon) reached settlement with the Missouri Department of Natural Resources (MDNR) regarding illegal disposal of solvents. The state court consent order required Harmon to clean up contaminated soil but did not impose any monetary penalties. The EPA decided substantial penalties should be imposed and filed its own administrative enforcement action that resulted in a $586,716 penalty.

---

[5] Under the Comprehensive Environmental Response, Compensation, and Liability Act (42 U.S.C. §§ 6901 to 6975) cost recovery actions, recovery of attorney's fees is generally not available.

Harmon appealed the federal decision and the Eighth Circuit Court of Appeals issued a decision in 1999 that found for Harmon. It reasoned that the plain language of section 6926(b) revealed a "congressional intent for an authorized state to supplant the federal hazardous waste program in all respects including enforcement."

The EPA holds that the *Harmon* decision applies only within the boundaries of the Eighth Circuit and only if an authorized state has initiated an enforcement action. For the EPA's interpretation of the decision, see http://www.epa.gov/region5/orc/articles/rcra_overfile.htm. At some point, the U.S. Supreme Court will decide the issue, but for now the decision should not be relied on as a bar to federal enforcement during a state proceeding.

Conclusion

The Resource Conservation and Recovery Act was enacted with the purpose to provide "cradle-to-grave" management of solid waste, including hazardous wastes. Congress's stated goal in enacting RCRA is that "wherever feasible, the generation of hazardous waste is to be reduced or eliminated as expeditiously as possible. Waste that is nevertheless generated should be treated, stored, or disposed of so as to minimize the present and future threat to human health and the environment."

Paralegals will typically be involved in the complicated waste facility siting process. Siting is usually a complex and time-consuming operation. Much research will have to be done on waste generation and transportation throughout the region of the proposed site. The siting application will be a complex document that will require a lot of organizational skill. Reports and exhibits to support the siting application may also need to be prepared and may need review and comment.

Paralegals may also be involved in the complicated permitting and permit reporting processes and in subsequent compliance evaluations.

Paralegals will also be actively involved in the RCRA enforcement process, in both administrative and judicial proceedings, as discussed in more detail in the Introduction and in Chapter Nine of this book.

GLOSSARY OF RCRA TERMS

characteristic waste. A waste that exhibits one of the four hazardous characteristics:

1. ignitability
2. corrosivity
3. reactivity
4. toxicity

Characteristic wastes are identified by a three-digit number preceded by a "D" and are generally called "D wastes." A waste may have more than one characteristic, and all documentation referring to the waste should include all applicable identifiers.

closure. The act of closing a facility in accordance with an approved facility closure plan and all applicable closure requirements.

D wastes. Characteristic wastes are identified by a three-digit number preceded by a "D" and are generally called "D wastes." Wastes with an ignitability characteristic are identified as D001 wastes. Corrosive wastes are identified as D002 wastes. Reactive wastes are identified as D003 wastes. Toxicity characteristic wastes are identified as D004 through D043 wastes, depending on the compound detected.

delisted waste. In some cases, the treatment of hazardous waste is sufficient to remove or encapsulate all hazardous components from the waste. If so, in some cases the resulting residue can be "delisted" by EPA if the waste generated by the treatment process does not "meet any of the criteria under which the waste was listed."

"derived from" rule. The "derived from" rule provides that residues from the treatment of listed hazardous wastes generally remain listed hazardous wastes regardless of whether the resulting residue is truly hazardous. However, if a waste was "listed" solely due to ignitability, corrosivity, or reactivity characteristics and that characteristic is removed through treatment, the treatment residue is no longer a listed hazardous waste. Characteristic waste treatment residues are hazardous *only* if the residue exhibits a hazardous waste characteristic.

discarded material. A solid waste is any "discarded material" that is not subject to one or more of a variety of exclusions. For purposes of the rules, discarded material is any material that is abandoned, recycled, or inherently wastelike.

discharge or hazardous waste discharge. The accidental or intentional spilling, leaking, pumping, pouring, emitting, emptying, or dumping of hazardous waste into or on any land or water.

disposal. The discharge, deposit, injection, dumping, spilling, leaking, or placing of any solid waste or hazardous waste into or on any land or water so that such solid waste or hazardous waste or any constituent thereof may enter the environment or be emitted into the air or discharged into any waters, including groundwaters.

F wastes. The F wastes are general classes of compounds listed as hazardous by the EPA. An example is waste F001, which is defined as "halogenated solvents used in degreasing."

facility. All contiguous land, structures, other appurtenances, and improvements on the land, used for treating, storing, or disposing of hazardous waste. A facility may consist of several treatment, storage, or disposal operational units (e.g., one or more landfills, surface impoundments, or combination of them).

generator. Any person, by facility, whose act or process produces hazardous waste or whose act first causes a hazardous waste to become subject to regulation. An exemption was developed that allows these generators to store hazardous waste on site for up to ninety days without a permit. Generators are required to apply for and obtain an EPA generator identification number. They must also comply with the RCRA regulations for personnel training requirements, tank storage standards, contingency planning, and facility preparedness. Generators must also prepare manifests for all hazardous waste shipments and keep records of these manifests for three years following shipment.

hazardous waste. RCRA defines "hazardous waste" as a solid waste, or combination of solid wastes, that because of its quantity, concentration, or physical, chemical, or infectious characteristics may

1. cause, or significantly contribute to an increase in mortality or an increase in serious irreversible, or incapacitating reversible, illness; or
2. pose a substantial threat or potential hazard to human health or the environment when improperly treated, stored, transported, or disposed of, or otherwise managed.

Note that, to be a hazardous waste, the material must first be a solid waste. If it meets that test, then one must look at its impact on human health or the environment.

household waste. Any solid waste, including garbage, trash, and sanitary waste in septic tanks, derived from households, including single and multiple residences, hotels and motels, bunkhouses, ranger stations, crew quarters, campgrounds, picnic grounds, and day-use recreational areas.

HSWA. Hazardous and Solid Waste Disposal Act Amendments of 1984. See RCRA.

interim status. When RCRA first became effective, there were many facilities that were already in the hazardous waste treatment, storage, and disposal business. Those that wished to continue in the business after the effective date were required to file a Part A of the RCRA TSD permit application. These facilities are known as "interim status" facilities until such time as they receive a full RCRA TSD permit.

K wastes. Wastes listed as hazardous by the EPA that are industry- or process-specific. An example is K005, which is "wastewater treatment sludge from the production of chrome green pigments."

LDRs. Land Disposal Restrictions. Congress determined that, for a number of listed hazardous wastes, disposal in a hazardous waste landfill is not sufficiently protective of human health and the environment. It decided that some degree of treatment for these wastes is required prior to land disposal.

leachate. Any liquid, including any suspended components in the liquid, that has percolated through or drained from hazardous waste.

liner. A continuous layer of natural or man-made materials, beneath or on the sides of a surface impoundment, landfill, or landfill cell, that restricts the downward or lateral escape of hazardous waste, hazardous waste constituents, or leachate.

listed hazardous waste. The EPA was given the authority to list wastes as hazardous wastes based on the waste's toxicity, persistence, and degradability in nature, potential for accumulation in tissue, and other related factors such as flammability, corrosiveness, and other hazard characteristics. The EPA examined a number of typical industrial waste streams and determined that a number of them nearly always have either one of the four characteristics identified above or contain compounds that have been determined to meet one of the other statutory criteria. These compounds or compound classes are listed as hazardous by the EPA. The tables of wastes are divided into four groups. The F wastes are general classes of compounds. K wastes are those that are industry- or process-specific. Finally, there are the P and U wastes.

manifest. The EPA has developed a system for keeping track of hazardous waste shipments. Each shipment is to be accompanied by a six-part hazardous waste manifest prepared by the generator. The manifest includes information on the identity of the generator, the nature and quantity of the waste being shipped, and the transporter's identity.

mixture rule. The so-called "mixture" rule holds that any nonhazardous waste that a hazardous waste is mixed with also becomes a part of that hazardous waste.

MSWL. Municipal Solid Waste Landfill. The MSWL rules apply only to landfills that accept household waste and provide minimum design and performance criteria for covered landfills. These include such things as siting criteria, liner standards, leachate collection standards, groundwater monitoring standards, and closure requirements. The rules also provide standards for corrective action if the landfill begins to affect the surrounding environment.

NIMBY. Not-in-My-Back-Yard syndrome. Many states have special siting criteria for new or modified waste facilities that are the direct result of the NIMBY syndrome. Community activists have been unsatisfied with the response they have received from state regulatory agencies and, as a result, have persuaded state legislators in those states to provide them with a statutory right to review siting decisions on a local basis.

operator. The person responsible for the overall operation of the facility.

owner. The person who owns the facility or part of the facility.

P wastes. Wastes listed as hazardous by EPA that are compound-specific and include spill residues and contaminated soil. P106 is, for example, material contaminated with sodium cyanide.

Part A and Part B permit application. When RCRA became effective, TSD facilities that wished to continue in the business were required to file a Part A of the RCRA TSD permit application. Those facilities are known as "interim status facilities" until such time as they receive a full RCRA TSD permit. To receive the full permit, the interim status facility must also file Part B of the application. Deadlines for the filing of the Part B applications for certain interim status facilities are found in the RCRA regulations. Also, the EPA (or the state administrator) may, at its discretion, call for the Part B application. If the interim status facility fails to file its Part B by the required date, it loses its interim status and thereafter is operating without a permit. Once the interim facility has filed the Part B, it may continue to operate as an interim facility until the full permit is granted or denied by the appropriate federal or state authority. New facilities must file both Part A and Part B and have the permit issued *prior* to initiating TSD activity.

person. An individual, trust, firm, joint stock company, federal agency, corporation (including a government corporation), partnership, association, state, municipality, commission, political subdivision of a state, or any interstate body.

RCRA. Resource Conservation and Recovery Act of 1976 at 42 U.S.C. §§ 6901–6992k. Popular name for the Solid Waste Disposal Act (SWDA), most recently amended by the Hazardous and Solid Waste Disposal Act Amendments of 1984 (HSWA).

RCRA hazardous waste. Applies to certain types of hazardous wastes that appear on the EPA's regulatory list or that exhibit characteristics of ignitability, corrosiveness, reactivity, or toxicity.

siting criteria. Generally, the standards used by regulators, the regulated community, and the public in determining whether a new waste management facility may be located within a community.

solid waste. For purposes of RCRA, a solid waste is any garbage, refuse, sludge from a waste treatment plant, water supply treatment plant, or air pollution control facility and other discarded material, including solid, liquid, semisolid, or contained gaseous material resulting from industrial, commercial, mining, and agricultural operations, and from community activities, but does not include solid or dissolved material in domestic sewage, or solid or dissolved material in irrigation return flows, or industrial discharges that are point sources subject to permits under § 1342 of Title 33, or source, special nuclear, or byproduct material as defined by the Atomic Energy Act of 1954, as amended (68 Stat. 923).

SQG. Small-Quantity Generator. Those that generate more than 100 kilograms but less than 1000 kilograms of hazardous waste within a calendar month may store waste on site for up to ninety days without a permit or for up to 180 days, provided certain additional requirements are met. Small-quantity generators who must transport their wastes more than 200 miles are allowed to store for up to 270 days without a permit.

SWDA. Solid Waste Disposal Act. Predecessor of RCRA.

tank. A stationary device, designed to contain an accumulation of hazardous waste, constructed primarily of non-earthen materials (e.g., wood, concrete, steel, plastic) that provide structural support.

TCLP. Toxicity Characteristic Leaching Procedure. The toxicity of a material is determined by using the toxicity characteristic leaching procedure. The TCLP is a laboratory method whereby a sample of the material is mixed with acetic acid solution for a specified period of time. The acetic acid solution is then analyzed for a number of heavy metals and organic compounds. A waste is hazardous if those compounds are detected in the solution in quantities greater than the limits provided in RCRA rules.

transporter. A person engaged in the off-site transportation of hazardous waste by air, rail, highway, or water.

treatment. Any method, technique, or process, including neutralization, designed to change the physical, chemical, or biological character or composition of any hazardous waste so as to neutralize such waste, or so as to recover energy or material resources from the waste, or so as to render such waste nonhazardous, or less hazardous; safer to transport, store or dispose of; or amenable for recovery, amenable for storage, or reduced in volume.

TSD facility. Treatment, Storage, or Disposal facility. RCRA rules provide very specific and highly technical standards for the design, construction, operation, and closure of TSD facilities. The rules are provided for interim status facilities and for RCRA-permitted facilities. There are separate sections in both parts for certain types of treatment operations, for storage operations, and for certain types of disposal operations. There are also general requirements for all TSD facilities such as "Preparedness and Prevention," "Contingency Planning and Emergency Procedures," and manifesting requirements.

U wastes. Wastes listed as hazardous by the EPA that are compound-specific and include off-spec materials and waste commercial products. An example is U019, which is benzene.

UST. Underground Storage Tank. A stand-alone portion of RCRA is the Underground Storage Tank program. The rules for this program apply to all nonexempt USTs.

BIBLIOGRAPHY

A Better Way: Guide to the RCRA Permitting Process (U.S. EPA 1986).

Final RCRA Comprehensive Ground-Water Monitoring Evaluation (GME) Guidance, OSWER Directive No. 9950.2 (U.S. EPA 1986).

Final Revised Guidance Memorandum on the Use and Issuance of Administrative Orders Under Section 7003 of RCRA (U.S. EPA 1984).

Fortuna, Richard C., & David J. Lennett, *Hazardous Waste Regulation: The New Era—An Analysis and Guide to RCRA and the 1984 Amendments* (McGraw-Hill 1987).

RCRA Civil Penalty Policy (U.S. EPA 1990).

RCRA Ground-Water Monitoring Technical Enforcement Guidance (TEG) Document OSWER Directive No. 9950.1. (U.S. EPA 1986).

The RCRA Practice Manual (Theodore L. Garrett ed., 2d ed. A.B.A., Section of Environment, Energy, and Resources 2004).

Teets, John W., & Dennis Reis, with Danny G. Worrell, *RCRA: Resource Conservation and Recovery Act* (A.B.A., Section of Environment, Energy, and Resources 2003).

Wagner, Travis. *The Computer Handbook of Hazardous Waste Regulation: A Comprehensive, Step-by-Step Guide to the Regulation of Hazardous Wastes Under RCRA, TSCA, and Superfund* (Perry-Wagner 1988).

DISCUSSION QUESTIONS

1. What is the difference between a solid waste and a hazardous waste?
2. What distinguishes a "characteristic" hazardous waste from a "listed" hazardous waste? Why is the difference important?
3. Why should a hazardous waste generator be required to manifest its wastes?

4. Why does the EPA believe that the "derived from" and "mixture" rules are critical to the regulation of hazardous waste? Is there some better way to bring the waste streams covered by those rules into RCRA?
5. What is all the fuss about underground storage tanks?

COMPUTER LABORATORY PROJECTS

1. Locate the EPA's OSWER section on the Internet. Compile a list of policy and guidance documents that relate to the closing of a solid waste municipal landfill. Report on the substance of the documents found.
2. Run a search on the EPA's RCRA facility information database at http://www.epa.gov/enviro for a list of local RCRA facilities.

INTERNET SITES

- The full text of the Resource Conservation and Recovery Act (RCRA) is on the Internet at http://www.law.cornell.edu/uscode/html/uscode42/usc_sup_01_42_10_82.html.

- The EPA's RCRA Web site is on the Internet at http://www.epa.gov/epaoswer/osw.

CHAPTER 4

The Toxic Substances Control Act

James F. Berry[1]

OBJECTIVES

The objectives of this chapter are for students to:

- Learn the terminology associated with the TSCA.
- Learn the concepts and ideas that underlie the TSCA law and regulatory program.
- Learn about specific sections and provisions of the TSCA law and regulations.
- Learn about the processes and procedures used by the government and other parties to comply with and to enforce the law under TSCA.
- Learn about the particular jobs and functions that are performed by paralegals working for attorneys in TSCA cases.

History of the Act

This chapter covers the Toxic Substances Control Act, 15 U.S.C. §§ 2601 to 2671 (1991) (**"TSCA"** or the "Act"). The chapter covers four main areas under TSCA:

- Authorization to market chemical substances
- Regulation of unreasonable risk under § 6 of TSCA, including polychlorinated biphenyls and asbestos
- Reporting and record-keeping requirements
- Enforcement and penalties under TSCA

---

[1] The author acknowledges and thanks Jeffrey C. Fort and Kirk M. Minckler for their work on earlier drafts of this chapter.

The primary purpose of TSCA is to regulate chemical substances and mixtures. It does so by regulating both the distribution of existing chemicals and the manufacture of new chemicals based on their risks to health and the environment. The scope of the term "new chemical substances and mixtures" is defined in the statute and in the EPA's regulations. Regulations under the Act are found at 40 C.F.R. §§ 700 to 799 (1997).

Certain substances are exempt from TSCA. For example, the statute does not regulate pesticides, tobacco, drugs, food products, cosmetics, and certain nuclear materials. These materials are regulated by other federal statutes.

The TSCA regulatory scheme is different from other environmental laws. Federal statutes such as the Clean Air Act, the Clean Water Act, and the Resource Conservation and Recovery Act (RCRA) are designed to control discharges of hazardous materials into the environment. The Comprehensive Environmental Response, Compensation, and Liability Act (CERCLA) attempts to clean up historical hazardous waste disposal sites.

TSCA takes a different approach than "end-of-pipe" or remedial statutes. It seeks to control hazardous inputs into commerce and industry rather than regulating by-products from manufacturing processes. In this regard, TSCA's goal is to screen out dangerous chemicals from the marketplace, thereby controlling human and environmental exposure to those substances.

> The TSCA seeks to control hazardous inputs into commerce and industry rather than by-products from manufacturing processes.

TSCA accomplishes this goal by screening the initial manufacture of chemicals to be used in commerce. TSCA is designed to protect the public from "unreasonable risk" by identifying potentially harmful substances *before* they are manufactured and placed on the market. The statute is carried out, however, under the condition that control of chemical substances and mixtures should not impede or create unnecessary economic barriers to technological innovation.

Authorization to Market Chemical Substances

The TSCA Inventory

TSCA was enacted in 1976, and the EPA was directed to compile an inventory of chemicals that were in commerce at the time. The inventory was intended as the starting point for the critical regulatory portion of the law. Under the TSCA § 5 program, any person who manufactures, processes, or imports a new chemical substance or mixture for commercial purposes must submit a notice of intent (known as a **Premanufacture Notice** or **PMN**) to the EPA at least ninety days before he or she begins manufacturing or processing. The person must submit test data for the substance, which must be performed under carefully controlled circumstances spelled out in the TSCA § 4 and the regulations. The EPA subsequently determines if the new chemical or mixture presents an unreasonable risk to health and environment or if testing on the new chemical must be performed.

The EPA's initial inventory was compiled from information submitted by chemical manufacturers. This input allowed the Agency to construct a list of "each chemical substance which is manufactured or processed in the United States"—more than 60,000 chemicals and chemical groups. The original inventory is periodically updated to add new chemicals for which PMNs are filed. There are currently over 75,000 chemicals in the database.

While the EPA's primary focus has been on new chemicals and new uses, TSCA authorizes the Agency to require testing of the inventoried chemicals. This authority allows the EPA to direct a manufacturer to perform tests on chemicals. Depending on the results of the tests, the EPA may then place controls on a chemical. For example, the EPA has instituted controls on a variety of substances in the original inventory, such as chlorofluorocarbons, polychlorinated biphenyls, and asbestos building materials.

Premanufacture Notices

Theoretically, the EPA's TSCA Inventory lists all of the chemical substances manufactured or in use in the United States. If a company plans to import, manufacture, or process a new chemical substance, it must give the EPA at least ninety days' notice. Before a company can give notice, it must decide whether its proposed substance is, in fact, "new."

> Theoretically, the TSCA Inventory lists all of the chemical substances manufactured or in use in the United States.

This decision is essentially made by comparing the proposed substance with the TSCA Inventory. The EPA defines two classes of substances for the purposes of determining whether a chemical is new.

Class 1 consists of chemicals whose composition can be represented by a unique chemical structural diagram. EPA's Office of

Pollution Prevention and Toxics (OPPT) has grouped PMN chemicals with shared chemical and toxicological properties into categories, enabling both PMN submitters and EPA reviewers to benefit from the accumulated data and past decisional precedents. There are currently forty-five categories. The EPA takes action to control potential risks to health or the environment on approximately 10% of the PMNs submitted. Only 2%–3% of these undergo a more stringent standard review, while the remaining 7%–8% are identified as members of the New Chemicals Program chemical categories.

Class 2 consists of chemicals whose composition cannot be identified by a unique molecular formula or chemical structure diagram. This is known as a "standard review."

For Class 1 chemicals, the determination as to whether a proposed substance is, in fact, new comes from comparing that substance with molecular formulas and chemical structures in the TSCA Inventory.

The Class 2 comparison is more complex. In the TSCA Inventory, these substances are identified by molecular formula and chemical structure and by reactants and reaction processes in which the substances are synthesized.

For Class 2 materials, a "new" substance determination is made by comparing molecular formula and chemical structure information with the similar TSCA Inventory information and by comparing reactant and reaction information with similar information maintained on file by the EPA.

Further details on the PMN process, as well as online forms, can be found at EPA's Office of Pollution Prevention and Toxics (OPPT) Web site at http://www.epa.gov/opptintr/newchems/invntory.htm.

Once a substance is determined to be new, a company planning to import, manufacture, or process the chemical must submit a PMN to the EPA. Premanufacture notice is given to the EPA on a standard form found at 40 C.F.R. § 720, Appendix A (1997). Figure 4-1 presents the PMN form along with annotations provided by the EPA for completing the form. The complete annotated form is available on the Internet at http://www.epa.gov/opptintr/newchems/pmnforms.pdf.

The PMN form, and the PMN process in general, requires the submitter to provide a variety of information on the new chemical. That information is detailed in 40 C.F.R. §§ 720.45 and 720.50 (1997) and, in general, includes the following.

1. A description of the substance:
   - Detailed description of chemical structure, molecular formula, the process by which it is formed, and information on immediate precursors and reactants
   - Impurities anticipated to be present
   - Synonyms and trade names

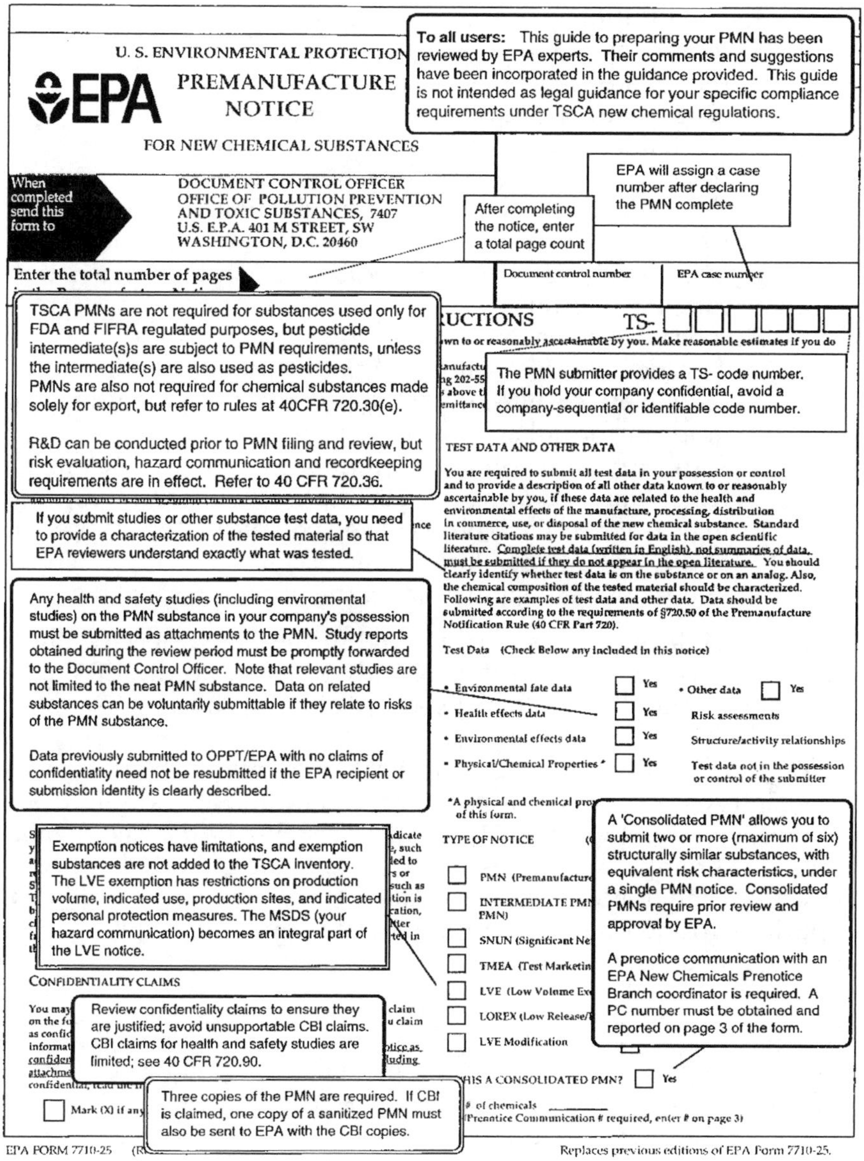

U. S. ENVIRONMENTAL PROTECTION

EPA PREMANUFACTURE NOTICE

FOR NEW CHEMICAL SUBSTANCES

To all users: This guide to preparing your PMN has been reviewed by EPA experts. Their comments and suggestions have been incorporated in the guidance provided. This guide is not intended as legal guidance for your specific compliance requirements under TSCA new chemical regulations.

When completed send this form to

DOCUMENT CONTROL OFFICER
OFFICE OF POLLUTION PREVENTION AND TOXIC SUBSTANCES, 7407
U.S. E.P.A. 401 M STREET, SW
WASHINGTON, D.C. 20460

After completing the notice, enter a total page count

EPA will assign a case number after declaring the PMN complete

Enter the total number of pages

Document control number | EPA case number

TS-

TSCA PMNs are not required for substances used only for FDA and FIFRA regulated purposes, but pesticide intermediate(s)s are subject to PMN requirements, unless the intermediate(s) are also used as pesticides.
PMNs are also not required for chemical substances made solely for export, but refer to rules at 40CFR 720.30(e).

R&D can be conducted prior to PMN filing and review, but risk evaluation, hazard communication and recordkeeping requirements are in effect. Refer to 40 CFR 720.36.

The PMN submitter provides a TS- code number. If you hold your company confidential, avoid a company-sequential or identifiable code number.

If you submit studies or other substance test data, you need to provide a characterization of the tested material so that EPA reviewers understand exactly what was tested.

TEST DATA AND OTHER DATA

You are required to submit all test data in your possession or control and to provide a description of all other data known to or reasonably ascertainable by you, if these data are related to the health and environmental effects of the manufacture, processing, distribution in commerce, use, or disposal of the new chemical substance. Standard literature citations may be submitted for data in the open scientific literature. Complete test data (written in English), not summaries of data, must be submitted if they do not appear in the open literature. You should clearly identify whether test data is on the substance or on an analog. Also, the chemical composition of the tested material should be characterized. Following are examples of test data and other data. Data should be submitted according to the requirements of §720.50 of the Premanufacture Notification Rule (40 CFR Part 720).

Any health and safety studies (including environmental studies) on the PMN substance in your company's possession must be submitted as attachments to the PMN. Study reports obtained during the review period must be promptly forwarded to the Document Control Officer. Note that relevant studies are not limited to the neat PMN substance. Data on related substances can be voluntarily submittable if they relate to risks of the PMN substance.

Data previously submitted to OPPT/EPA with no claims of confidentiality need not be resubmitted if the EPA recipient or submission identity is clearly described.

Test Data (Check Below any included in this notice)

- Environmental fate data ☐ Yes
- Health effects data ☐ Yes
- Environmental effects data ☐ Yes
- Physical/Chemical Properties * ☐ Yes
- Other data ☐ Yes
  Risk assessments
  Structure/activity relationships
  Test data not in the possession or control of the submitter

*A physical and chemical pro... of this form.

Exemption notices have limitations, and exemption substances are not added to the TSCA Inventory. The LVE exemption has restrictions on production volume, indicated use, production sites, and indicated personal protection measures. The MSDS (your hazard communication) becomes an integral part of the LVE notice.

TYPE OF NOTICE

☐ PMN (Premanufacture...
☐ INTERMEDIATE PMN...
☐ SNUN (Significant Ne...
☐ TMEA (Test Marketin...
☐ LVE (Low Volume Ex...
☐ LOREX (Low Release/...
☐ LVE Modification

A 'Consolidated PMN' allows you to submit two or more (maximum of six) structurally similar substances, with equivalent risk characteristics, under a single PMN notice. Consolidated PMNs require prior review and approval by EPA.

A prenotice communication with an EPA New Chemicals Prenotice Branch coordinator is required. A PC number must be obtained and reported on page 3 of the form.

CONFIDENTIALITY CLAIMS

Review confidentiality claims to ensure they are justified; avoid unsupportable CBI claims. CBI claims for health and safety studies are limited; see 40 CFR 720.90.

Three copies of the PMN are required. If CBI is claimed, one copy of a sanitized PMN must also be sent to EPA with the CBI copies.

IS A CONSOLIDATED PMN? ☐ Yes

# of chemicals

Prenotice Communication # required, enter # on page 3)

☐ Mark (X) if any

EPA FORM 7710-25

Replaces previous editions of EPA Form 7710-25.

Figure 4-1 The Annotated PMN Form Provided by the EPA.

- By-products resulting from manufacture, processing, use and disposal

2. The submitter's plans for production:
   - Estimated maximum amounts to be manufactured or imported during the first year of production and during any twelve-month period during the first three years of production

- The location of manufacturing sites
- A drawing of the production process
- Anticipated worker exposure
- Anticipated releases to the environment
3. The intended use:
   - Intended categories of use by function and application
   - The estimated percentage of production volume devoted to each category of use
   - The percentage of the new substance in the formulation for each consumer use
4. The health and environmental effects:
   - Test data in the submitter's possession on the health or environmental effects of the substance in its pure, technical grade or formulated form
   - A full report or standard literature citation of health effects data (including human exposure information), ecological effects data, physical and chemical properties data, and environmental fate characteristics
   - Other data known to exist on the proposed substance

Certain information is not required in the PMN. Specifically, a submitter need not provide data already provided to the EPA, efficacy data, or data that relate to exposure of humans or environment outside the United States.

TSCA regulations exempt from PMN requirements "substances manufactured or imported only in small quantities solely for research and development." 40 C.F.R. § 720.36 (1997). The regulations also exempt substances manufactured or imported for test-marketing and for export. Also exempt are certain by-products, impurities formed ancillary to a chemical reaction or production process, and certain polymers.

> A paralegal might typically be involved in gathering and processing information to be submitted with a premanufacture notice.

EPA Review of Premanufacture Notices

Once the EPA receives a PMN, the Agency publishes a notice in the *Federal Register*. When the PMN is complete (meaning the Agency has received all required information from the submitter), the EPA has ninety days (in some circumstances, 180 days) to decide whether to prohibit or regulate manufacture of the new chemical.

The EPA reviews PMNs in six stages. These stages include prenotice communication, process start-up, initial review, detailed review, regulatory response, and closeout. During this review, the EPA will consider economic benefits and will consider if the proposed chemical will displace a more toxic substance already on the market. If the EPA takes no action on the notice within ninety days, the manufacturer may begin production. The manufacturer must supply the EPA with further notice that manufacture will commence.

At that point, the EPA adds the chemical to the TSCA Inventory. Once listed, the substance is considered an **existing chemical.** This step essentially legalizes the manufacture of the substance.

At the PMN stage, the EPA can impose regulations on the use and manufacture of the new chemical. Under § 5(e) of TSCA, the Agency may issue orders if it determines that the PMN information is insufficient for an evaluation of the chemical's effects. The EPA may also issue an order under § 5(e) if it determines that the chemical would be produced in large quantities causing substantial human exposure to the substance. In this case, the order can prohibit or limit the manufacture, processing, or distribution of the chemical until sufficient data can be obtained.[2]

A manufacturer can avoid a § 5(e) order by responding with sufficient material. The burden is on the manufacturer to satisfy the Agency with specific information the Agency requests. If a manufacturer does respond, the proposed order does not go into effect. The EPA's redress is to seek an injunction in a U.S. district court. The injunction would force compliance with the proposed order.

At the PMN stage, the EPA can also issue orders under § 5(f) of the Act. When the Agency finds that a chemical presents an unreasonable risk, it can issue an order under § 5(f) to protect against that risk. The EPA can link its § 5(f) order with a proposed rule under § 6(a). Under this approach, the Agency can restrict the amounts and uses of a chemical and can prescribe precautionary measures to be taken in the use and manufacture of a chemical. As an alternative under § 5(f), the EPA can issue a proposed order to prohibit the manufacture, processing, or distribution in commerce of the new chemical. In this case, similar to the situation with a § 5(e) order, the manufacturer can file specific objections. The objections effectively preclude the order's effectiveness. The EPA must then seek a court injunction to enforce the proposed order.

---

[2] Between 1976 and 2003, the EPA received a total of over 32,000 PMNs and subjected less than 1000 of them to § 5(e) orders.

TSCA Testing Provisions

Another important aspect of TSCA concerns testing of chemicals under TSCA § 4. The EPA can require a manufacturer to test its chemical if the substance may pose an unreasonable risk or if potential exposure to humans and the environment is substantial. In both situations, the EPA must make specific factual findings. EPA maintains a Web site with useful testing information at http://www.epa.gov/opptsfrs/home/testmeth.htm.

If the EPA requires testing, it must devise a test rule. The rule dictates how the manufacturer must test the substance. In drafting test rules, the Agency must account for relative costs of the various test protocols and methodologies. A manufacturer can challenge a test rule in the federal courts of appeals. A test rule will only withstand such a challenge if there is "substantial evidence" as to the need for testing.

Significant New Use Rules

TSCA provides the EPA with authority beyond the regulation of new chemicals. In addition to requiring PMNs for new chemicals, the EPA can require PMNs for new uses of existing chemicals. Under § 5(a)(2) of TSCA, the EPA has authority to issue a **Significant New Use Rule** or **SNUR** if the EPA determines that a use of a chemical substance is a significant new use. Once an SNUR is issued, a PMN is required for the specified new uses of the existing chemical. Similar to the PMN process for new chemicals, the SNUR/PMN process requires the manufacturer to show that new uses will be safe.

The EPA might issue an SNUR for a variety of reasons. Some chemicals might present minimal risk when manufactured in small quantities or when used in a manner that minimizes exposure to humans or the environment. If increased output or a change in the intended application increases risk, the chemical is a candidate for an SNUR.

Regulation of Unreasonable Risk Under Section 6, Including Polychlorinated Biphenyls and Asbestos

If the EPA determines in a PMN review or in screening of the TSCA Inventory that there is a "reasonable basis to conclude that the manufacture, processing, distribution in commerce, use or disposal of a chemical substance . . . presents or will present an unreasonable risk of injury to health or the environment," the EPA may regulate the chemical under § 6 of TSCA. 15 U.S.C. § 2605 (1991). Likewise, if a chemical is already in the marketplace, it can be regulated through § 6. Similar to the provisions in § 5, a § 6 EPA action can include a demand for chemical testing in order to determine if a chemical meets the unreasonable risk threshold.

If the EPA decides that a chemical presents an unreasonable risk, it can take a variety of administrative or judicial measures under § 6. Specifically, the Agency can

- completely prohibit manufacture;
- prohibit or limit certain use;
- prescribe quantity and concentration limits in manufacture;
- specify quality control measures that must be used by the manufacturer or processor;
- require tests that are reasonable and necessary to assure compliance with regulations issued under § 6;
- establish record-keeping requirements;
- control disposal; or
- impose labeling and other public disclosure requirements.

Section 6 is clearly an important component of TSCA: it allows the Agency a wide array of options in regulating a chemical. Yet this section has been used sparingly. The Agency has been reluctant to bring § 6 enforcement actions because regulations under that section are vulnerable to attack in court. If challenged, the EPA must show that a regulation is supported by substantial evidence on the Agency's entire record in promulgating the regulation. This is an extremely burdensome standard. Hence, the Agency has been hesitant to implement rigorous enforcement under § 6.

Regulation of PCBs Under TSCA

TSCA contains explicit provisions with respect to **polychlorinated biphenyls (PCBs).** PCBs are a group of highly stable chemicals that achieved widespread industrial use by the time of TSCA's enactment. PCBs are synthetic chemicals that fall within the group known as **chlorinated hydrocarbons.** PCBs have been produced since 1929 and were generally used as cooling liquids in electrical equipment. PCBs were also used as heat transfer and hydraulic fluids. PCBs have been used in these applications because of their high boiling point, chemical stability, and low electrical conductivity.

PCBs were specifically included in the TSCA legislation due to growing concern about their environmental effects and due to evidence that PCBs are highly toxic in animals. Tests on laboratory animals showed that PCBs could cause cancers, tumors, birth defects, and reproductive failures.

CASES FOR DISCUSSION

United States v. Holloway Oil Co., 1988 WL 148608, 28 ERC 1190 (M.D. Fla. 1988).

In this case, where the company was found liable for violations of TSCA in a default order issued by an EPA administrative law judge, the court found that the company may not challenge the bases for the order in proceedings before a federal district court because: (1) the company's failure to participate in the EPA proceedings led to Agency's issuance of the judgment by default, (2) the administrative law judge relied on the same procedural rights and materials that would have been available in court proceedings, (3) the company and its owner were both privy to the EPA proceedings, and (4) the issues before the court were essentially same as those already resolved before the Agency.

PCB health effects are exacerbated through a process known as **bioaccumulation.** Because PCBs are stable compounds, they do not break down when released into the environment. They work their way into the food chain and can accumulate in significant concentrations at the top of the chain. By some estimates, 150 million pounds of PCBs have been irretrievably lost into the environment, with another 290 million pounds placed in landfills and dumps.

TSCA prohibited the manufacture of PCBs after January 1, 1979, and prohibited their processing and distribution in commerce after July 1, 1979.

TSCA exempts PCBs that are totally enclosed (i.e., will not be exposed to humans and the environment) and also exempts PCBs whose manufacture, processing, distributions, or use "will not present an unreasonable risk of injury to health or the environment." The EPA initially defined certain uses of PCBs in electrical transformers and capacitors as totally enclosed. The EPA also established a fifty **parts per million (PPM)** cutoff: substances containing less than fifty PPM PCBs were deemed as not presenting unreasonable risk.

The totally enclosed and fifty PPM use exemptions were successfully challenged in *Environmental Defense Fund v. EPA,* 636 F.2d 1267 (D.C. Cir. 1980), which ultimately led the EPA to promulgate a series of follow-up rules. Under the current system, PCBs are regulated for use in certain types of equipments.

The EPA has issued regulations on use and retirement of PCB-containing transformers in or near commercial buildings. The Agency also regulates the unintended by-product manufacture of PCBs. The

PCB regulations also include certain record-keeping requirements. The EPA regulations governing PCBs are found at 40 C.F.R. part 761 (1997).

> PCBs are regulated for use in certain types of equipment.

Figure 4-2 illustrates an example of how PCB materials must be labeled.

Regulation of Asbestos Under TSCA

In 1989, the EPA issued a final rule under TSCA to phase out the use of asbestos in commercial products.[3] The rule was designed to ban the use of asbestos in new products by 1997. The ban on the manufacture, import, and processing of asbestos in certain products was staged as follows:

1990—Felt used in construction, pipeline wrap, cement sheet, floor tile, and clothing

1993—Friction products such as gaskets, clutches, automatic transmission components, and new brake linings

1996—Cement pipe, corrugated paper, specialty paper, roof coatings, and replacement brake linings

The phaseout was set aside in *Corrosion Proof Fittings v. EPA*, 947 F.2d 1201 (5th Cir. 1991), but the EPA may attempt to revive an asbestos phaseout program.

Reporting and Record-Keeping Requirements

Section 8 of TSCA contains several important programs for reporting and record-keeping requirements. The two most important programs are contained in §§ 8(e) and 8(c), 15 U.S.C. §§ 2607(e) and (c) (1997).

---

[3] Apart from the asbestos rule, which applies primarily to manufacturing concerns, Congress amended TSCA in 1986 to address asbestos in schools. Under the Asbestos Hazard Emergency Response Act of 1986 (AHERA), Title II of TSCA, 15 U.S.C. §§ 2641–2655 (1991), the EPA was directed to promulgate regulations requiring Local Education Agencies (LEAs) to address asbestos problems in their school buildings. Consequently, LEAs are required to inspect school buildings for Asbestos Containing Materials (ACMs), develop management plans, and implement response actions.

Figure 1

Figure 2

[44 FR 31542, May 31, 1979. Redesignated at 47 FR 19527, May 6, 1982]

Figure 4-2   PCB Labels Required Under 40 C.F.R. Part 761.45.

The EPA maintains several related and useful Web sites and databases that are accessible at http://www.epa.gov/opptintr/opptdb.htm.

The § 8(e) program requires manufacturers, importers, processors, and distributors who obtain information "which reasonably supports the conclusion that [a] substance or mixture presents a substantial risk of injury to health or the environment" to inform the EPA immediately. Simply put, when manufacturers become aware that a chemical presents a health hazard, they are required to report that information to the EPA. The risk presented may arise from new technical information about a chemical, or it may arise from an environmental release of a well-known substance. Note that § 8(e) does not apply strictly to laboratory results. Rather, it is broad enough to cover certain types of environmental contamination.

Note that the EPA has recently revised a long-standing policy relating to § 8(e) reporting. *See* the "TSCA § 8(e): Notification of Substantial Risk Policy Clarification and Reporting Guidance," published at 68 Fed. Reg. 33129 (June 3, 2003). The Agency indicated in its notice that:

> EPA is hereby finalizing revisions to certain parts of EPA's "Statement of Interpretation and Enforcement Policy; Notification of Substantial Risk" (policy statement) issued March 16, 1978, concerning the reporting of "substantial risk" information pursuant to § 8(e) of the Toxic Substances Control Act (TSCA).

Figure 4-3 shows the first page of this EPA § 8(e) notice.

Section 8(e) notification is required within fifteen working days of the date the manufacturer learns of the substantial risk. No notice is required if the manufacturer has actual knowledge that the EPA has been adequately apprised of the substantial risk. This last condition means that if the EPA has been informed by other sources, the manufacturer is not required to make a report.

Figure 4-4 shows the EPA's more recent "TSCA § 8(e) Reporting Guidance, Correction, Clarification of Applicability, and Announcement Regarding the Issuance of Questions and Answers," published at 70 Fed. Reg. 2162 (January 12, 2005).

Reviewing EPA guidance and policy is critical to complying with the Agency's rules and regulations. Finding and collecting EPA policy and guidance often will fall to paralegals. Paralegals may also be asked to review these documents substantially and to prepare a memorandum stating the EPA's position on particular issues.

A paralegal might also typically be involved in organizing and managing information under § 8(e) of TSCA. A specific task might include creating a system to process new toxicological, epidemiological, or release information. The system would be set up to collect and analyze information and to prepare § 8(e) submissions to the EPA.

Federal Register / Vol. 68, No. 106 / Tuesday, June 3, 2003 / Notices   33129

may not conduct or sponsor, and a person is not required to respond to a collection of information unless it displays a currently valid OMB control number. The OMB control number for EPAís regulations, after initial display in the final rule, are listed in 40 CFR part 9.

VI. References

1. U.S. EPA, OPPT. *I. Ethylene Dichloride (107ñ06ñ2).* Pp 24ñ27 *In:* ëëTSCA Section 4 Findings for 21 Hazardous Air Pollutants: A Supporting Document for Proposed Hazardous Air Pollutants (HAPs) Test Rule.íí (June 25, 1996).

2. The HAP Task Force. Letter from Peter E. Voytek to Charles M. Auer with attachment entitled: ëëProposal for Pharmacokinetics Study of Ethylene Dichloride, November 22, 1996.íí (November 22, 1996).

3. U.S. EPA. Letter from Charles M. Auer to Peter E. Voytek with attachment entitled: ëëPreliminary EPA Technical Analysis of Proposed Industry Pharmacokinetics (PK) Strategy for Ethylene Dichloride, June, 1997.íí (June 26, 1997).

4. The HAP Task Force. Letter from Peter E. Voytek to Charles M. Auer, U.S. EPA. (March 19, 1999).

5. U.S. EPA. Letter from Charles M. Auer to Peter E. Voytek, HAP Task Force, Re: ECA Development of Ethylene Dichloride (EDC) (OPPTS 42197C, with attachment: ëëEDC ECA6 DRAFT, dated February, 2001.íí (February 13, 2001).

6. Final Enforceable Consent Agreement for Ethylene Dichloride and Accompanying Testing Consent Order, signed by EPA on May 13, 2003.

7. DíSouza, R.W., Francis, W.R., Bruce R.D., and Andersen, M.E. *Physiologically based phamacokinetic model for ethylene dichloride and its application in risk assessment.* Pp 286ñ 301, *In:* Pharmacokinetics in Risk Assessment. National Academy Press. Washington, D.C. (1987).

8. DíSouza, R.W., Francis, W.R., and Andersen, M.E. *Physiological model for tissue glutathione depletion and increased resynthesis after ethylene dichloride exposure.* Journal of Pharmacology and Experimental Therapeutics 245(2):563ñ568. 1988.

9. Daniel, F.B., Robinson, M., Olson, G.R., Yore, R.G., and Condie, L.W. *Ten and ninety-day toxicity studies of 1,2-dichloroethane in Sprague-Dawley rats.* Drug and Chemical Toxicology 17: 463ñ 477. 1994.

10. Alumot, E., Nachtomi, E., Mandel, E., Holstein, P., Bondi, A., and Herzberg, M. *Tolerance and acceptable daily intake of chlorinated fumigants in the rat diet.* Food, Cosmetics and Toxicology 14: 105ñ110. (1976).

11. Rao, K.S., Murray, J.S., Deacon, M.M., John, J.A., Calhoun, L.L., and Young, J.T. *Teratogenicity and reproduction studies in animals inhaling ethylene dichloride.* Banbury Report 5: 149ñ166. (1980).

12. Lane, R.W., Riddle, B.L., and Borzelleca, J.F. *Effects of 1,2-dichloroethane and 1,1,1-trichloroethane in drinking water on reproduction and development in mice.* Toxicology and Applied Pharmacology 63: 409ñ421. 1982.

13. Payan, J.P., Saillenfait, A.M., Bonnet, P., Fabry, J.P., Langonne, I., and Sabate J.P. *Assessment of the developmental toxicity and placental transfer of the 1,2-dichloroethane in rats.* Fundamental and Applied Toxicology 28: 187ñ198. 1995.

14. Sherwood, R.L., OíShea, W., Thomas, P.T., Ratajczak, H.V., and Aranyi, C. *Effects of inhalation of ethylene dichloride on pulmonary defenses of mice and rats.* Toxicology and Applied Pharmacology 91: 491ñ496. 1987.

15. U.S. EPA, OPPTS. ëëBurden Estimates for the Enforceable Consent Agreement for Ethylene Dichloride.íí (January 31, 2002).

List of Subjects

Environmental protection, Hazardous chemicals.

Dated: May 13, 2003.
Stephen Johnson,
Assistant Administrator for Prevention, Pesticides and Toxic Substances.

[FR Doc. 03ñ13721 Filed 6ñ2ñ03; 8:45 am]
BILLING CODE 6560ñ50ñS

ENVIRONMENTAL PROTECTION AGENCY

[OPPTñ2002ñ0067; FRLñ7287ñ4]

TSCA Section 8(e); Notification of Substantial Risk; Policy Clarification and Reporting Guidance

AGENCY: Environmental Protection Agency (EPA).
ACTION: Notice.

SUMMARY: EPA is hereby finalizing revisions to certain parts of EPAís ëëStatement of Interpretation and Enforcement Policy; Notification of Substantial Riskíí (policy statement) issued March 16, 1978, concerning the reporting of ëësubstantial riskíí information pursuant to section 8(e) of the Toxic Substances Control Act (TSCA). EPA is making these revisions after having considered public comments that were solicited in 1993 and 1995. Specifically, the revisions address the reporting of information on the release of chemical substances to, and the detection of chemical substances in, environmental media, the reporting deadline for written ëësubstantial riskíí information, and the circumstances under which certain information need not be reported to EPA under section 8(e) of TSCA. EPA is republishing the policy statement in its entirety in this document, including both those portions of the policy statement that are revised and those portions that are not affected by any revisions. Since the policy statement was published in 1978, this republication is intended to ensure that a single reference source for the TSCA section 8(e) policy and guidance is easily available to the regulated community and other interested parties.

FOR FURTHER INFORMATION CONTACT: *For general information contact:* Barbara Cunningham, Director, Environmental Assistance Division (7408M), Office of Pollution Prevention and Toxics, Environmental Protection Agency, 1200 Pennsylvania Ave., NW., Washington, DC 20460ñ0001; telephone number: (202) 554ñ1404; e-mail address: TSCA-Hotline@epa.gov.

For technical information contact: Richard Hefter, Chief, High Production Volume Chemicals Branch, Risk Assessment Division, Office Pollution Prevention and Toxics, Environmental Protection Agency, 1200 Pennsylvania Ave., NW., Washington, DC 20460ñ 0001; telephone number: (202) 564ñ 7649; e-mail address: hefter.richard@epa.gov.

SUPPLEMENTARY INFORMATION:

I. General Information

A. Does this Action Apply to Me?

You may be potentially affected by this action if you manufacture, process, import, or distribute in commerce chemical substances and mixtures. Potentially affected entities may include, but are not limited to:

Chemical manufacturers, processors, and distributors (NAICS 325)
Petroleum refiners and distributors (NAICS 324)
Manufacturers of plastic parts and components (NAICS 325211)
Paints and coatings and adhesive manufacturing (NAICS 3255)
Cleaning compounds and similar products manufacturing (NAICS 3256)
Electronics manufacturing (NAICS 334 and 335)
Automobiles manufacturing (NAICS 3361)

Figure 4-3   TSCA § 8(e) Guidance Published at 68 Fed. Reg. 33129 (June 3, 2003).

A TSCA § 8(e) program might also include

- educating employees on § 8(e) information;
- collecting potential § 8(e) information company-wide;

2162   Federal Register / Vol. 70, No. 8 / Wednesday, January 12, 2005 / Notices

on disk or CD ROM, mark the outside of the disk or CD ROM as CBI and then identify electronically within the disk or CD ROM the specific information that is CBI). Information so marked will not be disclosed except in accordance with procedures set forth in 40 CFR part 2.

In addition to one complete version of the comment that includes any information claimed as CBI, a copy of the comment that does not contain the information claimed as CBI must be submitted for inclusion in the public docket and EPA's electronic public docket. If you submit the copy that does not contain CBI on disk or CD ROM, mark the outside of the disk or CD ROM clearly that it does not contain CBI. Information not marked as CBI will be included in the public docket and EPA's electronic public docket without prior notice. If you have any questions about CBI or the procedures for claiming CBI, please consult the person listed under **FOR FURTHER INFORMATION CONTACT**.

E. What Should I Consider as I Prepare My Comments for EPA?

You may find the following suggestions helpful for preparing your comments:

1. Explain your views as clearly as possible.

2. Describe any assumptions that you used.

3. Provide copies of any technical information and/or data you used that support your views.

4. If you estimate potential burden or costs, explain how you arrived at the estimate that you provide.

5. Provide specific examples to illustrate your concerns.

6. Offer alternative ways to improve the notice.

7. Make sure to submit your comments by the deadline in this document.

8. To ensure proper receipt by EPA, be sure to identify the docket ID number assigned to this action in the subject line on the first page of your response. You may also provide the name, date, and **Federal Register** citation.

II. Background

In the **Federal Register** of December 22, 2004 (69 FR 76732) (FRL–7688–7), EPA announced the issuance of EUP 524–EUP–96 to Monsanto Company, 800 N. Lindberg Blvd., St. Louis, MO 63167. Monsanto has requested to further extend this EUP to March 1, 2006 and to amend it by allowing an additional 3,023 acres to be planted. Plantings are still to include the plant-incorporated protectants ZMIR39 x MON810 combined insecticidal trait stacked corn hybrids along with

ZMIR39 and MON810 corn hybrids; *Bacillus thuringiensis* Cry3Bb1 protein and the genetic material necessary for its production (vector ZMIR39) in corn (ZMIR39) and *Bacillus thuringiensis* Cry1Ab delta-endotoxin and the genetic material necessary for its production (vector PV–ZMCT01) in corn (MON810) for breeding and observation nursery, inbred seed increase production, line per se, hybrid yield, and herbicide tolerance, insect efficacy, product characterization and performance/ labeling, insect resistance management, non-target organism and benefit, seed treatment, swine growth and feed efficiency, dairy cattle feed efficiency, beef cattle growth and feed efficiency, and cattle grazing feed efficiency trials. The program is proposed for the States of Alabama, California, Colorado, Hawaii, Illinois, Indiana, Iowa, Kansas, Kentucky, Maryland, Michigan, Minnesota, Mississippi, Missouri, Nebraska, New Mexico, New York, North Carolina, North Dakota, Ohio, Oklahoma, Pennsylvania, Puerto Rico, South Dakota, Tennessee, Texas, Virginia, Washinton, and Wisconsin.

III. What Action is the Agency Taking?

Following the review of the Monsanto Company application and any comments and data received in response to this notice, EPA will decide whether to issue or deny the EUP request for this EUP program, and if issued, the conditions under which it is to be conducted. Any issuance of an EUP will be announced in the **Federal Register**.

IV. What is the Agencyís Authority for Taking this Action?

The Agency's authority for taking this action is under FIFRA section 5.

List of Subjects

Environmental protection, Experimental use permits.

Dated: December 23, 2004.

Janet L. Andersen,

Director, Biopesticides and Pollution Prevention Division, Office of Pesticide Programs.

[FR Doc. 05–506 Filed 1–11–05; 8:45 am]

BILLING CODE 6560–50–S

ENVIRONMENTAL PROTECTION AGENCY

[OPPT–2002–0067; FRL–7690–4]

TSCA Section 8(e) Reporting Guidance; Correction, Clarification of Applicability, and Announcement Regarding the Issuance Questions and Answers

AGENCY: Environmental Protection Agency (EPA).

ACTION: Notice.

SUMMARY: EPA is correcting certain language that was inadvertently changed from the March 16, 1978, TSCA Section 8(e) Statement of Interpretation and Enforcement Policy; Notification of Substantial Risk (1978 TSCA Section 8(e) Policy Statement) when the Agency issued its TSCA Section 8(e); Notification of Substantial Risk; Policy Clarification and Reporting Guidance (2003 guidance document) on June 3, 2003. The 2003 guidance document clarified certain aspects of TSCA section 8(e) reporting guidance and included a re-publication of major portions of the Agency's 1978 TSCA Section 8(e) Policy Statement. This notice merely re-inserts, verbatim, certain language from the 1978 TSCA Section 8(e) Policy Statement into the June 3, 2003, guidance document. This notice also clarifies the applicability date of the June 3, 2003 guidance document, and announces the addition of questions and answers on the reportability of environmental releases to the Q&A section of the TSCA section 8(e) web page (*http://www.epa.gov/oppt/tsca8e/*).

FOR FURTHER INFORMATION CONTACT: *For general information contact:* Colby Lintner, Regulatory Coordinator, Environmental Assistance Division (7408M), Office of Pollution Prevention and Toxics, Environmental Protection Agency, 1200 Pennsylvania Ave., NW., Washington, DC 20460–0001; telephone number: (202) 554–1404; e-mail address: *TSCA-Hotline@epa.gov.*

For technical information contact: Terry O'Bryan, Risk Assessment Division (7403M), Office Pollution Prevention and Toxics, Environmental Protection Agency, 1200 Pennsylvania Ave., NW., Washington, DC 20460– 0001; telephone number: (202) 564– 7656; e-mail address: *obryan.terry@epa.gov.*

SUPPLEMENTARY INFORMATION:

I. General Information

A. Does this Action Apply to Me?

You may be affected by this action if you manufacture, process, import, or distribute in commerce chemical

Figure 4-4   EPA "TSCA § 8(e) Reporting Guidance."

- screening information against the standards under the statute and EPA guidance to determine whether a substance presents a substantial risk;
- preparing § 8(e) reports to the EPA;

- advising the company's officers and employees on the company's decision in reporting to the EPA;
- educating employees on their right to report to the EPA (should the company decide not to report); or
- educating officers and employees on the federal penalties for failure to report.

Once the EPA receives § 8(e) information, it may pursue additional information gathering, refer the § 8(e) information to other agencies, or consider the chemical for regulation under § 6 of TSCA.

The other important record-keeping requirement under TSCA is found in § 8(c), 15 U.S.C. § 2607(c) (1991). That section requires the manufacturer and processors of chemical substances to "maintain records of significant adverse reactions to health or the environment . . . alleged to have been caused by the substance or mixture." Under this requirement, a manufacturer must keep, for example, records of consumer allegations of personal injury, harm to health, occupational disease, or injury to the environment. The statute is not limited to feedback from consumers. The manufacturer or processor must retain this type of information as received from *any* source.

Allegations by employees of adverse reactions must be kept on file for thirty years. Hence, this section of TSCA presents a significant challenge in terms of document and information management. All other allegations must be kept for five years.

> Because allegations by employees of adverse reactions must be kept on file for thirty years, document and information management under TSCA § 8(c) presents a significant challenge.

The relationship between § 8(e) reporting requirements and § 8(c) record-keeping requirements is worth noting. Certain § 8(e) information may be ultimately screened from reporting to the EPA because the chemical substance is deemed not to present a substantial risk. Such information may be appropriate for retention under § 8(c) as an allegation of adverse reaction. The EPA does not require reporting or submission of allegation information (other than the § 8(e) requirement); however, the EPA may inspect such information and require submission of copies at any time. To facilitate accessibility, the Agency requires the § 8(c) database to be maintained so that information may be retrieved by chemical name, type of process, or type of discharge to the environment. A paralegal might typically be involved in the control and management of a TSCA § 8(c) database.

CASES FOR DISCUSSION

EPA v. Alyeska Pipeline Service Co., 836 F.2d 443, 26 ERC 2129, 18 Envtl. L. Rep. 20,491 (9th Cir. 1988).

In this case, the company contended that the EPA improperly used the investigatory powers under TSCA to further its CWA investigation of its plant. The EPA maintained that it was conducting a separate investigation under TSCA. In particular, the EPA was investigating reported incidents in which tankers dumped contaminated tank washings from ships as ballast at the Valdez terminal before loading crude oil. These incidents, according to EPA, were outside the scope of a CWA relicensing investigation because the terminal was not designed (or licensed) to handle water soluble chemical mixtures or solutions that may have been involved in the suspected dumpings.

The court found that the EPA has authority under TSCA to subpoena information from a company about discharges, even though the Agency did not allege that the company violated the law, because: (1) the Agency has authority to investigate facilities under TSCA; (2) the EPA's request for information on chemical substances at the plant was within the scope of a TSCA investigation; (3) the EPA is not required to allege knowledge or suspicion about violations at the facility; and (4) although other environmental laws might also provide subpoena power, the EPA was unsure about which laws were appropriate to remedy any problems at the plant.

Enforcement and Penalties Under TSCA

Section 11 of TSCA, 15 U.S.C. § 2610 (1991), allows the EPA to inspect any facility where chemical substances are manufactured, processed, or stored. The Agency must give written notice prior to the inspection, and the inspection must be carried out in a reasonable manner. Between 1983 and 1992, the EPA conducted 2405 TSCA § 5 new chemical inspections and 2749 TSCA § 8 chemical reporting inspections.

Beyond its inspection powers, the Agency has authority to enforce TSCA under §§ 15 and 16, 42 U.S.C. §§ 2614 and 2615 (1991). These provisions allow the EPA to pursue civil penalties of up to $25,000 per day for each violation of the statute. The Agency can also seek criminal fines of up to $25,000 per day and imprisonment of up to one year.

The EPA maintains an active enforcement docket under TSCA. In these proceedings, the EPA will use the **TSCA Civil Penalty Policy** to determine appropriate penalties for alleged violations. Under the Policy, penalties are determined in two steps. The Agency calculates a **gravity-based penalty** and then applies appropriate adjustments to that penalty. In calculating the gravity component, the Agency considers the nature of the violation, the circumstances of the violation, and the potential for harm that could result from the alleged violation. Once the gravity component has been calculated, upward or downward adjustments are made considering culpability, history of similar violations, ability to pay, ability to continue in business, and such other matters as justice may require. The Agency's TSCA enforcement actions typically propose penalties of $15,000 to $25,000. Proposed penalties, however, can run as high as $17 million.

Miscellaneous Information

Additional information on TSCA is available directly from the EPA. The appropriate contact within EPA headquarters is the TSCA Assistance Office and Information Service, Office of Toxic Substances, Environmental Protection Agency, Mail Code 7408, 401 M Street SW., Washington, DC 20460. That office can be reached directly at the TSCA Hotline: (202)554-1404, Fax: (202)554-5603. Each of the EPA's ten regional offices can also provide additional information of specific programs under the statute.

Conclusion

TSCA is the primary statute regulating chemical substances. Under the Act, thousands of "chemical substances and mixtures" are regulated. The four main areas under TSCA are

- Authorization to market chemical substances
- Regulation of unreasonable risk under § 6 of TSCA, including polychlorinated biphenyls and asbestos
- Reporting and record-keeping requirements
- Enforcement and penalties under TSCA

Under TSCA, paralegals may be involved in gathering and processing information to be submitted with a premanufacture notice. Paralegals will research and analyze EPA policy, guidance, and rules. Paralegals may also be involved in organizing and managing information under § 8(e) of TSCA, such as creating a system to process new toxicological, epidemiological, or release information. Paralegals may be involved in the control and management of a TSCA § 8(c) database.

Paralegals will also be actively involved in the TSCA enforcement process, in both administrative and judicial proceedings, as is discussed in more detail in the Introduction to this book.

GLOSSARY OF TSCA TERMS

ACM. Asbestos containing material. See AHERA.

AHERA. Asbestos Hazard Emergency Response Act of 1986. Under AHERA, Title II of TSCA, 15 U.S.C. §§ 2641–2655 (1991), the EPA was directed to promulgate regulations requiring Local Education Agencies (LEAs) to address asbestos problems in their school buildings by inspecting school buildings for Asbestos Containing Materials (ACMs), developing management plans, and implementing response actions.

bioaccumulation. The effects of PCBs when released into the environment and the food chain.

chemical substances and mixtures. TSCA is the primary statute regulating chemical substances. Under TSCA, thousands of chemical substances and mixtures are regulated.

existing chemical. Once listed in the TSCA Inventory, a substance is considered an "existing chemical," a step essentially legalizing the manufacture of the substance.

LEAs. Local Education Agencies. See AHERA.

PCBs. Polychlorinated biphenyls. TSCA contains explicit provisions with respect to PCBs, a group of highly stable chemicals that achieved widespread industrial use by the time of TSCA's enactment. PCBs, synthetic chemicals falling within the group known as chlorinated hydrocarbons, have been produced since 1929, generally for use as cooling liquids in electrical equipment.

PMN. Premanufacture notice. A notice given to the EPA on a form found at 40 C.F.R. § 720, Appendix A (1997) when a company plans to import, manufacture, or process a substance determined to be new. The submitter provides a variety of information detailed in 40 C.F.R. §§ 720.45 and 720.50 (1997).

PPM. Parts per million.

Section 8(c) Record-Keeping and Section 8(e) Reporting. There is a regulatory relationship between § 8(c) record-keeping requirements and § 8(e) reporting requirements. Certain § 8(e) information may be ultimately screened from reporting to the EPA because the chemical substance is deemed not to present a substantial risk. Such information may be appropriate for retention under § 8(c) as an allegation of adverse reaction.

SNUR. Significant New Use Rule. In addition to requiring PMNs for new chemicals, the EPA can require PMNs for new uses of existing chemicals. Under TSCA § 5(a)(2), the EPA has authority to issue an SNUR. Once an SNUR is issued, a PMN is required for the specified new uses of the existing chemical.

substantial evidence. A manufacturer can challenge a chemical test rule in the federal courts of appeals. A test rule will only withstand such a challenge if there is "substantial evidence" as to the need for testing.

TSCA. The Toxic Substances Control Act, 15 U.S.C. §§ 2601 to 2671 (1991).

TSCA Inventory. In 1976, the EPA was directed to compile an inventory of chemicals that were in commerce at the time. The EPA's initial inventory was compiled from information submitted by chemical manufacturers. This input allowed the Agency to construct a list of "each chemical substance which is manufactured or processed in the United States"—more than 60,000 chemicals and chemical groups. The original inventory is periodically updated to add new chemicals for which PMNs are filed. Approximately 23,000 chemicals have been added to the original database.

BIBLIOGRAPHY

Beagles, Cynthia, *Survey of Recent Developments in Third Circuit Law—Environmental Law—Toxic Substances Control Act*, 23 Seton Hall L. Rev. 792 (1993).

Bergeson, Lynn L., *TSCA: The Toxic Substances Control Act* (A.B.A., Section of Environment, Energy, and Resources 2000).

BNA Chemical Regulation Reporter, Current Report (Oct. 1, 1993).

Brown, Elizabeth C., et al., *TSCA Deskbook*, Envtl. L. Rep. (Envtl. L. Inst. 1999).

Fort, Jeffrey C., *Designing an Effective Environmental Compliance Program* (CBC 1993).

Hanan, Andrew, *Pushing the Environmental Regulatory Focus—A Step Back: Controlling the Introduction of New Chemicals Under the Toxic Substances Control Act*, 18 Am. J.L. & Med. 395 (Note) (1992).

Merritt, Joyce, *Standard of Review Under the Toxic Substances Control Act: Corrosion Proof Fittings v. EPA*, 8 J. Nat. Resources & Envtl. L. 167 (Comment) (1992/93).

Novick, S., *Law of Environmental Protection* (CBC 1993).

Ruggerio, Cynthia, *Referral of Toxic Chemical Regulation Under the Toxic Substances Control Act: EPA's Administrative Dumping Ground*, 17 B.C. Envtl. Aff. L. Rev. 75 (1989).

Sorell, Louis S., *Biotechnology Regulation Under the Toxic Substances Control Act*, 3 Pace Envtl. L. Rev. 57 (1985).

Stever, D., *Law of Chemical Regulation and Hazardous Waste* (CBC 1993).

Sussman, Robert M., & David J. Hayes, *EPA Activities Under the Toxic Substances Control Act*, Hazardous Wastes, Superfund and Toxic Substances (Oct. 31, 1991).

Trost, Marc W., *The Regulation of Polychlorinated Biphenyls Under the Toxic Substances Control Act*, 31 A.F. L. Rev. 117 (1989).

DISCUSSION QUESTIONS

1. Where would you go to find printed or online information on the TSCA inventory?
2. What would be involved in a literature search for the health effects of a specific chemical substance?
3. What information is required in a premanufacture notice?
4. Where would you research administrative law decisions on TSCA?
5. What is involved in preparing a § 8(e) report? What information must be reported?
6. Under § 8(c) of TSCA, what information must be retained by a company? How must the information be organized? How long must the information be retained?

COMPUTER LABORATORY PROJECTS

1. Prepare a report on the toxicological effects of methyl mercury (MeHg). (*See*, for instance, http://books.nap.edu/books/0309071402/html/index.html or a related site).
2. Research and draft a premanufacture notice for the client described by your instructor.

INTERNET SITES

- The full text of the Toxic Substances Control Act (TSCA) is on the Internet at http://www.epa.gov/region5/defs/html/tsca.htm.

- The EPA Office of Prevention, Pesticides, and Toxic Substances (OPPT) Web site is on the Internet at http://www.epa.gov/oppt.

CHAPTER 5

The Comprehensive Environmental Response, Compensation, and Liability Act

Craig B. Simonsen

OBJECTIVES

The objectives of this chapter are for students to:

- Learn the terminology associated with CERCLA.
- Learn the concepts and ideas that underlie the CERCLA law and regulatory program.
- Learn about specific sections and provisions of the CERCLA law and regulations.
- Learn about the processes and procedures used by the government and other parties to comply with and to enforce the law under CERCLA.
- Learn about the particular jobs and functions that are performed by paralegals working for attorneys in CERCLA cases.

History of the Act

The **Comprehensive Environmental Response, Compensation, and Liability Act** of 1980 (**CERCLA** or **Superfund**), 42 U.S.C. §§ 9601 to 9675 (1991), was the first of the federal emergency cleanup response statutes. The statute was significantly amended by the **Superfund Amendments and Reauthorization Act** of 1986 **(SARA)**. Regulations under the Act are found at 40 C.F.R. §§ 300 to 311 (1997).

CERCLA was enacted in response to tragedies such as the Valley of the Drums, Times Beach, and other notorious hazardous waste sites that caused national outrage during the 1970s and 1980s. The Valley of the Drums, near Louisville, Kentucky, drew national attention in 1979 as one of the country's worst abandoned hazardous waste sites. Thousands of drums—accumulated over a ten-year period—were strewn in pits and trenches over a twenty-three-acre site. The drums at the site were deteriorating quickly; and, when it rained, they overflowed and leaked into a nearby creek, a tributary of the Ohio River. The drums were found to have the chemicals benzene, toluene, and methylmethacrylate.

In 1982, at Times Beach, Missouri, the EPA ended up closing down the town after measuring dangerous levels of dioxin. The Agency finally blocked off roads to the town and placed security guards to patrol the site around the clock. That began one of the most extensive cleanups in Superfund history. Years prior, the town regularly had waste oil sprayed on its streets and parking lots to control dust. Unfortunately, some of that oil was contaminated with dioxin, an unwanted chemical by-product of certain manufacturing processes. Upon discovering the contamination, the EPA decided to permanently relocate more than 2000 people and to demolish all of their homes and businesses.

CERCLA, as amended by SARA, provides for a number of programs that work to effect cleanups of hazardous or potentially hazardous waste sites. CERCLA portions of SARA amendments are dealt with here; other substantial portions are discussed separately in Chapter Six.

Removal and Remedial Programs

The main focus of CERCLA programs is the removal and remedial programs. The removal program establishes the minimum requirements for the immediate removal of hazardous substances so as to isolate them or stop them from release into the environment. The remedial program establishes the minimum requirements for the complete remediation of releases or threatened releases of hazardous substances into the environment.

National Contingency Plan

CERCLA and the **National Contingency Plan (NCP),** 40 C.F.R. § 300 (1997), comprise the national plan for the cleanup and remediation of thousands of contaminated hazardous waste sites across the

United States. The NCP is the EPA's basic policy directive for federal response actions under CERCLA. The NCP includes the procedures and standards for responding to releases of hazardous substances; the **Uncontrolled Hazardous Waste Site Ranking System (HRS),** found in Appendix A of the NCP; and the **National Priorities List (NPL),** found in Appendix B of the NCP.

> CERCLA and the NCP make up the national plan for the cleanup and restitution of thousands of contaminated hazardous waste sites across the United States.

The NCP is required by § 105 of CERCLA, 42 U.S.C. § 9605, as amended by the SARA, and by § 311(c)(2) of the CWA, as amended. In Executive Order No. 12,580, 52 Fed. Reg. 2,923 (1987), the President delegated to the EPA the responsibility for the amendment of the NCP. Prior to publication, amendments to the NCP are coordinated with members of the **National Response Team (NRT)** for notice and comment. This includes coordination with the **Federal Emergency Management Agency (FEMA)** and the **Nuclear Regulatory Commission (NRC)** in order to avoid inconsistent or duplicative requirements in the emergency planning responsibilities of those agencies. The NCP is applicable to response actions taken pursuant to the authorities under CERCLA and the CWA.

The Hazard Ranking System and the National Priorities List

The **Uncontrolled Hazardous Waste Site Ranking System,** Appendix A to the NCP, is the method used by the EPA to evaluate the relative potential of hazardous substance releases to cause health or safety problems, or ecological or environmental damage at a site. The HRS score attempts to quantify what the risk is to the "maximally exposed individual" for the site.

The National Priorities List, Appendix B to the NCP, is the list compiled by the EPA under CERCLA of uncontrolled hazardous substance release sites in the United States that are priorities for long-term remedial evaluation and response. Only those releases included on the NPL will be considered eligible for Fund-financed remedial action.

Removal actions (including remedial planning activities, remedial investigation/feasibility studies, and other actions taken pursuant to CERCLA § 104(b)) are not limited to NPL sites. Inclusion on the NPL is not a precondition to action by the lead agency under CERCLA §§ 106 or 122 or to action under CERCLA § 107 for recovery of non-Fund-financed costs or Fund-financed costs other than Fund-financed remedial construction costs.

CERCLA Liability: Section 106

Under § 106 of CERCLA, the government may bring an enforcement action either in U.S. district court or administratively with a unilateral administrative order to abate an imminent and substantial endangerment to the public health or welfare or the environment because of an actual or threatened release of a hazardous substance from a facility. In such case, paralegals may be involved in obtaining and organizing information for responding to and complying with the government action or order. The participation will involve many of the activities described in the Introduction to this book, such as document and information organization, allocation breakdown (NBAR) analysis, and steering committee administration and management.

CERCLA Liability: Section 107

Under § 107(a) of CERCLA, responsible parties are liable for all response costs incurred by the U.S. government or a state or an Indian tribe not inconsistent with the NCP. Responsible parties are also liable for necessary costs of response actions to releases of hazardous substances incurred by any other person consistent with the NCP. The NCP defines that, for the purpose of cost recovery under § 107(a)(4)(B) of CERCLA:

> A private party response action will be considered consistent with the NCP if the action, when evaluated as a whole, is in substantial compliance with the applicable requirements and results in a CERCLA-quality cleanup; and that any response action carried out in compliance with the terms of an order issued by the EPA pursuant to § 106 of CERCLA, or a consent decree entered into pursuant to § 122 of CERCLA, will be considered consistent with the NCP.

Responsible parties are liable for necessary costs of response actions to releases of hazardous substances incurred by any other person.

CASES FOR DISCUSSION

United States v. South Carolina Recycling and Disposal, Inc., 653 F. Supp. 984, 20 ERC 1753, 14 Envtl. L. Rep. 20,272 (D.S.C. 1984).

This case was instituted by the United States pursuant to § 107 CERCLA to recover the costs of removing hazardous substances from the surface of the Bluff Road site, a hazardous waste site located near Columbia, South Carolina. Named as defendants in this action were four hazardous waste "generators," the two owners of the Bluff Road property, a lessee of at least a portion of the site, and the site operator.

The United States filed for partial summary judgment on the issue of each defendant's joint and several liability for costs incurred in responding to the hazardous conditions posed by the site. The generator defendants likewise filed motions for summary judgment against plaintiff.

The Court noted that, stripping away the excess language of the statute, a generator may be held liable under § 107(a)(3) of CERCLA if the government can prove that:

a. The generator's hazardous substances were, at some point in the past, shipped to a facility;
b. The generator's hazardous substances or hazardous substances like those of the generator were present at the site;
c. There was a release or threatened release of a or any hazardous substance at the site;
d. The release or threatened release caused the incurrence of response costs.

The Court concluded that:

It is clear that each of the generator defendants made arrangements with SCRDI [South Carolina Recycling and Disposal, Inc.] or its predecessors for disposal or treatment of wastes containing hazardous substances and that, as evidenced by the identification of each generator's drums at the Bluff Road site, such wastes were shipped to the site. It is further undisputed that hazardous substances like those of each of the generator defendants were present at the site at the time of cleanup, as shown by samples taken at the site; that there were releases and threatened releases of hazardous substances at the site; and that the government incurred costs in responding to those releases and threatened releases. Thus, based on the undisputed facts, each of these generator defendants is subject to liability under Section 107 of CERCLA.

***

(continued)

CASES FOR DISCUSSION

This court conclude that, based on undisputed facts, the harm at the Bluff Road site was indivisible. Because of the deleterious condition of the site at the time of cleanup, it is impossible to divide the harm in any meaningful way. There were thousands of corroded, leaking drums at the site not segregated by source or waste type. Unknown, incompatible materials comingled to cause fires, fumes, and explosions. Because of the constant threat of further fires, explosions, and other reactions, all of the materials at the site were, if not actually oozing out, in danger of being released. Thus, while all of the substances at the site contributed synergistically to the threatening condition at the site, it is impossible to ascertain the degree of relative contribution of each substance. Clearly, the harm was indivisible, and defendants have failed to meet their burden of proving otherwise.

Generator defendants have argued that there may be a means of roughly apportioning the costs of cleanup among responsible parties by calculating their relative volumetric contributions from shipping documents, and that, therefore, the harm is divisible. But, as noted by the court in *Chem-Dyne*, "the volume of waste of a particular generator is not an accurate predictor of the risk associated with the waste because the toxicity or migratory potential of a particular hazardous substance generally varies independently of the volume." *Chem-Dyne, supra*, at 18. Such arbitrary or theoretical means of cost apportionment do not diminish the indivisibility of the underlying harm, and are matters more appropriately considered in an action for contribution between responsible parties after plaintiff has been made whole. Because the harm at the Bluff Road site was indivisible, each defendant against whom summary judgment was granted was jointly and severally liable for costs incurred at the site.

Figure 5-1 shows a § 107(a) consent decree published for comment by the U.S. Department of Justice in *United States v. Aetna Inc., et al.*

CERCLA Liability: Section 113

Section 113 of CERCLA provides authority for joint and several liability of responsible parties and for the use of contribution

**IN THE UNITED STATES DISTRICT COURT
FOR THE WESTERN DISTRICT OF PENNSYLVANIA**

UNITED STATES OF AMERICA,	)	
	)	
Plaintiff,	)	Civ. Action No. 04-_____
v.	)	Judge Ziegler
	)	Magistrate Judge Caiazza
AETNA INC., et al.	)	
Defendants.	)	
	)	

I. BACKGROUND

A. The United States of America ("United States"), on behalf of the Administrator of the United States Environmental Protection Agency ("EPA"), simultaneously with lodging this First Round De Minimis Consent Decree, is filing a complaint against the above-named defendants pursuant to Section 107(a) of the Comprehensive Environmental Response, Compensation and Liability Act of 1980, as amended, ("CERCLA"), 42 U.S.C. § 9607(a), for the recovery of response costs previously incurred by the United States in responding to releases or threatened releases of hazardous substances at or from the Breslube-Penn Superfund Site (the "Site") located in Moon Township, Allegheny County, Pennsylvania. In its complaint, the United States also seeks a declaration of the defendants' liability for all unreimbursed future response costs to be incurred by the United States in connection with the Site.

B. As a result of the release or threatened release of hazardous substances, EPA has undertaken response actions at or in connection with the Site pursuant to Section 104 of CERCLA, 42 U.S.C. § 9604, and it will undertake response actions in the future. In performing these response actions, EPA has incurred and will continue to incur Response Costs at or in connection with the Site. EPA has conducted several inspections of the Site since 1988, which

Figure 5-1   A § 107(a) Consent Decree Published for Comment by the U.S. Department of Justice in *United States v. Aetna Inc., et al.*

claims. The provision details the specific relevant criteria that a court may use in equitably allocating the response costs at a Superfund site.

Paralegals may be actively involved both in bringing and in defending CERCLA § 107 cost recovery and § 113 liability suits. For instance, research in the waste site documents and analysis of the waste-in data may be necessary to determine responsible parties for the site. The research may involve reviewing documents obtained from the site owners and operators, or a Freedom of Information Act request may need to be prepared to obtain agency records about the site.

Once the responsible parties are known, they can be invited to join with the other Superfund cleanup parties for the purpose of remediating the site. These parties joined together are known as steering committee members in the remediation of the site. For nonparticipants, § 107 suits may be brought to obtain contributions toward costs at the site.

> Superfund cleanup steering committees are typically made up of the largest contributing generators of waste to a site. These companies agree to work together in order to minimize costs and oversee the cleanup project. They are those companies that the Agency has identified and "asked" or ordered to do the cleanup. As new responsible parties are found, they can be added to the steering committee.

CERCLA Information Gathering

Section 104 of CERCLA allows the federal government and authorized state governments to make broad inquiries to persons who may have documents and other information or beliefs concerning a hazardous, potentially hazardous, or suspected hazardous waste site. These inquiries are generally referred to as "104(e) requests." The EPA has published *Transmittal of Guidance on Use and Enforcement of CERCLA Information Requests and Administrative Subpoenas*, August 25, 1988. The guidance indicates that it provides an overview of the information-gathering tools under CERCLA 104(e) and 122(e)(3)(B), and it focuses on the steps to be taken in the process. A copy of the guidance is available on the Internet at http://www.epa.gov/compliance/resources/policies/cleanup/superfund/cerc-infreq-mem.pdf. The guidance is shown in Figure 5-2.

OSWER # 9834.4-A

UNITED STATES ENVIRONMENTAL PROTECTION AGENCY
WASHINGTON, D.C. 20460

AUG 25 1988

OFFICE OF
ENFORCEMENT AND
COMPLIANCE MONITORING

MEMORANDUM

SUBJECT: Transmittal of Guidance on Use and Enforcement of
CERCLA Information Requests and Administrative
Subpoenas

FROM: Thomas L. Adams, Jr.
          Assistant Administrator

TO: Regional Administrators, Regions I - X
          Regional Counsel, Regions I - X
          Directors, Waste Management Divisions, Regions I - X

     With this memorandum, I am transmitting guidance on the use
and enforcement of EPA's information gathering authorities under
CERCLA §§ 104(e) and 122(e)(3)(B). The attached guidance
document replaces existing guidance entitled, "Policy on
Enforcing Information Requests in Hazardous Waste Cases," dated
September 10, 1984, to the extent that the earlier guidance
addressed information gathering under CERCLA §104(e).

Attachment

cc: Bruce Diamond, Director, Office of Waste Programs
        Enforcement
    Lloyd Guerci, Director, CERCLA Enforcement Division,
        Office of Waste Programs Enforcement
    Frank Russo, Chief, Compliance Branch, Office of Waste
        Programs Enforcement
    Robert J. Mason, Acting Chief, Guidance and Oversight
        Branch, Office of Waste Programs Enforcement
    Lisa K. Friedman, Associate General Counsel, Office of
        General Counsel
    David Buente, Chief, Environmental Enforcement Section,
        Department of Justice
    Nancy Firestone, Deputy Chief, Environmental Enforcement
        Section, Department of Justice
    Office of Regional Counsel Hazardous Waste Branch Chiefs,
        Regions I - X
    Clem Rastatter, Executive Assistant, Office of Emergency and
        Remedial Response

Figure 5-2 Transmittal of Guidance on Use and Enforcement of CERCLA
Information Requests and Administrative Subpoenas.

An example of an actual 104(e) information request letter is
shown in Figure 5-3.

UNITED STATES ENVIRONMENTAL PROTECTION AGENCY
REGION IX
75 Hawthorne Street
San Francisco, CA 94105

Certified Mail:
Return Receipt Requested

March 19, 2004

Bob Ferguson, Superintendent
El Dorado Union High School District
4675 Missouri Flat Road
Diamond Springs, CA 95619

Re: Request for Information
    Oak Ridge High School Site
    1120 Harvard Way
    El Dorado Hills, CA 95762

Dear Mr. Ferguson:

The United States Environmental Protection Agency ("EPA") is spending public funds to respond to actual or threatened releases of asbestos in the soils at the Oak Ridge High School ("Site"), located at 1120 Harvard Way in El Dorado Hills, California.

Since the spring of 2003, EPA has been working closely with the El Dorado Union School District ("the District") to address issues related to potential exposure to asbestos fibers from asbestos in disturbed soils. In addition to completing an initial soil assessment at the Site, EPA performed removal assessment of certain exposed soils at the site, which indicated the presence of hazardous substances.

EPA now is conducting an investigation to identify activities and potentially responsible parties ("PRP") with respect to the hazardous substances present at the Site. EPA believes you have information that may assist the Agency in its investigation of the Site. The purpose of this letter is to request information you may have that pertains to this Site.

We encourage you to give this matter your immediate attention and request that you provide a complete and truthful response to this Information Request and attached questions (Enclosure B) within thirty (30) calendar days of your receipt of this letter.

Under Section 104(e) of the Comprehensive Environmental Response, Compensation, and Liability Act ("CERCLA"), 42 U.S.C. § 9604(e), EPA has broad information gathering authority that allows EPA to require persons to furnish information or documents relating to:

Figure 5-3   Request for Information—Oak Ridge High School Site.

Paralegals may be involved in the collection and organization of responsive information and documents and in drafting of the § 104 information response.

CERCLA Cleanup

Section 106 of CERCLA allows the unilateral or consensual ordering of **potentially responsible parties (PRPs)** to remove hazardous substances or to remediate hazardous or potentially hazardous waste sites from threat of or potential threat of release. An example of a CERCLA § 106(a) administrative order by consent (AOC) is shown in Figure 5-4.

A potentially responsible party is someone who has either generated, stored, transported, treated, or disposed of CERCLA hazardous substances. The Superfund program allows the EPA and authorized state agencies to order the PRPs to remove hazardous substances and to remediate hazardous or potentially hazardous waste sites from threat of or potential threat of release.

Under CERCLA, PRPs may be unilaterally ordered to
- ➢ Remove hazardous substances
- ➢ Remediate hazardous or potentially hazardous waste sites from
  - ⌘ Threat of release or
  - ⌘ Potential threat of release

See the EPA's Web site on "CERCLA Section 106 Administrative Orders," at http://cfpub.epa.gov/compliance/resources/policies/cleanup/superfund/index.cfm?action=3&CAT_ID=&SUB_ID=28&templatePage=3&title=CERCLA%20Section%20106%20Administrative%20Orders.

CERCLA Settlements

CERCLA, as amended by SARA, includes comprehensive provisions in its § 122 for negotiations and settlements with PRPs to bring about removal and remedial actions. Section 122(e)(3), for instance, requires the EPA to develop guidelines for preparing **Nonbinding Preliminary Allocations of Responsibility (NBARs).** As defined in § 122(e)(3)(A), an NBAR is an allocation by EPA among PRPs of percentages of total response costs at a facility. SARA authorized the EPA to provide NBARs at its discretion. NBARs are a tool the EPA may use in appropriate cases to promote settlements.

NBARs will allocate 100% of response costs among the site PRPs. In preparing an NBAR, the EPA may consider such factors as volume, toxicity, and mobility of hazardous substances contributed

1̶67878

UNITED STATES ENVIRONMENTAL PROTECTION AGENCY
REGION 5

IN THE MATTER OF:	) Docket No. V-W-03-C-720
	)
RESOURCE RECOVERY GROUP/	)
CLAYTON CHEMICAL SITE	) ADMINISTRATIVE ORDER BY
Sauget, Illinois	) CONSENT PURSUANT TO
	) SECTION 106 OF THE
	) COMPREHENSIVE
	) ENVIRONMENTAL RESPONSE,
Respondents:	) COMPENSATION, AND
	) LIABILITY ACT OF 1980,
Listed in Attachment A	) as amended, 42 U.S.C.
	) §106(a)
	)

I. JURISDICTION AND GENERAL PROVISIONS

This Order is entered into voluntarily by the United States Environmental Protection Agency ("U.S. EPA") and the Respondents, which collectively includes the Performing Respondents and Non-Performing Respondents, each as defined in Section II below. The Order is issued pursuant to the authority vested in the President of the United States by Sections 106(a), 107 and 122 of the Comprehensive Environmental Response, Compensation, and Liability Act of 1980, as amended ("CERCLA"), 42 U.S.C. §§9606(a), 9607 and 9622. This authority has been delegated to the Administrator of the U.S. EPA by Executive Order No. 12580, January 23, 1987, 52 *Federal Register* 2923, and further delegated to the Region 5 Administrator as of January 16, 2002, by U.S. EPA Delegation Nos. 14-1 and 14-2, and to the Director, Superfund Division, Region 5, by Regional Delegation Nos. 14-1 and 14-2.

This Order provides for performance of a removal action and reimbursement of the liquids removal related past response and oversight costs incurred by the United States in connection with the Resource Recovery Group/Clayton Chemical Company property located at 1 Mobile Avenue, Sauget, Illinois (St. Clair County) (the "RRG/Clayton Chemical Site" or the "Site"). This Order requires the Performing Respondents to conduct removal actions described herein to abate an imminent and substantial endangerment to the public health, welfare or the environment that may be presented by the actual or threatened release of hazardous substances, as defined in CERCLA, Section 101, 42 U.S.C. §9601 (Hazardous Substances), at or from the Site, and this Order requires that Non-Performing Respondents provide certain of the financing for matters covered by this Order.

Figure 5-4 CERCLA Administrative Order by Consent.

to the site by PRPs, and other settlement criteria. The settlement criteria may include the strength of evidence tracing the wastes at a site to PRPs, ability of PRPs to pay, litigative risks in proceeding to trial, public interest considerations, precedential value, value of obtaining a present sum certain, inequities and aggravating factors, and the nature of the case that remains after settlement.

An NBAR is not binding on the government or PRPs. It cannot be admitted as evidence or reviewed in any judicial proceeding, including citizen suits. An NBAR is preliminary in the sense that PRPs are free to adjust the percentages allocated by the EPA among themselves. Should the EPA decide to prepare an NBAR, it will normally be

> CERCLA defines an "NBAR" as an allocation by the EPA among PRPs of percentages of total response costs at a facility.

prepared during the **remedial investigation/feasibility study (RI/FS)** stage and provided to PRPs as soon as practicable, but not later than completion of the RI/FS report for the site. The NBAR process will normally be used in cases in which the discretionary special notice procedures of § 122(e) are invoked.

Section 122(e) provides that:

Whenever the President determines that a period of negotiation under this subsection would facilitate an agreement with potentially responsible parties for taking response action (including any action described in section 9604(b) of this title) and would expedite remedial action, the President shall so notify all such parties and shall provide them with information concerning each of the following:

(A) The names and addresses of potentially responsible parties (including owners and operators and other persons referred to in section 9607(a) of this title), to the extent such information is available.

(B) To the extent such information is available, the volume and nature of substances contributed by each potentially responsible party identified at the facility.

(C) A ranking by volume of the substances at the facility, to the extent such information is available.

This sort of information sharing by the agency does really facilitate settlements, but unfortunately it is not seen that often.

Where the EPA does not prepare an NBAR, typically the PRPs will prepare one. Private NBARs serve the same purposes as those prepared by the EPA: that is, a tool to use among the PRPs to promote settlements and cooperation, and to allocate 100% of response costs among PRPs. Private NBARs are often prepared by paralegals. A model for a steering committee generated NBAR is provided for students at Appendix A: Data Analysis: Building a Non-Binding Allocation of Responsibility: A Model Data Structure.

The *de minimis* settlement provisions at § 122(g) provide a mechanism for minimal parties to obtain an early release from the EPA for the site. A ***de minimis* party** is someone who has been identified as a PRP at a Superfund site and where either

1. both the amount and the hazardous effects of the substance the PRP contributed are minimal in comparison to other hazardous substances at the facility; or
2. the PRP is the owner of the facility, did not allow generation, treatment, storage, or disposal at the facility, did not contribute to the release at the facility, and did not purchase the property knowing that it was used for the generation, transportation, treatment, storage, or disposal of hazardous substances.

CASES FOR DISCUSSION

United States v. Rohm & Haas Co., 721 F. Supp. 666, 30 ERC 1520 (D.C. N.J. 1989).

This case concerns CERCLA's § 122(g) authority, which indicates a congressional preference for the speedy settlement of cost recovery actions brought against parties meeting certain criteria. The President, by way of EPA, shall, whenever practicable and in the public interest, as promptly as possible, reach a final settlement with a defendant if the settlement involves a minor portion of the response costs at the facility and, in the President's judgment:

(1) The amount of hazardous substances contributed by the settling party is minimal in comparison to the other hazardous substances at the facility (minimal volumetric contribution); and

(2) The toxic or other hazardous effects of the substances contributed by the settling party is minimal in comparison to the other substances at the facility (minimal toxicity).

42 U.S.C. §§ 9622(g)(A)(i),(ii).

The Court, in its discussion, states that for this settlement to be reasonable, it must merely be reasonable when measured by the range of plausible interpretations of the record:

Compromise of litigation occurs precisely because there is uncertainty about the underlying factual circumstances and the

(continued)

CASES FOR DISCUSSION

range of possible recoveries. If a settlement is reasonable in light of those circumstances, it ought to be approved. On the other hand, if a settlement is based on a clear error of judgment, like a serious mathematical error, it may be appropriate to disapprove it because there is a likelihood that it is not a compromise intelligently entered into by the parties. But when a settlement is based on a plausible interpretation of the record evidence, and there has been no clear error of judgment, we do not believe that it is appropriate for the court to substitute its judgment for that of the statutorily appointed representatives of the public interest—the EPA and the Department of Justice.

* * *

[W]e will evaluate the reasonableness of the decree in light of the following factors: (1) the relative costs and benefits of litigating this case under CERCLA; (2) the strength of the plaintiff's case against the *de minimis* defendants, *i.e.,* the risks of establishing liability on the part of the settlors; (3) the good faith efforts and adversarial relationship of the negotiators who crafted the settlement; (4) the reasonableness of the settlement as compared to the settlor's potential volumetric contribution; (5) the ability of the settlors to withstand a greater judgment; and (6) finally, and most important, the effect of the settlement on the public interest as expressed in CERCLA. If the proposed decree is reasonable in light of these factors, we need not, based on our view of our role, separately consider the fairness of the decree to non-settling parties.

Public Participation

The public participation provisions under CERCLA § 117 require interactive community relations to inform and encourage public participation in the Superfund process and to respond to community concerns. The term "public" includes citizens directly affected by the site, other interested citizens or parties, organized groups, elected officials, and potentially responsible parties. The **Community Relations Coordinator (CRC)** is the agency staff person who works with the **On-Site Coordinator (OSC)** and **Remedial Project Manager (RPM)** to involve and inform the public about the Superfund process and response actions in accordance with the interactive community relations requirements in the NCP.

The **Community Relations Plan (CRP)** is the main tool that identifies community relations needs for a Superfund site. The CRP is developed prior to the beginning of remedial investigation field work to provide an early opportunity for the EPA to assess the level and nature of citizen concerns. The CRP can be the basis of an initial assessment to determine whether the site will require extensive community involvement. The EPA is required to revise the CRP after the **Record of Decision (ROD)** is signed, but the Agency recommends that if changes at the site occur, the RPM and the CRC update the CRP so that the document is accurate and timely.

The Superfund Site Process

One of the first events associated with a new Superfund site is the preparation by the agency of a **preliminary assessment (PA).** The PA is a review of existing information and an on-site and off-site reconnaissance, if appropriate, to determine if an apparent release may require additional investigation or action. *See* the EPA's "Guidance for Performing Preliminary Assessments Under CERCLA," September 1991, available from EPA libraries (document no. EPA 9345.0-01A).

A PA may be followed by a **site inspection (SI)** to determine whether there is a release or will be a potential release. The nature of the associated threats is also considered during the SI. The purpose is to augment the data collected in the PA and to generate, if necessary, sampling and other field data to determine if further action or investigation is appropriate. *See* the EPA's *Guidance for Performing Site Inspections Under CERCLA,* Interim Final, September 1992, available from the EPA libraries (Doc. No. EPA 9345.1-05).

Based on the PA and the SI, a site may be ranked or scored under the **Superfund Uncontrolled Hazardous Waste Site Ranking System.** If the site scores high enough, then the site may be proposed for listing on the NPL. Regardless of NPL listing, based on the findings of the PA and the SI, the site may be remediated under CERCLA § 106 or 107 authorities, or the EPA may do further investigation under its § 104 authorities.

If a site is proposed for the National Priorities List, it will be published with an explanation in the *Federal Register*. Public comments will be received by the EPA on the proposed listing. The EPA may then publish a final rule in the *Federal Register* responding to public comments as appropriate, either listing the site on the NPL or withdrawing the site from the proposal.

In support of the EPA's remedial activities, SARA mandated that the **Agency for Toxic Substances and Disease Registry (ATSDR)** perform specific public health activities associated with actual or potential exposure to toxic substances identified at hazardous waste sites. **Health assessments** are performed by the ATSDR at facilities on or proposed to be listed on the NPL and may be performed at other releases or facilities in response to petitions made to the ATSDR.

Where available, ATSDR health assessments may be used by the lead agency to assist in determining whether response actions should be taken or to identify the need for additional studies to assist in the assessment of potential human health effects associated with releases or potential releases of hazardous substances. SARA also directs the ATSDR to consider NPL schedules and the needs of the EPA in the remedial investigation/feasibility study process when determining its priorities and to complete health assessments promptly and to the maximum extent practicable before completion of the RI/FS.

The Cleanup Action

A Superfund cleanup action for an NPL-listed site will generally consist of either a removal action, where the danger is imminent, and/or a long-term remedial action that may take years to implement. In a removal action, there will be an immediate remedy, such as the removal of leaking drums or the isolation of certain areas of waste. The removal action will usually be followed by a long-term remedial action, where a permanent remedy will be selected and implemented.

A **removal action (RA)** under CERCLA is the cleanup or removal of released hazardous substances from the environment. Such actions as may be necessary are taken in the event of the threat of release of hazardous substances into the environment. Further actions may be necessary to monitor, assess, and evaluate the release or threat of release of hazardous substances. Actions may include the disposal of removed material or the taking of such other actions as may be necessary to prevent, minimize, or mitigate damage to the public health or welfare or to the environment that may otherwise result from a release or threat of release.

The removal action may include security fencing or other measures to limit access, provision of alternative water supplies, temporary evacuation and housing of threatened individuals not otherwise provided for, post-removal site control, and any emergency assistance. For the purpose of the NCP, the term also includes related enforcement activities.

Removal actions fall into three categories:

1. Classic emergency removal actions
2. Time-critical removal actions
3. Non-time-critical removal actions

> A cleanup action under Superfund will generally consist of either
> ➤ a removal action, where danger is imminent; and/or
> ➤ a long-term remedial action that may take years.

Classic emergency removal actions are initiated in response to a release or threat of release of hazardous substances that poses a risk to public health or welfare or the environment, such that the OSC determines that cleanup or stabilization actions must be initiated within hours or days after completion of the preliminary assessment. The emergency nature of the response is unrelated to the cost or duration of the response. Examples include responses to a fire in a chemical warehouse, a tanker truck spill that releases hazardous substances, or leaking drums that pose an explosion hazard.

Time-critical removal actions are actions initiated in response to a release or threat of release that poses a risk to public health or welfare or the environment, such that cleanup or stabilization actions must be initiated within six months following approval of the action memo. The time-critical response is unrelated to the cost or duration of the response. Classic emergencies are not included in this category. This six-month time frame within which response must be initiated is based on the determination that a threat exists that must be addressed within six months. This determination is independent of the question of resource or contractor availability to commence the action within that time frame, delays due to unexpected weather conditions, or other problems. Thus, if initiation of a time-critical action is delayed past six months for these reasons, it is still considered time-critical. Examples include responses to an industrial site in a residential area containing open tanks of hazardous substances and spilled materials, a facility containing eroding unlined waste lagoons, or an unregulated waste dump containing scattered piles of deteriorating drums.

Non-time-critical removal actions are actions initiated in response to a release or threat of release that poses a risk to public health or welfare or the environment, such that initiation of removal cleanup or stabilization actions may be delayed for six months or more following approval of the action memo. An example of a non-time-critical removal action might be response to an abandoned industrial dump isolated from public access that poses a potential threat to ground water if not cleaned up. Cleanup may also be delayed in situations where hazardous substances have been abandoned on a site but the substances are in stable containers and secured from public access. An example is an NPL site where containers are presently stable but are expected to deteriorate prior to the time that the remedial program can commence.

The two primary considerations in determining whether site response can be delayed are (i) the stability of the wastes and (ii) the potential for public contact with the wastes.

If the EPA decides to perform an **expedited response action (ERA)** at a site, an **engineering evaluation/cost analysis (EE/CA)** will be performed. The analysis of alternatives for an ERA in the EE/CA is like a focused feasibility study. As such, the EE/CA will consider all federal and state **applicable or relevant and appropriate requirements (ARARs)** and will stress the use of permanent solutions and alternative treatment technologies. Community responsiveness measures will apply for any EE/CA performed for a non-time-critical removal action, such as an ERA.

Selecting the Appropriate Remedy

The long-term remedial action cleanup plan or remedy selection, like the removal action, is closely regulated under the NCP. Under the NCP, there will first be a Remedial Investigation/Feasibility Study (RI/FS). The purpose of the RI/FS is to assess site conditions and evaluate alternatives to the extent necessary to select a remedy. The RI/FS goes far beyond the initial inquiry done during the PA and the SI.

It is at this point in the Superfund process when the Agency may invite the PRPs—with a § 122 special notice letter—to conduct the work for the RI/FS. This does assume that the PRPs for the site are identifiable and financially solvent.

The Agency will normally send notice letters to selected identifiable PRPs (i.e., just to the larger parties). Once these select parties are put on notice, they quite naturally may search out other (often smaller) PRPs and invite them to participate in the performance of the RI/FS. By joining the larger PRPs in the RI/FS project, these additional PRPs buy themselves some protection from the government and other parties for the other costs associated with the site.

The PRPs then form a steering committee to respond formally to the § 122 special notice letter and to coordinate and oversee the RI/FS performance and other negotiations with the Agency, contractors for the work, and other parties.

If the Agency has provided the PRPs with an NBAR, the work of allocation of the costs associated with the RI/FS will be easier—if the PRPs accept the work done by the agency. If there is not an NBAR, the task of building an allocation database may fall to a paralegal. It can be a large undertaking, and actually getting to a final allocation of costs can take years. A database design for a PRP-generated NBAR is provided in Appendix A.

The purpose of the RI/FS is

➤ To assess site conditions
➤ To evaluate alternatives to the extent necessary to select a remedy

---

Remedial Investigation

The remedial investigation (RI) is a process either supervised or undertaken by the lead agency (either the EPA or the state agency) to determine the nature and extent of the problem presented by a release. The purpose of the RI is to collect data necessary to characterize the site adequately to develop and evaluate effective remedial alternatives. To characterize the site, the RI will involve field investigations, including treatability studies, and a baseline risk assessment. The RI provides information to assess the risks to human health and the environment and to support the development, evaluation, and selection of appropriate response alternatives.

The EPA provides specific guidance for performance of the RI/FS. *Guidance for Conducting Remedial Investigations and Feasibility Studies Under CERCLA, Interim Final* (October 1988), shown in Figure 5-5 and available on the Internet at http://www.epa.gov/ superfund/ resources/remedy/pdf/540g-89004.pdf.

Site characterization may be conducted in one or more phases to focus sampling efforts and increase the efficiency of the investigation. Because estimates of actual or potential exposures and associated impacts on human and environmental receptors may be refined throughout the phases of the RI as new information is obtained, site characterization activities will be fully integrated with the development and evaluation of alternatives in the feasibility study. **Bench-** or **pilot-scale treatability studies** may also be conducted to provide additional data for the detailed analysis and to support the engineering design of the remedial alternatives.

EPA/540/G-89/004
OSWER Directive 9355.3-01
October 1988

Guidance for Conducting Remedial Investigations and Feasibility Studies Under CERCLA

Interim Final

Office of Emergency and Remedial Response
U.S. Environmental Protection Agency
Washington, D.C. 20460

Figure 5-5 *Guidance for Conducting Remedial Investigations and Feasibility Studies Under CERCLA, Interim Final* (October 1988).

Establishing the Applicable or Relevant and Appropriate Requirements

The RI will also establish what the applicable or relevant and appropriate requirements (ARARs) are. An ARAR is a requirement under other environmental laws that may be either "applicable" or "relevant and appropriate" to a CERCLA remedial action. A two-tier test may be applied: first, to determine whether a given requirement is applicable; then, if it is not applicable, to determine whether it is relevant and appropriate.

Applicable requirements are those cleanup standards, standards of control, and other substantive environmental protection requirements, criteria, or limitations promulgated under federal or state law that specifically address a hazardous substance, pollutant, contaminant, remedial action, location, or other circumstance at a CERCLA site. Applicability implies that the remedial action or the circumstances at the site satisfy all of the jurisdictional prerequisites of a requirement. For example, the minimum technology requirement for landfills under RCRA would apply if a new hazardous waste landfill unit (or an expansion of an existing unit) were to be built on a CERCLA site.

A **relevant and appropriate requirement** is a cleanup standard, standard of control, and other substantive environmental protection requirement, criteria, or limitation promulgated under federal or state law that, while not applicable to a hazardous substance, pollutant, contaminant, remedial action, location, or other circumstance at a CERCLA site, addresses problems or situations sufficiently similar to those encountered at the CERCLA site that its use is well suited to the particular site.

The relevance and appropriateness of a requirement can be judged by comparing a number of factors, including the characteristics of the remedial action, the hazardous substances in question, or the physical circumstances of the site with those addressed in the requirement. The objective and origin of the requirement may also be reviewed. For example, while RCRA regulations are not applicable to closing undisturbed hazardous waste in place, the RCRA regulation for closure by capping may be deemed relevant and appropriate.

> An ARAR is a requirement under other environmental laws that may be either "applicable" or "relevant and appropriate" to a CERCLA remedial action.

A requirement that is judged to be relevant and appropriate must be complied with to the same degree as if it were applicable; however, there is more discretion in this determination. It is possible in a given case for only part of a requirement to be considered relevant and appropriate, while other portions are dismissed as not relevant and appropriate.

Nonpromulgated advisories or guidance documents issued by federal or state governments do not have the status of potential ARARs. They may be considered, however, in determining the necessary level of cleanup for protection of health or environment. Such documents are also known as **TBCs,** meaning advisories or guidances **to be considered.**

ARAR Requirements

There are different types of ARAR requirements with which Superfund actions may have to comply. The classification of ARARs below is for illustrative purposes.

Ambient or chemical-specific requirements set health or risk-based concentration limits or ranges in various environmental media for specific hazardous substances, pollutants, or contaminants. Examples are CWA MCLs and CAA NAAQS. These requirements may set protective cleanup levels for the chemicals of concern in the designated media or, where one occurs in a remedial activity, may indicate an acceptable level of discharge (e.g., air emission or wastewater discharge taking into account water quality standards). If a chemical has more than one such requirement, the more stringent ARAR will be the level of compliance.

There are a limited number of actual ambient or chemical-specific requirements. In order to achieve remedies that are protective of health and the environment, it may frequently be necessary to use chemical-specific advisory levels such as **carcinogenic potency factors** or **reference doses**. While not actually ARARs, these chemical-specific advisory levels may factor significantly into the establishment of protective cleanup levels.

ARARs are triggered not by the specific chemicals present at a site but rather by the particular remedial activities that are selected to accomplish a remedy. Since there are usually several alternative actions for any remedial site, very different requirements can come into play. The action-specific requirements may specify particular performance levels, actions, or technologies, as well as specific levels (or a methodology for setting specific levels) for discharged or residual chemicals. Requirements function as action-specific requirements. Alternative remedial actions may be restricted or precluded, depending on the location or characteristics of the site and the requirements that apply to it.

Feasibility Study

A **feasibility study (FS)** is an analysis undertaken by or under the supervision of the lead agency (the state or federal agency in charge of the site) to develop and evaluate options for a remedial action. The primary objective of the FS is to ensure that appropriate remedial alternatives are developed and evaluated. Such relevant information concerning the remedial action options are presented to a decision maker and an appropriate remedy selected. The lead agency may develop a feasibility study to address a specific site problem or the entire site. The development and evaluation of alternatives will reflect the scope and complexity of the remedial action under consideration and the site problems being addressed. Development of alternatives will be fully integrated with the site characterization activities of the remedial investigation. The lead agency may include an alternatives screening step, when needed, to select a reasonable number of alternatives for detailed analysis.

CASES FOR DISCUSSION

General Electric Co. v. EPA, 360 F.3d 188, 58 ERC 1114 (C.A. D.C. 2004).

This case presents both a challenge of a decision and CERCLA's constitutionality. GE filed suit against the EPA seeking a declaratory judgment that the provisions of CERCLA relating to the unilateral administrative orders (§§ 106(a), 107(c)(3), and 113(h)) are unconstitutional under the Due Process Clause of the Fifth Amendment. GE alleged that the combination of the absence of pre-enforcement review and massive penalties for noncompliance with a UAO "imposes a classic and unconstitutional Hobson's choice: Either do nothing and risk severe punishment without meaningful recourse or comply and wait indefinitely before having any opportunity to be heard on the legality and rationality of the underlying order."

EPA moved to dismiss the amended complaint for lack of jurisdiction on the ground that § 113(h) postpones judicial review of any action under CERCLA until EPA seeks to enforce its remedial orders in court or the ordered party sues to recoup its expenses for undertaking the cleanup.

(continued)

Remedial Design/Remedial Action Costs Allocation

During the RI/FS phase, the PRP steering committee may once again find itself steeped in allocation negotiations. The RI report may have and usually does provide information on the particular chemicals and substances that are "driving" the **remedial design/remedial action (RD/RA)**. For instance, if much of the cost for the RD/RA is based on polychlorinated biphenyls (PCBs) at the site, it is likely that non-PCB-generating PRPs are not going to accept an RI/FS allocation based on each party paying an equal percentage of the costs. As such, in the RD/RA phase, the PRP group will probably have to renegotiate allocation based on waste-in material types and amounts to factor in things that are driving the RD/RA costs.

Remedial Design/Remedial Action

When the agency's Superfund **Record of Decision (ROD)** selecting a remedy is published, the remedial design/remedial action phase will begin. The RD/RA stage includes the development of the actual design of the selected remedy and implementation of the remedy through construction. A period of operation and maintenance may follow the RA activities.

The remedial design is the technical analysis and sets out procedures that follow the selected remedy for a site, and results in a detailed set of plans and specifications for implementation of the remedial action.

The remedial action for a site is the action or actions consistent with the permanent remedy taken instead of or in addition to a removal action at a site.

The remedial action may include such actions at the location of the release such as

- storage;
- confinement;
- perimeter protection using dikes, trenches, ditches, fences, earthen berms, or other enclosures;
- clay or other (asphalt or concrete) cover;
- neutralization;
- cleanup of released hazardous substances and associated contaminated materials;
- recycling or reuse, diversion, destruction, or segregation of reactive wastes;
- dredging or excavations, repair or replacement of leaking containers;
- collection of leachate and runoff;
- on-site treatment or incineration;
- provision of alternative water supplies; and
- any monitoring reasonably required to assure that such actions protect the public health and welfare and the environment and, where appropriate, post-removal site control activities.

> The remedial design/remedial action phase begins when the ROD is published.

The remedial action includes the costs of permanent relocation of residents and businesses and community facilities where the EPA determines that, alone or in combination with other measures, such relocation is more cost-effective than and environmentally preferable to the transportation, storage, treatment, destruction, or secure disposition off-site of such hazardous substances, or may otherwise be necessary to protect the public health or welfare.

A remedial action may include off-site transport and off-site storage, treatment, destruction, or secure disposition of hazardous substances and associated contaminated materials. For the purpose of the NCP, a remedial action also includes any related enforcement activities.

Figure 5-6 provides an example table of contents for an actual Superfund site ROD. The complete Record of Decision for the Final Remedial Action, J-Field Study Area Edgewood Area, Aberdeen Proving Ground, Maryland, is available on the Internet at http://www.epa.gov/superfund/sites/rods/fulltext/r0301025.pdf.

Brownfields Redevelopment

In an effort to bring back into productive use some low-level contaminated sites, now known as brownfields, a number of steps were taken. **Brownfields** are described in many ways by many different people, but generally, brownfields are abandoned pieces of land—usually in inner-city areas of surrounding communities—that are contaminated from previous industrial use. These sites do not qualify as Superfund sites because they do not pose a serious public health risk to the community. However, because of the stigma of contamination and legal barriers to redevelopment, businesses do not buy the land and the sites have essentially remained roped off, unproductive, and vacant.

Starting in late 1993, the federal government has taken a series of actions designed to clean up and redevelop brownfields to return them to productive use in these communities. For example, in November 1993, EPA Administrator Carol Browner launched the Brownfields Initiative with a $200,000 grant to Cleveland, Ohio, for a pilot project with state and local officials to determine the best way to develop a national model for revitalizing these areas across the country. Since 1993, Cleveland has leveraged $4.5 million for environmental cleanup and improvements for the brownfields properties. Several new businesses have located in the area, over 180 new jobs have been created, and payroll tax base improvement alone netted over $1 million for the local economy.

Since January 1995, the federal government has worked to remove the legal obstacles to development of brownfields sites by taking more than 30,000 sites off the Superfund inventory. By taking these low-priority sites off the list, it has relieved potential developers of unnecessary red tape, removed the stigma of being on the Superfund inventory, and theoretically gotten the sites on track for redevelopment.

The federal government has also provided brownfields seed money across the country, with a total of 113 such grants of up to $200,000 each. As of mid-1997, a total of nearly $20 million has been awarded. The program brings together people who live near contaminated land,

Final Remedial Action, J-Field Study Area — RECORD OF DECISION

TABLE OF CONTENTS

Section — Page

1. DECLARATION OF THE RECORD OF DECISION (ROD) 1-1

1.1 SITE NAME AND LOCATION 1-1

1.2 STATEMENT OF BASIS AND PURPOSE 1-1

1.3 ASSESSMENT OF THE SITE 1-3

1.4 DESCRIPTION OF THE SELECTED REMEDY 1-6

1.5 STATUTORY DETERMINATIONS 1-8

2. DECISION SUMMARY 2-1

2.1 SITE NAME, LOCATION, AND DESCRIPTION 2-1

2.2 SITE HISTORY AND ENFORCEMENT ACTIVITIES 2-6

2.2.1 History of the J-Field Study Area 2-6
2.2.2 History Site Investigations and Enforcement Activities 2-6

2.3 HIGHLIGHTS OF COMMUNITY PARTICIPATION 2-12

2.4 SCOPE AND ROLE OF ACTION 2-12

2.5 SUMMARY OF SITE CHARACTERISTICS 2-13

2.6 CURRENT AND POTENTIAL FUTURE SITE AND RESOURCE USES 2-15

2.7 SUMMARY OF SITE RISKS 2-15

2.8 REMEDIATION OF THE J-FIELD SURFICIAL AQUIFER 2-15

2.8.1 Description of the Alternatives 2-19
2.8.2 Summary of Comparative Analysis of Alternatives 2-27
2.8.3 The Selected Remedy 2-38
2.8.4 The Statutory Determinations 2-39

2.9 PERFORMANCE STANDARDS 2-40

3. RESPONSIVENESS SUMMARY 3-1

3.1 OVERVIEW 3-1

3.2 BACKGROUND ON COMMUNITY INVOLVEMENT 3-1

3.3 SUMMARY OF COMMENTS RECEIVED DURING THE PUBLIC COMMENT PERIOD AND AGENCY RESPONSES 3-2

3.4 COMMENTS FROM THE MARCH PUBLIC MEETINGS 3-6

3.5 WRITTEN COMMENTS RECEIVED 3-6

4. BIBLIOGRAPHY 4-1

MKD1|O:\11785001.002\J-FIELD ROD\JFIELDFINALROD_FM3.DOC — iii — 09/20/01

Figure 5-6 Example Table of Contents for a Superfund ROD: Record of Decision, Final Remedial Action, J-Field Study Area Edgewood Area, Aberdeen Proving Ground, Maryland.

businesses that want to get land cleaned up, community leaders, investors, lenders, and developers. Together, they seek ways to restore abandoned sites to new uses, increasing property values, stimulating tax revenues, creating jobs and job training opportunities, and revitalizing inner-city neighborhoods.

President Clinton's fiscal year 1998 balanced budget plan contained a targeted tax incentive to spur the private sector to clean up and redevelop brownfields in economically distressed rural and urban areas. This $2 billion tax incentive was expected to leverage $10 billion in private sector investment, helping to revitalize some 30,000 brownfield sites. Under the proposal, businesses would be able to expense the costs of cleaning up these properties in the year in which the costs were incurred, rather than capitalizing such costs over the life of the property. This tax proposal provided financial incentives for the private sector to revitalize these areas.

Small Business Liability Relief and Brownfields Revitalization Act

On January 11, 2002, President George W. Bush signed the Small Business Liability Relief and Brownfields Revitalization Act (Brownfields Act). Pub. L. No. 107–118, 115 Stat. 2356. The Brownfields Act amended CERCLA in a number of ways, including granting liability relief to small businesses and establishing a municipal solid waste exemption. It also promoted the redevelopment of brownfield sites by establishing new grant programs and by providing protections for prospective purchasers, limiting EPA's enforcement authority over sites cleaned up under state programs and by other mechanisms.

De Micromis Exemption

The Brownfields Act, at 42 U.S.C. § 9607(o)(1, 2, and 3), provides that hazardous substance generators who arranged for the disposal or transportation of less than 110 gallons of liquid materials or less than 200 pounds of solid materials before April 1, 2001, are exempt from CERCLA liability at National Priorities List sites. An exception, though, is that the exemption does not apply if the EPA determines that the hazardous substances in question contributed significantly to the cost of the response action or natural resource restoration, or if the person has failed to respond to an information request or has otherwise impeded a response or natural resource damage action.

Strikingly, the EPA's determination in this regard is not subject to judicial review!

Municipal Solid Waste Exemption

The Brownfields Act, at 42 U.S.C. § 9607(p)(1, 2, and 3), provides that several types of entities are now exempt from CERCLA liability at NPL sites if all they sent to the site was municipal solid waste (MSW): (1) residential property owners, operators, and lessees; (2) businesses with 100 or fewer employees and that qualify as a small business under the Small Business Act; and (3) nonprofit organizations with 100 or fewer employees. The exemption does not apply if the EPA determines that the MSW could contribute significantly to the cost of the response action or natural resource restoration, or if the entity had failed to respond to an information request or was otherwise impeding a response or natural resource damage action. Again, the EPA's determination is not subject to judicial review.

Brownfields Revitalization

Title II of the Brownfields Act was designed to spur cleanup at contaminated sites where the federal government is not likely to become involved. It codified and increased funding for EPA's existing brownfield grant program and created new grant programs. It also included liability protection for prospective purchasers and bars the EPA from taking enforcement action at sites addressed by state cleanup programs.

Bona Fide Prospective Purchaser Defense

The Brownfields Act, at 42 U.S.C. § 9601(40), exempts "bona fide prospective purchasers" from CERCLA liability. Under this provision, a purchaser will not be liable if the purchaser bought the property after enactment of this Act and if

- the release occurred before its ownership;
- the purchaser conducted the appropriate inquiries into the previous ownership and uses of the site;
- the purchaser complies with release reporting requirements;
- the purchaser exercises due care regarding the contamination; and

- the purchaser complies with institutional controls, cooperates with EPA, responds to information requests, and is not affiliated with the party responsible for the contamination.

Innocent Landowners

The Brownfields Act also defined more precisely the degree of appropriate inquiry required to establish innocent landowner status. The EPA was required to issue new regulations that established the standards and practices for carrying out the appropriate inquiries, including the use of an environmental professional for the inquiry, interviews with past and present owners and occupants of the site, and reviews of historical sources. The new final rule, published in the *Federal Register* on November 1, 2005, will apply to all property acquisitions that close on or after November 1, 2006.

Although the final rule dropped some of the harsher provisions of the EPA's proposed standard, the final rule differs from the industry standard in ASTM Standard E 1527-00 in several significant respects, which may have a significant effect upon the cost and scope of environmental site assessments conducted as part of property acquisitions. In response to the rule, ASTM published an updated standard, E 1527-05, which incorporates the new requirements of the EPA's final rule. Under the rule, prospective purchasers failing to follow the new requirements will not qualify for the "innocent purchaser," "adjacent landowner," or "bone fide prospective purchaser" defenses to liability under CERCLA in any post-closing litigation.

Contentious Superfund Issues

Contentious issues under CERCLA and in the implementation of the Superfund program are worth mentioning. For instance, can previous owners and operators of a Superfund site be held responsible for their activities if such activities occurred many years before CERCLA was enacted? In a quick answer: yes, they can. *See,* for example, *United States v. Reilly Tar,* 546 F. Supp. 1100 (D. Minn. 1982) and *Ohio v. Georgeoff,* 562 F. Supp. 1300 (N.D. Ohio 1983).

Joint and several liability is an issue that tends to generate animosity among CERCLA PRPs. Consider that, conceptually, a PRP with a .0035% waste-in volume is jointly and severally just as responsible for the site cleanup as a PRP that has a 50% waste-in volume. *See,* for instance. *United States v. A & F Materials,* 578 F. Supp. 1249 (S.D. Ill. 1984); *United States v. NEPACCO,* 579 F. Supp. 823 (W.D. Mo. 1984); and *United States v. Ward,* 618 F. Supp. 884 (E.D. N.C. 1985).

Can a parent corporation that actively participated in, and exercised control over, the operations of a subsidiary be held liable as an operator of a polluting facility owned or operated by the subsidiary? The Supreme Court, in *United States v. Bestfoods, et al,* 524 U.S. 51, 55 (1998), answered no, unless the corporate veil is pierced. But a corporate parent that actively participated in, and exercised control over, the operations of the facility itself may be held directly liable in its own right as an operator of the facility.

These issues and others continue to be reviewed by Congress, the EPA, and others.

Conclusion

CERCLA involves the federal law to clean up and remediate hazardous waste sites. In that process, paralegals are involved in obtaining and organizing information for responding and complying with government actions and orders under CERCLA § 106, including such activities as are described in the Introduction to this book. Paralegals may also be actively involved both in bringing and in defending CERCLA § 107 cost recovery and CERCLA § 113 contribution suits.

Section 104 of CERCLA allows paralegals to become involved in responding to the federal government and authorized state governments in their broad inquiries to persons that may have documents and other information or beliefs concerning a hazardous, potentially hazardous, or suspected hazardous waste site. Paralegals may be actively involved in the collection, organization, and drafting of the § 104 information response.

Finally, where the EPA does not prepare an NBAR, environmental paralegals may find themselves preparing one. Private NBARs serve as a tool to promote settlements and cooperation, and to allocate 100% of the response costs among the PRPs. Appendix A to this book, "Data Analysis: Building a Non-Binding Allocation of Responsibility: A Model Data Structure," is provided to assist paralegals in preparation of a private NBAR.

GLOSSARY OF CERCLA TERMS

ambient or chemical specific requirements. Under the CERCLA ARARs provisions, ambient or chemical specific requirements set health- or risk-based concentration limits or ranges in various environmental media for specific hazardous substances, pollutants, or contaminants. Examples are CWA MCLs and CAA NAAQS.

ARAR. Applicable or relevant and appropriate requirement. Requirements under other environmental laws that may be "applicable" or "relevant and appropriate" to a CERCLA remedial action.

ATSDR. Agency for Toxic Substances and Disease Registry.

Brownfield. A brownfield is, generally, an abandoned piece of land—usually in the inner-city areas of surrounding communities—that is contaminated from previous industrial use, making the property otherwise unusable.

CERCLA. Comprehensive Environmental Response, Compensation, and Liability Act (SARA or Superfund).

CERCLIS. Comprehensive Environmental Response, Compensation, and Liability Information System. The abbreviation for the CERCLA Information System, the EPA's database management system that inventories and tracks releases addressed or needing to be addressed by the Superfund program. CERCLIS contains the official inventory of CERCLA sites and supports the EPA's site planning and tracking functions.

cleanup. An action taken to deal with a release or threat of release of a hazardous substance that could affect humans, the environment, or both.

Community Relations Program. The EPA's program to inform and encourage public participation in the Superfund process and to respond to community concerns.

contaminant. Any physical, chemical, biological, or radiological substance or matter that has an adverse effect on air, water, or soil.

de micromis **exemption.** The Brownfields Act provides that hazardous substance generators who arranged for the disposal or transportation of less than 110 gallons of liquid materials or less than 200 pounds of solid materials before April 1, 2001, are exempt from CERCLA liability at National Priorities List sites.

de minimis **party.** Someone who has been identified as a PRP at a Superfund site, where either: (1) both the amount and the hazardous effects of the substance the PRP contributed are minimal in comparison to other hazardous substances at the facility, or (2) the PRP is the owner of the facility; did not allow generation, treatment, storage, or disposal at the facility; did not contribute to the release at the facility; and did not purchase the property knowing that it was used for the generation, transportation, treatment, storage, or disposal of hazardous substances.

EE/CA. Engineering evaluation/cost analysis.

ERA. Expedited response action.

facility. Physical structures of the plant.

Feasibility Study (FS). An analysis undertaken by the lead agency (the state or federal agency in charge of the site) under CERCLA authority to develop and evaluate options for a remedial action.

hazardous waste. By-products of society that can pose a substantial or potential threat to human health or the environment when improperly managed.

HRS. Hazard Ranking System. Method used by the EPA to evaluate relative potential of hazardous substance releases to cause health or safety problems or ecological or environmental damage.

NBAR. Nonbinding preliminary allocation of responsibility. An allocation by the EPA among potentially responsible parties of percentages of total response costs at a facility.

NCP. National Contingency Plan. The EPA's basic policy directive for federal response actions under CERCLA.

NPL. National Priorities List. The list of uncontrolled hazardous substance releases that are priorities for long-term remedial evaluation and response. Compiled by the EPA under CERCLA.

OSC. On-Scene Coordinator.

PA. Preliminary assessment. Review of existing information and an on-site and off-site reconnaissance, if appropriate, to determine if a release may require additional investigation or action.

PRPs. Potentially responsible party(ies). Persons who either generated, stored, transported, treated, or disposed of CERCLA hazardous substances.

RA. Remedial action. See RD/RA.

RD. Remedial design. See RD/RA.

RD/RA. Remedial design/remedial action. The RD/RA stage of a CERCLA remedial action that includes the development of the actual design of the selected remedy and implementation of the remedy through construction.

RI/FS. Remedial investigation/feasibility study. The remedial action cleanup plan or remedy selection closely regulated under the NCP. Under the NCP, there will first be an RI/FS. The purpose of the RI/FS is to assess site conditions (remedial investigation) and evaluate alternatives (feasibility study) to the extent necessary to select a remedy.

ROD. Agency's Superfund Record of Decision.

RQ. Reportable Quantities program requiring notification to the National Response Center.

SARA. Superfund Amendments and Reauthorization Act of 1986.

Section 104(e) information request. A form of information demand letter used by the EPA under the authority of CERCLA § 104(e). The EPA has published various policies and guidance documents that can be referred to in preparation of § 104(e) responses.

Section 106 enforcement action. Under CERCLA § 106, responsible parties can be ordered to institute an emergency removal action or to effect a remedial cleanup.

Section 107(a) cost recovery action. Under CERCLA § 107(a), responsible parties are liable for all response costs not inconsistent with the NCP incurred by the U.S. government, a state, or an Indian tribe. The costs of a cleanup that have been incurred may be recovered through the mechanism of a cost recovery action.

Section 113 contribution action. Under CERCLA § 113, responsible parties are subject to joint and several liability for response costs at a Superfund site. These provisions detail the specific relevant criteria that a court may use in equitably allocating the response costs.

site. The whole property in interest.

SI. Site inspection. On-site investigation to determine whether there is a release or potential release and the nature of the associated threats.

Superfund site. Any land in the United States that has been contaminated by hazardous waste and identified by the EPA or state agency as a candidate for cleanup because it poses a risk to human health, the environment, or both.

To be considered. Nonpromulgated advisories or guidance documents issued by federal or state governments do not have the status of potential CERCLA ARARs. They may be considered, however, in determining the necessary level of cleanup for protection of health or environment. Such documents are also known as TBCs.

BIBLIOGRAPHY

CERCLA Enforcement: A Practitioner's Compendium of Essential EPA Guidance and Policy Documents, 2 (Carole Stern Switzer et al. eds., A.B.A., Section of Environment, Energy, and Resources 2000).

Frank, William Harris, & Timothy B. Atkeson, *Superfund: Litigation and Cleanup* (BNA 1985).

Green, Janice L., *CERCLA and the Bankruptcy Code*, Temp. Envtl. L. & Tech. J. 171, 171–201 (1992).

Green, Michael D., *Successors and CERCLA: The Imperfect Analogy to Products Liability and an Alternative Proposal*, Nw. U. L. Rev. 897, 897–936 (1993).

Hyson, John M., *Private Cost Recovery Actions Under CERCLA* (Envtl. L. Inst. 2003).

Lazarus, Richard J., *Pursuing "Environmental Justice": The Distributional Effects of Environmental Protection*, Nw. U. L. Rev. 787, 787–857 (1993).

McGonigal, Melissa A., *Extended Liability Under CERCLA: Easement Holders and the Scope of Control*, Nw. U. L. Rev. 992, 992–1036 (1993).

OSWER Directives System Catalog Guidance and Policy Issued Through March, 1990 (U.S. EPA 1990).

Simonsen, Craig B., *Environmental Law Resource Guide* (CBC 1995).

Superfund Deskbook: 1988 Edition (Envtl. L. Inst. 1988).

Switzer, Carole Stern, & Lynn A. Bulan, *CERCLA: Comprehensive Environmental Response, Compensation, and Liability Act (Superfund)* (A.B.A., Section of Environment, Energy, and Resources 2000).

DISCUSSION QUESTIONS

1. CERCLIS is the abbreviation for the CERCLA Information System, the EPA's database management system that inventories and tracks releases addressed or needing to be addressed by the Superfund program. CERCLIS contains the official inventory of CERCLA sites and supports the EPA's site planning and tracking functions. Sites are not removed from the database after completion of evaluations in order to document that these evaluations took place and to preclude the possibility that they be needlessly repeated. Inclusion of a specific site or area in the CERCLIS database does not represent a determination of any party's liability, nor does it represent a finding that any response action is necessary.

   Q. How can a paralegal use information taken from the CERCLIS in support of:

      1. An environmental enforcement case against your new client?

      2. A citizens' group wishing to bring a suit against an alleged noncomplying source?

      3. A transaction in which you represent the buyer in a multiple facility purchase?

   Q. Where can paper and electronic sources of the CERCLIS be located?

2. In a typical CERCLA Superfund site case, there are many PRPs that generated the waste-in to the site. The waste-in was generated many years ago. The generators have copies of executed contracts and waste hauling and disposal agreements where, for a premium already long ago paid, the waste hauler/disposal site had accepted any liability for the generators' waste.

   Q. Is there equity in dividing the cost to clean up the site among the waste generators and the site owners and operators?

   Q. How does your previous answer change if the owners and operators are defunct or unfindable?

3. If the government has not prepared an NBAR for a Superfund site where your client appears to be the largest waste-in contributor:

   Q. In what ways can you justify to your client the cost of developing your own NBAR?

   Q. How would you propose to collect the information necessary to build the NBAR?

   Q. What structure would you propose for the NBAR database?

COMPUTER LABORATORY PROJECTS

1. Review and report on (in a memorandum) the key points and procedures given in the U.S. EPA *Final Guidance on Preparing Waste-In Lists and Volumetric Rankings Under CERCLA*, which is found on the Internet at http://www.epa.gov/compliance/resources/policies/cleanup/superfund/guide-volumet-rpt.pdf.

INTERNET SITES

- The full text of the CERCLA is on the Internet at http://www.epa.gov/superfund/action/law/cercla.htm.

- The EPA Office of Solid Waste and Emergency Response (OSWER) is on the Internet at http://www.epa.gov/swerrims.

CHAPTER 6

The Emergency Planning and Community Right-to-Know Act

James F. Berry[1]

OBJECTIVES

The objectives of this chapter are for students to:

- Learn the terminology associated with the EPCRA.
- Learn the concepts and ideas that underlie the EPCRA law and regulatory program.
- Learn about specific sections and provisions of the EPCRA law and regulations.
- Learn about the processes and procedures used by the government and other parties to comply with and to enforce the law under EPCRA.
- Learn about the particular jobs and functions that are performed by paralegals working for attorneys in EPCRA cases.

History of the Act

In 1986, Congress enacted the **Superfund Amendments and Reauthorization Act (SARA)** amending the **Comprehensive Environmental Response, Compensation, and Liability Act of 1980,** 42 U.S.C. §§ 9601 to 9675 (1997) **(CERCLA).**

Title III of SARA established a new law known as the **Emergency Planning and Community Right-to-Know Act,** 42 U.S.C. §§ 11001 to 11050 (1997) **(EPCRA).** With the passage of EPCRA, Congress

---

[1] The author acknowledges and thanks E. Lynn Grayson for her work on earlier drafts of this chapter.

expanded the role of the federal government into areas such as emergency planning that traditionally had been regulated by state and local governments and, in addition, granted citizens the right to obtain information about potential chemical hazards in their communities. Regulations under the Act are found at 40 C.F.R. §§ 350 to 372 (1997).

The passage of EPCRA resulted, in part, from the December 1984 tragedy in Bhopal, India, that focused worldwide attention on the dangers of hazardous materials. In India, a major release of methyl isocyanate killed more than 2000 people and injured 150,000 others. The statute is designed to bring together industry, government, and the general public to address the threat of accidental releases.

EPCRA has four major provisions:

1. Emergency planning (§§ 301–303)
2. Emergency release notification (§ 304)
3. Hazardous chemical storage reporting requirements (§§ 311–312)
4. Toxic chemical release inventory (§ 313)

Under EPCRA's Emergency Planning provisions, each state has designated a State Emergency Response Commission, or SERC. Each SERC is then responsible for implementing EPCRA provisions within its state.

In addition, each SERC has designated local emergency planning districts and appointed Local Emergency Planning Committees, or LEPCs (about 3500 so far), for each district. It is the responsibility of each SERC to supervise and coordinate the activities of each LEPC, to establish procedures for receiving and processing public requests for information collected under EPCRA, and to review local emergency response plans.

Additional information can be found at the EPA's Web site at http://yosemite.epa.gov/oswer/ceppoweb.nsf/content/epcraOverview. htm. Other EPA Web sites provide further information on SERCs at http://www.epa.gov/ceppo/serclist.htm on LEPCs at http://www.epa. gov/swercepp/lepclist.htm.

Local LEPC membership must include, at a minimum, local officials including police, fire, civil defense, public health, transportation, and environmental professionals, as well as representatives of facilities subject to the emergency planning requirements, community groups, and the media. The LEPCs must develop an emergency response plan, review it at least annually, and provide information about chemicals in the community to citizens.

The law requires states to receive and to disseminate two types of chemical data: **community right-to-know information** and **toxic chemical release information**.

The law requires states to receive and disseminate two types of chemical data:

➤ Community right-to-know information
➤ Toxic chemical release information

Community right-to-know data include information on both the hazards associated with certain chemicals and the amounts that are produced, stored, or handled in certain facilities. EPCRA § 311 requires businesses to submit **Material Safety Data Sheets (MSDSs)** or a list of all chemicals for all substances present at the facility if the substances are regulated by the U.S. **Occupational Safety and Health Administration (OSHA).** An inventory of these same chemicals is required by EPCRA § 312. Both types of right-to-know reports must be submitted to the SERC, the LEPC, and local fire departments. The U.S. **Environmental Protection Agency (EPA)** estimates that more than 50,000 chemicals and chemical mixtures are covered by these requirements.

The EPA, however, does make the list of EPCRA chemicals easy to find. Figure 6-1 shows the EPA's *Consolidated List of Chemicals Subject to the Emergency Planning and Community Right-to-Know Act*. The list is on the Internet at http://www.epa.gov/ceppo/pubs/title3.pdf.

The second type of chemical data collected concerns toxic chemical releases. Under EPCRA § 313, facilities must complete a special form (the **Form R**) reporting releases of listed toxic chemicals into the environment. Then the Form R must be submitted to the EPA and a state agency designated by the state's governor. Based on the information in these forms, the EPA must establish a national inventory of toxic chemical releases and make that inventory available to government officials and the public. Although the responsibility for establishing an accessible electronic database is given to the EPA, states must make the toxic release forms available. State agencies are often the focus of public information requests.

An important goal of EPCRA is improving state and local preparedness for hazardous materials incidents through more effective emergency planning and notification.

Emergency Planning

As suggested earlier, one important goal of EPCRA is to improve state and local preparedness for hazardous materials incidents through

United States Environmental Protection Agency	Office of Solid Waste and Emergency Response (5104)	EPA 550-B-01-003 October 2001 www.epa.gov/ceppo

EPA

CEPP

LIST OF LISTS

Consolidated List of Chemicals Subject to the Emergency Planning and Community Right-To-Know Act (EPCRA) and Section 112(r) of the Clean Air Act

- EPCRA Section 302 Extremely Hazardous Substances
- CERCLA Hazardous Substances
- EPCRA Section 313 Toxic Chemicals
- CAA 112(r) Regulated Chemicals For Accidental Release Prevention

Chemical Emergency Preparedness and Prevention Office   *Printed on recycled paper*

Figure 6-1   The EPA's *Consolidated List of Chemicals Subject to the Emergency Planning and Community Right-to-Know Act.*

more effective emergency planning and notification. Emergency planning requirements are designed to help communities prepare for and respond to emergencies involving hazardous substances. EPCRA contains three important planning requirements to assist states in emergency preparedness activities.

First, EPCRA requires the appointment of a State Emergency Response Commission in each state that will be responsible for implementing its provisions. As authorized by EPCRA, states had the option to designate one or more existing emergency response organizations as the SERC. States also had the option to create a new entity staffed with individuals with technical expertise in the emergency response field. Many states determined that the best selection for a SERC would be the existing emergency management agencies accustomed to managing natural and manmade emergencies. The identity and contact person for a state's SERC may be obtained by contacting the **EPA EPCRA Hotline,** contacting EPA regional offices, or at the EPA Web sites listed earlier.

The next planning requirement imposed by EPCRA is the designation of local emergency planning districts and the appointment of Local Emergency Planning Committees. Within the area served by each SERC, EPCRA requires the establishment of local emergency planning districts with LEPCs appointed in each district to direct and to manage local planning activities. In creating such districts, the SERC was authorized to designate existing political subdivisions in a state or to develop multijurisdictional planning organizations. Most SERCs opted to designate existing political subdivisions such as counties to act as emergency planning districts.

Following the designation of the local emergency planning districts, EPCRA required the formation of LEPCs within each district. Pursuant to EPCRA provisions, the SERC was required to appoint LEPCs consisting of representatives from the following groups or organizations:

- law enforcement;
- civil defense;
- firefighting;
- first aid;
- health;
- local environmental, hospital, and transportation personnel;
- broadcast and print media;
- community groups; and
- owners and operators subject to the provisions of EPCRA.

The main purpose of the LEPC is to develop an emergency plan for its jurisdictional area. The identity and contact person for any LEPC may be obtained by contacting that state's SERC.

The final emergency planning mandate imposed by EPCRA requires that each LEPC develop an emergency plan to respond to chemical emergencies in its district. The emergency plan should include the following elements (see the EPA's Web site at http://yosemite. epa.gov/oswer/ceppoweb.nsf/content/epcraOverview.htm):

- Identification of facilities and transportation routes of extremely hazardous substances
- A description of emergency response procedures, on and off site
- Designation of a community coordinator and facility coordinator(s) to implement the plan
- An outline of emergency notification procedures
- Descriptions of how to determine the probable affected area and population by releases
- Descriptions of local emergency equipment and facilities and the persons responsible for them
- An outline of evacuation plans
- Descriptions of training programs for emergency responders (including schedules)
- Methods and schedules for exercising emergency response plans

Once the emergency plans are submitted to the SERC, they are to be exercised and revised annually.

Reporting Requirements

In general, EPCRA reporting requirements are designed to assist state and local authorities to be better prepared to respond to chemical releases through increased awareness of releases. Reporting requirements also serve industry by improving communications between facility operators and emergency response personnel so that appropriate and timely actions are undertaken to address releases.

The reporting obligations and frequency of the reports required under EPCRA differ. Some reports are to be filed one time, while others may occur each time there is a chemical release beyond a certain reportable quantity from a facility. The differences in the reporting obligations involve the purpose for which the reports may be used. Some reports under EPCRA will be used solely for emergency planning objectives, while others are required to ensure timely emergency response actions. The various reporting obligations required under EPCRA are discussed in greater detail throughout the chapter. Also see Table 6-1 and Table 6-2 for additional reporting-related information.

EPCRA's reporting requirements are designed to assist state and local authorities to be better prepared to respond to chemical releases through increased and earlier awareness of releases.

TABLE 6-1   The Three Types of Chemical Information Required by EPCRA

Material Safety Data Sheets

Material Safety Data Sheets (MSDSs) are designed primarily to inform workers about the potential hazards associated with exposure to chemicals handled in the workplace. MSDSs typically are prepared by the industries that manufacture or handle the chemicals.

No standard format for the MSDS is specified but all required information must be included. The MSDS must be written in English and, at a minimum, must contain the following:

- The identity (any chemical or common name) that is used on the container label
- The chemical and common name of all ingredients having known health hazards if present in concentrations greater than 1%, and for carcinogens, if present at 0.1% or more
- The physical and chemical characteristics of the hazardous components
- The physical and health hazards including signs and symptoms of exposure and prior and/or existing contraindicating medical conditions
- The primary routes of entry
- Any known exposure limits (OSHA PELs or ACGIH TLVs)
- Whether the hazardous chemical is listed in the NTP Annual Report on Carcinogens or is a potential carcinogen according to IARC or OSHA
- Precautions for safe handling and use, and procedures for spill/leak cleanup
- Control measures
- Emergency first aid procedures
- Date of preparation
- The name, address, and telephone number of the company or the responsible employee distributing the MSDS

When an MSDS is prepared, the chemical has to be evaluated based on the mandatory hazards determination requirements. When uncertainty exists concerning a chemical's hazards, the preparer should be conservative in the evaluation to ensure employee protection. For further information, see the OSHA's Web site at http://www.osha-slc.gov/SLTC/hazardcommunications/index.html.

MSDSs are the cornerstone of worker and community right-to-know laws.

MSDSs must be distributed to workers and appropriate authorities under a variety of laws, including the federal Occupational Safety and Health Act (OSHA) of 1970, state worker and/or community right-to-know laws, and EPCRA. Under EPCRA § 311, facilities required to prepare MSDSs for OSHA regulations also must submit copies of MSDSs or a list of OSHA-regulated chemicals to the State Emergency Response Commission, the Local Emergency Planning Committee, and local fire departments. Given the quantity of hazardous chemicals, many states request lists as opposed to MSDSs.

(continued)

TABLE 6-1 The Three Types of Chemical Information Required by EPCRA—*continued*

Section 312 Chemical Inventory Form: Tier I and Tier II Information

Any facility owner or operator required to submit MSDSs must also submit a § 312 chemical inventory form to the SERC, LEPC, and local fire department. The inventory form can be either **Tier I (aggregate information by hazard type)** or **Tier II (chemical-specific information)**. Section 312 inventory forms differ from MSDSs in that they present information on the amount and location of hazardous chemicals that a facility handles on a daily basis as well as information on the hazard presented by the chemical.

The Tier I form requests aggregate information on a hazardous chemical according to the type of health and physical hazards that it presents. The Tier I form also requests an estimate, in ranges, of the maximum and average daily amounts of the hazardous chemical and its general location within the facility.

The Tier II form requests more chemical-specific information, including
* Chemical or common name as indicated on the MSDS
* Physical and health hazards of a specific chemical
* Estimates of the maximum and average daily amount of a chemical
* The number of days the chemical is present on site at the facility
* The manner of storage and its specific location within the facility
* An indication of whether a facility elects to withhold location information from public disclosure

The hazardous chemicals covered under § 312 are the same as those covered under § 311. Tier II includes Tier I information. In order to streamline the report processing, many states require facilities annually to submit Tier II rather than Tier I information.

Toxic Release Inventory Form (Form R)

The Toxic Release Inventory (TRI) Form R, revised and published annually by the EPA, must be filled out by owners and operators of facilities that release certain quantities of chemicals into the environment. The TRI consists of questions regarding the use of toxic chemicals and how they are disposed of or released into the environment during normal (and accidental) operation. Facility owners and operators must provide estimates of the range of chemicals released into the environment from **fugitive** or **nonpoint** air emission sources, stacks or other points sources, water discharge points, underground injection points, and land disposal. Amendments to the TRI Form R also require that certain pollution prevention information be reported.

Section 313 reporting is required for certain classes and quantities of listed toxic chemicals. The EPA administrator may, by rule, add or delete a chemical from the list at any time. **Covered facilities** (those with ten or more full-time employees and within the **Standard Industrial Classification (SIC) Codes** 20 through 39) that manufacture, process, or use any of the toxic chemicals above the threshold planning quantity limits established by EPCRA must annually submit TRI Form Rs on July 1. One Form R for each toxic chemical reported must be prepared and submitted to the EPA and the state agency designated by the governor.

TABLE 6-2 Key Deadlines

Requirement	Deadline
Covered manufacturing and reporting facilities submit hazardous chemical reports to EPA and designated state agencies.	Annually on March 1
Facilities submit toxic chemical release reports to EPA and designated state agencies.	Annually on July 1
Covered nonmanufacturing facilities submit hazardous chemical inventory reports to SERCs, LEPCs, and fire departments.	Annually on March 1

CASES FOR DISCUSSION

Fertilizer Institute v. EPA, 163 F.3d 774, 47 ERC 1545, 29 Envtl. L. Rep. 20,349, (3d Cir. 1998).

In this case, the EPA proposed a rule adding 313 chemicals to the Inventory pursuant to EPCRA. Subsequently, the EPA adopted a final rule that included 286 of the 313 chemicals originally proposed. Nitrate compounds were among the chemicals added based on chronic health effects, specifically because nitrate compounds cause human infants to develop methemoglobinemia, a condition that prevents proper transportation throughout the body of oxygen via red blood cells and causes damage to vital organs. The EPA characterized this consequence to be a "severe or irreversible . . . chronic health effect," one of the criteria for listing under the statute.

TFI, a trade association representing the fertilizer industry whose members use nitrate compounds, filed a complaint in the district court challenging the EPA's placement of nitrate compounds on the Inventory. TFI gave three reasons for its challenge to the nitrates listing: (1) inadequate notice of the EPA's intent to place nitrates on the list under the EPA's interpretation and application of chronic health effects; (2) inadequate response to the comments submitted by TFI; and (3) misapplication of the statutory criteria, which resulted in the EPA's overstepping its authority under § 11023(d).

(continued)

CASES FOR DISCUSSION

Reviewing the overall record, the district court held that the EPA provided adequate notice to the parties, including "particularly sophisticated commenters like TFI who are familiar with nitrate compounds." The district court also concluded that the EPA adequately responded to the comments submitted by several organizations, including TFI. The court observed that the criticisms challenged the EPA's conclusions but not the evidence the agency relied on in reaching them. Finally the district court concluded that the EPA had shown that the record supported the decision to include nitrates because of the chronic health effects they can produce in infants.

Thus, the district court upheld the agency's addition of nitrates to the Inventory and granted summary judgment in favor of the EPA. The Court of Appeals affirmed.

Section 302

EPCRA § 302 requires the owner or operator of any facility where **Extremely Hazardous Substances (EHSs)** are produced, used, or stored in quantities greater than the **Threshold Planning Quantity (TPQ)** to report. Any facility that has any of the listed chemicals at or above its threshold quantity must notify the SERC and LEPC within sixty days after it first receives a shipment or produces the substance on site. The facility also must notify the LEPC of a facility representative who will participate in the emergency planning process. The facility must promptly provide information to the LEPC necessary for developing and implementing the emergency plan if it is requested.

Paralegals may be instrumental in the compilation, analysis, and completion of the EPCRA § 302 submissions. When this type of information is deemed necessary in a particular case or for a facility or corporate transaction, paralegals may be asked to obtain these reports filed at some earlier time.

Section 304

EPCRA § 304 requires the owner or operator of a facility to report immediately a release of a CERCLA hazardous substance or EHS that meets or exceeds the **Reportable Quantity (RQ)**. The report must be provided to the SERC and the LEPC for any area likely to be affected by the release. This report is typically provided to the SERC and the LEPC by telephone.

Releases reported under EPCRA § 304 also require a written follow-up emergency notice. The purpose of this additional report is to provide the SERC and the LEPC with new information that may not have been known at the time of the original notification.

Under CERCLA § 103(a), a related reporting obligation exists requiring notification following certain chemical releases. CERCLA § 103(a) requires a person in charge of a vessel or an offshore or onshore facility to report certain releases of hazardous substances as soon as he or she has knowledge of such release. This report is to the **National Response Center (NRC)** and typically is provided by telephone or in person. As with EPCRA § 304, specific reportable quantities must be triggered before release reporting is required.

An emergency notification must include the following:

- The chemical name
- An indication of whether the substance is extremely hazardous
- An estimate of the quantity released into the environment
- The time and duration of the release
- Whether the release occurred into air, water, and/or land
- Any known or anticipated acute or chronic health risks associated with the emergency, and, where necessary, advice regarding medical attention for exposed individuals
- Proper precautions, such as evacuation or sheltering in place
- Name and telephone number of the contact person

In addition, a written follow-up notice must be submitted to the SERC and LEPC as soon as practicable after the release. The follow-up notice must update information included in the initial notice and provide information on actual response actions taken and advice regarding medical attention necessary for citizens exposed (see 40 C.F.R. part 355).

Section 311

EPCRA § 311 requires the owner or operator of any facility that must prepare or have material safety data sheets under the Occupational Safety and Health Administration Act of 1970 and regulations promulgated thereunder to submit copies of those MSDSs or a list of chemicals in those substances. EPCRA establishes threshold quantity levels that must be met before reporting is required. The MSDSs or the chemical list must have been submitted to the SERC, the LEPC, and the local fire department by October 17, 1987. After that, updates and revisions must be submitted within ninety days of any new submission to OSHA or awareness of significant new information.

Approximately 500,000 products have MSDSs. These are available in OSHA's hazard communication standard (see http://www.osha-slc.gov/SLTC/hazardcommunications/index.html). Section 311 requires facilities that have MSDSs for chemicals held above certain quantities to submit either copies of their MSDSs or a list of MSDS chemicals to the SERC, the LEPC, and local fire department.

Most SERCs, LEPCs, and local fire departments prefer to receive the chemical list, as opposed to the MSDSs. The storage and management of thousands and thousands of MSDSs from regulated facilities are, in many cases, more than the state and local entities are capable of handling.

Paralegals may be instrumental in the compilation, analysis, and completion of the EPCRA § 311 submissions. Just as with the § 302 submission, when this type of information is deemed necessary in a particular case or for a facility or corporate transaction, paralegals may be asked to obtain these reports filed at some earlier time.

Section 312

EPCRA § 312 requires the owner or operator of any facility subject to MSDS requirements for hazardous chemicals by OSHA to prepare and submit an emergency and hazardous chemical inventory form. This reporting obligation is triggered in the same manner as EPCRA § 311 by OSHA requirements. The reports, commonly referred to either as **Tier I** or **Tier II** forms, must have been submitted for the first time by March 1, 1988, and are required to be submitted on an annual basis thereafter. As with EPCRA § 311, certain threshold quantity levels must be met before reporting is required (see the EPA's Web site at http://yosemite.epa.gov/oswer/ceppoweb.nsf/content/epcraOverview.htm#hazardous).

The Tier I form is shown in Figure 6-2. A complete resource for EPCRA § 312 tier reporting is found on the Internet at http://yosemite.epa.gov/oswer/ceppoweb.nsf/content/tier2.htm.

Regulated entities may submit a Tier I form or a Tier II form to satisfy the EPCRA § 312 requirement. In many cases, states or local entities may require the submission of the Tier II form by statute or ordinance. Tier II forms provide the most complete information about chemicals at any specific facility and, accordingly, the Tier II form tends to be preferred by governmental entities. Refer to Table 6-1 for a further explanation of Tier I and Tier II forms.

OMB Control No. 2050-0072
Approval expires: XX/XX/XX

Paperwork Reduction Act - The public reporting and recordkeeping burden for this collection of information is estimated to average 3.1 hours per response. Send comments on the Agency's need for this information, the accuracy of the provided burden estimates, and any suggested methods for minimizing respondent burden, including through the use of automated collection techniques to the Director, Collection Strategies Division, U.S. Environmental Protection Agency (2822T), 1200 Pennsylvania Ave., NW, Washington, D.C. 20460. Include the OMB control number in any correspondence. Do not send the completed form to this address.

Tier One	EMERGENCY AND HAZARDOUS CHEMICAL INVENTORY	FOR OFFICIAL USE ONLY	ID#
	Aggregate Information by Hazard Type		Date Received

Important: Read instructions before completing form   Reporting Period   From January 1 to December 31, 20_____

Facility Identification

Name _____

Street _____

City _____ County _____ State_____ Zip_____

SIC Code ☐☐☐☐   ☐☐ - ☐☐☐ - ☐☐☐☐
                              Dun & Brad Number

Owner/Operator

Name _____

Mail Address _____
Phone _____

Emergency Contacts

Name _____

Title _____

Phone (____) _____

24 hour Phone (____) _____

Name _____

Title _____

Phone (____) _____

24 hour Phone (____) _____

☐ Check if information below is identical to the information submitted last year.

☐ Check if site plan is attached

Physical Hazards

Hazard Type	Max Amount	Average Daily Amount	Number Of Days On-Site	General Location
Fire	☐☐	☐☐	☐☐☐	
Sudden Release of Pressure	☐☐	☐☐	☐☐☐	
Reactivity	☐☐	☐☐	☐☐☐	

Health Hazards

Immediate (acute)	☐☐	☐☐	☐☐☐	
Delayed (acute)	☐☐	☐☐	☐☐☐	

Certification *(Read and sign after completing all sections)*

I certify under penalty of law that I have personally examined and am familiar with the information submitted in pages one through ____, and that based on my inquiry of those individuals responsible for obtaining the information , I believe that the submitted information is true, accurate and complete.

_____
Name and official title of owner/operator OR owner/operator's authorized representative

_____   _____
Signature   Date Signed

Range Code	* Reporting Ranges Weight Range in pounds From.....	To......
01	0	99
02	100	999
03	1000	9,999
04	10,000	99,999
05	100,000	999,999
06	1,000,000	9,999,999
07	10,000,000	49,999,999
08	50,000,000	99,999,999
09	100,000,000	499,999,999
10	500,000,000	999,999,999
11	1 billion	Higher than 1 billion

EPA Form 8700-29

Figure 6-2   The EPA's EPCRA Tier I Form.

Section 312 of EPCRA requires the owner or operator of any facilities subject to MSDS requirements for hazardous chemicals by OSHA to prepare and submit an emergency and hazardous chemical inventory form.

Paralegals may be instrumental in the compilation, analysis, and completion of the EPCRA § 312 Tier I and Tier II forms. Just as with the § 302 submission, when this type of information is deemed necessary in a particular case or for a facility or corporate transaction, paralegals may be asked to obtain these reports filed at some earlier time.

Section 313

EPCRA § 313 requires the owner or operator of regulated facilities to submit a toxic chemical release form. This report, commonly referred to as the Form R, must have been submitted to the EPA and the other state officials designated for the first time by July 1, 1988, and annually thereafter. Form R must be filed with the EPA and with the state agency having jurisdiction over EPCRA § 313. The report is and must be submitted for certain facilities manufacturing, processing, or using materials identified as toxic chemicals by the EPA. Revisions to Form R now require that regulated facilities also submit key information about their pollution prevention activities, subject to the **Pollution Prevention Act of 1990**, 42 U.S.C. §§ 13101 to 13109 (1997).

There are three criteria in § 313 of the Emergency Planning and Community Right-to-Know Act that must be met in order to be required to file a Form R (see the EPA's Web site at http://www.epa.gov/tri/report/index.htm#forms). A facility must file a separate Form R for each chemical used that exceeds the threshold amounts. If the facility does not meet all three requirements, a Form R is not required. The criteria are:

- The facility has a Standard Industrial Classification (SIC) code between 2000 and 3999 (codes assigned to manufacturing facilities).
- The facility has ten or more full-time employees or an equivalent combination of full-time or part-time employees, with total work hours of 20,000 during the calendar year.
- The facility manufactures (defined to include importing) or processes any listed toxic chemical in quantities equal to or

greater than 25,000 pounds; or the facility otherwise uses any listed toxic chemical in quantities equal to or greater than 10,000 pounds during the calendar year.

The information reported on Form R includes primarily the following:

- Identification of the chemical and chemical-specific data used at the facility
- The amount of chemical released to the air, land, and/or water
- The source reduction and waste minimization activities conducted at the facility

The § 313 Form R is shown in Figure 6-3.

Beginning with the 1995 reporting year, facilities that meet certain criteria may submit an abbreviated report, called Form A, for a reportable chemical. After a facility determines that it must report on a given chemical, the facility is eligible to use the Form A for that chemical if

1. the sum of the annual releases, transfers, and wastes managed on site (known as the "reportable amount") does not exceed 500 pounds; and
2. the total annual amount of the chemical manufactured, processed, or otherwise used does not exceed one million pounds.

Form A is a two-page report that provides facility information (essentially the same as the Form R) and the identification of the chemical, but no release, transfer, and waste management data.

Section 313 of EPCRA requires the owner or operator of regulated facilities to submit a toxic chemical release form.

The EPA provides a wealth of information on the Toxic Release Inventory program, including forms and instructions, at http://www.epa.gov/tri/report/index.htm. For instance, *see* "Section 313 Release and Other Waste Management Reporting Requirements," February 2001, shown in Figure 6-4 and available on the Internet at http://www.epa.gov/tri/guide_docs/2001/brochure2000.pdf.

Paralegals may be instrumental in the compilation, analysis, and completion of the EPCRA § 313 Form Rs. Just as with the § 302 submission, when this type of information is deemed necessary in a particular case or for a facility or corporate transaction, paralegals may be asked to obtain these reports filed at some earlier time.

Form Approved OMB Number: 2070-0093
Approval Expires: 01/31/2006   Page 1 of 5

(IMPORTANT: Type or print; read instructions before completing form)

♦EPA

United States
Environmental Protection
Agency

FORM R

Section 313 of the Emergency Planning and Community
Right-to-Know Act of 1986, also Known as Title III of the
Superfund Amendments and Reauthorization Act

TRI Facility ID Number

Toxic Chemical, Category or Generic Name

WHERE TO SEND COMPLETED FORMS: 1. TRI Data Processing Center   2. APPROPRIATE STATE OFFICE
P. O. Box 1513   (See instructions in Appendix F)
Lanham, MD 20703-1513
ATTN: TOXIC CHEMICAL RELEASE INVENTORY

Enter "X" here if
this is a revision
For EPA use only

IMPORTANT: See instructions to determine when "Not Applicable (NA)" boxes should be checked.

PART 1. FACILITY IDENTIFICATION INFORMATION

SECTION 1. REPORTING YEAR _____

SECTION 2. TRADE SECRET INFORMATION

2.1 Are you claiming the toxic chemical identified on page 2 trade secret?
☐ Yes (Answer question 2.2; Attach substantiation forms)   ☐ No (Do not answer 2.2; Go to Section 3)

2.2 Is this copy ☐ Sanitized   ☐ Unsanitized
(Answer only if "YES" in 2.1)

SECTION 3. CERTIFICATION   (Important: Read and sign after completing all form sections.)

I hereby certify that I have reviewed the attached documents and that, to the best of my knowledge and belief, the submitted information is true and complete and that the amounts and values in this report are accurate based on reasonable estimates using data available to the preparers of this report.

Name and official title of owner/operator or senior management official: Signature: Date Signed:

SECTION 4. FACILITY IDENTIFICATION

4.1 TRI Facility ID Number

Facility or Establishment Name   Facility or Establishment Name or Mailing Address (If different from street address)

Street   Mailing Address

City/County/State/Zip Code   City/State/Zip Code   Country (Non-US)

4.2 This report contains information for:
(Important: Check a or b; check c or d if applicable) a. ☐ An entire facility   b. ☐ Part of a facility   c. ☐ A Federal facility   d. ☐ GOCO

4.3 Technical Contact Name   Telephone Number (include area code)
Email Address

4.4 Public Contact Name   Telephone Number (include area code)

4.5 SIC Code (s) (4 digits)   Primary a.   b.   c.   d.   e.   f.

4.6 Latitude   Degrees   Minutes   Seconds   Longitude   Degrees   Minutes   Seconds

4.7 Dun & Bradstreet Number (s) (9 digits)	4.8 EPA Identification Number (RCRA ID No.) (12 characters)	4.9 Facility NPDES Permit Number(s) (9 characters)	4.10 Underground Injection Well Code (UIC) I.D. Number(s) (12 digits)
a.	a.	a.	a.
b.	b.	b.	b.

SECTION 5. PARENT COMPANY INFORMATION

5.1 Name of Parent Company   NA ☐

5.2 Parent Company's Dun & Bradstreet Number   NA ☐

EPA Form 9350 -1 (Rev. 02/2004) - Previous editions are obsolete.

Figure 6-3 Section 313 Form R.

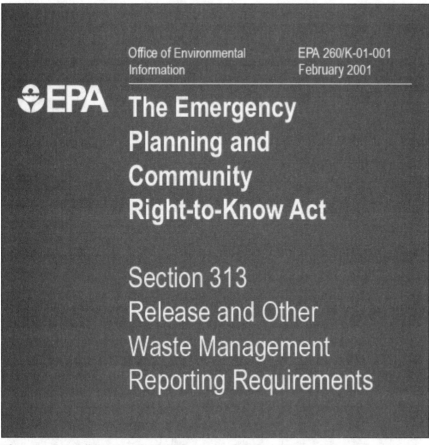

Office of Environmental
Information

EPA 260/K-01-001
February 2001

♦EPA The Emergency
Planning and
Community
Right-to-Know Act

Section 313
Release and Other
Waste Management
Reporting Requirements

Figure 6-4 "Section 313 Release and Other Waste Management Reporting Requirements," February 2001.

CASES FOR DISCUSSION

Steel Co. v. Citizens for a Better Environment, 523 U.S. 83, 118 S. Ct. 1003, 46 ERC 1097 (1998).

In this case, the Supreme Court is considering an EPCRA civil suit brought for wholly past violations. The citizen-suit provision is EPCRA, 42 U.S.C. § 11046(a)(1), which authorizes civil penalties and injunctive relief. It provides that "any person may commence a civil action on his own behalf against . . . [a]n owner or operator of a facility for failure" to "[c]omplete and submit an inventory form

(continued)

CASES FOR DISCUSSION

under section 11022(a) of this title . . . [and] section 11023(a) of this title." As a prerequisite to bringing such a suit, the plaintiff must, sixty days prior to filing his complaint, give notice to the Administrator of the EPA, the State in which the alleged violation occurs, and the alleged violator. The citizen suit may not go forward if the Administrator "has commenced and is diligently pursuing an administrative order or civil action to enforce the requirement concerned or to impose a civil penalty."

The complaint asks for (1) a declaratory judgment that the petitioner violated EPCRA; (2) authorization to inspect periodically petitioner's facility and records (with costs borne by the petitioner); (3) an order requiring the petitioner to provide respondent copies of all compliance reports submitted to the EPA; (4) an order requiring the petitioner to pay civil penalties of $25,000 per day for each violation of §§ 11022 and 11023; (5) an award of all respondent's "costs, in connection with the investigation and prosecution of this matter, including reasonable attorney and expert witness fees, as authorized by Section 326(f) of [EPCRA]"; and (6) any such further relief as the court deems appropriate.

The Court found that "none of the specific items of relief sought, and none that we can envision as 'appropriate' under the general request, would serve to reimburse respondent for losses caused by the late reporting, or to eliminate any effects of that late reporting upon respondent."

The Court in its opinion cites to a couple of related cases:

> *O'Shea v. Littleton*, 414 U.S. 488, 496–497 (1974). "Past exposure to illegal conduct does not in itself show a present case or controversy regarding injunctive relief . . . if unaccompanied by any continuing, present adverse effects." . . . .; *see also Renne v. Geary*, 501 U.S. 312, 320 (1991) "[T]he mootness exception for disputes capable of repetition yet evading review . . . will not revive a dispute which became moot before the action commenced."

The court concluded that:

> Because respondent alleges only past infractions of EPCRA, and not a continuing violation or the likelihood of a future violation, injunctive relief will not redress its injury. Having found that none of the relief sought by respondent would likely remedy its alleged injury in fact, we must conclude that respondent lacks standing to maintain this suit, and that we and the lower courts lack jurisdiction to entertain it.

IN THE UNITED STATES DISTRICT COURT
FOR THE DISTRICT OF NEBRASKA

UNITED STATES OF AMERICA,   )
and THE STATE OF NEBRASKA,   )
ex rel. MICHAEL J. LINDER,   )
DIRECTOR, NEBRASKA DEPARTMENT)
OF ENVIRONMENTAL QUALITY,   )
)
                          Plaintiffs,)
)
    v.   )   Civil Action No. 8:00-CV-28
)
IBP, inc.,   )
)
            Defendant.   )
_____)

SECOND AND FINAL PARTIAL CONSENT DECREE

WHEREAS, The United States of America ("United States"),

on behalf of the Administrator of the United States

Environmental Protection Agency ("EPA"), has filed a Second

Amended Complaint in this matter ("Complaint"), pursuant to

Sections 325(b)(3) and (c)(4) of the Emergency Planning and

Community Right to Know Act ("EPCRA"), 42 U.S.C.

§ 11045(b)(3), Section 109(c) of the Comprehensive

Environmental Response and Compensation Liability Act

("CERCLA"), 42 U.S.C. § 9609(c), Section 113(b) of the Clean

Air Act, as amended ("CAA"), 42 U.S.C. § 7413(b), Sections

309(b) and (d) of the Clean Water Act ("CWA"), 33 U.S.C.

§ 1319(b) and (d), and Sections 3008(a) and (g) of the Solid

Waste Disposal Act ("SWDA"), as amended by the Resource

Conservation and Recovery Act and the Hazardous and Solid

Figure 6-5   Consent Decree in the Iowa Beef Packers (IBP), Inc., Multimedia Settlement.

Other EPCRA-Related Considerations

EPCRA also contains numerous other important provisions of which paralegals should be aware. These other provisions relate to but are not limited to the public availability of EPCRA information and civil and criminal enforcement.

In conducting legal research involving EPCRA, paralegals should be aware that many state and local governmental entities have promulgated right-to-know type laws and ordinances that may be very similar to federal EPCRA provisions. State and local authorities also may have notification requirements in addition to EPCRA requirements, particularly in regard to reporting obligations. It is important to note that states also may have enforcement authority for state right-to-know laws.

Enforcement of EPCRA provisions has been of increasing priority to the EPA. Since the passage of EPCRA in 1986, enforcement actions for violations of EPCRA provisions have greatly increased. The majority of EPCRA enforcement efforts tends to focus on violations of the immediate notification requirements under EPCRA § 304. In many instances, EPCRA enforcement cases involve alleged violations of all or most EPCRA reporting obligations.

Figure 6-5 shows an EPA multimedia consent decree that includes enforcement pursuant to §§ 325(b)(3) and (c)(4) of EPCRA for failure to report releases.

Conclusion

The Emergency Planning and Community Right-to-Know Act expanded the role of the federal government into areas such as emergency planning that traditionally had been regulated by state and local governments and, in addition, granted citizens the right to obtain information about potential chemical hazards in their communities.

Under EPCRA, paralegals may be instrumental in the compilation, analysis, and completion of the EPCRA § 302 and § 311 submissions. For instance, for doing EPCRA reporting it is necessary to compile copies of all MSDSs for products that the company uses. The compilation will need indexing and specific information for the MSDSs will need to be culled out for further reporting analyses.

When this type of information is deemed necessary in a particular case or for a facility or corporate transaction, paralegals may be asked to obtain and analyze EPCRA reports filed at some earlier time.

Paralegals may be instrumental in the compilation, analysis, and completion of the EPCRA § 312 Tier I and Tier II forms, and the § 313 Form Rs. Just as with the § 302 and § 311 submissions, when this type of information is deemed necessary in a particular case or for a facility or corporate transaction, paralegals may be asked to obtain and analyze reports filed at some earlier time.

Paralegals will also be actively involved in the EPCRA enforcement process, in both administrative and judicial proceedings, as is discussed in more detail in the Introduction to this book.

GLOSSARY OF TITLE III TERMS

administrator. Administrator of the U.S. Environmental Protection Agency.

carcinogen. Any substance that is proven to cause or to contribute to the production of cancer.

CERCLA. Comprehensive Environmental Response, Compensation, and Liability Act of 1980, commonly referred to as the Superfund Law.

CERCLA hazardous substance. A hazardous substance listed in Table 302.4 of 40 C.F.R. § 302.4 (1997) that subjects facilities to CERCLA and Title III release notifications.

contingency plan. An emergency plan to be followed in case of fire, accident, or, in some instances, chemical releases to respond to an emergency situation.

EHS. Extremely hazardous substance listed in Appendices A and B of 40 C.F.R. part 355 (1997).

environment. Water, air, land, and the interrelationship that exists among and between water, air, and land, including all living things.

facility. All buildings, equipment, structures, and other stationary items that are located on a single site, or on contiguous or adjacent sites, that are owned or operated by the same person (or by any person who controls, is controlled by, or under common control with, such person). For the purpose of emergency release notification, the term includes motor vehicles, rolling stock, and aircraft.

federally permitted release. Release exempted from CERCLA and Title III reporting requirements as designated in CERCLA.

fire department. A paid or voluntary professional fire department with jurisdiction over a facility.

Form R. Toxic Release Inventory Form under EPCRA § 313 that must be completed to report releases of listed toxic chemicals into the environment and submitted to EPA and the state agency designated by the state's governor.

hazardous chemicals. All chemicals that constitute a physical hazard or a health hazard, as defined by 29 C.F.R. § 1910.1200 (1997), with the exceptions listed in EPCRA § 311(e). This term comprises approximately ninety percent of all chemicals.

HCS. Hazard Communication Standard. The OSHA standard cited in 29 C.F.R. § 1910.1200 (1991).

health hazard. A chemical for which there is statistically significant evidence based on at least one study conducted in accordance with established scientific principles that acute or chronic health effects may occur in exposed employees.

inventory form. See Tier I or Tier II.

LEPC. Local Emergency Planning Committee.

manufacture. To produce, prepare, import, or compound a toxic chemical. *Manufacture* also applies to substances that are produced coincidentally during the manufacture, processing, use, or disposal of another substance or mixture, including by-products and co-products that are separated from that other substance or mixture, and impurities that remain in that substance or mixture.

MSDS. Material Safety Data Sheet. Compilation of the health, flammability, and reactivity hazards of a chemical. A legal document required by the OSHA 1910.1200 (1991) Hazard Communication Standard.

NRC. National Response Center. Established under CERCLA and operated under the supervision of the National Response Team at U.S. Coast Guard Headquarters, Washington, D.C.

OSHA. U.S. Occupational Safety and Health Administration.

person. Any individual, trust, firm, joint stock company, corporation (including a government corporation), partnership, association, state, municipality, commission, political subdivision of state, or interstate body.

release. Any spilling, leaking, pumping, pouring, emitting, emptying, discharging, injecting, escaping, leaching, dumping, or disposing into the environment (including the abandonment or discarding of barrels, containers, and other closed receptacles) of any hazardous chemical, extremely hazardous substance, or CERCLA hazardous substance that enters the environment.

RQ. Reportable quantity. That amount of a CERCLA hazardous substance or extremely hazardous substance listed in 40 C.F.R. part 302, Table 302.4, or 40 C.F.R. part 355, Appendix A (1997) that, when exceeded as a release, requires reporting.

SARA. Superfund Amendments and Reauthorization Act of 1986.

SERC. State Emergency Response Commission.

SIC Code. Standard Industrial Classification Code.

state. Any state of the United States, the District of Columbia, the Commonwealth of Puerto Rico, Guam, American Samoa, the United States Virgin Islands, the northern Mariana Islands, and any other territory or possession over which the United States has jurisdiction.

Tier I or Tier II. Inventory form for reporting hazardous chemicals under EPCRA § 312.

Title III. Emergency Planning and Community Right-to-Know Act of 1986.

Toxic Release Inventory Form. See Form R or Form A.

TPQ. Threshold planning quantity. The amount of an extremely hazardous substance present in a facility at any one time that, when exceeded, subjects the facility to the emergency planning requirements.

BIBLIOGRAPHY

Chemicals in Your Community: A Guide to the EPCRA (U.S. EPA 1988).

Common Synonyms for Chemicals Listed Under Section 313 of the EPCRA, EPA 744-B-92-001 (U.S. EPA 1992).

Final Penalty Policy for Sections 302, 303, 304, 311, and 312 of EPCRA and Section 103 of CERCLA, OSWER Directive No. 9841.2 (U.S. EPA 1990).

Grayson, E. Lynn, *The Pollution Prevention Act of 1990: Emergence of a New Environmental Policy*, Envtl. L. Rep. (June 1992).

Grayson, E. Lynn, & Joseph F. Madonia, *Title III Enforcement: One State's Perspective*, Nat'l Envtl. Enforcement J. (Sept. 1989).

Interim Strategy for Enforcement of Title III and CERCLA Section 103 Notification Requirements, OSWER Directive No. 9841.0 (U.S. EPA 1988).

Kuszaj, James M., *The EPCRA Compliance Manual: Interpreting and Implementing the Emergency Planning and Community Right-to-Know Act of 1986* (A.B.A., Section of Natural Resources, Energy, and Environmental Law 1997).

Right-to-Know Planning Guide (BNA 1996).

Spill Reporting Procedures Guide, 1997 Edition (BNA 1997).

Title III List of Lists: Consolidated List of Chemicals Subject to Reporting Under EPCRA, EPA 560/4-92-011 (U.S. EPA 1996).

Treatability Studies Under EPCRA, OSWER Directive No. 9380.3-02 (U.S. EPA 1989).

DISCUSSION QUESTIONS

1. In many business transactions, the environmental compliance status of a particular facility may be very important in evaluating whether to purchase certain property or perhaps in considering a stock purchase of a company owning certain properties.

   Q. If a client were interested in obtaining information about the environmental compliance status of a specific facility or, alternatively, the type of operations it conducts, what types of information might be available under EPCRA?

   Q. How would you obtain this information for your client and from what specific source?

2. Reportable quantities are established under CERCLA and EPCRA for hazardous substances and extremely hazardous substances respectively. A client informs your firm that a release of vinyl chloride is taking place at the client's facility and emergency response activities are underway. So far it is estimated that 1500 pounds of vinyl chloride have spilled next to the aboveground storage tank (AST) within the client's site boundaries. The client needs to know if this is a reportable event.

   Q. What actions can a paralegal take under these circumstances to work together with the case attorney in determining the appropriate reporting requirements?

   Q. Where would the reportable quantity for vinyl chloride be listed?

   Q. What is the urgency for owners and operators of facilities associated with notification requirements?

COMPUTER LABORATORY PROJECTS

1. Research a local company on the EPA's EnviroFacts database and prepare an oral report to the class on what Form R chemicals it reported on last year and in what quantities.

INTERNET SITES

- The full text of the EPCRA is on the Internet at http://www.epa.gov/region5/defs/html/epcra.htm.

- The Emergency Planning and Community Right-to-Know Act (EPCRA) Fact Sheet is on the Internet at http://yosemite.epa.gov/oswer/Ceppoweb.nsf/vwResourcesByFilename/epcra.pdf/$File/epcra.pdf.

CHAPTER 7

The Endangered Species Act

Francine Shay and Jody L. Brooks

OBJECTIVES

The objectives of this chapter are for students to:

- Learn the terminology associated with the ESA.
- Learn the concepts and ideas that underlie the ESA law and regulatory program.
- Learn about specific sections and provisions of the ESA law and regulations.
- Learn about the processes and procedures used by the government and other parties to comply with and to enforce the law under the ESA.
- Learn about the particular jobs and functions that are performed by paralegals working for attorneys in ESA cases.

Overview of the Act

The stated purposes of the **Endangered Species Act of 1973 (ESA),** codified in 16 U.S.C. §§ 1531 through 1544, are to conserve the ecosystems (see Figure 7-1 for a photograph of the Upper Missouri/Yellowstone River Ecosystem) (defined as the dynamic and interrelating complex of plant and animal communities and their associated nonliving (e.g., physical and chemical) environment) upon which endangered and threatened species depend, to provide a program for the conservation of such endangered and threatened species, and to take steps to achieve the purposes of existing treaties and conventions affecting wildlife, fish, and plants. 16 U.S.C. § 1531(b). The federal regulations that implement ESA are found in 50 C.F.R. part 17.

Figure 7-1 The Upper Missouri/Yellowstone River Ecosystem.
Used with permission. U.S. Fish and Wildlife Service Photo by Kent Olson.

Congress gave the secretaries of the Department of Commerce and the Department of the Interior joint responsibility for implementation of the ESA. In turn, the Department of Commerce delegated its lead responsibility—the protection of marine species including both freshwater and ocean-dwelling fish—to the **National Marine Fisheries Service (NMFS).** The Department of the Interior delegated its lead responsibility—the protection of all land-dwelling species, freshwater species, some marine mammals, and migratory birds—to the **U.S. Fish and Wildlife Service (FWS).** In this chapter, the FWS and the NMFS will be referred to as the "agency" or "agencies."

The ESA is divided into the following discrete sections:

Section 2.	Congressional Findings and Declaration of Purposes and Policy
Section 3.	Definitions
Section 4.	Determination of Endangered Species and Threatened Species
Section 5.	Land Acquisition
Section 6.	Cooperation with States
Section 7.	Interagency Cooperation
Section 8.	International Cooperation
Section 8A.	Convention Implementation

Introduction

This chapter will primarily focus on §§ 4, 6, 7, 9, and 10 of the Act. These sections are the ones that are most utilized by the agencies and practitioners.

History of the Act

Prior to the enactment of ESA in 1973, the federal legislature attempted to protect **endangered species** through two acts: the 1966 Endangered Species Preservation Act, 80 Stat. 926 (1966), and the 1969 Endangered Species Conservation Act, 83 Stat. 275 (1969). In 1973, Congress completely revised and strengthened the earlier species protection legislation through the passage of the Endangered Species Act. The ESA's overall framework remains essentially unchanged since 1973 despite significant amendments that were subsequently enacted. The legislation amending the ESA—92 Stat. 3751 (1978), 92 Stat. 1225 (1979), and 96 Stat. 1411 (1983)—was enacted to improve the listing process and to balance conflicts that arise between economic development and species protection.

In enactment of the ESA, the Congress found that species of **fish, wildlife,** and **plants** are of aesthetic, ecological, educational, historical, recreational, and scientific value to the United States and its people. The ESA declares that its purpose is to provide a means whereby the ecosystems upon which endangered species and threatened species depend may be conserved and to provide a program for the conservation of such endangered and threatened species. 16 U.S.C. § 1531(a)(3) and (b).

Defining a Species

Species has been broadly defined to include a distinct vertebrate population segment that is both discrete and significant, as defined by the "Final Vertebrate Population Policy," 61 Fed. Reg. 4722 (1996). The ESA defines the term *species* to include any subspecies of fish, wildlife, or plants, or any distinct population segment of any species of vertebrate fish or wildlife that interbreeds when mature. 16 U.S.C. 1532(16).

A species is considered endangered when it is in danger of extinction throughout all or a significant portion of its range. 16 U.S.C. 1532(6). A species is considered a **threatened species** when the species is likely to become endangered within the foreseeable future throughout all or a significant portion of its range. 16 U.S.C. § 1532(20).

Listing of Species and Designation of Critical Habitat

With the exception of activities associated with candidate species, the ESA provides substantive protection only to those species **listed** as threatened or endangered in accordance with § 4 of the Act. Section 4 of the ESA, codified in 16 U.S.C. § 1533, provides a mechanism to list species the agencies determine to be endangered or threatened. Listings can include either an entire species or a distinct population, subspecies, or population segment of a species. Listings also include species similar in appearance to endangered or threatened species. 16 U.S.C. § 1533(e).

The agencies determine which species are to be placed on either the endangered or the threatened species list by reviewing certain factors that qualify species for listing. These factors are found in 16 U.S.C. § 1533(a)(1). The factors include

- present or threatened destruction, modification, or curtailment of its habitat or range;
- overutilization for commercial, recreational, scientific, or educational purposes;
- disease or predation;
- inadequacy of existing regulatory mechanisms; and
- other natural or man-made factors affecting the species' continued existence.

The agencies also determine which habitats qualify for designation as **critical habitats** by following the factors listed in 16 U.S.C. § 1532(5).

A critical habitat is a geographical area occupied by the species either at the time listed or at a later time on which are found physical or biological features that are determined to be both

- essential to the conservation of the species; and
- which may require special management considerations or protection.

Except for certain limited predetermined circumstances, a critical habitat cannot include the entire geographical area that can be occupied by a listed species. Also, sometimes subsequent to the listing of a species, specific areas that lie outside the geographical area occupied by the species are designated as critical habitats because the agencies determine at a later point in time that such areas are essential for the conservation of the listed species.

The FWS is required to publish lists of species it or the NMFS determines are endangered or threatened, as well as any designated critical habitat. The lists are found at:

- 50 C.F.R. § 17.11 (wildlife species)
- 50 C.F.R. § 17.12 (plant species)
- 50 C.F.R. § 17.95 (wildlife critical habitat)
- 50 C.F.R. § 17.96 (plants critical habitat)

The FWS and the NMFS are required to review and update the lists every five years. The FWS publishes its *Endangered Species Handbook* (1994), now in its fourth edition, as its internal procedural guidance.

Procedure for Listing

Section 4 of the ESA, 16 U.S.C. § 1533, provides a procedure for listing endangered and threatened species. The FWS and the NMFS make the lists for the species and habitats under their respective delegation. The agencies themselves may initiate the listing or delisting of species or critical habitats. In addition, any individual or any organization may file a petition with either the FWS or the NMFS to list, delist, or reclassify species or habitats. The petition process and requirements are outlined in 50 C.F.R. § 424.14.

Petitions regarding species must include certain information to be considered sufficient so that the agencies may evaluate whether the petition presents substantial biological data to indicate that the petitioned action may be warranted. The regulations found in 50 C.F.R. § 424.14(b)(2)(i)–(iv) provide that the petitions must

- clearly indicate the recommended administrative measures;
- provide the taxonomic identity, common name, and current status of the species; and
- present a narrative justification for the action with supporting biological documentation.

Petitions regarding critical habitat designations are required to provide sufficient information about the area recommended for designation and justify why the area meets the critical habitat criteria. The regulations for petitions regarding critical habitats are found in 50 C.F.R. § 424.14.

Additional guidance for drafting petitions can be found in the "Final Petition Management Guidance," published at 61 Fed. Reg. 36075 (July 1996).

Attorneys who are preparing ESA petitions may utilize paralegals in a number of ways. Among the tasks that might be assigned paralegals are

- to research the requirements and procedure for submitting petitions;
- to research case law regarding similar scenarios under ESA;
- to find an appropriate expert to either provide pretrial advice, to testify, or both;
- to compile and organize the biological data and supporting documentation obtained from the expert or consultant;
- to draft the petition for the attorney's review; and
- to compile the exhibits to the petition.

Agency's Determination

To the maximum extent practicable, the agency has ninety days after its receipt of the petition to make a finding, and then promptly publish its finding in the *Federal Register*. The agency's finding is whether the petition presents substantial biological data to indicate the petitioned action may be warranted. The agency's determination is based solely on the best scientific and commercial information available. 50 C.F.R. § 424.24(b)(1). However, the courts have determined that conclusive evidence is not required. *Defenders of Wildlife v. Babbitt*, 958 F. Supp. 670 (D.D.C. 1997). In any event, Congress intended to give the benefit of the doubt to the species.

If the agency's ninety-day review results in a finding that the petition does not satisfy the agency's "substantial information" requirement, the petitioner may appeal the decision to the federal district court. Appeals of agency or administrative decisions to the district court are conducted in the same manner as any other litigation at the trial court level. Attorneys utilize the assistance of paralegals in these litigation matters as they would in any other type of litigation: the drafting of pleadings, preparing discovery requests and responses, researching legal procedures and substantive issues, interviewing potential witnesses, finding expert witnesses, and coordinating the exchange of information and documents between these witnesses and the attorneys.

When an agency reviews a petition regarding the listing of species and finds that adequate biological data suggest the petitioned action may be warranted, the agency has twelve months after its receipt of the petition to initiate a review of the petitioned action and publish in the *Federal Register* its ultimate finding of whether listing the species may be warranted. When an agency reviews a petition regarding the designation of critical habitat, the agency has twelve months after its receipt of the petition to determine how the agency will proceed and promptly publish notice of its determination in the *Federal Register*.

At the conclusion of its twelve-month review of the petitioned action regarding the listing of species, the agency decides the petitioned action

- may be warranted;
- is warranted;
- is not warranted; or
- is warranted but precluded.

If the agency's final determination is that the action may be warranted but needs additional information to make a final determination, the agency publishes in the *Federal Register* a **Notice of Review (NOR)** to solicit additional data. Figure 7-2 shows an NOR, published at 67 Fed. Reg. 40657 (June 13, 2002).

If the agency determines that the petitioned action is warranted, the agency publishes proposed regulations in the *Federal Register* pursuant to the Administrative Procedures Act (5 U.S.C. § 501 *et seq.*) notice and comment rule-making procedures. The procedures include a sixty-day comment period and, if anyone requests it, at least one public hearing that must be held within fourty five days of the published notice. The agency then has one year to

- promulgate a final rule;
- find that the petitioned action should not be made;
- withdraw its proposed rule if the agency finds no adequate supporting evidence; or
- extend the review period for no more than six months.

If the determination is that the action is warranted but precluded because there exist other pending and imminent proposals to list species that are in greater biological danger, then the agency adds the petitioned species to the **candidate species list.** The agency publishes in the *Federal Register* its finding of "warranted but precluded." The finding must be reexamined every year until the petitioned action is either proposed as a rule or denied as not warranted. The agency

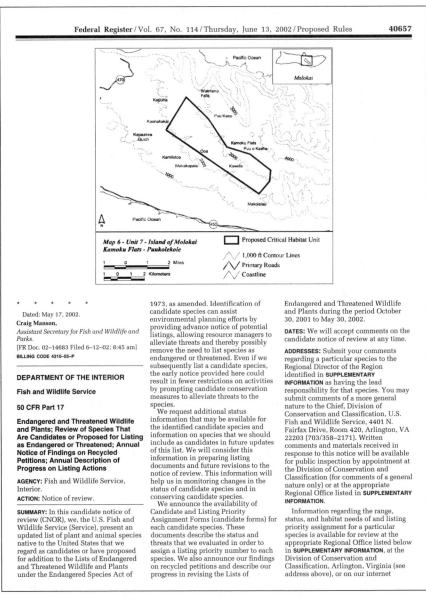

Federal Register / Vol. 67, No. 114 / Thursday, June 13, 2002 / Proposed Rules **40657**

Map 6 - Unit 7 - Island of Molokai
Kamoku Flats - Puukolekoie

1,000 ft Contour Lines
Primary Roads
Coastline

Proposed Critical Habitat Unit

* * * * *

Dated: May 17, 2002.

Craig Manson,
Assistant Secretary for Fish and Wildlife and Parks.

[FR Doc. 02–14683 Filed 6–12–02; 8:45 am]

BILLING CODE 4310–55–P

DEPARTMENT OF THE INTERIOR

Fish and Wildlife Service

50 CFR Part 17

Endangered and Threatened Wildlife and Plants; Review of Species That Are Candidates or Proposed for Listing as Endangered or Threatened; Annual Notice of Findings on Recycled Petitions; Annual Description of Progress on Listing Actions

AGENCY: Fish and Wildlife Service, Interior.

ACTION: Notice of review.

SUMMARY: In this candidate notice of review (CNOR), we, the U.S. Fish and Wildlife Service (Service), present an updated list of plant and animal species native to the United States that we regard as candidates or have proposed for addition to the Lists of Endangered and Threatened Wildlife and Plants under the Endangered Species Act of

1973, as amended. Identification of candidate species can assist environmental planning efforts by providing advance notice of potential listings, allowing resource managers to alleviate threats and thereby possibly remove the need to list species as endangered or threatened. Even if we subsequently list a candidate species, the early notice provided here could result in fewer restrictions on activities by prompting candidate conservation measures to alleviate threats to the species.

We request additional status information that may be available for the identified candidate species and information on species that we should include as candidates in future updates of this list. We will consider this information in preparing listing documents and future revisions to the notice of review. This information will help us in monitoring changes in the status of candidate species and in conserving candidate species.

We announce the availability of Candidate and Listing Priority Assignment Forms (candidate forms) for each candidate species. These documents describe the status and threats that we evaluated in order to assign a listing priority number to each species. We also announce our findings on recycled petitions and describe our progress in revising the Lists of

Endangered and Threatened Wildlife and Plants during the period October 30, 2001 to May 30, 2002.

DATES: We will accept comments on the candidate notice of review at any time.

ADDRESSES: Submit your comments regarding a particular species to the Regional Director of the Region identified in **SUPPLEMENTARY INFORMATION** as having the lead responsibility for that species. You may submit comments of a more general nature to the Chief, Division of Conservation and Classification, U.S. Fish and Wildlife Service, 4401 N. Fairfax Drive, Room 420, Arlington, VA 22203 (703/358–2171). Written comments and materials received in response to this notice will be available for public inspection by appointment at the Division of Conservation and Classification (for comments of a general nature only) or at the appropriate Regional Office listed in **SUPPLEMENTARY INFORMATION**.

Information regarding the range, status, and habitat needs of and listing priority assignment for a particular species is available for review at the appropriate Regional Office listed below in **SUPPLEMENTARY INFORMATION**, at the Division of Conservation and Classification, Arlington, Virginia (see address above), or on our internet

Figure 7-2 Notice of Review (NOR).

publishes in the *Federal Register* its annual notice of candidate species as a Notice of Review (NOR). The NOR solicits information needed to prioritize species. Through the Listing Priority System, the agency assigns a one through twelve listing priority to each candidate species according to the immediacy of the threat to the species.

CASES FOR DISCUSSION

National Association of Home Builders v. Interior Department, 340 F.3d 835, 56 ERC 2098 (C.A. 9 2003).

In this case, the National Association of Home Builders and others (Home Builders) appealed the district court's decision upholding the designation of a population of pygmy-owls in Arizona as a distinct population segment (DPS) pursuant to the Fish and Wildlife Service's *Policy Regarding the Recognition of Distinct Vertebrate Population Segments Under the Endangered Species Act*, 61 Fed. Reg. 4722 (Feb. 7, 1996) (DPS Policy). The Home Builders argued that this DPS designation violated the DPS Policy because the Arizona pygmy-owl population was neither discrete nor significant. The Court of Appeals held that although the FWS did not arbitrarily find the Arizona pygmy-owl population to be discrete, the FWS arbitrarily found the discrete population to be significant. It reversed the district court's decision and remanded the Listing Rule to the district court.

Paralegals assist in the process of the listing of species by following up on the publication of notices, attending public hearings, and reporting back to the attorney and petitioners through memoranda of the public hearing proceedings. Paralegals also assist by drafting Freedom of Information Act (FOIA) requests to the agencies and reviewing and obtaining copies of agency records on the comments received and the biological data and internal documents related to its decision-making processes.

A petitioner may challenge the agency's determination in federal district court if the agency determines that the petitioned request is not warranted, or warranted but precluded, or the agency fails to make a finding. Paralegals assist in these challenges in the same manner that they assist in any litigation action.

Listing Moratorium

In April 1995, Congress passed legislation creating a moratorium on the agency's function of listing endangered and threatened species and critical habitat. This legislation temporarily cut off funds for the agencies to make listings determinations. In April 1996, the moratorium expired and funding was restored to the amount of $4 million. The backlog of petitions resulted in the FWS's publication of its Listing Priority Guidance, which is found in 50 C.F.R. part 17, or 61 Fed. Reg. 64475 (December 5, 1996).

Delisting

Species may be delisted using the same standards as those for listing species: using the best scientific and commercial data available to substantiate that the species is either extinct or has recovered. A species may also be delisted if the original data that formed the basis for listing the species are now found to be in error. 50 C.F.R. § 424.11(d). A species is considered extinct if it is no longer found in its previous range. 50 C.F.R. § 424.11(d)(1). A species is considered recovered if, using the standards for listing and delisting, the data show it is no longer endangered or threatened. 50 C.F.R. § 424.11(d)(2). In fact, any listed species that no longer meets the ESA's definition of endangered or threatened species is removed from the list.

Critical Habitat Protection

The ESA prohibits all federal agencies from undertaking actions that would destroy or adversely modify habitat of listed species that the FWS or NMFS designates as critical habitat. 16 U.S.C. § 1536. The federal circuit courts are split as to whether NEPA requirements must be followed for designations of critical habitat. NEPA regulates federal agencies as to their procedures and priorities for the protection of environmental resources. The statutes regarding NEPA are found in 42 U.S.C. §§ 4321–4370(d).

Recovery Plans

Recovery plans assist the agencies in identifying, prioritizing, and scheduling management and research necessary to reverse the decline of a species and ensure its long-term survival.

Congress did not require the development of recovery plans until it amended the ESA in 1978. Additional amendments enacted in 1982 established priorities for the development of recovery plans, giving priority to species most likely to benefit from recovery efforts, especially species threatened by development. The agencies are responsible for developing and implementing recovery plans for endangered and threatened species, unless the agencies find that such a plan will not promote the conservation of the species. Legislation regarding recovery plans is codified in 16 U.S.C. § 1533(f).

In recovery planning, the agencies must give priority ranking to species most likely to benefit from the recovery plan, especially those that are or may be in conflict with development activities. Each plan must include

- a description of the site-specific management actions that may be necessary to achieve the plan's goal for the protection of the species;
- objective, measurable criteria that specify when the species may be removed from the endangered or threatened list; and
- estimates of the time and cost to carry out the plan.

The agencies may procure the services of other public agencies or private institutions, as well as qualified individuals, to develop and implement recovery plans. These entities comprise what are known as recovery teams.

Cooperation with States

Section 6 of the ESA, codified in 16 U.S.C. § 1535, authorizes the agencies to enter into management agreements with the states to implement the ESA. The agencies may enter into a management agreement with any state in the United States for the administration and management of any area established for the conservation of listed species. 16 U.S.C. § 1535 (b). In addition, the agencies are authorized to enter into cooperative agreements with any state that establishes and maintains an adequate and active program for the conservation of listed species. 16 U.S.C. § 1535(c).

Federal funds are provided to the states to implement the states' conservation programs. 16 U.S.C. 1535(c). The states participating in cooperative agreements are entitled to receive grants through the Cooperative Endangered Species Conservation Fund. States contribute twenty-five percent of the estimated program costs of approved projects, or ten percent when two or more states implement a joint project.

Takings—Civil and Criminal Sanctions (16 U.S.C. § 1538)

Section 9 of the ESA prohibits **"take"** of endangered fish and wildlife. "Take" means to "harass, harm, pursue, hunt, shoot, wound, kill, trap, capture, or collect, or to attempt to engage in such conduct." 16 U.S.C. § 1532(19).

"Harm" is defined by the FWS in 50 C.F.R. § 17.3 as an act that actually kills or injures wildlife, but the act may also include significant habitat modification or degradation that actually kills or injures wildlife by significantly impairing essential behavioral patterns, including breeding, feeding, or sheltering. The NMFS defines "harm" in 50 C.F.R. § 222.102. The NMFS's definition closely matches the definition of "harm" specified by the FWS, but the NMFS adds to its definition additional behavioral patterns of the species: spawning, rearing, and migrating.

In 16 U.S.C. § 1538(a)(1), the ESA lists the unlawful activities regarding endangered species of fish and wildlife:

- To import into or export out of the United States any endangered species
- To take any endangered species within the United States or the U.S. territorial sea or upon the high seas
- To possess, sell, deliver, carry, transport, or ship any endangered species that were taken
- To deliver, receive, carry, transport, or ship any endangered species in interstate or foreign commerce in the course of commercial activity
- To sell or offer for sale any endangered species
- To violate any regulation pertaining to any endangered species

Similarly, in 16 U.S.C. § 1538(a)(2), the ESA lists the unlawful activities regarding endangered species of plants:

- To import into or export endangered species of plants from the United States
- To remove and reduce to possession, or to maliciously damage or destroy, endangered species of plants from areas under federal jurisdiction
- To remove, cut, dig up, or damage or destroy any endangered species of plants on any area other than under federal jurisdiction or while violating any state law or regulation or while violating any state criminal trespass law
- To sell or offer for sale any endangered species of plants
- To violate any regulation pertaining to any endangered species of plants

Note that listed plants are not protected to the same extent as listed fish and wildlife because the prohibition against take applies only to listed animals. 16 U.S.C. § 1538(a)(1)(B).

It is unlawful to violate regulations pertaining to any threatened species of fish, wildlife, and plants. In addition, it is unlawful to attempt to commit, solicit another to commit, or cause to be committed the listed offenses.

Exemptions to the unlawful activities are listed in 16 U.S.C. §§ 1535(g)(2) and 1539. These include emergency situations, those involving certain cooperative agreements, approved scientific purposes, and if the taking is incidental to an otherwise lawful activity. Approved incidental takings and their accompanying conservation plans are discussed later in this chapter.

Responsibilities for enforcement of the provisions of the ESA are found in 16 U.S.C. § 1540. Public enforcement is undertaken by the Department of Justice, the Department of the Interior through the FWS, and through the Department of Commerce through the NMFS. The Coast Guard, the Customs Service, and the Department of Agriculture may develop the cases for the various agencies. Public enforcement results in criminal or civil penalty and forfeiture actions.

Citizen Suits

In addition, citizens may initiate private legal actions to enforce the ESA through citizen suits. 16 U.S.C. § 1540(g). A citizen suit may be brought in federal district court to enjoin any person or governmental entity alleged to violate any statute or regulation under the ESA. A citizen suit may also be brought against the FWS or the NMFS to compel the agency to apply the prohibitions set forth in the ESA with respect to the taking of any listed species within the United States, or if the agency fails to perform any nondiscretionary act or duty under 16 U.S.C. § 1533. In most situations, the plaintiff initiating a citizen suit must provide the agency and the alleged violator with written notice prior to filing the suit. The court, when issuing any final order in any suit brought by a citizen, may award the costs of litigation, including reasonable attorneys' and expert witness fees, to any party whenever the court determines that such award is appropriate. 16 U.S.C. § 1540(g)(4).

Anyone initiating a citizen suit must have standing to bring the suit. Standing issues have been decided in several Supreme Court cases. In *Lujan v. Defenders of Wildlife*, 504 U.S. 555, 560–561 (1992), the Court determined that a plaintiff must demonstrate he or she has suffered an "injury in fact," an invasion of a judicially recognizable interest, which is concrete and particularized, where there exists a casual connection between the injury and the conduct complained of, the injury is fairly traceable to the challenged action, and the injury is not merely speculative. However, any person may commence a civil suit if injury is produced by issuance of a biological opinion, thereby negating the traditional zone of interests test. *Bennett v. Spear*, 520 U.S. 154 (1997). The biological opinion is considered final agency action, which, pursuant to the APA found in 5 U.S.C. § 501 *et seq.*, makes it judicially reviewable under the arbitrary and capricious standard.

A review of case law reveals how courts have decided whether a take has occurred in various fact scenarios. For example, it has been determined that killing in self-defense or in the defense of others is not a taking, but the individual must report his or her action to the FWS within five days. *United States v. Clavette*, 135 F.3d 1308 (9th Cir. 1998). It has also been decided that a state can be held liable for take through its implementation of a licensing program. *Strahan v. Coxe*, 127 F.3d 155 (1st Cir 1997).

There are also court rulings deciding whether critical habitat modifications result in a taking. In these cases, the plaintiffs who initiate a citizen suit have the burden to establish with reasonable certainty that the modification action will result in significant habitat modification that would actually kill or injure listed species by impairing their essential behavior patterns. *United States v. West Coast Forest Resources L.P.*, No. Civ. 96-1575-HO, 2000 WL 298707 (D. Or. Mar. 13, 2000).

Civil Penalties

Civil penalties for any person or organization knowingly violating ESA, other than an administrative violation such as record keeping or report filing, are listed in 16 U.S.C. § 1540(a), which provides for monetary penalties after the receipt of proper notice and an opportunity for a hearing. No civil penalty is imposed if the accused violator can prove by a preponderance of the evidence that he or she committed the act based on a good-faith belief that he or she was acting to protect himself or herself, or any individual, from bodily harm from any listed species. 16 U.S.C. § 1540 (a)(3).

Civil penalties assessed against an individual or organization convicted of criminal violations of the ESA may include the modification, suspension, or revocation of its permit or license to import or export fish or wildlife, or any federal grazing permit, with no compensation for the loss of the permit or license. 16 U.S.C. § 1540(b)(2). Other civil penalties include civil forfeiture of listed plants and animals and of equipment used in furtherance of an unlawful act. These are enumerated in 16 U.S.C. § 1540(e)(5) and 19 U.S.C. §§ 1581 *et seq.*

In addition, the Department of Justice may sue to enjoin an alleged violator from the activity that is believed to violate the ESA or its regulations. 16 U.S.C. § 1540(e)(6).

Criminal Penalties

Criminal penalties of monetary fines or imprisonment may also await any person who knowingly violates the ESA. Criminal penalties are listed in 16 U.S.C. § 1540(b). It is a Class A misdemeanor for any person or organization to violate the ESA in a manner that affects endangered species. It is a Class B misdemeanor for ESA violations that affect threatened species. Although a defense to a criminal violation is a good-faith belief that the violator acted to protect himself, herself, or others from bodily harm (16 U.S.C. § 1540(b)(3)), it is not a defense if the violator acted merely to protect property.

Since the ESA does not provide for felony penalties, violations are often prosecuted as a Lacey Act charge. Violations are incorporated into the Lacey Act when the acts are considered as the "triggering" or as an underlying offense that falls under the Lacey Act. This would include a charge of knowingly importing, exporting, transporting, selling, receiving, acquiring, or purchasing any wildlife, fish, or plant taken, transported, or sold in prohibition of any U.S. law, including the ESA. 16 U.S.C. § 3372. Violators of the Lacey Act are charged with a Class D felony, which may result in up to five years' imprisonment, a fine of up to $250,000 for individuals, or $500,000 for organizations, or both.

An individual or organization may be criminally charged and prosecuted for multiple liability of violations of the ESA. A determination of units of prosecution is made when the violation involves more than one animal or protected species. For example, a unit of prosecution may be determined as one count per day, or one count for all animals taken per day, or one count per species per day, among other methods of calculations.

Assistance to Landowners

A 1993 study determined that half of listed species have at least eighty percent of their habitat on private lands. What can a landowner do when there are listed species on his or her property so that he or she will not violate § 9 of the ESA? Several programs provide mechanisms for private landowners, tribes, and local governments to assist the federal government in protecting listed species.

- Habitat conservation planning allows for development of land provided conservation measures are undertaken.
- The No Surprises Policy assures participating landowners that they will incur no additional mitigation requirements beyond those they agreed to in their **Habitat Conservation Plans (HCPs),** even if circumstances change. 63 Fed. Reg. 8859 (February 28, 1998).
- Safe Harbor Agreements are available to landowners that implement on their private land species-friendly measures that restore, enhance, or maintain habitat for listed species. The Agreements provide certain assurances, such as limitations on

future land use restrictions. Application requirements, issuance criteria, permit conditions, and assurances are found in 50 C.F.R. § 17.22(c) for endangered species, and in 50 C.F.R. § 17.32(c) for threatened species.

- The Candidate Conservation Agreements with Assurances Policy provides incentives for landowners to conserve candidate species, thereby making listing unnecessary for those species. Application requirements, permit conditions, and assurances in the event of various potential circumstances are found in 50 C.F.R. § 17.22(d) for endangered species, and in 50 C.F.R. § 17.32(d) for threatened species.
- The Private Stewardship Program provides grants and other assistance on a competitive basis to individuals and groups engaged in local, private, and voluntary conservation efforts that benefit listed, proposed, or candidate species, or other at-risk species. 67 Fed. Reg. 61649 (October 1, 2002).

Incidental take authorization and HCPs are discussed in greater detail later in this chapter.

Federal Agencies' Consultation Requirements

Section 7 of the ESA places a statutory duty on each **federal agency (action agency)** to consult with the FWS or the NMFS **(consulting agency)** to ensure that any action "authorized, funded, or carried out by such agency" is not likely to jeopardize the continued existence of any endangered or threatened species or result in the destruction or adverse modification of habitat. 16 U.S.C. § 1536(a)(2). To comply with the jeopardy prohibition, federal agencies must follow § 7 procedures when they consult with the FWS or the NMFS before proceeding with proposed "agency actions" to determine whether such actions are likely to jeopardize any endangered or threatened species.

See Figure 7-3, the *Endangered Species Act Consultation Handbook: Procedures for Conducting Section 7 Consultations and Conferences (Handbook)*, U.S. Fish and Wildlife Service, National Marine Fisheries Service, March 1998, for detailed information on the Consultation program. This document is available for review on the Internet at http://endangered.fws.gov/consultations/s7hndbk/s7hndbk.htm.

Any action "authorized, funded, or carried out" by a federal agency triggers consultation procedures under § 7. The consulting agencies' joint implementing regulations for consultation broadly construe the term "action":

Action means all activities or programs of any kind authorized, funded, or carried out, in whole or in part, by Federal

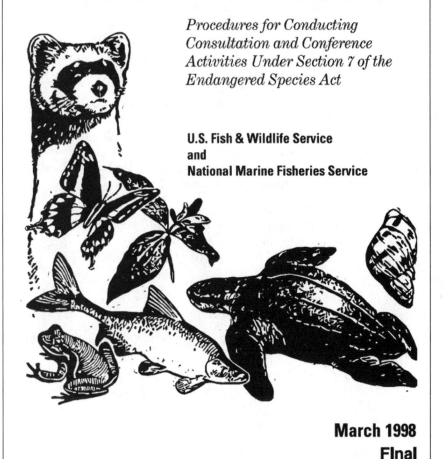

Figure 7-3 *The Endangered Species Act Consultation Handbook: Procedures for Conducting Section 7 Consultations and Conferences (Handbook)*, U.S. Fish and Wildlife Service, National Marine Fisheries Service, March 1998.

agencies in the United States or upon the high seas. Examples include but are not limited to

(a) actions intended to conserve listed species or their habitat;
(b) the promulgation of regulations;
(c) the granting of licenses, contracts, leases, easements, rights-of-way, permits, or grants-in-aid; or
(d) actions directly or indirectly causing modifications to the land, water or air. 50 C.F.R. § 402.2.

This statutory duty to consult applies only to federal "actions in which there is discretionary Federal involvement or control." 50 C.F.R. § 402.03.

To comply with § 7 requirements, the action agency first defines the action area, determines the presence of listed species or critical habitat within the action area, and establishes whether the project may have a direct or indirect impact to listed species or designated habitat. The action agency uses an incremental approach to assess the degree of the proposed action's impact on listed species or designated habitat. This incremental approach consists of

- an analysis of whether there will be any effect;
- an analysis of whether there will be any adverse effect; and
- an analysis of whether any listed species will be jeopardized or whether any critical habitat will be destroyed or adversely impacted.

The agencies examine whether a proposed action may affect listed species and designated habitat by

- holding early consultations with permittees and licensees (50 C.F.R. § 402.11);
- conducting biological assessment for major construction activities or other federal action that may be done as part of an NEPA requirement (50 C.F.R. § 402.12); and
- performing informal consultations pursuant to 50 C.F.R. § 402.13 to determine whether a formal consultation, as outlined in 50 C.F.R. § 402.14, is required.

Consultation may end immediately when agencies determine that the action will have "no effect" on listed species or critical habitat. An action agency can request that the consulting agencies concur with the "no effect" determination. If the consulting agency concurs with the "no effect" determination, consultation ends.

A biological assessment must be conducted when the action agency determines the proposed action is a major construction activity and listed species or designated habitat may be present in the action area. For nonconstruction or minor construction activities that may affect listed species or critical habitat, the action agency can do one of the following:

- voluntarily prepare a biological assessment;
- engage in "informal consultation" with the consulting agency; or
- engage in its own, independent analysis of the effects of the action.

Formal consultation is not required for actions that are not likely to adversely affect listed species or critical habitat. 50 C.F.R. § 402.14(b). Formal consultation is required if the action agency determines that its proposed action is likely to adversely affect listed species or critical habitat. 50 C.F.R. § 401.14(a) and (b). Formal consultation is "initiated" by a written request from the action agency to the consulting agency. Formal consultation must be concluded within ninety days from the date it is initiated, unless the agencies involved agree to extend the time period. The conclusion results in the consulting agency's issuance of a biological opinion.

Biological Opinion

"Biological opinion (BO)" is not defined in the ESA but is used to satisfy the provision within § 7(b) of the Act that requires a "written statement setting forth the Secretary's opinion, and a summary of the information on which the opinion is based, detailing how the agency action affects the species or its critical habitat."

Every BO must contain

- a summary of the information on which the opinion is based;
- a detailed discussion of the effects of the action on listed species or critical habitat;
- the consulting agency's opinion as to whether the action is likely to jeopardize the continued existence of a listed species or result in destruction or adverse modification of critical habitat; and,
- if jeopardy is determined, reasonable and prudent alternatives.

If the consulting agency's BO results in a finding of the existence of any adverse impact, then the consulting agency must determine the existence of any reasonable and prudent alternatives to avoid any jeopardy or adverse impacts to the listed species or habitat. 16 U.S.C. § 1536(b)(3). In light of the possibility of a potential alternative, from the time the action agency initiates the § 7 process, it is prohibited from making any "irreversible or irretrievable" commitment of resources that would foreclose the formulation or implementation of any reasonable and prudent alternative to the proposed action. The action agency may be challenged for injunctive relief to stop the action that may preclude the implementation of potential alternatives. 16 U.S.C. § 1536(d).

ESA allows for **incidental take** of listed species in connection with otherwise lawful activities. As long as an action can proceed, that is no jeopardy, any BO issued with respect to an otherwise lawful activity must include an **incidental take statement (ITS),** which is essentially a permit that allows for take of a listed species incidental to the agency action.

An action agency must reinitiate consultation for any one of the following events:

- The amount and extent of incidental take is exceeded.
- New information indicates that the proposed action may threaten endangered species or critical habitat.
- The action is modified in such a way as to cause an effect on listed species or critical habitat in a manner not considered in the BO.
- A new species is listed or critical habitat is designated that may be affected by the action.

The consulting agency's BO is considered final agency action that is subject to challenge in the federal courts. The challenger may be the action agency that disagrees with the BO. In that event, the action agency must articulate its reason for its disagreement with the BO. In fact, the action agency is technically free to disregard the BO and proceed with its proposed action. However, if the action agency proceeds with its proposed action, it runs a substantial risk. *Bennett v. Spear,* 520 U.S. 154 (1997). If the action agency turns out to be incorrect and the action indeed results in jeopardy to listed species or habitat, the action agency is not covered by the take provisions and may be subject to § 9 enforcement.

An alternative an action agency may take to avoid being subject to § 9 enforcement is for the action agency to apply to the Endangered Species Committee (ESC), commonly referred to as the "God Squad" or "God Committee," which is comprised of seven Cabinet secretaries and agency administrators. The committee may grant an action agency exemption from its § 7 duty to avoid jeopardy. The ESC has met only a handful of times since Congress created the ESA § 7 exemption process in 1978. On most occasions, the ESC has denied the application for the exemption. The ESC has granted at least two exemptions. One exempted the Bureau of Land Management for the timber sales that would impact the northern spotted owl. The other exempted a reservoir project in Wyoming contrary to adverse effects to whooping cranes.

CASES FOR DISCUSSION

Tennessee Valley Authority v. Hill, 437 U.S. 153 (1978).

In this landmark case, the court held that Congress had intended to afford species the highest of priorities, and that § 7 demanded that a nearly completed dam project be halted to protect the snail darter (a listed fish species). Subsequent to this decision, the ESC was convened for the first time, but it did not grant TVA an exception.

Application procedures for these exemptions are codified in 50 C.F.R. § 450 and outlined in the CRS publication titled *Endangered Species Act: The Listing and Exemption Processes,* CRS No. 90-242 ENR (May 8, 1990). Pursuant to 16 U.S.C. § 1536(h)(1)(A), in order to be granted an exemption, the applicant must satisfy the following conditions.

- There are no reasonable and prudent alternatives to the agency action.
- The benefits of the agency action is in the public interest and clearly outweigh the benefits of alternative courses of action to conserve the species.
- The action is of regional or national importance.
- Neither the action agency nor the exemption applicant made any irreversible or irretrievable commitment of resources.

Any decision made by the ESC may be challenged by any person by taking the action to the U.S. Court of Appeals. The laws regarding the ESA and applications for exemption are discussed in 16 U.S.C. § 1536(e) through (h).

Incidental Takes and Habitat Conservation Plans

A new section, § 10, was added to the ESA through the 1982 amendments, and was codified as 16 U.S.C. § 1539. The purpose for enacting § 10 was to reduce the conflicts that were occurring between the goal of protecting listed species and the economics of development activities. The legislation encourages "creative partnerships" between public and private sectors. Section 10 allows for incidental takes of endangered and threatened species of wildlife by non-federal entities. 16 U.S.C. § 1539(a)(1)(B); 50 C.F.R. §§ 17.22 and 17.23. An incidental take is a take that occurs incidentally during otherwise legal activities.

Upon application, anyone may request the FWS or the NFMS to issue an incidental take permit. 16 U.S.C. § 1539(a). The applicant submits a habitat conservation plan (HCP) that specifies

- an analysis of the impacts that will likely result from the taking;
- the actions the applicant plans to take to minimize and mitigate those impacts;
- an assurance of adequate funding to carry out the HCP; and
- the alternative actions the applicant considered and why the alternatives are not being used.

Figure 7-4 illustrates the incidental take permit application for native species. A complete copy of the permit application is available on the Internet at http://forms.fws.gov/3-200-56.pdf.

If the activities are minor in scope and effect, the submitted HCP is considered one of low effect and receives expedited permit processing. In addition, as an alternative to the agency's issuing an incidental take permit, the agency may make a recommendation to landowners on ways to avoid and minimize impacts to the listed species, making a permit unnecessary.

When the FWS makes a decision, it publishes its notice in the *Federal Register*, allowing for a public comment period. The incidental take permit is issued only if all of the following conditions are met (16 U.S.C. § 1539(a)(2)(B)):

- The taking will be incidental.
- The applicant will minimize and mitigate the impacts of taking.
- The applicant will ensure adequate funding for the conservation plan.
- The taking will not appreciably reduce the likelihood of survival and recovery of the species in the wild.

HCPs are addressed in the FWS's comprehensive *Habitat Conservation Planning Handbook and Incidental Take Permit Processing Handbook* (November 4, 1996). The entire handbook is published on the FWS Web site at http://endangered.fws.gov/hcp/hcpbook.htm and includes application requirements and processing procedures as well as the application forms.

Policy for Evaluation of Conservation Efforts

When the agencies evaluate conservation efforts when making listing decisions, they follow their Policy for Evaluation of Conservation Efforts (PECE), which was published on June 13, 2000,

Department of the Interior
U.S. Fish and Wildlife Service
Federal Fish and Wildlife Permit Application Form

Expires September 30, 2007
OMB No. 1018-0094

Return to: *Click here for addresses*

Type of Activity:

Native Endangered & Threatened Species –
Incidental Take permits Associated With A Habitat Conservation Plan

Complete sections A. OR B. and C. on this page, plus the attached pages of this application. Application will not be considered complete without all sections. See additional instructions on attached pages.

A.	Complete if applying as an individual		
1.a. Last name	1.b. First name	1.c. Middle name or initial	1.d. Suffix
2.a. Street address (line 1)	2.b. Street address (line 2)	2.c. Street address (line 3)	
3.a. City	3.b. Province	3.c. State	3.d. Zip code/Postal code:	3.e. Country
4. Date of birth (mm/dd/yyyy)	5. Social Security No.	6. Occupation	7.a. Home telephone number
7.b. Work telephone number	7.c. Fax number	8. E-mail address	9. County
10. List any business, agency, organizational, or institutional affiliation associated with the wildlife or plants to be covered by this permit (see C.1.)	11. Doing business as (dba)		

B.	Complete if applying as a business, corporation, public agency or institution		
1.a. Name of business, agency, or institution	1.b. Doing business as (dba)		
2.a. Street address (line 1)	2.b. Street address (line 2)	2.c. Street address (line 3)	
3.a. City	3.b. Province	3.c. State	3.d. Zip code	3.e. Country
4. Tax identification no.	5. Describe the type of business, agency, or institution and provide state of incorporation		
6.a. Principal officer (President, director, etc) Last name	6.b. First name	6.c. Middle name or initial	6.d. Suffix
7. Principal officer title:	8. Home telephone number		
9. Work telephone number	10. Fax number	11. E-mail address	12. County

C.	All applicants complete
1.	Do you currently have or have you had any Federal Fish and Wildlife permits? (For simplification, all licenses, permits, registrations, and certificates will be referred to as a permit.) Yes ☐ If yes, list the number of the most current permit you have held: _____ No ☐
2.	Have you obtained all required State, Federal, or foreign government approval(s) to conduct the activity you propose? Yes ☐ If yes, provide a copy of the approval(s). Have applied ☐ Not required ☐
3.	Enclose check or money order payable to the U.S. FISH AND WILDLIFE SERVICE in the amount of $25 [50 CFR 13.11(d)(2)]. Institutions which qualify under 50 CFR 13.11(d)(3) may be exempt from the application processing fee.
4.	Certification: I hereby certify that I have read and am familiar with the regulations contained in Title 50, Part 13, of the Code of Federal Regulations and the other applicable parts in subchapter B of Chapter I of Title 50, and I certify that the information submitted in this application for a permit is complete and accurate to the best of my knowledge and belief. I understand that any false statement herein may subject me to the criminal penalties of 18 U.S.C. 1001.
5.	Signature (in blue ink) of applicant/person responsible for permit in Section A. or B. (Photocopied signatures are not accepted.) 6. Date (mm/dd/yyyy):

Form 3-200-56 (Rev. 6/2004)   **Please continue to next page**   1

Figure 7-4 Incidental Take Permit Application for Native Species.

in 64 Fed. Reg. 37102. The purpose of the policy is to ensure consistent and adequate evaluations of future or recently implemented conservation efforts identified in the various methods, such as conservation agreements, conservation plans, management plans, and other documents when making listing decisions.

Implementation of CITES

Section 9 of the ESA provides for the implementation of the **Convention on International Trade in Endangered Species of Wild Flora and Fauna (CITES).** About 140 nations list species and provide a sliding scale of protection. The sliding scale is reflected as three appendices that are listed in 50 C.F.R. § 23.23. Appendix 1 provides the greatest protection to the listed species, and Appendix 3 provides the least protection.

The importation requirements of CITES species are found in 50 C.F.R. part 23. Violators of the CITES requirements are charged with a Class A misdemeanor. 16 U.S.C. § 1538(c). It is unlawful to engage in trade, or to **import** fish, wildlife, or plants contrary to the CITES, or to possess any fish, wildlife, or plants that have been unlawfully imported.

Freedom of Religion Exemptions

There are no exemptions from the ESA for Native Americans in Hawaii and the mainland United States. However, there are some exemptions for Alaskan natives, particularly for sustenance purposes. 16 U.S.C. § 1539(e)(1). For example, the U.S. Supreme Court held that the Bald and Golden Eagle Protection Act abrogated any Indian treaty right to hunt bald eagles. The 1962 amendment to the Act, which authorizes the issuance of permits for Indian eagle hunting, indicated legislative intent that eagle hunting by Native Americans is inconsistent with the ESA unless authorized by permit. *United States v. Dion*, 476 U.S. 734, on remand 800 F.2d 771 (8th Cir. 1986). Also, in *United States v. Billie*, 667 F. Supp. 1485 (S.D. Fla. 1987), the court held that the taking prohibitions of the ESA apply to activities of the Native Americans on their reservation.

Latest Developments

At the time of the writing of this chapter, the FWS proposed a change to its taking regulation that would permit American hunters, circuses, and the pet industry to kill, capture, and import endangered species in other countries. The rationale is that the current regulations provide no incentive for poor countries of the world to protect endangered species, and that taking fixed numbers of animals from the wild would pay for conservation programs for remaining animals. Other Western countries are already trading in endangered and threatened species, but the ESA and its regulations, as currently written, preclude such takings.

Other recent developments could result in changes to the ESA, including

- ongoing debate over whether critical habitat adds any additional protection to listed species and the role of "sound science" in making critical habitat designations (2003 U.S. Senate Committee on Environment and Public Works, Hearing on Critical Habitat Designations Under the ESA (April 10, 2003) and GAO-03-803, Additional Guidance Needed for Critical Habitat Designations (Aug. 29, 2003)).
- whether the FWS and the NMFS "no surprises" rule is valid and whether landowners will continue to participate in the HCP process if no assurances are given through the "no surprises" rule (*Spirit of the Sage Council v. Babbitt*, 98-1873 EGS, D.D.C.); and
- whether the Department of Defense should be exempt from portions of the ESA for military operations.

GLOSSARY OF ESA TERMS

action agency. A federal agency proposing an action that may affect species or habitat that consults with either the FWS or the NMFS to comply with its § 7 requirements under the ESA.

Biological Opinion. In a § 7 consultation, the determination made by the consulting agency of whether an action agency's proposed action is likely to directly or indirectly jeopardize the continued existence of any species that is listed or proposed to be listed, or is likely to result in the destruction or any adverse impact to any designated or proposed critical habitat.

candidate species list. A list of species that is published annually in the *Federal Register* that the FWS or the NMFS determines are warranted to be included in either the endangered or threatened species lists but precluded for specific reasons.

CITES. Convention on International Trade in Endangered Species of Wild Flowers and Fauna, a multilateral international trade and conservation convention currently made up of 144 countries.

commercial activity. All activities of industry and trade, including the buying or selling of commodities and activities, conducted for the purpose of facilitating such buying and selling but not for exhibition by museums or similar cultural or historical organizations.

conserve, conserving, and conservation. The use of all methods and procedures that are necessary to bring any listed species to the point at which the measures provided in the ESA are no longer necessary.

consulting agency. Either the FWS or the NMFS when it is consulted by a federal agency to comply with its § 7 requirements.

critical habitat. The specific areas within the geographical area occupied by the species, at the time it is listed, on which are found the physical or biological features that are essential to the conservation of the species and that may require special management considerations or protection, and also the specific areas outside the geographical area occupied by the species, at the time it is listed, that are determined essential for the conservation of the species.

endangered species. Any species in danger of extinction throughout all or a significant portion of its range whose protection under the provisions of the ESA, other than a species of the Class Insecta, determined by the agency to constitute a pest and would present an overwhelming and overriding risk to man.

ESA. Endangered Species Act, codified in 16 U.S.C. §§ 1531 to 1544, the primary federal statute regulating the protection of species of fish, wildlife, and plants so depleted in numbers they are in danger of or threatened with extinction.

federal agency. Any department, agency, or instrumentality of the United States.

fish or wildlife. Any member of the animal kingdom, including without limitation any mammal, fish, bird, amphibian, reptile, mollusk, crustacean, arthropod, or other invertebrate, and including any part, product, egg, or offspring thereof, or the dead body or parts thereof.

foreign commerce. Any transaction between persons within one foreign country, between persons in two or more foreign countries, between a person within the United States and a person in a foreign country, or between persons within the United States, where the fish and wildlife in question are moving in any country or countries outside the United States.

FWS. The U.S. Fish and Wildlife Service, the federal agency that is delegated lead responsibility for protecting all land-dwelling species, freshwater species, some marine mammals, and migratory birds.

Habitat Conservation Plan (HCP). A report submitted to the FWS or the NMFS that details the steps an incidental take permit applicant will undertake to minimize, mitigate for, and monitor the impacts to listed species.

harm. Defined by the FWS as an act that actually kills or injures fish or wildlife or significant habitat modification or degradation that actually kills or injures wildlife by significantly impairing essential behavioral patterns, including breeding, feeding, or sheltering. The NMFS adds spawning, rearing, and migrating to the behavior patterns affected by the habitat modification or degradation.

import. To land on, bring into, or introduce into, or attempt to land on, bring into, or introduce into, any place subject to the jurisdiction of the United States, whether or not such landing, bringing, or introduction constitutes an importation within the meaning of the customs laws of the United States.

incidental take. A take that occurs from, but is not the purpose of, carrying out an otherwise lawful activity conducted by a federal agency or applicant.

incidental take statement (ITS). A permit that allows for take of a listed species incidental to a lawful agency action.

listed species. Species that are listed in the *Federal Register* by the FWS or the NMFS either as endangered or threatened.

NMFS. National Marine and Fisheries Service, the federal agency that is delegated lead responsibility for protecting marine species, including both freshwater and ocean-dwelling fish.

Notice of Review (NOR). The annual notice of candidate species that is published in the *Federal Register* to solicit information needed to prioritize species.

plant. Any member of the plant kingdom, including seeds, roots, and other parts thereof.

recovery plan. A plan that identifies, justifies, and schedules the research and management actions necessary to reverse the decline of a species and ensure its long-term survival.

species. Any subspecies of fish or wildlife or plants, and any distinct population segment of any species of vertebrate fish or wildlife that interbreeds when mature.

take. To harass, harm, pursue, hunt, shoot, wound, kill, trap, capture, or collect any listed species, or to attempt to engage in any such conduct.

threatened species. Any species that is likely to become an endangered species within the foreseeable future throughout all or a significant portion of its range.

BIBLIOGRAPHY

Baur, Donald C., & Wm. Robert Irvin, *Endangered Species Act: Law, Policy, and Perspective* (A.B.A. 2002).

Brightman, Richard S., & Gabriel E. Nieto, *Incidental Take Permitting and Habitat Conservation Planning*, Fla. Envtl. & Land Use L. (The Florida Bar Feb. 2002).

Brown, Mark, *Overview of the Endangered Species Act and Highlights of Recent Litigation* (U.S. Dept. of Justice, Wildlife and Marine

Resources Section of the Environment and Natural Resources Division 1991).

Endangered Species—Fish and Wildlife Service Uses Best Available Science to Make Listing Decision, but Additional Guidance Needed for Critical Habitat Designations, U.S. General Accounting Office Report to Congressional Requestors No. GAO-03-803 (Aug. 2003).

Ergas, Luna, *Section 9 of the Endangered Species Act: Prohibitions on Taking Listed Species*, Fla. Envtl. & Land Use L. (The Florida Bar Feb. 2001).

McGowan, Paul, *The Endangered Species Act Listing Process*, Fla. Envtl. & Land Use L. (The Florida Bar Feb. 2001).

Rizzardi, Keith, *ESA Section 7 Consultation*, Fla. Envtl. & Land Use L. (The Florida Bar Feb. 2001).

Sullins, Tony A., *ESA Endangered Species Act*, Basic Practice Series (A.B.A. 2001).

White, David J., *Enforcement and Judicial Review of the Endangered Species Act*, Fla. Envtl. & Land Use L. (The Florida Bar Feb. 2001).

DISCUSSION QUESTIONS

1. What is the difference between an endangered species and a threatened species?
2. What is the difference between a biological assessment and a biological opinion?
3. Under what situations may anyone "take" an endangered or threatened species?
4. An owner of a large vacant property adjacent to a large state park would like to have it developed as a mixed use development, incorporating residential, commercial, and natural areas.

    Q. In light of the ESA, what is one of the preliminary steps the owner needs to take in order to plan for the development?

    Q. What should the owner do if an endangered or threatened species is found on the property?

    Q. What are some of the alternatives available to the landowner who wishes to develop property on which an endangered or threatened species is found?

5. Do you believe that taking endangered species from the wild in poor countries is an effective means to conserve remaining endangered species in those countries? Explain your response.

COMPUTER LABORATORY PROJECTS

1. Research and report on federal or state programs that might undermine endangered species protection.

INTERNET SITES

- The full text of the Endangered Species Act (ESA) is on the Internet at http://www.epa.gov/region5/defs/html/esa.htm.

- The Fish and Wildlife Service is on the Internet at http://www.fws.gov.

- The National Marine Fisheries Service is on the Internet at http://www.nmfs.noaa.gov.

CHAPTER 8

The National Environmental Policy Act

James F. Berry[1]

OBJECTIVES

The objectives of this chapter are for students to:

- Learn the terminology associated with NEPA.
- Learn the concepts and ideas that underlie the NEPA law and regulatory program.
- Learn about specific sections and provisions of the NEPA law and regulations.
- Learn about the processes and procedures used by the government and other parties to comply with and to enforce the law under NEPA.
- Learn about the particular jobs and functions that are performed by paralegals working for attorneys in NEPA cases.

History of the Act

The **National Environmental Policy Act of 1969 (NEPA),** 42 U.S.C. §§ 4321 to 4370d (2003), is considered to be the cornerstone of environmental law. The statute is unique because it is one of the few environmental laws that apply solely to the federal government. Regulations under the Act are found at 40 C.F.R. §§ 1500 to 1517 (2003).

NEPA was proposed by Senator Henry M. Jackson on February 18, 1969, as Senate Bill S. 1075. NEPA passed the Senate on a voice vote

---

[1] The author acknowledges and thanks Patricia L. McCarthy for her work on earlier drafts of this chapter.

on July 10, 1969. Following negotiations in conference committee with representatives of the House, NEPA was adopted by the Congress on December 22, 1969. President Richard M. Nixon signed the bill into law on January 1, 1970.

The enactment of NEPA was not the only event focusing on the environment in 1970. In April 1970, the United States celebrated its first Earth Day. In July of that same year, President Nixon created the Environmental Protection Agency.

NEPA was designed to regulate federal agencies such as the Department of Defense, Department of the Interior, Fish and Wildlife, the Federal Aviation Administration, the Federal Highway Administration, the Bureau of Land Management, the U.S. Army Corps of Engineers, and the Department of Energy. Almost every federal agency had, and continues to have, responsibilities that affect the environment. The goal of NEPA was to change the procedures and priorities of the federal agencies to incorporate the idea of stewardship of our nation's resources.

NEPA is organized into three titles. The first, Title I, 42 U.S.C. §§ 4331 to 4335 (2003), containing the purpose of NEPA, declares six national environmental goals, provides the means for accomplishing those goals, and gives guidance on how NEPA relates to other federal laws.

Title II, 42 U.S.C. §§ 4341 to 4347 (2003), created the **Council on Environmental Quality (CEQ)** and defines CEQ's responsibilities.

Title III, 42 U.S.C. §§ 4361 to 4370d (2003), addressed other miscellaneous issues.

> The goal of NEPA was to change the procedures and priorities of federal agencies to incorporate the idea of stewardship of our nation's resources.

Section 2 of the Act details the purpose of NEPA, which is to adopt a national environmental policy:

> The purposes of this chapter are: To declare a national policy which will encourage productive and enjoyable harmony between man and his environment; to promote efforts which will prevent or eliminate damage to the environment and biosphere and stimulate the health and welfare of man; to enrich the understanding of the ecological systems and natural resources important to the Nation; and to establish a Council on Environmental Quality.

National Environmental Policy Act of 1969, 42 U.S.C. § 4331 (2003).

NEPA's Goals

In order to achieve NEPA's purpose for a national environmental policy, Congress commanded the federal government "to use all practicable means" to attain the following six goals:

1. Fulfill the responsibilities of environmental trustee for future generations.
2. Assure "safe, healthful, productive and aesthetically and culturally pleasing surroundings" for all Americans.
3. Provide the widest range of beneficial uses of the environment without degradation, health or safety risks, or other unwanted consequences.
4. Preserve important historic, cultural, and natural aspects of national heritage and protect the environment's diversity.
5. Balance between population and resource use.
6. Increase the quality of renewable resources and achieve the maximum recycling of depletable resources.

42 U.S.C. § 4331(b) (2003).

NEPA establishes important substantive goals for the nation with respect to the environment, yet the obligations for the agencies to comply with NEPA are "essentially procedural." *Strycker's Bay Neighborhood, Inc. v. Karlen*, 444 U.S. 223 (1980). NEPA commands the decision-making process to evaluate environmental concerns for the purpose of informed agency action. The statute does not mandate particular results.

NEPA has twin aims. First, the federal agency has an absolute "obligation to consider every significant aspect of the environmental impact of the proposed action." *Baltimore Gas & Elec. Co. v. NRDC*, 462 U.S. 87 (1983). Congress enacted NEPA to require that federal agencies take a "hard look" at the environmental effects of their decisions before taking action.

Second, NEPA ensures that environmental information is available to public officials and citizens before any decision is made or action is taken. 40 C.F.R. § 1500.1(b) (2003).

> A federal agency has an absolute obligation to consider every significant aspect of the environmental impact of a proposed action.

The method for achieving NEPA's goals originates from § 102(2) of NEPA. Congress authorized the Council on Environmental

Quality to develop procedures for the compliance with NEPA's goals. The CEQ regulations present these procedures. 40 C.F.R. §§ 1500 to 1508 (2003).

NEPA and the CEQ regulations are binding on all federal agencies. All agencies must use the **NEPA process** to identify and evaluate the alternatives to proposed agency actions in order to avoid or minimize adverse effects on the environment. 40 C.F.R. §§ 1500.3 and 1500.2(e) (2003). The regulations define "NEPA process" as the measures necessary to comply with § 2 of NEPA. 40 C.F.R. § 1508.21 (2003). The federal agencies must also integrate NEPA requirements with the agency's planning process so that the procedures "run concurrently rather than consecutively." The NEPA process must begin at the earliest possible time so that all planning and decisions "reflect environmental values."

> NEPA ensures that environmental information is available to public officials and citizens before decisions are made and actions are taken.

The NEPA process provides for encouraging public involvement in agency decisions that affect the environment. 40 C.F.R. §§ 1500.2(b), (c), and (d) and 1501.2 (2003).

The Environmental Assessment

The NEPA process begins with the **Environmental Assessment (EA).** A federal agency, under circumstances described below, must prepare an environmental assessment, a concise public document for which a federal agency is responsible, that serves to

1. provide brief sufficient evidence and analysis for determining whether to prepare an environmental impact statement or a finding of no significant impact;
2. aid an agency's compliance with the Act when no environmental impact statement is necessary; and
3. facilitate preparation of an environmental impact statement when one is necessary.

40 C.F.R. § 1508.9(a) (2003).

The EA is not necessary if the agency has decided to prepare an environmental impact statement. 40 C.F.R. § 1501.3(a) (2003). If the agency's planning procedures, which include NEPA procedures, call for an EA, then the EA is prepared by the federal agency. The EA can, however, be prepared by a permit applicant and reviewed by the agency for compliance with NEPA. 40 C.F.R. § 1506.5(b) (2003).

The EA can be prepared by the state if the major federal action is federally funded to the state under a grant. State involvement is essential when the state receives federal grants for highway construction. The state's EA will satisfy NEPA if

- the state agency or official has statewide jurisdiction and is responsible for the action;
- the responsible federal official provides guidance and participates in the preparation of the related **Environmental Impact Statement (EIS)**;
- the responsible federal official independently evaluates the EIS prior to approval and adoption; and
- the responsible federal official both provides early notice to and requests the views of other state or federal land management agencies that may have impacts from the project. If other state agencies or federal agencies have comments, oppose the project, or disagree on the impacts of the project, those views must be documented in a written report and incorporated into the EA.

42 U.S.C. § 4332(2)(D) (2003).

The CEQ regulations expect cooperation among agencies. 40 C.F.R. § 1501.1(b) (2003). The agencies must be involved in the process at the beginning to assist with the NEPA process.

A vehicle to exclude the EA process entirely is the **categorical exclusion.** The agency has the flexibility to determine if a category of actions does not individually or cumulatively have a significant environmental impact. 40 C.F.R. §§ 1501.4(a)(2) and 1508.4 (2003). The categorical exclusion regulations are specific to each agency's program.

The majority of federal actions will require an EA and thereby reach the initial decision of whether a **Finding of No Significant Impact (FONSI)** exists or whether the agency should prepare an EIS. A FONSI is a document prepared by the federal agency that briefly explains the reasons why the proposed action will not have a significant impact on the environment. 40 C.F.R. § 1508.13 (2003). The FONSI document will include the EA prepared by the agency.

Whether the agency prepares an EA or a FONSI, paralegals may be involved in reviewing these documents for their clients to summarize and criticize the agency's conclusion.

CASES FOR DISCUSSION

Greater Yellowstone Coalition v. U.S. Forest Service, 209 F. Supp. 2d 156, 54 ERC 1864, 32 Envtl. L. Rep. 20,681 (D. D.C. 2002).

In this case the plaintiffs claimed that the defendants violated NEPA by failing to conduct an environmental assessment before reissuing a livestock grazing permit on federal public lands.

In November 1994, in response to various court decisions, the Forest Service implemented a policy to conduct NEPA analyses for the reissuance of grazing permits. However, the Forest Service was unprepared to handle this new slate of NEPA reviews, and it quickly became apparent that the Service would not be able to complete all NEPA analyses in time to reissue expiring permits.

In response to the looming threat that many permits would not be reissued for failure to complete the NEPA review, Congress enacted the Rescission Act, Pub. L. No. 104-19, 109 Stat. 194.8 (1995). The Rescission Act established a temporary exemption from NEPA review for those permits that were up for reissuance before the NEPA review for that allotment had been completed. The Act directed each national forest to establish and adhere to a schedule for conducting NEPA reviews on all of the grazing allotments in that forest. It also provided that if a grazing permit came up for reissuance before the time stated in the schedule for NEPA review, the Service must automatically reissue the permit. If implemented properly, no rancher would be left with an expired permit solely because the Service had not completed NEPA analysis in accordance with the schedule the Service had adopted.

Pursuant to the Rescission Act, in November 1995, the Gallatin National Forest established a NEPA compliance schedule that set a 1998 environmental analysis and decision date for the Horse Butte allotment. This compliance date was later included in a national list compiled by the Forest Service's national headquarters. By the summer of 1997, officials at the Gallatin National Forest anticipated that the 1998 deadline would not be met.

Meanwhile, the Munns Brothers' permit was due to expire on December 31, 2000. The permit was reissued on December 19, 2000. The district ranger, invoking § 504(b) of the Rescission Act, reissued the permit for another ten years on the same terms, subject to modification upon completion of the NEPA analysis. The reissuance allowed the Munns Brothers to continue to graze 147 head of cattle and thirty horses on the allotment.

The plaintiffs contend that the Service's reissuance of the Horse Butte permit violated NEPA and thereby constituted an unlawful

(continued)

CASES FOR DISCUSSION

agency action under the Federal Administrative Procedures Act. The court concluded:

> [T]he Service failed to adhere to the schedule that it initially adopted, [so] then it cannot invoke § 504(b) to justify the permit's reissuance. By the time it was reissued, the original schedule as it pertained to Horse Butte had been modified and amended out of existence. The permit reissued to the Munns brothers in December 2000 was certainly not issued pursuant to the original schedule that set the date for the completion of Horse Butte NEPA process in 1998. Plaintiffs are therefore correct in stating that since no exemption was available under the Rescission Act, the Service's granting of the permit was in violation of NEPA.

Section 102(2) and the Environmental Impact Statement

Section 102(2) of NEPA is paramount to NEPA's goal of informed decision making. This "action-forcing" provision is activated when the agency's EA determines that the proposed action is "a major federal action that significantly affects the quality of the human environment." An Environmental Impact Statement is required for every report or recommendation on proposals, for legislation, and for other major federal actions significantly affecting the quality of the human environment. 40 C.F.R. § 1502.3 (2003).

This list constitutes the statutory criteria for preparing an EIS. Each criterion will be explained below, as will the requirements of an EIS.

"Major Federal Action" is defined as "actions with effects that may be major and that are potentially subject to federal control and responsibility. "Major" reinforces but does not have a meaning independent of 'significantly." 40 C.F.R. § 1508.18 (2003).

An assumption exists that there are objective criteria by which most environmental choices can be evaluated. With that assumption, the cost-benefit analysis was adopted by Congress for the federal government in making resource allocation choices. The cost-benefit analysis produces a ratio of costs for a proposed project and compares one project over another.

The current mandate on cost-benefit analysis, outlined in Executive Order 12,291 at 46 Fed. Reg. 13193 (February 19, 1981), sets out how federal agencies are to weigh cost-benefit factors, including

    a. refraining from regulation unless the potential benefits outweigh the potential costs;
    b. choosing the objective that maximizes net benefits to society;
    c. selecting alternatives with the least cost to society; and
    d. setting regulatory priorities that maximize net benefits to society.

Action also includes the failure of an agency to act, and that failure to act can be reviewed by the court or by an administrative law judge under the **Federal Administrative Procedure Act (FAPA),** 5 U.S.C. §§ 500 to 596 (2003).

This definition for "major federal action" includes

- proposed legislation;
- adoption of rules, regulations, and policy;
- adoption of formal plans; and
- approval of specific projects.

Actions taken by federal agencies, operation of agency programs, and construction of agency facilities are also eligible for an EIS. The regulations (40 C.F.R. § 1508.18(b) (2003)) detail four categories of federal action, which include

    a. adoption of official policy such as rules, regulations, and interpretations adopted pursuant to the FAPA; treaties and international conventions or agreements; or formal documents establishing an agency's policies that will result in or substantially alter agency programs;
    b. adoption of formal plans such as official documents prepared or approved by federal agencies that guide or prescribe alternative uses of federal resources, upon which future agency actions will be based;
    c. adoption of programs such as a group of concerted actions to implement a specific policy or plan; systematic and connected agency decisions allocating agency resources to implement a specific statutory program or executive directive; and
    d. approval of specific projects such as construction or management activities located in a defined geographic area. Projects include actions approved by permit or other regulatory decision, as well as federal and federally assisted activities.

The consequence of the action includes all impacts caused by the action, whether those impacts are direct or indirect. 40 C.F.R. § 1508.8 (2003).

Federal permits, licenses, loans, grants, and leases may also require an EIS even though federal involvement is very minimal. Appropriation requests do not qualify as major federal action. *Andrus v. Sierra Club*, 442 U.S. 347 (1979).

An EIS is required for **proposals.** A proposal exists when an agency has a goal or idea and the agency is actively preparing to make a decision on one or more alternatives. The EIS on the proposal should be completed before any recommendation or report on the proposal. 40 C.F.R. § 1508.23 (2003).

The CEQ regulations specify that an EIS is required for all **legislation.** 40 C.F.R. § 1502.3 (2003). "Legislation" includes a bill or legislative proposal to Congress that was developed by or with the support of a federal agency. Requests for appropriations are expressly excluded from this definition of "legislation." The regulations define a test for determining the degree of agency cooperation: "whether the proposal is in fact predominantly that of the agency rather than another source." 40 C.F.R. § 1508.17 (2003). An agency's drafting of a bill or legislation is not enough.

Proposals of legislation also specifically include requests for ratification of treaties. The agency that has primary responsibility for the bill or legislation is the one responsible for preparing a legislative environmental impact statement.

Significantly affecting the quality of the human environment also extends to a broad spectrum of activities. "Significantly" requires consideration of both context and intensity. By "context," the regulations explain that the significance of an action must be analyzed in multiple contexts. These contexts include

- society as a whole, both human society and our national society;
- the region affected by the agency action;
- the interests impacted by the action; and
- the location of the project.

The significance of an agency's action will vary. Both short-term and long-term effects are relevant and must be evaluated. 40 C.F.R. § 1508.27 (2003).

"Significantly" also requires analysis of the intensity of the proposed action. The severity of the impact of the proposal will be reviewed. Agency cooperation is required if the proposed action may involve more than one agency, and all agencies must evaluate the impact. This intensity component requires the consideration of numerous issues. The impacts can be both beneficial and adverse. Even when the agency believes the balance weighs in favor of beneficial, the agency must evaluate the adverse impact.

Public health and safety are critical evaluations. If a cumulative significant impact can be reasonably anticipated, then this criterion has been satisfied. The responsible agency must consider whether the effects on the human environment may be controversial and, if so, to what degree. 40 C.F.R. §§ 1508.27 and 1508.27 (b)(1), (2), and (7) (2003).

For example, the court in *Hanley v. Kleindienst (II)*, 471 F.2d 823 (2d Cir. 1972), found that the agency must evaluate the controversial effect on the environment for the construction of a prison in an urban setting. The agency must determine whether the action may threaten or adversely affect an endangered or threatened species or its habitat.[2] 40 C.F.R. § 1508.27(b)(9) (2003).

If the proposed action satisfies the criteria, then an Environmental Impact Statement is required. An EIS is a detailed statement by the responsible agency official that presents the environmental impact of the proposed action. There are several purposes of an EIS.

First, an EIS ensures that policies and goals of NEPA are infused into ongoing federal programs and actions.

Second, an EIS provides fair and full discussion of significant environmental impacts.

Third, the document informs the public and decision makers of reasonable alternatives. The EIS also is used by federal officials to plan actions and make decisions.

The EIS document is the final product of an intense review. Preparation for the EIS must begin early when the agency begins developing the proposed action. The EIS should be included in any report or recommendation for the project. The EIS serves as a contribution to the decision-making process.

> An EIS is a detailed statement by the responsible agency official presenting the environmental impact of a proposed action.

It is essential for the federal agency to use a systematic, interdisciplinary approach in preparing the EIS. 42 U.S.C. § 4332(2)(A) (2003). The EIS must identify

- the environmental impact of the proposed action;
- any adverse environmental effects that cannot be avoided if the proposed action is adopted;
- the alternatives to the proposed action;
- the relationship between short-term uses and long-term productivity; and

---

[2] The Endangered Species Act of 1973 governs for any adverse effect on an endangered or threatened species or its habitat. (See Chapter 7)

- "any irreversible and irretrievable commitments of resources" involved with the proposed action.

42 U.S.C. § 4332(2)(C) (2003).

The CEQ regulations introduce an EIS tool: **scoping.** Scoping is the process for early and open evaluation of the issues relating to the proposed action. 40 C.F.R. § 1501.7 (2003). Scoping includes the range of actions, alternatives, and impacts that must be considered in the EIS. The regulations demand agencies to consider three types of actions, three types of alternatives, and three types of impacts. 40 C.F.R. § 1508.25 (2003).

The actions that must be considered are (i) connected actions, (ii) cumulative actions, or (iii) similar actions.

Connected actions are closely related actions. These include actions that "automatically trigger other actions" that may require an EIS. A connected action is one that cannot or will not proceed unless other actions are taken, either before or simultaneously with the proposed action. "Connected" also means those actions that are interdependent parts of a larger project and depend on that larger action for their justification. All connected actions should be included in the same impact statement. 40 C.F.R. § 1508.25(a)(1) (2003).

The second type, **cumulative actions,** results from the combination of other proposed actions, whether by the same agency or another agency. The concern is that the combination will have cumulative significant impacts. The cumulative impacts should be discussed in the same impact statement. 40 C.F.R. § 1508.25(a)(2) (2003).

Similar actions are those proposed or future actions dealing with the same location, similar geography, or actions occurring at the same time. 40 C.F.R. § 1508.25(a)(3) (2003). The agency is encouraged to analyze the similar actions in the same EIS. The CEQ regulations require one EIS for similar actions as the best way to assess the combined impacts of similar actions or the reasonable alternatives to the similar actions.

Pursuant to 40 C.F.R. § 1508.25(b) (2003), the agency must consider three types of alternatives:

1. Should no action be proposed?
2. What are other reasonable actions?
3. What mitigation measures must be taken?

"Scoping" means the early and open evaluation of issues that must be addressed to identify significant issues relating to a proposed action.

The final scoping requirement is for the agency to identify the impacts of the action. The three impacts are (i) direct, (ii) indirect, or (iii) cumulative. The agency must evaluate all three types of impact. 40 C.F.R. § 1508.25(c) (2003).

When a federal agency has determined from the EA that an EIS is needed (because the proposal is a major federal action that significantly affects the quality of the human environment), the agency must prepare a draft EIS **(DEIS)** and make it available to the public. 40 C.F.R. § 1502.9(a) (2003).

An agency must consider three types of alternatives:

1. Should no action be proposed?
2. What are other reasonable actions?
3. What mitigation measures must be taken?

The EIS must be concise and written in plain language. 40 C.F.R. § 1502.8 (2003). A minimum of forty-five days must be provided for comments.

EPA Review of the DEIS

The U.S. Environmental Protection Agency, like other federal agencies, prepares and reviews NEPA documents. However, the EPA also has a unique responsibility in the NEPA review process. Under § 309 of the Clean Air Act, the EPA is required to review and publicly comment on the environmental impacts of major federal actions including actions that are the subject of EISs. If the EPA determines that the action is environmentally unsatisfactory, it is required by § 309 to refer the matter to CEQ.

In addition, in accordance with a Memorandum of Agreement between EPA and CEQ, EPA carries out the operational duties associated with the administrative aspects of the EIS filing process. See Figure 8-1, EPA Filing System Guidance for Implementing 1506.9 and 1506.10 of the CEQ Regulations, 54 Fed. Reg. 9592 (March 7, 1989), on the Internet at http://www.epa.gov/compliance/resources/policies/nepa/fileguide.pdf. The EPA's Office of Federal Activities has been designated the official recipient of all EISs prepared by federal agencies.

The EPA has a significant role in rating the environmental impact of a proposed action. The EPA has developed a set of criteria, or a rating system, that provides a basis upon which it makes recommendations to the lead agency for improving the draft (see, for instance, the

9592   Federal Register / Vol. 54, No. 43 / Tuesday, March 7, 1989 / Notices

ENVIRONMENTAL PROTECTION AGENCY

Filing System Guidance for the Implementation of 1506.9 and 1506.10 of the CEQ Regulations Implementing the Procedural Provisions of the NEPA

Preamble

In 1978, the Council of Environmental Quality (CEQ) and the Environmental Protection Agency (EPA) entered into a Memorandum of Agreement on the allocation of responsibilities of the two agencies for assuring the government-wide implementation of the National Environmental Policy Act of 1969 (NEPA). These responsibilities are consistent with the 1978 CEQ NEPA-Implementing Regulations (40 CFR Parts 1500–1508).

The Memorandum of Agreement transferred to EPA operational duties associated with the administrative aspects of the environmental impact statement (EIS) filing process. The Office of Federal Activities has been designated the official recipient in EPA of all EISs. It should be noted that the operational duties associated with the administrative aspects of the EIS process are totally separate from the substantive EPA reviews performed pursuant to both NEPA and section 309 of the Clean Air Act.

The purpose of the EPA Filing System paper is to provide guidance to federal agencies on filing EISs, including draft, final, and supplemental EISs. Information is provided on (1) Where to file; (2) number of copies required; (3) information required in the transmittal letter; (4) steps to follow when a federal agency is adopting an EIS or when an EIS is being withdrawn, delayed or reopened; (5) review periods; (6) notice of availability in the Federal Register; and, (7) retention of filed EISs.

On August 10, 1988, following consultation with CEQ, EPA sent the draft paper to 26 federal agencies for comment prior to its submission to the Federal Register for formal publication and implementation. EPA received comment letters from 16 agencies. Although this preamble does not respond to each comment individually all were carefully considered. A synopsis of the comments, other than editorial, and EPA's response follow:

Section 3—Filing an EIS-Draft, Final and Supplemental

As requested, clarification has been made that completion of the transmittal of an EIS is accomplished simultaneously with the filing with EPA.

It was recommended that the cover letter include the official issuing agency number for the EIS being filed. EPA does not use an agency's number for the EIS being filed; therefore, it is not needed in the cover letter. An agency may, if it wishes, include the number because of internal requirements.

Information has been added to clarify that, in the case of filing an EIS that is not hand carried, the cover letter should state that transmittal has been completed. In addition, EPA will telephone the filing agency to verify that EPA has received the EIS.

At the recommendation of a commenter, EPA will now include a reference in the Notice of Availability when an agency adopts an EIS that does not require recirculation. This will not reopen the public comment period, but will complete the public record.

Several agencies commented on EPA's role in checking an EIS for "completeness and compliance." In response the specific subsection of the CEQ Regulations that recommends the standard format that an agency should follow unless the agency determines that there is a compelling reason to do otherwise has been identified—§ 1502.10 of the CEQ Regulations—for clarification. EPA's review is to assure that the document meets certain minimum administrative requirements, i.e., there is a cover sheet, a summary of the statement, a table of contents, the name, address and telephone number of the agency is included, cooperating agencies are listed, etc. The format and explanation of each is found in § 1502.10 of the CEQ regulations. The review does *not* address the quality of the document's substance. Further, it is totally independent of EPA's review on environmental impacts under Section 309 of the Clean Air Act.

One commenting agency suggested deleting the sentence concerning reopening an EIS review period after a substantial amount of time has passed since the original review period closed. The commenting agency objected to the use of the word "substantial" without defining the term. EPA believes that the word substantial stands on its own merits and suggests that agencies use their best judgment in deciding what is reasonable. The intent is to keep the public informed. EISs reopened for review will be published in the Notice of Availability to inform all interested parties and to keep the public record current.

Section 4—Notice in the Federal Register

Language has been added to clarify that the Notice of Availability is

published each Friday in the Federal Register for those EISs filed during the preceding week—e.g., the notice is published on January 13th for EISs filed between January 2nd and January 6th.

The last paragraph of this section has been deleted at the request of CEQ. CEQ will remain solely responsible for notification to the public of referral actions due to the process timeframes called for in the current CEQ Regulations.

Section 5—Time Periods

The section heading and opening paragraph have been edited to address many comments requesting clarification of time periods for draft and final EISs. The time period for review and comment on draft EISs shall not be less than 45 "calendar" days. CEQ Regulations do not address a review period for a final EIS. It is a 30 "calendar" day wait period during which no decision may be made to proceed with the proposed action.

Additional information has been added to address the question concerning calculated time periods ending on non-work days. When a calculated time period ends on a non-working day, the assigned time period will be the next working day.

Section 1506.10(b) of the CEQ Regulations allows for an exception to the rules of timing. Language has been included on exceptions relating to cases of an agency decision which is subject to a formal internal appeal. When exceptions are made by an agency, it is important to inform EPA so that it is accurately reflected in the Notice of Availability.

It was requested that the paper cite examples where both extensions and reductions of time periods have been granted by EPA and where CEQ has approved special cases. EPA appreciates the point but has declined to present examples since these are done on a case-by-case basis and each case is considered on its individual merits.

One commenting agency was concerned with having to request reductions and extensions of time periods in writing to EPA. The agency felt this put too much stress on a formal, and possibly time-consuming, process. Language has been added indicating EPA will accept these requests by telephone, but agencies should follow up in writing to ensure that EPA can maintain a complete record of the decision-making process.

One commenting agency requested that guidance be provided for filing of non-federal EISs, i.e., those prepared by state and local governments where

Figure 8-1 EPA Filing System Guidance for Implementing 1506.9 and 1506.10 of the CEQ Regulations, 54 Fed. Reg. 9592 (March 7, 1989).

EPA's Web site at http://www.epa.gov/compliance/nepa/comments/ratings.html). There are four possible EPA responses to a DEIS:

- **Lack of Objections (LO).** The review has not identified any potential environmental impacts requiring substantive changes to the preferred alternative. The review may have disclosed opportunities for application of mitigation measures that could be accomplished with no more than minor changes to the proposed action.
- **Environmental Concerns (EC).** The review has identified environmental impacts that should be avoided in order to fully protect the environment. Corrective measures may require changes to the preferred alternative or application of mitigation measures that can reduce the environmental impact.
- **Environmental Objections (EO).** The review has identified significant environmental impacts that should be avoided in order to adequately protect the environment. Corrective measures may require substantial changes to the preferred alternative or consideration of some other project alternative (including the no action alternative or a new alternative). The basis for Environmental Objections can include several situations, including where an action might violate or be inconsistent with achievement or maintenance of a national environmental standard, where the federal agency violates its own substantive environmental requirements that relate to the EPA's areas of jurisdiction or expertise, or where proceeding with the proposed action would set a precedent for future actions that collectively could result in significant environmental impacts.
- **Environmentally Unsatisfactory (EU).** The review has identified adverse environmental impacts that are of sufficient magnitude that the EPA believes the proposed action must not proceed as proposed. The basis for an environmentally unsatisfactory determination consists of identification of environmentally objectionable impacts one or more conditions including the potential violation of or inconsistency with a national environmental standard is substantive and/or will occur on a long-term basis; there are no applicable standards but the severity, duration, or geographical scope of the impacts associated with the proposed action warrant special attention; or the potential environmental impacts resulting from the proposed action are of national importance because of the threat to national environmental resources or to environmental policies.

The EPA also rates the adequacy of the DEIS as

- **Adequate.** The DEIS adequately sets forth the environmental impact(s) of the preferred alternative and those of the alternatives reasonably available to the project or action. No further analysis or data collection is necessary, but the reviewer may suggest the addition of clarifying language or information.

- **Insufficient Information.** The DEIS does not contain sufficient information to fully assess environmental impacts that should be avoided in order to fully protect the environment, or the reviewer has identified new reasonably available alternatives that are within the spectrum of alternatives analyzed in the DEIS, which could reduce the environmental impacts of the proposal. The identified additional information, data, analyses, or discussion should be included in the final EIS.

- **Inadequate.** The DEIS does not adequately assess the potentially significant environmental impacts of the proposal, or the reviewer has identified new, reasonably available, alternatives that are outside of the spectrum of alternatives analyzed in the draft EIS, which should be analyzed in order to reduce the potentially significant environmental impacts. The identified additional information, data, analyses, or discussions are of such a magnitude that they should have full public review at a draft stage. This rating indicates the EPA's belief that the draft EIS does not meet the purposes of NEPA and/or the § 309 review and, thus, should be formally revised and made available for public comment in a supplemental or revised DEIS.

The Final EIS

The final EIS must respond to all comments submitted on the draft EIS. 40 C.F.R. § 1503 (2003). The final EIS must be filed with the EPA, and a notice must be published in the *Federal Register*. The agency may prepare supplements to the EIS if substantial changes are made to the proposed action that are relevant to the environment. 40 C.F.R. § 1502.9(c) (2003).

The agency is also required to prepare a **Record of Decision (ROD)** at the time of its decision or recommendation concerning the project. 40 C.F.R. § 1505.2 (2003).

Paralegals may be involved in the EIS process. They may be asked to evaluate a draft EIS, in contemplation of filing comments, and to review the final EIS, for consideration and factual review of whether the agency has complied with its mandates under NEPA. The ROD may also need close review or summary.

If more than one agency is involved in the proposed federal action, a lead agency must supervise the EIS preparation. 40 C.F.R. § 1508.16 (2003). If the agencies cannot agree on a lead agency, then the Council on Environmental Quality may designate a lead agency. 40 C.F.R. § 1501.5 (2003). The lead agency must solicit cooperation from other federal agencies, and from state or local agencies. The lead agency must determine who will undertake which responsibilities and must respond to all substantive issues raised by the draft EIS.

In the event that an agency fails to perform an EIS or a party believes the EIS is insufficient, the party can sue the agency if **standing** is satisfied. In the environmental context, standing is generally available and depends on

- a protected interest;
- being adversely affected by the agency action; and
- the **zone-of-interest** test.

The zone-of-interest test is not always satisfied if the party alleges an economic interest. The party must allege that such party actually uses or enjoys the area at issue. Proof of injury is required. See, for example, *Lujan v. National Wildlife Federation*, 497 U.S. 871 (1990).

Assuming the party satisfies the standing requirements, the court will hear the case. The standard of review is an arbitrary and capricious basis. The court's task is to determine whether the agency complied with NEPA. This compliance includes whether an EA was prepared, whether a FONSI was issued, and whether an EIS was prepared. The court will defer to the agency for its decision on the impact of the project, the possible alternatives and the agency's decision on whether to proceed with the project.

In essence, NEPA is a procedural statute. The goals are clear, and the mission to encourage thoughtful decision making is achieved through the EIS. Many states have expanded the reach of NEPA by enacting state **Environmental Policy Acts.** These requirements are generally parallel to the federal policy.

Figure 8-2 provides, in the *Final Chesapeake Bay Special Resource Study Report and Final Environmental Impact Statement*, an example of a completed, final, and approved EIS. The full report is available on the Internet at http://www.chesapeakestudy.org/final report.htm.

The success of NEPA is the creation of a national policy to protect our environment. The NEPA process still continues for all agency actions.

> In essence, NEPA is a procedural statute.

Chesapeake Bay Special Resource Study and Final Environmental Impact Statement

ABSTRACT

PRODUCED BY:
National Park Service
U.S. Department of the Interior
Chesapeake Bay Program Office
August 2004

Responding to a request from Congress, the National Park Service (NPS) has explored the potential for a new unit of the National Park System focused on the Chesapeake Bay. The *Chesapeake Bay Special Resource Study (SRS) and Final Environmental Impact Statement* examines whether having additional Chesapeake Bay resources within the National Park System would make sense and would advance partnership efforts to conserve and celebrate the Chesapeake Bay; defines any concepts for how resources or areas of the Bay might fit within the National Park System; and makes recommendations regarding these findings. The *Chesapeake Bay Special Resource Study (SRS) and Final Environmental Impact Statement* describes a series of conceptual alternatives for how the National Park System might best represent the national significance of the Chesapeake Bay.

The study compares four action alternatives against a no action alternative that calls for the continuation of existing initiatives:

Alternative A: Today's Programs – No New Initiatives—This alternative assumes the National Park Service would simply continue its existing roles related to Chesapeake Bay conservation, restoration and interpretation.

Alternative B: An Enhanced Chesapeake Bay Gateways Network – A Permanent Watershed-wide System of Special Bay Places for Experiencing the Chesapeake--This alternative would enhance and build upon the existing Chesapeake Bay Gateways Network, the partnership system of 140-plus parks, refuges, maritime museums, historic sites and trails around the Bay watershed.

Alternative C: Chesapeake Bay Estuary National Park – Conserving and Exploring the Bay's Waters – The Chesapeake Bay is a vast estuary – 2,500 square miles of water – known not just for its size, but also its high productivity as a natural system. This alternative would create a water-based national park that exemplifies the larger Bay's estuarine character with limited land resources for access and interpretation.

Alternative D: Chesapeake Bay National Reserve – Protecting Bay Maritime & Rural Heritage – Unlike national parks, national reserves protect and sustain the working landscape, recognizing the vital role of continued human uses in the heritage of a special place. This alternative would create a reserve representative of the Chesapeake's maritime and agricultural heritage.

Alternative E: Chesapeake Bay Watershed National Ecological & Cultural Preserve – A Living Example for the Bay and the Nation--The Bay is fed by 124,000 miles of rivers and streams from a 64,000 square mile watershed. This alternative would establish a national ecological and cultural preserve focused on one exemplary Bay tributary, from headwater stream to open Bay, representative of the larger watershed.

Preferred Alternative: Alternative B represents a remarkably efficient and effective approach to advancing public understanding and enjoyment of Chesapeake resources and stimulating resource conservation. The Chesapeake Bay Gateways Network should be a permanent partnership system for experiencing the Chesapeake. For this to occur, alternative B would be implemented in its entirety: the Gateways Network would be designated a permanent program of the National Park System with an on-going funding commitment; creation of two new partnership Chesapeake Bay interpretive/education centers would be stimulated through two matching grants; and the Gateways Network would enhance links to surrounding working landscapes. At some time in the future, a unit of the National Park System encompassing either one or several of alternatives C, D, and E could make a significant contribution to protection and public enjoyment of the Chesapeake Bay.

Questions regarding this document should be directed in writing to the Director, National Park Service Chesapeake Bay Program Office, 410 Severn Avenue, Suite 109, Annapolis, Maryland 21403.

Figure 8-2   The *Final Chesapeake Bay Special Resource Study Report and Final Environmental Impact Statement.*

CASES FOR DISCUSSION

Westlands Water District v. Interior Department, 58 ERC 2024 (9th Cir. 2004).

In this case, the court noted that for forty years most of the Trinity River's water has been diverted to the Sacramento River basin. Congress then mandated that some of that water be returned to the Trinity River in order to revive its chinook salmon, coho salmon, and steel-head trout populations, which have been decimated by the decades of reduced water flows. California municipal water agencies and power districts challenged the plan to redirect Trinity River water, arguing that the procedural requirements of NEPA and the Endangered Species Act were not met.

Ruling on cross-motions for summary judgment, the district court enjoined parts of the restoration program devised by federal agencies and the Hoopa Valley Tribe, mandated that nonflow restoration measures be implemented, and ordered the federal agencies to supplement their EIS to cover issues neglected or inadequately addressed in previous studies.

The circuit court affirmed in part and reversed in part. The court reversed the conclusion that the scope of the EIS and the range of alternatives considered therein were unreasonable and reversed the district court's injunctive orders to supplement the EIS to address the issues raised on appeal.

The court affirmed the district court's ruling that two of the mitigation measures insisted upon by the Fish and Wildlife Service (FWS) and the National Marine Fisheries Service (NMFS) in their biological opinions exceeded the statutory authority for such opinions.

Conclusion

Paralegals can be involved in the NEPA process in various ways. For instance, whether the agency prepares an EA or a FONSI, paralegals may be involved in reviewing these documents for their clients to summarize and criticize the agency's conclusions. Paralegals may also be involved in the EIS process. They may be asked to evaluate a draft EIS, in contemplation of filing comments, and to review the final EIS, for consideration and factual review of whether the agency has complied with its mandates under NEPA. The ROD may also need close review or summary.

GLOSSARY OF NEPA TERMS

categorical exclusion. A vehicle to exclude the EA process entirely. The agency has the flexibility to determine if a category of actions does not individually or cumulatively have a significant environmental impact. The categorical exclusion regulations are specific to each agency's program.

CEQ. Council on Environmental Quality. Created by Title II of NEPA.

cost-benefit analysis. Based on the assumption that objective criteria do exist by which most environmental choices can be evaluated, cost-benefit analysis was adopted by Congress for the federal government in making resource allocation choices. The cost-benefit analysis produces a ratio of costs for a proposed project and compares one project to another. The current mandate on cost-benefit analysis, outlined in Executive Order 12,291, at 46 Fed. Reg. 13,193 (February 19, 1981) sets out how federal agencies are to weigh cost-benefit factors.

EA. Environmental Assessment; beginning of the NEPA process. A federal agency, under certain circumstances, must prepare an environmental assessment, which is a concisely written public document.

EIS. Environmental Impact Statement. Required for every report or recommendation of federal agencies: (1) on proposals, (2) for legislation, and (3) for other major federal actions significantly affecting the quality of the human environment. If a proposed action satisfies certain criteria, then an EIS is required. A detailed statement by the responsible agency official that presents the environmental impact of the proposed action.

FAPA. Federal Administrative Procedure Act (5 U.S.C. §§ 500 to 596 (1991)).

FONSI. Finding of No Significant Impact. Document prepared by a federal agency briefly explaining the reasons why a proposed action will not have a significant impact on the environment. The FONSI document will include the EA prepared by the agency.

major federal action. Action with effects that may be major and that are potentially subject to federal control and responsibility.

NEPA. National Environmental Policy Act of 1969, 42 U.S.C. §§ 4321 to 4370(d) (1991), considered to be the cornerstone of environmental law.

NEPA process. Process used by all federal agencies to identify and evaluate the alternatives to proposed agency actions in order to avoid or minimize adverse effects on the environment.

proposal or proposed action. Proposal exists when an agency has a goal or idea and the agency is actively preparing to make a decision on one or more alternatives. The EIS on the proposal should be complete before any recommendation or report on the proposal.

ROD. Record of Decision. Requirement to be prepared by an agency at the time of its decision or recommendation concerning a NEPA project.

scoping. An EIS tool for early and open evaluation of the issues that must be addressed and for identifying the significant issues relating to the proposed action. Scoping includes the range of actions, alternatives, and impacts that must be considered in the EIS. The regulations demand agencies to consider three types of actions, three types of alternatives, and three types of impacts.

BIBLIOGRAPHY

Burleson, David G., *NEPA at 21: Over the Hill Already*, 24 Akron L. Rev. 623 (Spring, 1991).

Caldwell, Lynton K., *NEPA Revisited: A Call for a Constitutional Amendment*, 18 Envtl. Forum (Nov.–Dec. 1989).

Heer, John E., Jr., & D. Joseph Hagerty, *Environmental Assessments and Statements* (Van Nostrand Reinhold 1977).

Littell, Richard, *Endangered and Other Protected Species: Federal Law and Regulation* (BNA 1992).

Parenteau, Patrick A., *NEPA at Twenty: Shining Knight or Tilting at Windmills*, 14 Environmental Forum (Sept.–Oct. 1989).

DISCUSSION QUESTIONS

1. In the state of Apple, the second largest city is constructing a new airport. The funding of the airport is from state appropriations. The airport will be regulated by the Federal Aviation Administration. The state also is receiving federal government highway funds for new roads leading to the new airport. Is the state required to comply with NEPA?

   Q. Should the federal government prepare an environmental assessment? If an environmental assessment should be prepared, which federal agency—the Federal Highway Administration or the FAA—is responsible? Would the federal agency consider the projects separately or cumulatively?

2. Scout Troop 211 uses the Indian Hills Campground for camping events throughout the year. The Henderson River flows next to Camp Indian Hills. The power authority wishes to build a dam to generate hydroelectric power. The

proposed action will decrease the flow of the Henderson River.

Q. Does NEPA apply? Would it make a difference if other people used the campground or the river? Would your analysis change if the river was a habitat for a threatened species of turtle?

COMPUTER LABORATORY PROJECTS

1. Research notices of environmental impact statements that have been published for a project that is in your area. Find a copy of the EIS and outline its findings.

INTERNET SITES

- NEPAnet is a CEQ NEPA Task Force Web site on the Internet at http://ceq.eh.doe.gov/nepa/nepanet.htm, with links to the Act, rules, and policy documents.

- The Council on Environmental Quality is on the Internet at http://www.whitehouse.gov/ceq.

CHAPTER 9

Administrative Law and Procedure

David A. Piech, Esq.

OBJECTIVES

The objectives of this chapter are for students to:

- Learn the terminology associated with FAPA.
- Learn the concepts and ideas that underlie the FAPA law and regulatory program.
- Learn about specific sections and provisions of the FAPA law and regulations.
- Learn about the processes and procedures used by the government and other parties to comply with and to enforce the law under FAPA.
- Learn about the particular jobs and functions that are performed by paralegals working for attorneys in FAPA cases.

Introduction

Environmental laws and regulations are constantly in a state of flux, changing to meet today's and tomorrow's needs. An understanding of environmental laws and regulations requires a knowledge of how these laws and regulations are born and how they mature.

The Role of Agencies

The basis for modern environmental laws and regulations in the United States flows from the development of **administrative agencies.**

These agencies are, in effect, extensions of the legislative and executive branches of government. These agencies administer and execute laws. Many of these agencies are also known under a host of other names such as boards, departments, bureaus, commissions, or divisions. Their functions are, however, the same: to execute and administer the law.

This chapter will highlight various topics in and requirements of administrative law and regulations. These topics are directly related to environmental laws and regulations, since, to be effective, those laws and regulations must abide by administrative law and procedure. This chapter will also highlight research techniques that can be useful in analyzing legal questions under environmental law.

Although this chapter focuses on federal law, the concepts and techniques reviewed are useful for research and activities involving administrative bodies under federal, state, and local laws, regulations, and ordinances. An overall understanding of administrative law has practical application in each of these jurisdictions and is useful for tasks such as research, writing, and filing of papers and materials. While the chapter is limited to administrative law, it focuses on rule making rather than on the judicial aspects of administrative law.

Other parallel concepts and issues may arise under administrative law but are not considered in this review. These include constitutional issues such as procedural and substantive due process, search warrants, and other constitutional rights. On a state level, these rights may be further expanded by state constitutions.

Finally, this chapter reviews the enabling law or ordinance that allows the agency to create and administer rules and regulations. This empowering law or ordinance defines the power of the agency to enact and enforce rules and regulations. The **Federal Administrative Procedure Act (FAPA)** is only effective against federal agencies and may be further limited by other federal laws and the Constitution. State agencies and governments are unaffected by FAPA but must provide the minimum rights bestowed by the U.S. Constitution. Some state administrative procedure acts may be limited to certain state agencies and may not be applicable to county or municipal boards or agencies.

FAPA is only effective against federal agencies and may be further limited by other federal laws and the Constitution.

Research Tools and References

Several research and reference tools and hints are included in this chapter. These tools represent skills that an environmental law paralegal will need to acquire in order to support attorneys and clients in this area of law. Although these tools and hints are good for all aspects of environmental law, those reviewed are not exclusive. There are many other reference sources and tools besides those included herein. For instance, *Computer-Aided Legal Research (CALR) on the Internet* (Pearson Prentice Hall 2006), by Craig B. Simonsen, provides lists and links to Internet sources of administrative and environmental law and reference materials. Paralegals are encouraged to seek out this type of desk reference.

The basic tools include online services such as LEXIS® (http://www.lexis.com) and Westlaw® (http://www.westlaw.com),[1] that include materials on federal and state cases and statutes. Other computer databases, provided by the U.S. EPA, provide a variety of information.[2]

Printed environmentally based reference materials are plentiful. They include publications like *Environment Reporter,* published by the Bureau of National Affairs (BNA) (http://www.bna.com), the *Environmental Law Reporter* (ELR) (http://www.elr.com), published by the Environmental Law Institute, law review articles, *Shepard's Case and Statutory Citations*, and other books and compilations on environmental law. State reference materials may also be available for administrative codes and registers, in addition to state cases. Federal and state agencies may maintain copies and an index of their policy documents and decisions.

Perhaps the most important resources are the various agency personnel. Several agencies maintain help lines providing for additional leads research. For instance, see Appendix D.

---

[1] LEXIS® and Westlaw® include general federal and state statutory, regulatory, and case law information. Administrative cases and decisions may also be available through these databases. Contact your nearest LEXIS® and Westlaw® representative for assistance.

[2] A starting place is the EPA Web site at http://www.epa.gov or through various Internet search engines. At http://www.epa.gov, laws, regulations, rule-making dockets, and guidance documents can be found. See Simonsen, *Computer-Aided Legal Research (CALR) on the Internet,* for a complete listing and description of this and other similar resources at the EPA. Many such resources are found on the Internet.

Statutes and Regulations

Statutes or laws may direct an agency to develop rules that would govern a person's or company's actions under the law. These rules are known as **regulations.**[3] The law may be specific as to what the rules must require, or it may empower the agency with broad discretion as to the substance of the rules.

Under the law, an agency may be directed to create rules that would govern a person's or company's actions as they may relate to the law. The proposed and final rules may be published in a public journal, such as the *Federal Register.* Normally, the agency develops a proposed rule. This may be developed in cooperation with affected parties or wholly within the agency. Comments on a proposed rule are usually solicited by the agency.

Finally, the agency drafts the regulation into final form. The final rule has the same effect as law. A violation of the rule is a violation of the law.

> The final rule has the same effect as the law from which it was derived. A violation of the rule is a violation of the law.

Federal Administrative Procedure Act

With the growth of administrative agencies in the middle of this century, Congress enacted the Federal Administrative Procedure Act (FAPA) in 1946.[4] FAPA is found at 5 U.S.C. §§ 551 to 706 (2000). FAPA was created to define a federal agency's actions as they related to creating public rules and granting permits and licenses. FAPA is very similar to other laws in that it is broken down into functional sections. These include definitions, creation of rules and regulations, and appeals from imposition of those rules and regulations.

---

[3] Do not be confused by the more generic term "code." While some "codes" refer to regulations that are derived through statutes, other "codes" actually refer to the statute. For example, the *United States Code* is a compilation of statutes, while the *Code of Federal Regulations* is a compilation of the regulations that are developed from their respective statutes.

[4] Most state administrative procedure acts were enacted after 1955.

FAPA Definitions—Section 551

FAPA's definitions[5] describe those agencies and governmental bodies that are covered by FAPA. For example, an **agency** does not include a federal court. This list is exclusive. This means that, if the governmental body is not listed, the term "agency" encompasses that body and, therefore, the governmental body is regulated by FAPA.

The definitions also describe a **person.** A "person" generally would only mean an individual. For the purposes of FAPA, however, a "person" also includes public and private organizations, corporations, and associations.

Another important definition is that of a **rule** or **regulation.** FAPA specifically limits a rule to those agency statements with "future effect designed to implement, interpret, or prescribe law or policy . . ." 5 U.S.C. § 551(4) (2000). This definition closely follows the concept of a rule as compared to the concept of adjudication.

Rules and regulations are designed to have a future effect. All actions, from a certain date forward, must conform themselves to the rule. Past actions are not encompassed by the rule. In comparison, an adjudication examines actions that have already happened.

FAPA also defines an agency **order.** For a person to contest an order, it must be final. This finality must effectively conclude the matter before the agency. For example, if the IRS sends you a notice concerning an audit of your taxes, the notice you receive is not a final agency action on whether your tax return is in error. You must wait for the IRS to state specifically that your return is erroneous.

Agency decision making at times may not be so straightforward as to state a final decision or order. In this case, the effect of the agency's decision or order must be determined. In the IRS example above, assume the IRS stated in its notice that your failure to conduct the audit before a certain date would subject you to penalties for an erroneous tax return. Under this scenario, you might be able to argue that, after that date, the IRS had, by default, determined that your tax return was in error. Therefore, after that date, the IRS's actions were "final" as to your tax return. Since the IRS took no enforcement action against you after that date, the IRS might argue that the determination had not been "finalized." The differences between these approaches are continually being argued in court.

---

[5] Each law and regulation usually includes a section of definitions. Before diving into the specific section of the law or regulation, first scan its definitions section. This will provide an overview of the specific items covered by the law and regulation.

FAPA also defines what constitutes an **agency action.** This term refers to an agency rule, order, sanction, or even an agency's failure to act. Note that "sanctions," "orders," and "rule" are also included within the definitions.

Finally, *ex parte* communications are defined. *Ex parte* communications are oral or written communications that are not included on the public record of the rule or case. Most *ex parte* communications are forbidden.[6] A proponent of a special rule exemption cannot present the rule maker with data and other materials in an effort to persuade that rule maker into adopting the proponent's position.

Public Information—Section 552—FOIA

Agencies must make available to the public any information, orders, and procedures that would affect the public. This means that essentially all agency files and documents except those exempted from disclosure (as described below) must be released to the public if requested. In the rule-making context, this public information, commonly known as the **Record,** traces the development of rules or the decision of an administrative case. The Record is important because, as we will see in administrative appeals, an administrative appeal can only be brought pertaining to that information contained in the Record. There are some exceptions to this rule that will be discussed in more detail later.

Additionally, agencies operate under internal and external administrative procedures. These procedures describe when the agency must develop a rule, what sort of information or data can be used in formulating the rule, and how the public must submit information for the rule making. Internal procedures include items such as what forms must be used and, more important, agency guidelines and statements that govern how the agency will determine a rule or case before it. External procedures include procedures governing the formal rule-making or appeal procedures before the agency, such as those contained in FAPA. These procedures and information do not include such items as agency personnel policies, trade secrets, national

---

[6] A paralegal should be extremely careful in communicating with governmental agencies and personnel. From the law firm or company's viewpoint, various information may be extremely useful in ongoing negotiations with the agency on a specific topic. Disclosure of this information could put your firm or company at a severe disadvantage in these negotiations. More important, this disclosure could conceivably be considered an *ex parte* contact. Most *ex parte* contacts are illegal and may carry criminal and civil penalties. Furthermore, the contact could also present your firm or company in a negative light, a severe disadvantage to the firm or company in promoting specific aspects of the rule.

defense matters, and any other information specifically exempted by law. 5 U.S.C. § 552(b) (2000).

Possibly the most significant aspect of this public information is obtaining these procedures and statements from the agency. Within the limits of the **Freedom of Information Act (FOIA),** found at 5 U.S.C. § 552(a)(6) (2000), anyone can obtain information from an agency. Such a request for information is commonly referred to as an **FOIA** request.[7]

> Within the limits of FOIA, anyone can obtain information from an agency.

The type of information that an agency may divulge is governed by the general limits in § 522(b). To obtain agency information, a person may submit a request to the agency indicating that the request is under FOIA and briefly describing the type of information sought.

Be aware, however, that some information may be limited or restricted under this section or the statute governing the agency's directive.[8]

Paralegals will often be the point person in preparing and processing FOIA requests. As noted in Chapter One, the information gathered through FOIA requests can be used for corporate intelligence and for many other purposes, including case support.

Rule Making—Section 553

Rule makings define how agencies develop rules and regulations as required by law. Specific examples include requirements for rules and regulations under the Clean Air Act and other laws. See 42 U.S.C. § 7412(d) (2000).

> Rulemakings are how agencies develop rules and regulations required by law.

---

[7] The student of environmental law must become familiar with an abundance of acronyms.
[8] Many FOIA requests can take several weeks or months to compile and, depending on their extent, can cost hundreds of dollars. Very broad FOIA requests can further delay their completion. If possible, make your requests as specific as possible, citing any applicable statutory or regulatory sections in which you are interested.

Rule makings can be either formal or informal proceedings. Formal proceedings may include hearings and presentation of testimony and data very similar to a judicial proceeding. Informal proceedings may include only written presentation of data and comments to the agency. In informal proceedings, there may be no opportunity to rebut or argue against an opponent's position.

As is discussed in the Introduction and in other chapters of this book, paralegals may be involved in the rule-making process. Paralegals may assist in the preparation of comments and hearing testimony, including the drafting of testimony and collecting and analyzing other information for submission into the administrative record. Paralegals may also attend and participate in administrative meetings and hearings.

Generally, the agency publishes a notice when it is considering promulgating a rule or when it has drafted a proposed rule. FAPA requires publication of a **Notice of Proposed Rule Making,** also known as an **NPRM,** in the *Federal Register.* Later, when the agency is ready or has otherwise been required to act, the agency publishes the rule in final form known as a **Final Rule.**

Alternatively, an agency may adopt a rule for immediate use, but that agency may revise the rule in the future. This intermediate rule is known as an **Interim Rule.** An Interim Rule is as effective as a Final Rule, but the agency may continue to solicit comments on the Interim Rule. As such, an Interim Rule has many of the same features of both an NPRM and a Final Rule.

The federal government also provides a comprehensive "rule-making" Web site for public information and participation in the process. The Web site is, appropriately, http://www.regulations.gov; its homepage is shown in Figure 9-1.

Code of Federal Regulations

The *Code of Federal Regulations* and the *Federal Register* contain actual and proposed rules and regulations. The ***Code of Federal Regulations,*** or **C.F.R.,** is an annual compilation of federal rules. An entire C.F.R. Title, such as Title 40, Environment, is very large and can take up several shelves on a bookcase.

Each annual C.F.R. is color-coded for that year. The environmental rules are primarily contained in Titles 33 and 40. Title 40 contains rules for air, water, and waste. These environmental rules are updated every July 1.

A typical C.F.R. page is shown in Figure 9-2. The C.F.R. provides which edition it is (7-1-2004 Edition), a summary index with general headings, an authority section (AUTHORITY), and the rules themselves.

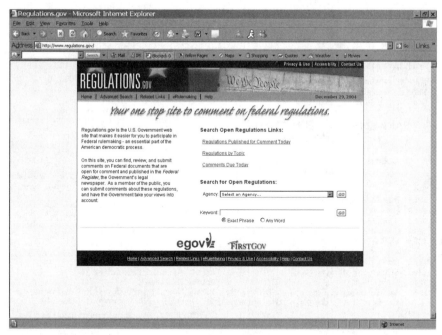

Figure 9-1   The http://www.regulations.gov Web site.

The C.F.R., in full text searchable and mirror image form, is available on the Internet at http://www.access.gpo.gov/cgi-bin/cfrassemble. cgi?title=200240.

Federal Register

The **Federal Register,** also known as the **Fed. Reg.,** is a daily journal of federal agencies.[9] The Fed. Reg. is published Monday through Friday, except for legal holidays. In comparison, the C.F.R. is published only once a year. Many states have similar journals or registers and administrative code compilations.

> Many states have similar journals or registers and administrative code compilations.

---

[9] Do not confuse the *Federal Register* with the *Congressional Record*, which is a compilation of daily activities of Congress. Many bills that may eventually become laws are included in the *Congressional Record*. Various amendments proposed to the bills are also included in the *Congressional Record*.

State law, nor does it affect the validity of actions by the State prior to withdrawal.

[48 FR 14178, Apr. 1, 1983; 50 FR 6941, Feb. 19, 1985, as amended at 57 FR 5335, Feb. 13, 1992; 63 FR 45123, Aug. 24, 1998]

PART 124—PROCEDURES FOR DECISIONMAKING

Subpart A—General Program Requirements

Sec.
124.1 Purpose and scope.
124.2 Definitions.
124.3 Application for a permit.
124.4 Consolidation of permit processing.
124.5 Modification, revocation and reissuance, or termination of permits.
124.6 Draft permits.
124.7 Statement of basis.
124.8 Fact sheet.
124.9 Administrative record for draft permits when EPA is the permitting authority.
124.10 Public notice of permit actions and public comment period.
124.11 Public comments and requests for public hearings.
124.12 Public hearings.
124.13 Obligation to raise issues and provide information during the public comment period.
124.14 Reopening of the public comment period.
124.15 Issuance and effective date of permit.
124.16 Stays of contested permit conditions.
124.17 Response to comments.
124.18 Administrative record for final permit when EPA is the permitting authority.
124.19 Appeal of RCRA, UIC, NPDES, and PSD Permits.
124.20 Computation of time.
124.21 Effective date of part 124.

Subpart B—Specific Procedures Applicable to RCRA Permits

124.31 Pre-application public meeting and notice.
124.32 Public notice requirements at the application stage.
124.33 Information repository.

Subpart C—Specific Procedures Applicable to PSD Permits

124.41 Definitions applicable to PSD permits.
124.42 Additional procedures for PSD permits affecting Class I areas.

Subpart D—Specific Procedures Applicable to NPDES Permits

124.51 Purpose and scope.
124.52 Permits required on a case-by-case basis.
124.53 State certification.
124.54 Special provisions for State certification and concurrence on applications for section 301(h) variances.
124.55 Effect of State certification.
124.56 Fact sheets.
124.57 Public notice.
124.58 [Reserved]
124.59 Conditions requested by the Corps of Engineers and other government agencies.
124.60 Issuance and effective date and stays of NPDES permits.
124.61 Final environmental impact statement.
124.62 Decision on variances.
124.63 Procedures for variances when EPA is the permitting authority.
124.64 Appeals of variances.
124.65 [Reserved]
124.66 Special procedures for decisions on thermal variances under section 316(a).

AUTHORITY: Resource Conservation and Recovery Act, 42 U.S.C. 6901 *et seq.*; Safe Drinking Water Act, 42 U.S.C. 300f *et seq.*; Clean Water Act, 33 U.S.C. 1251 *et seq.*; Clean Air Act, 42 U.S.C. 7401 *et seq.*

SOURCE: 48 FR 14264, Apr. 1, 1983, unless otherwise noted.

Subpart A—General Program Requirements

§ 124.1 Purpose and scope.

(a) This part contains EPA procedures for issuing, modifying, revoking and reissuing, or terminating all RCRA, UIC, PSD and NPDES "permits" (including "sludge-only" permits issued pursuant to § 122.1(b)(2) of this chapter. The latter kinds of permits are governed by part 270. RCRA interim status and UIC authorization by rule are not "permits" and are covered by specific provisions in parts 144, subpart C, and 270. This part also does not apply to permits issued, modified, revoked and reissued or terminated by the Corps of Engineers. Those procedures are specified in 33 CFR parts 320–327. The procedures of this part also apply to denial of a permit for the active life of a RCRA hazardous waste management facility or unit under § 270.29.

(b) Part 124 is organized into four subparts. Subpart A contains general

Figure 9-2 40 C.F.R. Part 124 (July 1, 2004).

The Fed. Reg. includes all notices required to be published by federal agencies. Many agencies may publish notices, and the daily Fed. Reg. can be several hundred pages long. A general index by agency is contained in the beginning of each Fed. Reg. and contains an index only for that Fed. Reg. A year-to-date index is published at the end of each month and at the end of each year. The Fed. Reg. also contains a short index of C.F.R. sections affected by notices in this Fed. Reg.[10]

A typical Fed. Reg. for a Final Rule is shown in Figure 9-3. There are several important and regular or customary features of a Fed. Reg. The general Fed. Reg. information is at the top of the printed page and shows the date of the Fed. Reg. (January 2, 1998), the volume and issue number (Vol. 63, No. 1), and the Fed. Reg. page number (26).

Typically, a Fed. Reg. is referenced by its volume and page number.[11] The Final Rule includes the agency involved (ENVIRONMENTAL PROTECTION AGENCY), sections affected (40 C.F.R. part 52), a general title (Final Determination to Extend Deadline for Promulgation of Action on Section 126 Petitions), and the action intended (Final Rule). The body of the rule includes a short summary (SUMMARY), important dates (EFFECTIVE DATE), contact information such as addresses and telephone numbers (FOR FURTHER INFORMATION), and a history of the rule (SUPPLEMENTARY INFORMATION).

The "Background" section highlights the statutory authority for the rule making and also provides any previous Fed. Reg. notices connected with this rule making.[12] The "SUPPLEMENTARY INFORMATION" section is commonly known as the "preamble" to the final rule. It contains the EPA's analysis of comments, proposals, and its decision on the rule making. These analyses may provide further explanation of definitions and covered or exempted activities or may further explain the rule. Finally, the last section in the Final Rule contains the actual rules and regulations.

An environmental paralegal may keep busy just following EPA rule-making activities. Monitoring the daily *Federal Register* for notices, proposals, and final rules that may affect current or potential clients is an important task in staying abreast of developments.

---

[10] While the *C.F.R.-Affected Sections* is a useful research tool, the year-to-date Fed. Reg. index does not contain this same index. There is a useful C.F.R. index that includes sections affected by Fed. Reg. notices. The *List of Sections Affected* index is usually published on a monthly basis. This C.F.R. index contains a cumulative list of affected C.F.R. sections since the C.F.R. was last published.

[11] For example, the notice in Figure 9-3 would be referenced as 63 Fed. Reg. 26 (January 2, 1998).

[12] In Figure 9-3, under Background, 62 Fed. Reg. 54769 and 62 Fed. Reg. 61914 are referenced. These may provide additional information on the same rule making and should be used as a research reference.

26   **Federal Register** / Vol. 63, No. 1 / Friday, January 2, 1998 / Rules and Regulations

2. Paragraphs (f) and (g) are redesignated as paragraphs (g) and (h), respectively.

3. A new paragraph (f) is added.

4. Paragraph (h), as redesignated, is revised.

The addition and revisions read as follows:

ß48.4082±5   Diesel fuel; Alaska

*   *   *   *   *

(b) * * *

Qualified dealer means any person that holds a qualified dealer license from the state of Alaska or has been registered by the district director as a qualified retailer. The district director will register a person as a qualified retailer only if the district director–

(1) Determines that the person, in the course of its trade or business, regularly sells diesel fuel for use by its buyer in a nontaxable use; and

(2) Is satisfied with the filing, deposit, payment, and claim history for all federal taxes of the person and any related person.

*   *   *   *   *

(f) *Registration.* With respect to each person that has been registered as a qualified retailer by the district director, the rules of ß 48.4101±1(g), (h), and (i) apply.

*   *   *   *   *

(h) *Effective date.* This section is applicable with respect to diesel fuel removed or entered after December 31, 1996. A person registered by the district director as a qualified retailer before April 2, 1998 may be treated, to the extent the district director determines appropriate, as a qualified dealer for the period before that date.

ß48.6416(b)(4)±1   [Removed]

Par. 7. Section 48.6416(b)(4)-1 is removed.

ß48.6421±3   [Amended]

Par. 8. In ß 48.6421±3, paragraph (d)(2) is amended by removing the last sentence.

ß48.6427±3   [Amended]

Par. 9. In ß 48.6427±3, paragraph (d)(2) is amended by removing the last sentence.

Par. 10. In ß 48.6715±1, paragraph (a)(3) is revised to read as follows:

ß48.6715±1   Penalty for misuse of dyed diesel fuel.

(a) * * *

(3) The alteration or attempted alteration occurs in an exempt area of Alaska after September 30, 1996.

*   *   *   *   *

ß48.6715±2T   [Removed]

Par. 11. Section 48.6715±2T is removed.

Approved: November 6, 1997.

Michael P. Dolan,

Acting Commissioner of Internal Revenue.

Donald C. Lubick,

Acting Assistant Secretary of the Treasury.

[FR Doc. 97±33988 Filed 12±31±97; 8:45 am]

BILLING CODE 4830±01±P

ENVIRONMENTAL PROTECTION AGENCY

40 CFR Part 52

[FRL±5937±7]

Final Determination to Extend Deadline for Promulgation of Action on Section 126 Petitions

AGENCY: Environmental Protection Agency (EPA).

ACTION: Final rule.

SUMMARY: The EPA is extending by an additional three-day period the deadline for taking final action on petitions that eight States have submitted to require EPA to make findings that sources upwind of those States contribute significantly to nonattainment problems in those States. Under the Clean Air Act (CAA), EPA is authorized to grant this time extension if EPA determines that the extension is necessary, among other things, to meet the purposes of the Act's rulemaking requirements. By this document, EPA is making that determination.

EFFECTIVE DATE: This action is effective as of December 15, 1997.

FOR FURTHER INFORMATION CONTACT: Howard J. Hoffman, Office of General Counsel, MC±2344, 401 M St., SW, Washington, D.C. 20460, (202) 260± 5892.

SUPPLEMENTARY INFORMATION:

I. Background

Today's action follows closely EPA's final actions taken by notice dated October 22, 1997 (62 FR 54769) and November 20, 1997 (62 FR 61914). Familiarity with those documents is assumed, and background information in them will not be repeated here.

In the November 20, 1997 document, EPA extended by one month, pursuant to its authority under CAA section 307(d)(10), the time-frame for taking final action on petitions submitted by Connecticut, Maine, Massachusetts, New Hampshire, New York, Pennsylvania, Rhode Island, and Vermont under CAA section 126. This

extension established the deadline at December 14, 1997, but because that date fell on a Sunday, the deadline became the following Monday, December 15, 1997. In the November 20, 1997 document, EPA indicated that it was reserving its option to extend the date for final action by all or part of the remaining four months of the six-month extension period provided under section 307(d)(10).

EPA is today extending the deadline for an additional three days, to December 18, 1997. In the November 20, 1997 document, EPA justified the second one-month extension as necessary in part to allow the agency, working with the section 126 petitioners and other interested parties, to conclude the process for determining an appropriate schedule for action on the section 126 petitions. This schedule would include, as important elements, timetables for proposed rulemaking, a public hearing, and a public comment period. In this manner, the extension furthered the purposes of section 307(d)(10) by promoting public participation in the rulemaking process.

EPA believes that these same reasons continue to apply to favor another, brief extension, at this time. In particular, EPA seems to be in the final stages of finalizing with the section 126 petitioners an appropriate schedule for section 126 rulemaking. Accordingly, EPA again concludes today that extending the date for action on the section 126 petitions for another three days is necessary.

As EPA indicated in its previous notices, EPA, even with today's action, continues not to use the entire six months provided under section 307(d)(10) for the extension. EPA continues to reserve the right to apply the remaining period, or a portion thereof, as an additional extension, if necessary, immediately following the conclusion of the three-day period, or to apply the remaining time to the period following EPA's proposed rulemaking.

II. Final Action

A. Rule

Today, EPA is determining, under CAA section 307(d)(10), that an additional three-day period is necessary to assure the development of an appropriate schedule for rulemaking on the section 126 petitions, which schedule would allow EPA adequate time to prepare a notice for proposal that will best facilitate public comment, as well as allow the public sufficient time to comment. Under this extension, the date for action on each of the section 126 petitions is December 18, 1997.

Figure 9-3   Final Determination to Extend Deadline for Promulgation of Action on Section 126 Petitions, 63 Fed. Reg. 26 (January 2, 1998).

Hearings and Other Matters—Sections 555 and 556

If necessary, the agency may hold hearings to discuss the proposed rule. Interested persons and parties affected by the rule may appear and give testimony and present evidence.

The agency may decide to propose an Interim Rule. A primary reason may be time and schedule constraints imposed upon the agency by law. An Interim Rule operates, for all practical purposes, as a Final Rule. The agency may, however, solicit additional comments concerning the Interim Rule or portions of the Interim Rule for further review and analysis. At a later date, those portions of the Interim Rule or the Interim Rule itself could be incorporated as a Final Rule or could later be withdrawn.

After the agency has accepted and reviewed comments and, if necessary, held hearings on the proposed rule, the agency will review this information and may promulgate a Final Rule. As described above, the Final Rule will be published in the Fed. Reg.

The Fed. Reg. will list an effective date of the Final Rule. Often the agency's reasoning for adopting the rule will be included, which may further aid in defining the scope of the actual rule.

Agency Decisions, *Ex Parte* Contacts, and the Record—Section 557

During a rule-making procedure, the agency will create a **Record** of its decision for a Final Rule. The Record comprises all the various comments, testimony, and exhibits presented to the agency concerning the matter. The agency's proposed findings and conclusions will also constitute part of the Record. 5 U.S.C. § 557(c) (2000).

The Record is an extremely important concept and compilation. Most appeals of rules and regulations promulgated under certain laws are restricted only to those items contained in the Record.

> During a rule making, the agency will create a Record of its decision on a Final Rule.

See 42 U.S.C. § 6976(a)(2) (2000). Therefore, items not in the Record cannot usually be scrutinized by a reviewing court in its review of the regulation or the agency's actions in promulgating the regulation.

Under some circumstances, however, a reviewing court may consider information not contained in the Record. Generally, this information concerns agency policy and decisions in similar cases or circumstances.[13] Nevertheless, use of these exceptions is very limited.

As previously noted, *ex parte* contacts are forbidden. Those items derived from the *ex parte* contact may be stricken from the Record. This may result in the dismissal of the proponent's petition or request for a rule making. 5 U.S.C. § 557(d)(1)(D) (2000).

Permits

An agency may grant a person or company a **permit** to operate its facility. A permit allows the discharge of pollutants into the environment.[14] A typical permit to discharge into waters and streams is governed by the **National Pollutant Discharge Elimination System (NPDES)** under the **Clean Water Act (CWA).** See 33 U.S.C. § 1342 (2000).

Permits may contain specific limitations on the types and amounts of pollutants that may be discharged. A violation of any of the discharge limits is a violation of the applicable statute. These violations can carry significant fines.[15]

A permit application must be submitted to the agency. The permit application process may be governed by specific procedures. See 40 C.F.R. § 124 (1997). The permit application may require specific information on the facility and associated discharges. Public hearings may be required to allow the surrounding community to voice its opinions on the anticipated facility. See 40 C.F.R. § 124.71 (1997).

Finally, after review of the permit application, hearing testimony and other information, the agency may issue the permit. The permit applicant can appeal the agency's final permit determination. See 40 C.F.R. § 124.125 (1997). These appeals are discussed below.

---

[13] Such items as public policy documents and public information may be used to understand ambiguous or unclear language in the rule. Additionally, agencies may rely upon "guidance documents" to further clarify regulations or answer specific questions. See http://www.epa.gov/guidance. However, such "guidance documents" have no legal authority as do regulations. See *Appalachian Power v. EPA*, 208 F.3d 1015 (D.C. Cir. 2000).

[14] Few, if any, processes are pollutant-free. Physical and chemical laws limit the efficiency of production processes and determine the types of by-products created; therefore, some sort of "pollution" is inevitable. These permits are an ongoing effort to minimize the amounts and types of pollutants.

[15] Civil fines can range up to $32,500 per day per violation. See 33 U.S.C. § 1319 (2000) as amended by 69 Fed. Reg. 7121 (February 13, 2004). Each day could, conceivably, be construed as a separate violation. A violation over three days could therefore accrue a maximum of $97,500 in penalties. Criminal fines can carry monetary fines along with imprisonment.

Adjudication—Section 554

In addition to rule making, an agency may also hold hearings to determine whether the rules have been violated. These hearings are called **administrative adjudications.** These adjudications include appeals of an agency's permit decision and are very similar to a court trial. The parties may be represented by attorneys and can obtain information from the other party by subpoena.[16] 5 U.S.C. § 555 (2000).

> Administrative adjudications include appeals of an agency's permit decision and are similar to a court trial.

Additionally, the parties may present information and evidence on their behalf, conduct depositions and questioning of witnesses, and make appropriate motions during the course of the hearing. 5 U.S.C. § 556 (2000). An agency may require special procedures for conduct during these hearings. 5 U.S.C. § 555 (2000).

At the conclusion of the hearing, the agency will issue its decision. The decision must be based upon the information and testimony presented during the hearing. This decision, testimony, and information constitute the Record for the hearing. 5 U.S.C. § 557 (2000). Appeals from the agency's decision will refer to this Record. 5 U.S.C. § 706(2)(E) (2000).

The agency may also impose appropriate sanctions upon a party based upon its decision in the hearing. 5 U.S.C. § 558 (2000).

Appeals

Appeals from FAPA rule making or permit decisions are governed by §§ 701 to 706. These sections describe the type of actions that can be appealed and the permissible scope of review. Additionally, the statute under which an appeal is brought may also provide procedures for an appeal of an agency's action.

This section of the chapter highlights some of the legal concepts and issues involved in administrative appeals. From a practical

---

[16] Subpoenas are demands to produce data and information from another party. A *subpoena duces tecum* is an administrative subpoena on a witness who is in possession or control of documents or paper pertinent to the issues of the case.

standpoint, research skills in the case and the statutory and regulatory materials will figure significantly in administrative appeals. However, even apparently minor procedural items, such as filing requirements and computation of filing dates, type size, and paper color are also important. They could significantly affect whether a document is properly filed in a timely manner.[17]

> A paralegal's research skills will figure significantly in administrative appeals.

The appeal procedures are also governed by court rules for federal civil and appellate procedures.[18] These rules govern the printed form of the papers filed, timing of filing, and other required court procedures.

Definitions—Section 701

This section of FAPA contains definitions that delineate what type of actions may be appealed.

Right of Review—Section 702

Any person suffering a legal wrong is entitled to a review of the agency's action or determination. These legal wrongs may include improper agency rule-making determinations and permit decisions. Actions against the United States must specify the acting head of the agency or department at the time the appeal is begun. 5 U.S.C. § 702 (2000).

---

[17] Minor procedures are important. Local court rules may govern such items as type size and spacing, paper size and color, and number of pages allowed. It will be embarrassing to have a "perfect" brief and arrive at the clerk's office to file, only to find that because you used the incorrect type and spacing, the clerk refuses to accept your document for filing.

[18] The majority of rules are contained in the Federal Rules of Civil Procedure (FRCP) and Federal Rules of Appellate Procedure (FRAP). There may also be local court rules governing form and substance of papers, motions, and appeals. Generally, before work on an appeal or brief is begun, these general and local rules should be reviewed to determine any special requirements for submitting court papers.

Form and Location of Proceeding—Section 703

The statute may require that an appeal be heard before a specific court or in a certain location. This location is also known as **venue.** For example, the **Resource Conservation and Recovery Act (RCRA)** provides that certain actions must be brought in the federal district court in which an alleged violation occurred. 42 U.S.C. § 6972(a) (2000). In comparison, actions against the EPA concerning the promulgation of regulations under RCRA require the action to be brought in the United States Court of Appeals for the District of Columbia. 42 U.S.C. § 6976(a) (2000).

Actions Reviewable—Section 704

Generally, only final agency actions are judicially reviewable. An intermediate decision is reviewable upon issuance of the final decision. 5 U.S.C. § 704 (2000). As previously discussed, "finality" may be difficult to ascertain. Extensive case law has defined what types of agency decisions are considered final.

> Generally, only final agency actions are judicially reviewable.

CASES FOR DISCUSSION

Appalachian Power Co. v. EPA, 135 F.3d 791, 46 ERC 1001, 28 Envtl. L. Rep. 20,521 (D.C. Cir. 1998).

This case concerns rule making under Title IV of the Clean Air Act, which directs the EPA to promulgate limits on the emission of nitrogen oxides from various electric utility boilers. A number of electric utilities and industry groups challenged the EPA's promulgated emission limits. The Court agreed with the EPA and concluded that, cognizant of the deference due to an agency dealing with largely scientific and technical matters, the EPA had not exceeded its authority. It vacated, however, a portion of the final rule that reclassified certain retrofitted cell burner boilers as wall-fired boilers and remanded it to the EPA for reconsideration or a more adequate justification.

Relief Pending Review—Section 705

The agency can delay the effective date of the rule against the appealing party or appellant during the pendency of the case before the court. This will, in effect, allow a reprieve from conforming to the new rules or requirements for the appellant. 5 U.S.C. § 705 (2000).

Scope of Review—Section 706

Finally, a reviewing court has limited discretion as to what type of agency actions can be reviewed or how it may review those actions. FAPA lists several reasons that a court may set aside an agency's actions. 5 U.S.C. § 706(2) (2000). There is a significant body of case law for rule-making and permit appeals under the various environmental laws.

If the agency's action was arbitrary and capricious, there may be significant reason for appealing. **"Arbitrary and capricious"** means that the agency's actions were not based on the Record in the rule-making or permit decision.

Other reasons the court may give in setting aside the agency's decision include (i) the agency's acting beyond its statutory authority, (ii) its failure to abide by procedural requirements, or (iii) the decision's being found unwarranted by the facts in the rule-making or permit decision.

CASES FOR DISCUSSION

Central and South West Services Inc. v. EPA, 220 F.3d 683, 51 ERC 1065, 31 Envtl. L. Rep. 20,058 (5th Cir. 2000).

In this case, the petitioners challenged the EPA's Final Rule concerning the use and disposal of polychlorinated biphenyls (PCBs). The petitioners argued that discrete portions of the EPA's Final Rule are too restrictive.

In June 1998, approximately three-and-one-half years after the NPRM and seven years after the advanced notice of proposed rule making (ANPR), the EPA promulgated this Final Rule. The rule adopted significant amendments affecting the use, manufacture, processing, distribution in commerce, and disposal of PCBs. 63 Fed. Reg. 35384 (June 29, 1998). Two sets of petitioners challenged discrete aspects of the Final Rule, arguing essentially that the revisions do not go far enough in

(continued)

CASES FOR DISCUSSION

relaxing regulatory controls on PCB storage and disposal. In a third petition, it is argued that the rule goes too far and thus allows unreasonably risky disposal practices.

The court confirmed that:

TSCA states that the Administrative Procedure Act's scope of review provision, 5 U.S.C. § 706, shall apply to *review of rules* under TSCA section 6(e) except that "the court shall hold unlawful and set aside such rule if the court finds that the rule is not supported by substantial evidence in the rulemaking record . . . taken as a whole." TSCA § 19(c)(1)(B)(i); U.S.C. § 2618(c)(1)(B)(i).

The substantial evidence standard requires reviewing courts "to ask whether a 'reasonable mind might accept' a particular evidentiary record as 'adequate to support a conclusion.'" *Dickinson v. Zurko*, 527 U.S. 150, 162, 119 S. Ct. 1816, 1823, 144 L. Ed. 2d 143 (1999) (citations omitted). "Substantial evidence requires 'something less than the weight of the evidence, and the possibility of drawing two inconsistent conclusions from the evidence does not prevent an administrative agency's finding from being supported by substantial evidence.'" *Corrosion Proof Fittings v. EPA*, 947 F.2d 1201, 1213, 33 ERC 1961 (5th Cir. 1991) (quoting *Consolo v. Federal Maritime Comm'n*, 383 U.S. 607, 620 (1966)). As this Court emphasized, "Congress put the substantial evidence test in the statute because it wanted the courts to scrutinize [EPA's] actions more closely than an arbitrary and capricious standard would allow." *Id.* at 1214.

***

[W]e conclude that the statutory language creates a rebuttable presumption that uses of PCBs pose an unreasonable risk to health and the environment.

Accordingly, we hold that the substantial evidence standard of review provided for under section 19(c)(1)(B)(i) applies only when a petitioner challenges EPA's decision to depart from the outright ban and permit the use or expand the use of PCBs. When a petitioner challenges an EPA rule restricting or prohibiting the use of PCBs, courts must review EPA's action under the arbitrary and capricious standard of review.

Conclusion

Environmental laws and regulations are constantly in a state of flux, changing to meet today's and tomorrow's needs. An understanding of environmental laws and regulations requires a knowledge of how these laws and regulations are born and how they mature. The basis for modern environmental laws and regulations in the United States flows from the development of administrative agencies and administrative law.

Research and reference tools and hints in administrative law represent skills that an environmental law paralegal will need in support of environmental law attorneys and clients. Paralegals who are going to work in this area are encouraged to seek out a desk reference, such as *Computer-Aided Legal Research (CALR) on the Internet* (Pearson Prentice Hall 2006), by Craig B. Simonsen, to provide them with ready reference to resource and reference materials that they may need.

In administrative law and in working with the EPA, paralegals will often be the point persons in preparing and processing FOIA requests. An environmental paralegal may keep busy just following EPA rule-making activities. As discussed in the Introduction and in other chapters of this book, paralegals may be involved in the rule-making process. Paralegals may assist in the preparation of comments and hearing testimony, including the drafting of testimony and collecting and analyzing other information for submission into the administrative record. Paralegals may also attend and participate in administrative meetings and hearings. For more information on the administrative process, see *Administrative Law for Paralegals* (Pearson Prentice Hall 1999), by Joseph W. Teague. Paralegals will also be actively involved in the administrative enforcement proceedings, as discussed in more detail in the Introduction to this book.

GLOSSARY OF FAPA TERMS

administrative adjudication. In addition to rule makings, an agency can determine whether its rules have been violated. Hearings for this purpose are called "administrative adjudications." These adjudications include appeals of an agency's permitting decisions. Adjudications are very similar to a judicial proceeding in that parties may be represented by attorneys and can obtain information from the other party by subpoena.

agency. FAPA's definitions describe what agencies and governmental bodies are covered by FAPA. For example, an "agency" does not include a federal court. This list is exclusive. This means that, if the governmental body is not listed, the term "agency" encompasses that body and, therefore, the governmental body is regulated by FAPA.

agency action. FAPA defines "agency action" as an agency rule, order, sanction, or even an agency's failure to act.

BNA. Bureau of National Affairs.

CAA. Clean Air Act (42 U.S.C. § 7401 (2000)).

CERCLA. Comprehensive Environmental Response, Compensation, and Liability Act (42 U.S.C. § 9601 (2000)). Also known as "Superfund."

C.F.R. *Code of Federal Regulations.*

CWA. Clean Water Act. See FWPCA.

de novo **review.** Considering the matter as if it had not been heard before, and as if no decision previously had been rendered.

ELR. *Environmental Law Reporter.*

EPA. United States Environmental Protection Agency.

ex parte. A contact or communication outside of the formal rule-making, permit, or adjudication procedure.

FAPA. Federal Administrative Procedure Act (5 U.S.C. § 551 (2000)).

Fed. Reg. *Federal Register.*

FOIA. Freedom of Information Act (5 U.S.C. § 552 (2000)).

FWPCA. Federal Water Pollution Control Act (33 U.S.C. § 1251 (2000)). Also known as the CWA.

HSWA. Hazardous and Solid Waste Disposal Act Amendments of 1984. See RCRA.

NPDES. National Pollutant Discharge Elimination System. An agency may grant a person or company a permit to operate a facility. A permit allows the discharge of pollutants into the environment. A typical permit to discharge into waters and streams is governed by the FWPCA National Pollutant Discharge Elimination System (NPDES). Permits may contain specific limitations on the types and amounts of pollutants that may be discharged. A violation of any of these limits is a violation of the applicable statute. Such violations can carry significant fines. A person must submit a permit application to the agency. The permit application process may be governed by specific procedures. The permit application may require specific information on the facility and associated discharges. Additionally, public hearings may be required to allow members of the surrounding community to voice their opinions on the anticipated facility.

NPRM. Notice of Proposed Rule Making. In an NPRM, the agency publishes a notice that it is either considering or has proposed a rule on a certain subject. The notice may require comments and other materials for the Record to be submitted by a date certain. It may also list references to the laws or regulations affected. FAPA requires publication of the NPRMs in the *Federal Register.*

OAQPS. Office of Air Quality Planning and Standards.

person. For the purposes of FAPA, a "person" includes public and private organizations, corporations, and associations.

RCRA. Resource Conservation and Recovery Act (42 U.S.C. § 6901 (2000)). Also known as the Hazardous and Solid Waste Disposal Act Amendments of 1984 (HSWA) and the Solid Waste Disposal Act (SWDA).

Record. Information and testimony created during a rule-making procedure or permit application. Many appeals are based exclusively on the Record.

rule or regulation. FAPA specifically limits a rule to those agency statements with "future effect designed to implement, interpret, or prescribe law or policy . . ." 5 U.S.C. § 551(4) (2000). This definition closely follows the concept of a rule as compared to the concept of adjudication.

rule making. The process through which agencies develop rules and regulations required by law. Specific examples include requirements for rules and regulations under the Clean Air Act and other laws.

subpoena duces tecum. An administrative subpoena on a witness in possession or control of documents or paper pertinent to the issues of a case.

Superfund. See CERCLA.

SWDA. Solid Waste Disposal Act. See RCRA.

U.S.C. *United States Code.*

venue. A requirement that an appeal be heard before a specific court or in a certain location is found in many statutes. This location is known as "venue." For example, the Resource Conservation and Recovery Act provides that certain actions must be brought in the federal district court in which an alleged violation occurred.

BIBLIOGRAPHY

Anderson, Frederick R., et al., *Environmental Protection: Law & Policy* (Little, Brown & Co. 1990).

Bonfield, A., *State and Federal Administrative Law* (West 1989).

Bureau of National Affairs, *Environmental Reporter* (BNA 1997).

Clean Air Act: Law and Explanation (Commerce Clearing House 1990).

Environmental Laws & Statutes (West 1996).

Federal Civil Judicial Procedure & Rules (West 1996).

Simonsen, Craig B., *Computer-Aided Legal Research (CALR) on the Internet* (Pearson Prentice Hall 2006).

Teague, Joseph W., *Administrative Law for Paralegals* (Pearson Prentice Hall 1999).

DISCUSSION QUESTIONS

1. What is your state's administrative procedure act? What additional items or issues are covered in your state's administrative procedure act as compared with FAPA?
2. Locate a recent Fed. Reg. containing a Final Rule on an environmental topic. Trace the history of this Final Rule back to the initial NPRM.
3. Review the CWA, CAA, and RCRA. What appeal or rule-making procedures in FAPA are limited or changed by these laws?

COMPUTER LABORATORY PROJECTS

1. Find the *Code of Federal Regulations* (C.F.R.), Titles 33 and 40 in the library and on the Internet. For the library print version, report on how many volumes and how many pages make up the contents for the most recent but complete year available (in some cases, all volumes for the present year may not be available, so use last year's instead). For the Internet version, explore a C.F.R. section. Can the Internet version be word searched and blocked/copied-and-pasted into word processing documents?
2. Find a recent EPA-related *Federal Register* (Fed. Reg.) Proposed Rule and prepare a detailed summary of it for presentation to the class.

INTERNET SITES

The full text of the Federal Administrative Procedure Act (FAPA) is on the Internet at http://www.archives.gov/federal_register/public_laws/acts.html.

Data Analysis: Building a Nonbinding Allocation of Responsibility: A Model Data Structure

Craig B. Simonsen

This appendix illustrates the formatting of a CERCLA/Superfund-type "nonbinding allocation of responsibility" (NBAR) database structure. This structure has been used for preparation of allocation waste-in databases to facilitate equitable allocation and settlements at several Superfund sites.

A graphic depiction of the function of an NBAR database structure is shown in Figure A-1.

Waste-In Database

The waste-in database table is key to an NBAR database structure. In the database table structure that follows, an "A" followed by a

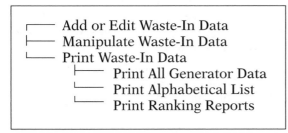

Figure A-1   Function of an NBAR Database Structure.

number represents an alphanumeric field type. For instance, an "A50" field type would allow fifty alpha or numeric characters entered into that field. A "D" field type represents a date field. An "N" field type represents a numeric field type, where only numeric characters may be entered.

The Waste-In Database Table

A typical waste-in database table would contain the following field structure:

Field Name	Field Type
Generator	A50
Transporter	A50
Transaction Date	D
Doc. Type	A35
Doc. I.D. #	A35
Waste Name	A50
Container Type	A100
Unit Type	A35
Waste Volume	N
Converted Pounds	N

The types of data entry and information that are suggested for entry into each of the waste-in database table fields are reviewed next.

Generator

The original source of the waste materials should be entered into this field. Fifty alphanumeric characters are allowed for the company or individual name. It is recommended that normal caps and lowercase letters be utilized in data entry. For instance:

Ace Metals Company

It is critical for data entry operators to enter the generator name exactly the same for each record entered for the same generator. This continuity is critical to sort and rank all generators correctly. If a single entity is listed under two or more different spellings, it will be ranked as two or more separate entities. In a more complicated database application, a "lookup table" for generator names could be specified.

Transporter

The transporter of the waste materials should be entered into this field. Fifty alphanumeric characters are allowed for the company or individual name. It is recommended that normal caps and lowercase letters be utilized in data entry. For instance:

Waste Transportation, Inc.

Trans. Date The date of the waste materials transaction document (e.g., waste manifest form) should be entered here. The date should be entered with slashes, as follows:

01/31/2006

Doc. Type The document type should be entered into this field. Thirty-five alphanumeric characters are allowed for the document type. It is recommended that normal caps and lowercase letters be utilized in data entry. For instance:

Manifest

Doc. I.D. # The identification number of the document reference, if available, should be entered into this field. Ideally, this will be a "Bates" type number, that can identify the document source (e.g., with a prefix like "EPA" for documents produced by the EPA). Thirty-five alphanumeric characters are allowed for the document I.D. number. For instance:

EPA000035

Waste Name The name of the waste material should be entered into this field. Fifty alphanumeric characters are allowed for the waste name. It is recommended that normal caps and lowercase letters be utilized in data entry. For instance:

Waste Solvent

Container Type The container name should be entered into this field. One hundred alphanumeric characters are allowed for the container name. It is recommended that normal caps and lowercase letters be utilized in data entry. For instance:

Drum

Unit Type The unit name should be entered into this field. Thirty-five alphanumeric characters are allowed for the unit name. It is recommended that normal caps and lowercase letters be utilized in data entry. For instance:

Gallons

Waste Volume

This is a numeric field where the total waste volume should be entered. For example, if the units listed in the unit type field for the current transaction document are in gallons, then the data entry operator should enter the total gallons listed. Commas in numbers are not necessary. Decimal points may be used. For instance:

1250.5555

Converted Lbs.

In data entry, the converted pounds field should be left blank. Ideally, the database application (by the operator) should be able to convert all units to pounds automatically.

Document File Organization, Indexing, and File Management in Environmental Cases: Computer Database and Programming Techniques

Craig B. Simonsen

The management of the document file, together with well-organized document indexes that facilitate document retrieval, is key to the successful support of environmental cases. In support of case organization and analysis, generally and specifically in environmental law, the ability to retrieve selected documents and information concerning documents is critical. This appendix provides an outline for document and file organization and document indexes and concludes with a discussion of computer automation of this information.

Document File Organization Concepts

A file, as used in the case support context, is a compilation or group of related documents, records, or other information. There are certain generalities concerning file organization that remain fairly consistent from case to case and from practice to practice (whether law firm or business entity) that can be illustrated and utilized for this purpose. These file creation and maintenance techniques will, if vigorously applied, provide a basis for an initial document indexing and organization and will allow document retrieval and information analysis.

For instance, a general rule is that each client's file will be maintained in a segregated fashion. That is, all of client ABC's files will be

I.	Correspondence
	A. Ongoing correspondence
	B. Selected correspondence
	Strategy and case memoranda files
II.	Pleadings
	A. Instant case pleadings (court or administrative)
	B. Related and other venue pleadings files
III.	Occurrence/Discovery Documents
	A. Client documents
	B. Discovery documents
	C. Deposition, hearing, and trial documents
	D. Witness documents
IV.	Expert/Technical Documents
	A. Separate file for each expert
V.	Research Documents
VI.	Case Preparation Outlines, Documents, and Notes

Figure B-1   Document File Organization.

maintained in the same file drawer or file cabinet. For each of your client's individual matters, there will be further segregation. For example, client ABC's air-permitting files will be maintained separately from its RCRA permit files.

Beyond this initial segregation, the documents will be organized and indexed such as is outlined in Figure B-1. This outline depicts a general filing system based on categories of documents that can be modified to suit any organizational situation.

There are certain general rules for implementing this file organization. For instance, documents in correspondence files should be maintained in a chronological order. The correspondence file can be clipped or affixed to the correspondence folder to assure the integrity of the chronological order.

Pleadings (documents that are filed with the court or other adjudicative bodies) should be maintained in chronological order. Pleadings can be clipped or affixed to a pleadings folder to assure the integrity of the chronological order. An ongoing index to the pleadings should be maintained. On the other hand, pleadings files can be maintained by creating a separate individual folder for each pleadings document. These folders can then be maintained in chronological order in the file. The index to the main file would then become the pleadings index as well.

For the occurrence/discovery document files, generally the greater the subdivision, the better. The case documents are, after all, the base evidence for or against your case. Therefore, by creating and maintaining individual folders for each of these documents, you necessarily create a rough-cut document index that may be used by the case management team to distinguish those documents that need further analysis.

The expert/technical document files are the basis for arguing your position on the facts of the case. In environmental law cases, experts can make or end a case. Breaking down these documents into individual folders and creating and maintaining indexes to these documents are critical to the retrieval of the documents and in the preparation and understanding of the "expert case."

Research document files are often created and maintained by the case attorney for ongoing reference. If a paralegal is to create these types of files, he or she should have close guidance from the attorney generating the file material. Generally, separate folders and indexes will be appropriate.

Case preparation, outlines, documents, and notes files are often created and maintained with close guidance from the supervising attorney. If a third person is to create these types of files, again, he or she should have close guidance from the attorney generating the file material. Generally, separate folders and indexes will be appropriate.

Document Indexing

In initial review of the client files, certain key information should be extracted for the creation of retrievable files and useful indexes. After the initial review, the "first cut" document indexes can then be the basis for identifying those documents that require further review, in-depth indexing, and, possibly, abstraction.

In-depth document indexes and document abstracts, if prepared, will become a key source of information as to the facts of the case and will be the basis for review and retrieval of evidence to support or discredit your client's position.

Initial Indexes

In the preparation of the first cut document indexes, which can also be the basis for a file organization, certain key information (or "fields") needs to be extracted from the documents. The fields include the document date, the document type, the document title, and an arbitrarily assigned file retrieval number.

The document date will normally be the date that is on the face of the document. Usually it will be the date that the document author originally gave the document. In certain instances, however, this general rule is modified. For instance, pleadings will always have the date on which they were filed with the court. Documents that have been revised or modified will take the date of that revision or modification.

To determine the document type, refer to the file organization outline at Figure B-1. Documents will always be from one of those categories. Note that by classifying documents into one of the categories above, sorting information by document type after completing the initial index will provide a file creation and maintenance tool for the index.

The document title field can be more difficult to determine. In many cases, a proper title cannot be given without a thorough review of the document. Even after review, some documents may be so obscure as to avoid any useful title. These documents should be put aside, and the reviewer should seek further guidance from the case management team before arbitrarily giving difficult documents a title. If a document title still remains obscure after consultation, then a title should be arbitrarily given. The selected title should contain whatever information is known about the document (such as unidentified invoices, selected pages from unknown manuscripts, etc.).

The arbitrarily assigned file number field may be stipulated after the complete file review and indexing. Once the base information on the file (document date, type, and title) is collected, the information can then be sorted and appropriate file numbers can be assigned based on the document type.

A sample of this type of document file index follows.

SUPERFUND SITE - INDEX TO DOCUMENT DEPOSITORY
Client #99999-00001

August 31, 1996

I.   Correspondence

Correspondence (Wallet #: 001001)

    (A)   Correspondence January 1995—December 1995

II.   Pleadings

107 Notice of Removal Action (Wallet #: 002001)

    (A)   General Notice of Potential Liability, July 1, 1995
    (B)   Response of Group PRPs to General Notice, August 15, 1995

III.   Occurrence/Discovery Documents

104(e) Request (Wallet #: 003001)

    (A)   104(e) Request from U.S. EPA and IEPA, 5/21/93

IEPA FOIA Response: DLPC Files (Wallet #: 003002)

    (A)   IEPA DLPC FOIA Response—FOS File, 1 of 2
    (B)   IEPA DLPC FOIA Response—FOS File, 2 of 2
    (C)   IEPA DLPC FOIA Response—Groundwater File

IV.   Expert/Technical Documents

RI/FS Final Work Plan (Wallet #: 004001)

    (A)   IEPA Conditional Acceptance of Revised Draft RI/FS
           Work Plan, November 2, 1992
    (B)   Transmittal of Final Work Plan for Remedial
           Investigation/Feasibility Study, November 20, 1992
    (C)   Final Work Plan for Remedial
           Investigation/Feasibility Study, November 20, 1992

V.   Research Documents

News clippings (Wallet #: 005001)

    (A)   Miscellaneous News Clippings

VI.   Case Preparation Outlines, Documents, and Notes

Allocation Meeting Documents and Handouts (Wallet #: 006001)

    (A)   Allocation Alternatives Prepared for Allocation
           Subcommittee Meeting, March 3, 1992

In-Depth Document Indexing and Abstraction

Once the initial document indexes are prepared, they can be used to make the first cut to identify which documents need further review. This determination should be made by the case management team.

The in-depth document indexes will include the information already extracted from the documents in the initial indexes, plus more detailed and substantive information, possibly including document abstracts. Information to extract from the documents may include the following:

    Date   (from initial index)
    Type   (from initial index)
    Title   (from initial index)
    File Number (from initial index)

Author
Recipient
Carbon Copies
Names In-Text
Abstract
Comments

The document's author, recipient, carbon copies, and names in-text may or may not be clear on the face of the document. If so, list that information. If not, leave the field blank until the information is clearly established (e.g., obtained through discovery in interrogatories or in deposition).

The document abstract field should provide a brief, concise summary of the substance of the document. The purpose of the abstract is to establish those documents that are on point with respect to issues in the case and will require further analysis. The case management team should be able to review the in-depth document indexes and abstracts and thereby have a good understanding for the evidence to support and contest the case.

The comments field allows the document reviewer and the case attorneys and paralegals to add analysis about the documents. In reviewing a document, the reviewer may decide that this document represents the essence of what the client has proclaimed—or just the opposite. The comments field allows the reviewer an opportunity to add comments concerning the document as it relates to the issues of the case.

In-Depth Index Preparation Process

In preparing the in-depth indexes, the document indexers should be in constant consultation with the case management team. A recommended process would be to review initially a sample amount of the in-depth index entries in the document database—let's say, five percent of the documents. Use this sample group to prepare the in-depth document indexes, and then seek consultation and feedback of the work-product from the case management team.

The sample review process will serve a dual purpose. First, in reviewing the in-depth indexes at an early stage, the case management team may conclude that the work product is incomplete in some regard. Or the team may find the indexes overbroad and in too much detail. In either case, with only a sample of the project completed, it would still be early enough in the process to allow correction.

The second purpose of the sample review is to allow both the case management team and the document indexers to analyze the format in which the document indexes are presented. An index created in a database environment can be manipulated to show various data in various perspectives. By modifying the index or printed reports, or by adding multiple reports that summarize the same data in varying ways, new insights to the in-depth document index may be acquired. Making the report specifications analysis from a sample of the database will save time, effort, and material.

Computer Database and Document Index Programming

In reviewing the above sections, you may have gleaned an inkling of what is to follow here. In the preparation and maintenance of file and document indexes, there is no more useful tool than a computer database. This is because a computer database will, with a little planning, easily store, modify, sort, and print (report) information.

For purposes of this appendix, the term "computer" is synonymous with an IBM[1]-compatible personal computer (PC). The database terminology is applicable to most relational database software.

To prepare document indexes in a PC database environment, significant planning must be done. For instance, the design of the database will reflect its usefulness and flexibility as an information tool. Data entry screens may need to be developed to provide an efficient and effective interface to the database. Printed reports will be the media for presentation of the data. Multiple reports are the norm and should be considered.

In the creation of the database, the programmer must stipulate the field names and the field types. The field names for the creation of the file and document indexes have already been mentioned above and are discussed below. A field type describes whether the field will be alphanumeric, numeric, a date, currency/money, or a memo (full-text) field. The difference between these field types will affect the kind and the flexibility of the database sorting and reporting capabilities in relation to the data. These particular field types will be discussed in reference to the file and document index database structure given below.

In the previous sections, the suggested field names for document indexes were given. Here is a database structure that incorporates

---

[1] IBM™ is a trademark of International Business Machines, Inc.

those field names and adds the field types that are appropriate for this application:

Field Name	Field Type
Date	D
Type	A100
Title	A255
File Number	A6
Author	A255
Recipient	A255
Carbon Copies	A255
Names In-Text	A255
Abstract	Memo
Comments	Memo

In this database structure, the first field is a date (D) field. This type of field will only accept an actual date, such as January 1, 1995 (01/01/1995). This field will be useful in sorting the database chronologically and looking for documents with a certain date.

The remaining field types are alphanumeric (A#) and full-text (Memo) fields. Next to the A is a number that represents the number of alphanumeric characters that may be entered into that field. Therefore, in the document type field, a maximum of 100 characters, of any kind (e.g., a, A, 1, *, #, !, ?, -) will be allowed. Memo fields will allow unlimited text entry.

Once the database structure is designed, forms or data entry screens may be created, if appropriate. The form provides a more sophisticated data entry system for the data operators. Otherwise, the data may be entered through the table or spreadsheet format.

As discussed in the previous appendix, modified and/or multiple reports of the file and document indexes may be necessary. By designing reports in the database environment, flexibility and ease of preparation are ensured. Previously designed reports are easy to modify and to update.

Document Organization Techniques: Building an Adobe[1] "pdf" Library

Craig B. Simonsen

These days it is common to have multiple offices, lawyers, and their clients all connected by computer networks across the Internet. This is to suggest a technique for creating a case library of document images or files in Adobe pdf format, to facilitate and enlarge access to case documents. As with the paper files, the management of the case image documents will enable document retrieval.

This is not to suggest an alternative to imaging and abstraction of the case discovery and production documents, which are usually programmed in litigation support databases, such as Summation,[2] but rather to suggest an electronic file organization for key documents and for those documents that are typically not included in the litigation support databases, such as pleadings, attorney case research memoranda, and case indexes. Interestingly, these traditional databases, such as Summation, are now also supporting the linking of network computer hard drives and folders, making seamless the access to all case documents through the litigation support database environment.

An Accessible Drive Location

In order for the image library to be useful, it has be accessible by all team members. For instance, building a pdf library on the "C:\" drive

---

of the local computer will make the library inaccessible to all but the creator. Ideally, the image collection should be created on a computer network drive that is accessible to all team members' computer workstations.

Alphanumerical Organization

Computer drives, that is, hard-disk storage space, with operating systems such as Windows XP,[3] allow for the easy organization of information into logical folders. Folders can be created for current cases, with each folder titled to encourage recognition for case team members. Within each top-level or "root" case folder, there would be general documents, like service lists and other key information relating to the case, and additional subfolders to organize the additional case documents.

For instance, where the case at issue is *Johnson v. Smith*, the top-level network pdf folder could be named either Johnson or Smith. For this illustration we will use "Johnson." In the Johnson folder, we will also have the following additional subfolders to organize the information and documents as they are collected:

- Expert Documents
  - Johnson Experts
  - Smith Experts
- Indexes
- Research Memos
- Pleadings
- Selected Production Documents
  - Johnson Documents
  - Smith Documents
- Witness Documents

Expert Documents Folder

In the Expert Documents folder, there would be two subfolders: one for Johnson Experts and one for Smith Experts. In these subfolders, there would be selected pdf files of either the Johnson Experts or the Smith Experts. In this example, "expert documents" means those key documents that have been identified with case experts, such as expert

---

[3] Copyright ©2004 Microsoft Corporation. All rights reserved.

reports and résumés. Having pdf copies of these documents available in an easy-to-find network location can save time and effort.

Using this system, copies of the pdf or Word or other format files named after the related expert would be compiled in each related sub-folder. To sort alphabetically by expert, files need to be labeled first with the expert's last name, then first initial or first name (if necessary), then by the substance of the file, as shown here:

- Madison—Report.pdf
- Madison—Résumé.pdf
- Samson—Report.pdf
- Samson—Résumé.pdf
- Samson—Supp Report.pdf

Indexes Folder

In the Indexes folder, there would be current copies of the indexes of discovery production documents, lists of depositions taken, plead-ings indexes, chronologies, and so on. These indexes could be either in their original file format (Access, Excel, Word), or they could be printed copies in pdf format.

Files in any format should be named so that they provide other team members with a sense of what is indexed. In this example, then, the files in the Indexes folder might be named:

- Johnson Documents.pdf
- Key Documents.pdf
- Pleadings.pdf
- Smith Documents.pdf

Note that the documents above are listed in alphabetical order. This is because in a Windows XP environment, the operating system—or "My Computer"—will automatically organize and list the files in each folder opened or viewed in alphabetical order.

Pleadings Folder

The Pleadings folder would contain pdf format files of all or selected substantive pleadings. These would be pdf files saved and named first by the date and then by the abbreviated name of each document. For example, the first five files in this folder might be named:

- 040201—Complaint.pdf
- 040228—Answer and Affirm Defs.pdf
- 040315—Plts 1st Set Int and Req for Prod Docs.pdf

- 040415—Defs Resp to Plts 1st Set Int and Req for Prod Docs.pdf
- 040615—Order re Status.pdf

In this example, in order for the pleadings to sort properly, the proper naming convention will first list the year (04), then the month (02), and then the day (01). By using this naming convention, the files in the Pleadings folder will always sort chronologically. Pleading name abbreviation is suggested as pleadings names can be unwieldy, and shorter names are easier to read in list of files.

Research Memos Folder

It seems that finding historical research that has been done in a case is always difficult. Attorneys sometimes remember that there may have been a research memo written some time ago on a particular topic, but staff is often left looking through the entire file to find the remembered memo. This system would place pdf or other format copies of research memos and even related case law in the Research Memos folder, so that this sort of historical work-product is always at hand.

There are mixed views about whether the files in this sort of collection should be named chronologically, so that they can easily be found by date, or topically, so that the right topical file is easy to find. Take your pick.

Selected Production Documents Folder

In the Selected Production Documents folder, there would two subfolders: one for Johnson Documents and one for Smith Documents. In these subfolders would be selected pdf files of either the Johnson Documents or the Smith Documents. In this example, "selected" means those key documents that have been identified as important to the case, or that are constantly referred to. Having pdf copies of key documents available in an easy-to-find network location can save time and effort.

For instance, the documents in the Johnson Documents subfolder would be pdf files saved and named after the first Bates label of each document, accompanied by a short description. For example, the first five files in this subfolder would be named:

- JOH000001—Contract for Services.pdf
- JOH000026—Letter from Smith to Johnson-8-12-2001.pdf
- JOH000123—Contract Amendment.pdf

- JOH000126—Letter from Johnson to Smith-9-25-2001.pdf
- JOH000201—Affidavit of Davidson.pdf

In this example, the first Johnson document goes from Bates number JOH000001 through JOH000025, the second one goes from JOH000026 through JOH000122, and so on. By using this naming convention, the files will always sort correctly (that is, in Bates number order), and so finding copies of needed documents by Bates number will never be an issue.

Witness Documents Folder

The Witness Documents folder would contain pdf or other formatted files that concern witnesses in the case. For instance, deposition summaries or witness summaries are often prepared and placed in the hard-copy paper witness folder. Using this system, copies of the Word and other format files, named after the witnesses, would be compiled in this folder. To sort alphabetically by witness, files need to be labeled with the witness's last name, then first initial or first name, (if necessary) them by the substance of the file, as shown here:

- Johnson—Affidavit.pdf
- Johnson—Dep Ex No 01.pdf
- Johnson—Dep Sum.doc
- Smith—Dep Ex No 01.pdf
- Smith—Dep Sum.doc

Key U.S. EPA Contacts

U.S. EPA National Contacts

Environmental Protection Agency
Ariel Rios Building
1200 Pennsylvania Avenue NW
Washington, DC 20460
(202) 272-0167

Agency Locator Service
(202) 260-2090

Endangered Species Protection Program (Pesticides) Information Line
(800) 447-3813
e-mail: opp-web-comments@epa.gov

Enforcement Investigations Center Laboratory
Box 25277, Bldg. 53
Denver Federal Center
Denver, CO 80225
(303) 236-5132

Environmental Appeals Board
(202) 233-0122; (202) 233-0121 (fax)

Environmental Education Clearinghouse
(800) 424-4372

Environmental Justice Hotline
(800) 962-6215
e-mail: environmental-justice-epa@epa.gov

Freedom of Information Officer
U.S. EPA, Records, FOIA and Privacy Branch
1200 Pennsylvania Avenue, NW (2822T)
Washington, DC 20460
(202) 566-1667, (202) 566-2147 (fax)
e-mail: hq.foia@epa.gov

National Compliance Assistance Clearinghouse
(202) 564-7071
e-mail: cfpub.epa.gov/clearinghouse/contact_us.cfm

Office of Public Affairs
(202) 260-4361

Pollution Prevention Information Clearinghouse (PPIC)
(202) 566-0799; (202) 564-8899 (fax)
e-mail: ppic.@epa.gov

Public Information Center
(202) 475-7751

RCRA, Superfund and EPCRA Call Center
(800) 424-9346; (703) 412-9810 (Washington, DC Area Local)
http://www.epa.gov/epaoswer/osw/comments.htm

Safe Drinking Water Hotline
(800) 426-4791; (703) 412-3333 (fax)
e-mail: hotline-sdwa@epa.gov

Superfund Document Center
(202) 566-0276; (202) 566-0224 (fax)
e-mail: superfund.docket@epa.gov

Toxic Release Inventory—Community Right to Know—EPCRA
Hotline
(800) 424-9346; (703) 412-9810 (Washington, DC Area Local)
e-mail: tri.us@epa.gov

Toxic Substances Control Act (TSCA) Hotline
(202) 554-1404; (202) 554-5603 (fax)
e-mail: tsca-hotline@epa.gov

WasteWise Helpline
(800) EPA-WISE ((800) 372-9473); (703) 308-8686 (fax)
e-mail: ww@cais.net

Regional Contacts

Region 1 (States: CT, ME, MA, NH, RI, VT)

Environmental Protection Agency
1 Congress St. Suite 1100
Boston, MA 02114-2023
(617) 918-1111; (617) 565-3660 (fax)

Regional Freedom of Information Officer
U.S. EPA, Region 1
JFK Federal Bldg
1 Congress St. Suite 1100 (OARM)
Boston, MA 02114-2023
(617) 918-1103; (617) 918-1809 (fax)
e-mail: r1foia@epa.gov

Region 2 (States: NJ, NY, PR, VI)

Environmental Protection Agency
290 Broadway
New York, NY 10007-1866
(212) 637-3000; (212) 637-3526 (fax)

Regional Freedom of Information Officer
U.S. EPA, Region 2
290 Broadway, 26th Floor
New York, NY 10007-1866
(212) 637-3668, (212) 637-5046 (fax)
e-mail: r2foia@epa.gov

Region 3 (States: DE, DC, MD, PA, VA, WV)

Environmental Protection Agency
1650 Arch Street
Philadelphia, PA 19103-2029
(215) 814-5000; (215) 814-5103 (fax)
Toll free: (800) 438-2474
e-mail: r3public@epa.gov

Regional Freedom of Information Officer
U.S. EPA, Region 3
1650 Arch Street (3CG10)
Philadelphia, PA 19103
(215) 814-5553; (215) 814-5102 (fax)
e-mail: r3foia@epa.gov

Region 4 (States: AL, FL, GA, KY, MS, NC, SC, TN)

Environmental Protection Agency
Atlanta Federal Center
61 Forsyth Street, SW
Atlanta, GA 30303-3104
(404) 562-9900; (404) 562-8174 (fax)
Toll free: (800) 241-1754

Regional Freedom of Information Officer
U.S. EPA, Region 4
AFC Bldg, 61 Forsyth Street, SW, 9th Flr (4PM/IF)
Atlanta, GA 30303-8960
(404) 562-9891; (404) 562-8054 (fax)
e-mail: r4foia@epa.gov

Region 5 (States: IL, IN, MI, MN, OH, WI)

Environmental Protection Agency
77 West Jackson Boulevard
Chicago, IL 60604-3507
(312) 353-2000; (312) 353-4135 (fax)

Regional Freedom of Information Officer
U.S. EPA, Region 5
77 West Jackson Boulevard (MI-9J)
Chicago, IL 60604-3590
(312) 886-6686; (312) 886-1515 (fax)
e-mail: r5foia@epa.gov

Region 6 (States: AR, LA, NM, OK, TX)

Environmental Protection Agency
Fountain Place 12th Floor, Suite 1200
1445 Ross Avenue
Dallas, TX 75202-2733
(214) 665-2200; (214) 665-7113 (fax)

Regional Freedom of Information Officer
U.S. EPA, Region 6
1445 Ross Avenue (6MD-II)
Dallas, TX 75202-2733
(214) 665-6597; (214) 665-2146 (fax)
e-mail: r6foia@epa.gov

Region 7 (States: IA, KS, MO, NE)

Environmental Protection Agency
901 North 5th Street
Kansas City, KS 66101
(913) 551-7003
Toll free: (800) 223-0425

Regional Freedom of Information Officer
U.S. EPA, Region 7
901 N. 5th Street
Kansas City, KS 66101

(913) 551-7003, (913) 551-7066 (fax)
e-mail: r7foia@epa.gov

Region 8 (States: CO, MT, ND, SD, UT, WY)

Environmental Protection Agency
999 18th Street Suite 500
Denver, CO 80202-2466
(303) 312-6312; (303) 312-6339 (fax)
Toll free: (800) 227-8917
e-mail: r8eisc@epa.gov

Regional Freedom of Information Officer
U.S. EPA, Region 8
999 18th Street, Suite 300 (OC)
Denver, CO 80202-2466
(303) 312-6940; (303) 312-6961 (fax)
e-mail: r8foia@epa.gov

Region 9 (States: AZ, CA, HI, NV, AS, GU)

Environmental Protection Agency
75 Hawthorne Street
San Francisco, CA 94105
(415) 947-8000; (415) 947-3553 (fax)
e-mail: r9.info@epa.gov

Regional Freedom of Information Officer
U.S. EPA, Region 9
75 Hawthorne Street (OPPA-2)
San Francisco, CA 94105
(415) 947-4251; (415) 947-3591 (fax)
e-mail: r9foia@epa.gov

Region 10 (States: AK, ID, OR, NA)

Environmental Protection Agency
1200 Sixth Avenue
Seattle, WA 98101
(206) 553-1200; (206) 553-0149 (fax)
Toll free: (800) 424-4372

Regional Freedom of Information Officer
U.S. EPA, Region 10
Office of External Affairs
1200 6th Avenue (CEC-142)
Seattle, WA 98101
(206) 553-8665; (206) 553-0149 (fax)
email: r10.foia@epa.gov

Selected Environmental Resources on the Internet

Francine Shay[1]

As a working legal professional, you will find that you will perform far more research for environmental information and documents online than on paper. The most effective way to use Web sites as resources is to visit potentially useful sites and then surf the various links and pages the sites offer. Ideally, this is done casually and in your spare time—before you need to hastily obtain information during an emergency project. Save your frequently used sites in your Favorites folder. You'll be surprised how quickly your Favorites folder will fill up with site links, so keep them well-organized and renamed in a manner that makes sense to you. To find specific information on a site, either browse through the site's index or use the site's search function. Each site uses a different query method to run its searches. Therefore, to ensure you are using the most effective search method for a particular site, click onto the site's search instructions and learn its query language.

Although finding information on the Internet may appear quick and easy, keep in mind that the reliability of information is directly related to its source. Therefore, unless you obtain information from a government Web site, you must double-check the facts cited in the site. Many Web sites are hosted by individuals or groups with an agenda who will post anything to push that agenda forward.

The Web sites listed in this appendix offer far more information than what is described below, and their offerings are constantly changing. Web site addresses also change. Therefore, if an address listed

---

[1] Thanks to Adrienne Henry for preparing the first draft of this appendix.

below does not take you to the described Web site, you may search for the site on a search engine such as Google. Type in the name of the governmental agency, division, or organization in the search engine's search box, and the first few "hits" will likely be the Web site you are seeking.

FEDERAL GOVERNMENT SITES
Environmental Protection Agency and Related Sites

United States Environmental Protection Agency
http://www.epa.gov
The government agency charged with the mission of protecting human health and safeguarding the natural environment: air, water, and land. The Web site contains numerous links to agency rule-making dockets, publications, and online databases, and is useful for making FOIA requests. The site also provides the opportunity to join listservs, as discussed later in this appendix.

United States Environmental Protection Agency Rules, Regulations, and Legislation
http://www.epa.gov/epahome/cfr40.htm
Contains Title 40 of the *Code of Federal Regulations.*

EPA Regional Offices and State EPAs
http://www.epa.gov/regional/contact.htm
The EPA page that provides a comprehensive listing with links to EPA regional offices and their contact information.

EPA Information Sources
http://www.epa.gov/epahome/dockets.htm
The EPA page that provides access to electronic public dockets of the regulatory and nonregulatory process. For each rule-making and non-rule-making action, a docket is established. The dockets include *Federal Register* documents, supporting documentation, and public comments. The site also allows access to an online comment system.

EPA Office of Air and Radiation
http://www.epa.gov/air/index.html
Information on indoor and outdoor toxic air pollution, radon, motor vehicle emissions, stationary sources, radiation protection, acid rain, ozone depletion, and global warming. The site includes links to the Clean Air Act and related policies and regulations.

EPA Office of Enforcement and Compliance
http://www.epa.gov/oecaerth

The site provides information useful in achieving environmental law compliance, in compliance monitoring, in civil and criminal enforcement regarding air pollution, pesticides, NEPA, cleanup, toxic substances, water, and federal facilities, as well as community right to know. Resources include links to cases and settlements, consent decrees, and legal decisions.

EPA Office of Environmental Justice
http://www.epa.gov/compliance/environmentaljustice/
This office serves as a focal point for ensuring that communities comprised predominantly of people of color or low income populations receive fair treatment and meaningful involvement regarding development, implementation, and enforcement of environmental laws.

EPA Office of Freedom of Information
http://www.epa.gov/foia/
The EPA's homepage for its Freedom of Information Act office, this site provides an online form for making and submitting FOIA requests, a reading room providing final opinions, statements of policy and interpretation, administrative staff manuals and instructions, frequently requested records, and other reference materials.

EPA Office of Prevention, Pesticides, and Toxic Substances
http://www.epa.gov/oppts
This office develops national strategies for toxic substance control and promotes pollution prevention and the public's right to know about chemical risks. The site includes laws and regulations, test methods and guidelines, and a chemical library.

EPA Office of Solid Waste
http://www.epa.gov/epaoswer/osw/index.htm
This site provides information on solid wastes of various industries, pollution prevention, federal facilities restoration and reuse, hazardous waste technology innovations, recycling, permitting, voluntary partnership programs, special initiatives (brownfields), RCRA, the Superfund program, and underground storage tanks.

EPA Office of Transportation and Air Quality
http://www.epa.gov/omswww/
This office provides information on efforts to control air pollution from motor vehicles, engines, and the fuels used to operate them; voluntary programs; transportation and air quality; and modeling, testing, and research.

EPA Office of Water
http://www.epa.gov/ow

This site provides information on wetlands, oceans, coasts, estuaries, watersheds, monitoring water quality, polluted runoff, and the issue of water security.

U.S. EPA Technology Transfer Network
http://www.epa.gov/ttn
A collection of Web sites containing information about many areas of air pollution science, technology, regulation, measurement, and prevention. In addition, the TTN serves as a public forum for the exchange of technical information and ideas among participants and EPA staff. The sites on TTN include:

> AQS, Air Quality System
> AMTIC, Air Quality Monitoring
> ATW, Air Toxics Web site
> CATC/RBLC Prevention and Control Technologies
> CHIEF, Inventories and Emission Factors
> CICA, U.S. Mexico Information Center
> ECAS, Economic Analysis
> EMC, Emission Test Methods and Information
> FACA, Advisory Committee for Ozone and PM
> FERA Fate, Exposure, and Risk Analysis
> GEI, Geographical/Ecosystems Initiatives
> NAAQS, National Ambient Air Quality Standards
> NELAC, Lab Accreditation Performance Standards
> NSR, New Source Review Permitting
> OAR PG, OAR Rules, Policy & Guidance
> SBAP, Small Business Assistance Activities
> SCRAM, Regulatory Air Quality Models

OTHER FEDERAL GOVERNMENT SITES

United States Corps of Engineers Regulations and Policy
http://www.usace.army.mil/inet/functions/cw/cecwo/reg/index.htm
The U. S. Army Corps of Engineers' regulatory program reviews dredge and fill activities in U.S. waters, construction or dredging in navigable waterways, and spoil material disposal in offshore disposal sites. This page links to many other pages providing local district information, Corps regulations, administrative and judicial materials, regulatory programs, technical and biological resources, archives, and news.

United States Fish and Wildlife Service
http://www.fws.gov
The mission of the U.S. Fish and Wildlife Service (FWS) is to work with others to conserve and enhance fish, wildlife, and plants and their habitats for the continuing benefit of the American people.

United States Department of Labor, Occupational Safety and Health Administration

http://www.osha.gov

The mission of the Occupational Safety and Health Administration (OSHA) is to save lives, prevent injuries, and protect the health of America's workers. The site offers compliance assistance, laws and regulations, cooperative programs, and an opportunity to subscribe to biweekly e-news memos.

National Marine Fisheries Service

http://www.nmfs.noaa.gov

The National Marine Fisheries Service (MFS) is dedicated to the stewardship of living marine resources through science-based conservation and management, and to the promotion of healthy ecosystems.

United States Department of Transportation

http://www.dot.gov

The Department of Transportation is composed of several organizational entities such as the United States Coast Guard, the Federal Aviation Administration, the Maritime Administration, and the Federal Highway Administration, each of which has its own contracting office. The site includes an online database of regulatory and adjudicatory information, as well as the laws and regulations affecting the various agencies.

United States Department of Energy/Energy Efficiency and Renewable Energy

http://www.eere.energy.gov/.

The mission of the Office of Energy Efficiency and Renewable Energy is to lead the nation to a stronger economy, a cleaner environment, and a more secure future through development and deployment of sustainable energy technologies. The homepage advises that the Web site serves as a gateway to hundreds of Web sites and thousands of online documents related to energy efficiency and renewable energy.

Thomas Legislative Information

http://thomas.loc.gov

Contains federal legislative information including searchable House and Senate bills, *Congressional Record* text, bill summary and status, committee information, historical documents, and links to the *United States Code*.

Government Printing Office

http://www.access.gpo.gov

Access to the *Federal Register*, the *Congressional Record*, the *Code of Federal Regulations*, congressional bills, congressional documents, public laws, and Supreme Court decisions. The site includes a browse feature for congressional hearings.

STATE ENVIRONMENTAL AGENCIES

Alabama
http://www.adem.state.al.us
—Alabama Department of Environmental Management
http://www.dcnr.state.al.us
—Alabama Department of Conservation and Natural Resources

Alaska
http://www.dec.state.ak.us
—Alaska Department of Environmental Conservation

Arizona
http://www.azdeq.gov
—Arizona Department of Environmental Quality
http://www.gf.state.az.us
—Arizona Game and Fish Department

Arkansas
http://www.adeq.state.ar.us
—Arkansas Department of Environmental Quality

California
http://www.calepa.ca.gov/
—California Environmental Protection Agency
http://www.consrv.ca.gov/
—California Department of Conservation
http://www.arb.ca.gov/
—California Air Resources Board
http://www.dwr.water.ca.gov/
—California Department of Water Resources
http://www.ciwmb.ca.gov/
—California Integrated Waste Management Board

Colorado
http://www.cdphe.state.co.us/cdphehom.asp
—Colorado Department of Public Health and Environment

Connecticut
http://dep.state.ct.us
—Connecticut Department of Environmental Protection

Delaware
http://www.dnrec.state.de.us
—Delaware Department of Natural Resources and Environmental Control

Florida
http://www.dep.state.fl.us
—Florida Department of Environmental Protection

Georgia
http://www.gaepd.org/
—Georgia Department of Natural Resources

Hawaii
http://www.hawaii.gov/dlnr/
—Hawaii Department of Land and Natural Resources

Idaho
http://www.deq.state.id.us/
—Idaho Department of Environmental Quality
http://www.idwr.state.id.us/
—Idaho Department of Water Resources

Illinois
http://www.epa.state.il.us/
—Illinois Environmental Protection Agency
http://www.ipcb.state.il.us/
—Illinois Pollution Control Board

Indiana
http://www.ai.org/idem/
—Indiana Department of Environmental Management
http://www.state.in.us/dnr/
—Indiana Department of Natural Resources

Iowa
http://www.iowadnr.com/
—Iowa Department of Natural Resources

Kansas
http://www.kdhe.state.ks.us/
—Kansas Department of Health and Environment

Kentucky
http://www.kyeqc.net/
—Kentucky Environmental Quality Commission

http://www.naturalresources.ky.gov/
—Kentucky Department for Natural Resources
http://www.environment.ky.gov/
—Kentucky Environmental and Public Protection Cabinet

Louisiana
http://www.deq.state.la.us/
—Louisiana Department of Environmental Quality

Maine
http://www.state.me.us/dep/index.shtml
—Maine Department of Environmental Protection

Maryland
http://www.mde.state.md.us
—Maryland Department of the Environment
http://www.dnr.state.md.us/
—Maryland Department of Natural Resources

Massachusetts
http://www.magnet.state.ma.us/dep/dephome.htm
—Massachusetts Department of Environmental Protection

Michigan
http://www.michigan.gov/deq
—Michigan Department of Environmental Quality

Minnesota
http://www.dnr.state.mn.us/
—Minnesota Department of Natural Resources
http://www.pca.state.mn.us/
—Minnesota Pollution Control Agency

Mississippi
http://www.deq.state.ms.us/
—Mississippi Department of Environmental Quality

Missouri
http://www.dnr.mo.gov/
—Missouri Department of Natural Resources
http://www.mdc.mo.gov/
—Missouri Department of Conservation

Montana
http://www.deq.state.mt.us/index.asp
—Montana Department of Environmental Quality

http://www.nris.state.mt.us/
—Montana Natural Resource Information System

Nebraska
http://www.deq.state.ne.us/
—Nebraska Department of Environmental Quality

Nevada
http://www.forestry.nv.gov/
—Nevada Division of Forestry
http://www.dcnr.nv.gov/
—Nevada Department of Conservation and Natural Resources
http://www.ndep.nv.gov/
—Nevada Division of Environmental Protection

New Hampshire
http://www.des.state.nh.us/
—New Hampshire Department of Environmental Services

New Jersey
http://www.state.nj.us/dep/
—New Jersey Department of Environmental Protection

New Mexico
http://www.nmenv.state.nm.us/
—New Mexico Environmental Department

New York
http://www.dec.state.ny.us
—New York State Department of Environmental Conservation

North Carolina
http://www.enr.state.nc.us/
—North Carolina Department of Environment and Natural Resources
http://www.p2pays.org/
—North Carolina Division of Pollution Prevention and Environmental Assistance

North Dakota
http://www.swc.state.nd.us/
—North Dakota State Water Commission
http://www.state.nd.us/ndgs/
—North Dakota Geological Survey Division
http://www.health.state.nd.us/EHS/
—North Dakota Department of Health—Environmental Health Section

Ohio
http://www.epa.state.oh.us/
—Ohio Environmental Protection Agency
http://www.ohioairquality.org/
—Ohio Air Quality Development Authority

Oklahoma
http://www.okcc.state.ok.us/
—Oklahoma Conservation Commission
http://www.deq.state.ok.us/
—Oklahoma Department of Environmental Quality

Oregon
http://www.deq.state.or.us/
—Oregon Department of Environmental Quality
http://www.dfw.state.or.us/
—Oregon Department of Fish and Wildlife

Pennsylvania
http://www.dep.state.pa.us/
—Pennsylvania Department of Environmental Protection
http://www.dcnr.state.pa.us/
—Pennsylvania Department of Conservation and Natural Resources

Rhode Island
http://www.state.ri.us/dem/
—Rhode Island Department of Environmental Management

South Carolina
http://www.scdhec.net/
—South Carolina Department of Health and Environmental Control
http://water.dnr.state.sc.us/
—South Carolina Department of Natural Resources

South Dakota
http://www.state.sd.us/denr/
—South Dakota Department of Environment and Natural Resources

Tennessee
http://www.state.tn.us/environment/
—Tennessee Department of Environment and Conservation

Texas
http://www.tceq.state.tx.us/
—Texas Commission on Environmental Quality

Utah
http://www.eq.state.ut.us/
—Utah Department of Environmental Quality

Vermont
http://www.anr.state.vt.us/
—Vermont Agency of Natural Resources

Virginia
http://www.deq.state.va.us
—Virginia Department of Environmental Quality

Washington
http://www.ecy.wa.gov/
—Washington State Department of Ecology
http://www.dnr.wa.gov/
—Washington State Department of Natural Resources
http://www.wsdot.wa.gov/environment/
—Washington State Department of Transportation Environmental Services

West Virginia
http://www.dep.state.wv.us/
—West Virginia Department of Environmental Protection

Wisconsin
http://www.dnr.state.wi.us/
—Wisconsin Department of Natural Resources
http://www.dnr.state.wi.us/Environment.html
—Wisconsin DNR Environmental Protection

Wyoming
http://deq.state.wy.us/
—Wyoming Department of Environmental Quality

ENVIRONMENTAL AND RELATED PROFESSIONAL SITES
The descriptions here are those provided by the respective associations on their Web sites. Each Web site offers a wealth of information and additional resources.

Air and Waste Management Association
http://www.awma.org
International nonprofit, nonpartisan organization of environmental professionals promoting global environmental responsibility. It offers an online library of publications and articles that are free to

members and at a fee for nonmembers, including articles from its *Air & Waste Management Journal.*

Enfo.com
http://www.enfo.com
An independent server dedicated to facilitating the distribution of information related to the natural environment and society's interactions with it.

Envirolink Network
http://www.envirolink.org
A nonprofit organization and grassroots online community that unites hundreds of organizations and volunteers around the world with millions of people in over 130 countries. It provides access to "thousands" of online environmental resources.

Environmental Defense
http://www.environmentaldefense.org
Environmental Defense (formerly Environmental Defense Fund) is comprised of scientists, economists, attorneys, and others who work in teams to find solutions to environmental problems to protect human health, restore the oceans and ecosystems, and curb global warming.

Environmental Law Network
http://www.environmentallawnetwork.com
More than 100 environmental attorneys across the nation share ideas, information, experiences, and contacts to increase the value of legal representation to their respective clients. The Web site offers links to online environmental resources, as well as to other member environmental law firms.

Environmental News Network
http://www.enn.com
Founded in 1993, an online company committed to producing high quality, moderated content related to environmental and science topics. The company also offers cutting-edge Web site design and hosting services.

Greenpeace
http://www.greenpeace.org
An organization that describes itself as an independent, campaigning organization that uses nonviolent, creative confrontation to expose global environmental problems.

National Association of Environmental Professionals
http://www.naep.org
NAEP is a multidisciplinary association dedicated to the advancement of environmental professions in the United States and abroad.

Its goal is to provide a forum for state-of-the-art information on environmental planning, research, and management.

National Compliance Assistance Center
http://www.assistancecenters.net/
A product of partnerships between the EPA, industry, academic institutions, environmental groups, and other agencies to launch sector-specific Compliance Assistance Centers in agriculture, and industries such as auto recycling and repair, metal finishing, paints and coatings, chemicals, and more.

National Resources Defense Council
http://www.nrdc.org/
A nonprofit organization with more than 350,000 members nationwide, NRDC's mission is to preserve the environment, protect the public health, and ensure the conservation of wilderness and natural resources. With the help of a committed board of trustees, NRDC's staff in four offices across the country pursues these goals through research, advocacy, litigation, and public education.

The Nature Conservancy
http://nature.org
Its mission is to preserve the plants, animals, and natural communities that represent the diversity of life on Earth by protecting the lands and waters they need to survive.

Sierra Club
http://www.sierraclub.org
A nonprofit, member-supported, public interest organization that promotes conservation of the natural environment by influencing public policy decisions—legislative, administrative, legal, and electoral.

WaterWeb Consortium
http://www.waterweb.org
The Consortium is an organization that brings together educational, governmental, nonprofit, and commercial entities focused in water research, conservation, and management to advance water-related issues, promote the use of quality information, and share information with water use stakeholders and decision makers. The Web site is an excellent source of additional online resources.

World Wildlife Fund
http://wwf.org
An international organization dedicated to protecting the natural environment, focusing on endangered wildlife and conservation of their habitat, this site offers a wealth of information through its postings and e-newsletter.

ADDITIONAL INTERNET RESOURCES FOR PARALEGALS
http://www.lawsites.com
The National Law Net is a private law firm's remarkable collection of links to federal law materials on the Internet.

http://www.nala.org
The National Association of Legal Assistants (NALA) Web site offers professional and continuing educational information, along with its online NALA campus of paralegal virtual courses.

http://www.paralegals.org
The National Federation of Paralegal Associations (NFPA) offers links to legal resources and other professional development information on its Web site, as well as past issues of its *National Paralegal Reporter.*

http://www.roosevelt.edu/paralegal/resources.htm
Roosevelt University provides an impressive collection of links to legal and paralegal resources.

http://www.findlaw.com/01topics/13environmental/index.html
FindLaw.com's Web page on environmental law, providing resources such as law firms and expert witnesses, message boards, databases, government agencies, discussion groups, journals, newsletters and articles news and analysis, and case summaries.

Internet Mailing Lists and Newsgroup Mailing Lists

There are thousands of Internet mailing lists on every topic imaginable. Many are environmental in nature. You can subscribe to these mailing lists by sending the host computer a simple e-mail message. Once you subscribe, the host computer will automatically send you information by e-mail message. For example, when you subscribe to the correct distribution-only mailing list, the EPA will send you e-mail messages containing the full text of all *Federal Register* proposed and final regulations relating to air pollution on the same day those regulations are published in the *Federal Register*.

The second type of mailing list operates more like a discussion group or an interactive bulletin board. You subscribe in the same general manner that you use for distribution-only mailing lists. In addition, when you send an e-mail message to the interactive mailing list, everyone who subscribes to the mailing list will receive a copy of that message by e-mail. On unmoderated interactive mailing lists, any message will be forwarded to subscribers, regardless of whether it is relevant or appropriate. On moderated mailing lists, an individual—

the moderator—must first approve the message as relevant and appropriate for the discussion group before the message will be forwarded to subscribers.

Subscribing to a mailing list is easy. You simply send a specific e-mail message to the host computer. Usually, this message must contain only the word "subscribe," the name of the mailing list, and your first and last name. You should receive a message confirming your subscription to the mailing list shortly thereafter. To cancel your subscription, you typically send an e-mail message to the host computer containing only the word "unsubscribe," the mailing list name, and your first and last name.

Additional general information on using mailing lists can be retrieved from The Mailing List Gurus found at http://lists.gurus.com. This Web site also provides a list of mailing list directories, where you may search for mailing lists by keyword or by category.

The following list includes some mailing lists of interest to the environmental community.

EPA Mailing Lists

Directions for subscribing to one of the EPA mailing lists are found on http://yosemite.epa.gov/OEI/webguide.nsf/resources/deploylist1. Subscribing to a list is easy. Send a blank e-mail to "join-listname@ lists.epa.gov." where listname is the name of the list. For example, to subscribe to a list called "Brownfields," send a blank e-mail to: join-brownfields@lists.epa.gov. The available lists appear on the Web site page at the link: https://lists.epa.gov/read/all_forums/. Many of these lists are open to the public, while other lists require membership approval.

Other Mailing Lists

A variety of non-U.S.-EPA mailing lists are devoted to the environment. Because mailing lists change over time, it is prudent to find current mailing lists through online directories. Most directories can be searched using keywords; others can be searched by reviewing subject categories. Popular directories include the following.

http://www.topica.com/dir/?cid=0
Liszt, a popular mailing list directory, is now managed by Topica. Mailing lists may be found by using keywords or subject categories.

http://tile.net/lists/
This directory contains an alphabetical listing of lists by name and by domain. The lists may be searched by keyword.

http://groups.yahoo.com
In addition to searching for an existing group by keyword or category, you may register to join the groups or start a new group.

http://www.findlaw.com
You may find message boards run by FindLaw.® After searching for Environmental Law under Resources by Practice Area, click on the link titled "FindLaw Message Boards–Environmental Law." Or, you may find private message boards by clicking on the link "Other Message Boards," where registration instructions are provided under each mailing list and description.

WEBLOGS (BLOGS)

Weblogs, often referred to as "blogs," are personal Web sites run by individuals or groups who typically offer commentaries on their topic of choice, linking the visitor to other Web sites and articles. Blogs often develop an audience of regular visitors who provide their commentary as well. Good Weblogs are constantly updated. There are hundreds of thousands of Weblog sites, some of them focusing on the environment. Of course, any information obtained from a Weblog must be double-checked against more accurate sources. As is typical of mailing lists and other Web sites, addresses change often. Therefore, rather than listing individual addresses of blogs that focus on topics related to the environment, we have provided the Web sites of directories where these blogs may be found.

Environmental Blogs

http://www.wilsdomain.com/blogs/environmental-blogs.html

Blog Search Engine

http://www.blogsearchengine.com/environmental-blogs.html

Environmental Health

http://www.blogshares.com/industries.php?id=346

WIFLBlog

http://blogs.salon.com/0001455/

Network Centric Advocacy

http://www.network-centricadvocacy.net/weblogs/index.html

Index